FINANCIAL INSTITUTIONS IN EUROPE UNDER NEW COMPETITIVE CONDITIONS

FINANCIAL AND MONETARY POLICY STUDIES

Volume 20*

*Published on behalf of the
Société Universitaire Européenne de Recherches Financières (SUERF),
consisting the lectures given
at the 15th Colloquium, held in Nice, France, October 1989

FINANCIAL INSTITUTIONS IN EUROPE UNDER NEW COMPETITIVE CONDITIONS

Edited by

DONALD E. FAIR AND CHRISTIAN DE BOISSIEU

Published on behalf of the Société Universitaire Européenne de Recherches
Financières (SUERF)

with contributions from:

Ole Aerthøj
Patrick Artus
Forrest Capie
Ivo Caytas
Peter Cornet
Jean Dermine
Geoffrey Fitchew
Christopher Johnson
Leslie Johnson
Philippe Lagayette
José Leal Maldonado
François Léonard de Juvigny
André Levy-Lang
David Llewellyn

Catherine Lubochinsky
Ian Lumsden
Julian Mahari
Georges Martin
Rainer Masera
Joël Métais
Marco Onado
Jean-Paul Pollin
David Ravenscraft
Alfred Steinherr
Niels Thygesen
Marc van Turenhoudt
Norbert Walter
Geoffrey Wood

KLUWER ACADEMIC PUBLISHERS
DORDRECHT / BOSTON / LANCASTER

Library of Congress Cataloging-in-Publication Data

```
Financial institutions in Europe under new competitive conditions /
   edited by Donald E. Fair and Christian de Boissieu ; with
   contributions from Ole Aerthej ... [et al.].
       p.   cm. -- (Financial monetary policy studies ; 20)
   Papers presented at the 15th colloquium arranged by the Sociéte
universitaire européene de recherches financières (SUERF), Nice,
France, Oct. 1989.
   ISBN 0-7923-0673-2 (U.S. : alk. paper)
   1. Finance--Europe--Congresses.   2. Banks and banking--Europe-
-State supervision--Congresses.   3. Financial institutions--Europe-
-State supervision--Congresses.   I. Fair, Donald E.   II. Boissieu,
Christian de.   III. Aerthej, Ole.   IV. Sociéte universitaire
européene de recherches financières.   V. Series.
HG186.A2F56   1990
332.1'094--dc20                                              90-30763
```

ISBN 0-7923-0673-2

Published by Kluwer Academic Publishers,
P.O. Box 17, 3300 AA Dordrecht, The Netherlands.

Kluwer Academic Publishers incorporates the publishing programmes of
D. Reidel, Martinus Nijhoff, Dr W. Junk and MTP Press.

Sold and distributed in the U.S.A. and Canada
by Kluwer Academic Publishers,
101 Philip Drive, Norwell, MA 02061, U.S.A.

In all other countries, sold and distributed
by Kluwer Academic Publishers Group,
P.O. Box 322, 3300 AH Dordrecht, The Netherlands.

Printed on acid-free paper

Printed in the Netherlands

Contents

Preface ix
About the Editors and Authors xiii

Part A
OPENING ADDRESSES

Chapter I. Introduction
by *Niels Thygesen* 3

Chapter IIA. Implications Monétaires de l'Intégration Financière
Européenne
by *Philippe Lagayette* 9

Chapter IIB. Monetary Implications of European Financial
Integration (English translation of Philippe Lagayette's paper) 19

Chapter III. The European Regulatory and Supervisory Framework
by *Geoffrey E. Fitchew* 27

Chapter IV. Banking Strategies for the 1990s
by *André Levy-Lang* 39

Part B
COMPETITION IN BANKING SERVICES AND ITS IMPLICATIONS

Chapter V. Financial Innovation, Internationalization, Deregulation
and Market Integration in Europe: Why Does It All Happen Now?
by *Alfred Steinherr* 49

Chapter VI. La Banque à Géométrie Variable: Un Nouveau Facteur
de Compétitivité
by *Catherine Lubochinsky* and *Joël Metais* 65

Chapter VII. Les Pouvoirs Publics Français et les Résistances à la
Création d'un Marché Bancaire Intérieur Unifié
by *François Leonard de Juvigny* 83

Chapter VIII. Competition in Banking Services and Its Implications:
The Italian Case
by *Marco Onado* 95

Chapter IX. Le Secteur Bancaire Espagnol et le Problème des
Fusions
by *José Luis Leal Maldonado* 107

Part C
IS THERE AN EFFICIENCY/STABILITY TRADE-OFF?
ISSUES IN BANKING SUPERVISION AND REGULATION

Chapter X. Competition, Diversification and Structural Change in
the British Financial System
by *David T. Llewellyn* 117

Chapter XI. Frankfurt Financial Centre Challenged by 1992
by *Norbert Walter* 147

Chapter XII. The European Insurance Industry and the Impact
Competition from Banks Will Exert on It
by *Ole Aerthøj* 157

Chapter XIII. Competition in the British Housing Finance Market
by *Ian M. Lumsden* 175

Chapter XIV. Competition in Retail Banking: Threat or Promise?
by *Leslie T. Johnson* 191

Chapter XV. La Concurrence dans le Domaine des Valeurs Mobilières
by *Georges Martin* and *Marc van Turenhoudt* 203

Part D
THE ROLE OF THE BANKS IN THE RESTRUCTURING OF EUROPEAN INDUSTRY

Chapter XVI. Why Do We Have This M & A Wave?
by *Ivo G. Caytas* and *Julian I. Mahari* 223

Chapter XVII. The Merger Game: Playing Against the Odds
by *David J. Ravenscraft* 235

Part E
COMPETITION IN TRADITIONAL NON-BANK AREAS; SECURITIES TRADING, HOUSING FINANCE AND INSURANCE; FINANCIAL CONGLOMERATES

Chapter XVIII. Les Effets de la Réglementation et le Comportement des Banques
by *Patrick Artus* and *Jean-Paul Pollin* 253

Chapter XIX. Issues in Banking Supervision and Regulation from the Perspective of a Banking Supervisor
by *Peter A. A. M. Cornet* 275

Chapter XX. Home Country Control and Mutual Recognition
by *Jean Dermine* 293

Chapter XXI. Banking Structure and Banking Stability after 1992
by *Forrest H. Capie* and *Geoffrey E. Wood* 305

Chapter XXII. Issues in Financial Regulation: Efficiency, Stability, Information
by *Rainer S. Masera* 319

Part F
CONCLUDING ADDRESS

Chapter XXIII. General Report on the Colloquium
by *Christopher Johnson* 347

Preface

The papers collected in this volume are those presented at the fifteenth Colloquium arranged by the Société Universitaire Européenne de Recherches Financières (SUERF), which took place in Nice in October 1989.

The Society is supported by a large number of central banks and commercial banks, by other financial and business institutions and by personal subscriptions from academics and others interested in monetary and financial problems. Since its establishment in 1963, it has developed as a forum for the exchange of information, research results and ideas among academics and practitioners in these fields, including central bank officials and civil servants responsible for formulating and applying monetary and financial policies, national and international.

A major activity of SUERF is to organise and conduct Colloquia on subjects of topical interest to its members. The titles, places and dates of previous Colloquia for which volumes of the collected papers were published are noted on the last page of this volume. Volumes were not produced for Colloquia held at Tarragona, Spain in October 1970 under the title 'Monetary Policy and New Developments in Banking' and at Strasbourg, France in January 1972 under the title 'Aspects of European Monetary Union'.

In choosing "Financial Institutions in Europe under New Competitive Conditions" as the general theme for the Nice Colloquium the SUERF Council felt that banks and other financial institutions in Europe were entering a phase of increasing pressures of competition. This resulted from factors in global financial markets, supplemented in Europe by the removal of residual capital controls and liberalization of financial services. These external pressures, intensified by competition induced by technological developments and by the efforts of financial institutions to transcend national regulatory frameworks, have implications for, first, the strategies of banks and the likely banking structure of the 1990s; secondly, the authorities regulating financial markets and institutions and exercising prudential supervision in an increasingly coordinated manner; thirdly, the role of financial institutions in the restructuring of European industry and, lastly, the future of non-bank financial institutions. These broad themes were expected to be of particular interest to bankers, regulators and financial economists as the time approaches during 1990-92 for implementing the major decisions taken in the European Communities.

The Colloquium was attended by 175 participants, representing a wide range of financial activities and academic teaching and research in the financial field. The Chairman of the Colloquium as a whole was the President of SUERF, Professor Dr. Niels Thygesen. After his introductory remarks, opening addresses were given by Mr Philippe Lagayette, Deputy Governor of the Bank of France, Mr Geoffrey Fitchew, Director-General for Financial Services in the Commission of the European Communities and by Mr André Levy-Lang, President of Compagnie Bancaire. These contributions appear in Part A of this volume, Chapters I–IV.

The contributed papers that followed had been distributed beforehand and were discussed in four separate Commissions meeting simultaneously. The themes of the Commissions were: "Competition in Banking Services and its Implications", chaired by Mr R. Raymond and Dr H. E. Scharrer (Part B, Chapters V–VIII); "Is there an Efficiency/Stability Trade-Off? Issues in Banking Supervision and Regulation" chaired by Professor Christian de Boissieu and Dr Warren McClam (Part C, Chapters X–XV); "The Role of the Financial Institutions in the Restructuring of European Industry" chaired by Professor Jean-Paul Abraham and Mr Alois Schwietert (Part D, Chapters XVI and XVII) – this Commission also conducted case studies of the Swiss Watch Industry and the Sociéte Générale de Belgique, introduced by Mr Alois Schwietert and Mr Georges Ugeux, respectively; and "Competition in Traditional Non-bank Areas; Securities Trading, Housing Finance and Insurance; Financial Conglomerates" chaired by Professor Niels Thygesen and Professor J. S. G. Wilson (Part E, Chapters XVIII–XXII).

The Colloquium reassembled for a final plenary session to which Mr Christopher Johnson gave his reflections on the Colloquium as a whole (Part F, Chapter XXIII).

In some cases minor changes have been made to the papers before publication.

As on previous occasions the Colloquium was strongly supported by the local financial community. Generous financial contributions were made by the Banque de France, Association Française des Banques, Association Monégasque des Banques, Communauté Financière de Nice et des Alpes Maritimes, Banque Nationale de Paris, Crédit Lyonnais, Société Générale, Banque Paribas, Crédit Populaire de France, Caisse Nationale de Crédit Agricole, Société Marseillaise de Crédit, Compagnie Bancaire, Crédit du Nord, Banque d'Escompte, Compagnie Financière Edmond de Rothschild, Banque Pallas France, Société Nancéienne Varin-Bernier, Banque Franco-Allemande, Banque Centrale Monégasque de Crédit and Banque Commerciale pour l'Europe du Nord.

The Colloquium was most successful not only in the quality of the papers presented but also in the opportunity it provided for contacts and discussions between experts from many different countries and financial institutions. Particular thanks were given to the French members of the SUERF Council, Professor Christian de Boissieu and Mr Robert Raymond, and to Professor Hans Bosman, the Secretary-General, and Miss Annelies Vugs, the Executive Secretary, for their excellent organisation and ever-ready assistance.

About the Editors and Authors

EDITORS

Donald E. Fair, formerly Economic Adviser, The Royal Bank of Scotland Group and The Northern Trust Company of Chicago, London
Christian de Boissieu, Professor of Economics, University of Paris I

AUTHORS

Ole Aerthøj, Vice-President, Baltica Holding, Copenhagen
Patrick Artus, Head of Department of Economic and Financial Studies, Caisse des Dépôts et Consignations, Paris
Forrest H. Capie, Professor of Economic History, City University Business School, London
Ivo G. Caytas, Caytas K. G., Corporate Control Consultants, St. Gallen, Switzerland
Peter A. A. M. Cornet, Chief of Banking Supervision, De Nederlandsche Bank
Jean Dermine, Professor of Finance, INSEAD, Fontainebleau
Geoffrey E. Fitchew, Director-General for Financial Services, Commission of the European Communities
Christopher Johnson, Chief Economic Adviser, Lloyds Bank
Leslie T. Johnson, Senior Research Fellow in Banking, University College of North Wales
Philippe Lagayette, Deputy Governor, Bank of France
José Luis Leal Maldonado, Economic Adviser, Banco Bilbao-Vizcaya, Madrid
François Leonard de Juvigny, Deputy Director, Association Française des Banques
André Levy-Lang, President, Compagnie Bancaire, Paris
David T. Llewellyn, Professor of Money and Banking, University of Loughborough
Catherine Lubochinsky, Adviser, Société Marseillaise de Crédit, Paris
Ian M. Lumsden, Divisional Manager, European Operations, Halifax Building Society

Julian I. Mahari, Lecturer in Finance, University of St. Gallen
Georges Martin, Head of Economics Department, Association Belge des Banques
Rainer S. Masera, Director General, Instituto Mobiliare Italiano, Rome
Joël Metais, Professor, University of Paris IX
Marco Onado, Professor of Economics, University of Bologna
Jean-Paul Pollin, Professor of Economics, University of Orleans
David J. Ravenscraft, Professor of Finance, University of North Carolina
Alfred Steinherr, Director, Financial Research Department, European Investment Bank
Niels Thygesen, Professor, Institute of Economics, University of Copenhagen
Marc van Turenhoudt, Adviser, Association Belge des Banques
Norbert Walter, Senior Economist, Deutsche Bank
Geoffrey E. Wood, Professor of Economics, City University Business School, London

Part A
Opening Addresses

I. Introduction

NIELS THYGESEN

On behalf of the Council of Management of SUERF I welcome participants to the fifteenth Colloquium. The broad theme: "Financial Institutions in Europe Under New Competitive Conditions" has attracted to Nice about 170 participants for two and a half days of discussions.

The list of authors reflects closely, we believe, the purpose of our association: to further the exchange of research results and ideas within the wide-ranging membership of SUERF in universities, the private financial sector and national or international policy-making institutions. SUERF does not have the ambition to offer to participants an overview of the latest financial techniques or of the most recent developments in financial theory which has now become a major field of application for rigorous economic theory; others, whether commercial organisers or professional associations, can do that better than we could hope to. But SUERF does have the ambition to encourage dialogue within our heterogenous membership on a number of analytical and policy-related issues that arise out of recent developments in European and global financial markets and in new analytical approaches to them.

The perspective of discussion at SUERF Colloquia obviously depends on the particular theme chosen. At our previous Colloquium in Helsinki in May 1988 – as well as at the forthcoming one at Lisbon in May 1991 – the perspective was and will be primarily that of economic policy. The views and methods of analysis of central banks, governments and macroeconomists are more fully represented on such occasions than is the case in the present Colloquium. Here in Nice we shall aim to adopt a more microeconomic perspective of the functioning of financial markets in a broad sense. The behaviour of individual economic agents and, particularly, of financial institutions, subjected to intensified international competition in an environment of simpler and more unified national and international regulation over a widening range of financial activity, will be at the centre of attention.

In the SUERF Council we attach some significance in this change of perspective to the fact that the present Colloquium is organised in a major city other than a capital, where the perspective of traditional economic policy is less likely to dominate. We have been happy to choose as site for this

D. E. Fair and C. de Boissieu (eds), Financial Institutions in Europe Under New Competitive Conditions, 3–7.
© 1990 *Kluwer Academic Publishers, Dordrecht. Printed in the Netherlands.*

year's Colloquium a city and a region undergoing rapid economic growth and change, where all the major challenges to financial markets are evident. Nice has become an important financial centre, as testified by the presence of leading French and foreign institutions. The region which she serves is, not unlike California in the United States, attracting a remarkable inflow of human and financial capital. The fact that many citizens of France – and other countries – find it attractive to move to the Côte d'Azur, or as near to it as possible, as they approach the age of retirement has long been observable. But in recent years this inflow of capital has been matched by the growth of new, technologically advanced industries or service activities requiring imaginative use also of financial resources. To this one may add the demands on the financial sector to contribute to the strengthening of links with contiguous regions along the Mediterranean, extending into Italy and Spain. We hope that the substantial participation from financial institutions from this region in rapid economic evolution will push the discussion of our chosen subjects towards concrete problems and opportunities.

Admittedly SUERF has had another incentive in planning the Colloquium for Nice, a very positive reception of our plan by the banking community in terms of financial contributions and of splendid hospitality offered to our participants by the Communauté Financière des Alpes Maritimes and by the Groupement des Banques de Monaco. The SUERF Council is most grateful for this very active support and I want to put on record also our appreciation of the major part played by our two French Council members, Christian de Boissieu and Robert Raymond in helping to bring it forward.

Turning to the questions which the SUERF Council has formulated over the general theme of the Colloquium and circulated to members with the invitation, I want to recall briefly the central subjects for each of the four Commissions. When we approach authors we do not try to enforce any strict discipline on them; they are asked to regard our outline as suggestive only. Occasionally, therefore, the resulting papers may offer answers to questions different from those formulated in the outline, and the distinction between the subjects treated in the four Commissions may have become more blurred than originally imagined. Since our main effort has been to invite speakers known for deeper insight into a particular subject area than we can muster in our Council, we have felt that a liberal attitude as to how authors choose to approach the subject area assigned to them is called for and, indeed, to the advantage of participants.

In one sense I cannot help but congratulate SUERF on a particular discipline observed by authors: nearly all papers have been available for circulation to participants well in advance of the Colloquium. This is in some contrast to most international conferences and I congratulate our authors.

If some participants still, despite the opportunity they have had to look at the papers, retain a residual doubt as to which Commission they would like to attend, let me restate some of the guiding ideas from the programme outline. (For an overview of what the papers actually bring out and how they were received in the Commissions readers are referred to the concluding chapter of the Rapporteur General, Mr. Christopher Johnson.)

Commission I has been asked to discuss competition in banking services and its implications. For banks a new competitive environment has been prompted by several factors: financial innovation, deregulation, internationalization and despecialization. Some of these factors will intensify as remaining controls on short-term capital movements are removed in France and Italy in 1990, in Spain and Ireland in 1992 and by the mid-1990s in Greece and Portugal, and as trade in financial services is increasingly liberalized as part of the 1992 programme. Will the increased competition drive banks towards offering non-bank services, or will rewards be available to banks that remain specialized or even respecialize? What are the likely strategies by a bank in terms of containing costs, sharing production facilities and increasing equity capital?

What are the implications for the structure of the banking industry? Will the emphasis be on concentration through mergers or on various forms of cooperative arrangements? What are the likely locational aspects of banking activities within countries and in Europe? Will trends in concentration and size generate new attention on banking by the national and EC competition authorities? More philosophically, is the market for financial services perfectly contestable and how does the pressure of potential entrants make itself felt? What are the costs of exit from the market?

Commission II has been encouraged to address the central issue whether there is a trade-off between financial efficiency and stability.

How will competitive pressures affect the performance of the banking industry in terms of efficiency and of stability? Will there be an increase in the operational efficiency of banks and in the allocative efficiency of the banking industry? Which nonbank sectors in the economy will benefit most from the resulting improvement in the quality and cheapening of banking services? Will there be a cost in terms of increased risk of instability as the profitability of banking is squeezed further? How will the efficiency-stability trade-off be perceived by the economy, by the banking industry and by the authorities?

What is the nature of the interaction of the globalization of financial markets (and the efforts to face up to it, notably through the proposals of the Cooke Committee on capital requirements) and the EC's Second Banking Directive and other parts of the financial aspects of the Internal Market programme? Is there in the EC a danger of a competitive deregulation (minimal taxation of income from financial instruments, low prudential standards etc.) and, if so, what are the potential consequences for financial stability? Or has that danger been checked? What is the role of deposit insurance in the light of EC proposals, recent national experiences in Europe and the alarming difficulties of the US deposit insurers.

Recent experience and expected effects of the removal of controls on short-term capital flows planned in France and Italy, should be evaluated. What are the minimal requirements imposed on harmonization of the fiscal régime and of financial regulation to prevent important delocalization of financial activity and hence instability? Is the concept of mutual recognition being overloaded? Are differences in national regulatory frameworks effectively narrowing? There is also a need to review the balance between controls of institutions and on activities. Is a functional approach preferable to an institutional approach? If yes, is the former feasible?

Commission III will look at the role of financial institutions in the restructuring of European industry.

In the restructuring of Europe's industry banks (and, in general, financial institutions) are centrally involved in strategic choices for their main clients, and in particular in advising them on mergers and acquisitions. How do banks fill this role? Are they increasingly taking on the role of consultants? Are they assuming increased risks whether in hostile or friendly takeovers or in organizing leveraged and management buy-outs?

The US and UK experience with mergers and acquisitions is wider than that of the rest of Europe. How important have they been in terms of numbers of companies and/or capital involved? What have been the main features by size of company and main cause? What is there to learn from the US/UK experience – illustrated by typical success or failure stories – in the Continental European context, keeping in mind that the regulatory framework, shareholder attitudes and other institutional differences may make analogies difficult?

The role of the financial institutions in mergers and acquisitions – banks in Europe have widely different institutional backgrounds (investment banks, brokers, commercial banks, universal banks etc.) which may make difficult an answer to the question: what should be the role of the financial institution? A disinterested adviser or a "banque d'affaires"? In practice, conflicts of interest may arise regardless of the degree of impartiality or arm's length aimed for (Glass-Steagall Act, universal banking, broker/dealer or agents/consultants with and without taking positions). Possible types of conflict are: self-interest of the institution versus clients' interests, interests of one client versus that of another client, self-interest of the bank versus interest of other units of the same group, conflicts with a perceived public interest. There is also an important choice between self-regulation by the institution and regulation by law.

Two case studies (from Switzerland and Belgium) will be discussed.

Commission IV will extend the perspective of Commission I beyond banking activities and the institutions traditionally engaged in them. Competitive pressures also arise from the blurring of borderlines between banks and financial institutions specialized in housing finance, insurance and market-making and trading of securities. Non-financial institutions have also become major providers of intermediate financial services. The emergence of financial conglomerates and the blurring of traditional specializations have been prompted but the trend observable in several countries in recent years towards an improved self-financing capacity in the enterprise sector and by the growing relative importance of the household sector as a borrower. Financial institutions including banks, have increasingly aimed at providing comprehensive financial services to households. What are the implications of this growing reliance on the personal sector and on retail banking? What are the leading examples of competition across traditional financial borderlines? How does the internationalization of both financial an non-financial enterprises contribute to the process of despecialization?

What will be the competitive position of London and Frankfurt, respectively, as a financial centre, taking into account that London is a dominant centre now and that Frankfurt is the financial centre of the country with the strongest currency among the EC currencies?

With these introductory remarks I have already taken up too much time in this opening session the main purpose of which is to listen to our three very distinguished speakers: M. Philippe Lagayette, Deputy Governor of Banque de France, Mr. Geoffrey Fitchew, Director-General for Financial Services in the Commission of the European Communities and M. André Lévy-Lang, President of Compagnie Bancaire. We are honoured to be able to lead off our Colloquium with this excellent panel.

IIA. Implications Monétaires de l'Intégration Financière Européenne

PHILIPPE LAGAYETTE

INTRODUCTION

C'est avec un grand plaisir que je m'adresse à vous aujourd'hui à l'occasion du colloque organisé par la SUERF. Votre société a contribué à l'émergence et au développement d'un esprit européen dans le domaine de la recherche financière. Aujourd'hui, le processus d'intégration des marchés est bien avancé, même s'il reste des obstacles à surmonter, et l'idée d'une unification monétaire européenne aborde une étape décisive. Cette perspective est précisément au coeur de votre programme et je me réjouis que vous ayez choisi cette époque et mon pays pour en traiter.

Même si elle représente des objectifs et des contraintes spécifiques, l'intégration financière européenne ne peut être isolée du mouvement global d'ouverture des marchés de capitaux, sous l'effet de l'innovation financière et de la déréglementation. A lui seul, ce phénomène suffit à modifier les conditions d'activité des institutions financières et d'exercice de la politique monétaire. La Banque de France a d'ailleurs adapté ses instruments à cette situation nouvelle au cours des années récentes, en renonçant à l'encadrement du crédit et en privilégiant le rôle de ses interventions sur le marché monétaire.

Aux effets de la globalisation des marchés s'ajoutent en Europe les disciplines imposées par un régime de taux de change nominaux de plus en plus fixes, tant est grande la volonté d'espacer le plus possible les réalignements. La pratique du SME, par laquelle je commencerai, nous a préparés à une intégration européenne. Il n'empêche que la libéralisation complète des mouvements de capitaux, prévue pour juillet 1990, et la réalisation du grand marché intérieur, en 1993, auront de sérieuses implications, et cela à brève échéance. Enfin, la perspective de l'union économique et monétaire, dont les grandes étapes ont été tracées dans le rapport du Comité pour l'étude de l'union économique et monétaire, discuté lors du Sommet de Madrid en juin dernier, conduit à réexaminer le rôle et l'élaboration des politiques nationales.

D. E. Fair and C. de Boissieu (eds), Financial Institutions in Europe Under New Competitive Conditions, 9–17.
© 1990 *Kluwer Academic Publishers, Dordrecht. Printed in the Netherlands.*

1. LA PRATIQUE DES POLITIQUES MONETAIRES APRES DIX ANS DE FONCTIONNEMENT DU SME

1.1 Les principes

La mise en oeuvre du SME en 1979 a reflété à l'origine une volonté commune de la part des pays fondateurs de renoncer aux dévaluations compétitives ou aux surévaluations excessives, source d'inflation dans le pays dont la monnaie se déprécie, et de distorsion des courants d'échange. La philosophie qui est à la base du SME va même au-delà. Elle recommande de respecter le plus longtemps possible un objectif de taux de change nominal, laissant au pays qui dévie le soin de réorienter sa politique. Cette contrainte s'est révélée très forte, notamment au cours des premières années de fonctionnement du SME, pour les pays à monnaie comparativement faible; et si des réalignements de parités, concernant une ou plusieurs monnaies, ont du être opérés à onze reprises entre 1979 et 1987 (dont 7 au cours des 4 premières années), la philosophie générale que j'ai indiquée est demeurée.

Cet effort de convergence n'aurait pas de sens, et pourrait même avoir des effets pervers, s'il ne s'accompagnait d'une ferme volonté de juguler l'inflation: c'est d'abord aux pays dont les monnaies voient leur pouvoir d'achat le plus érodé par l'inflation qu'il appartient accomplir les efforts les plus intenses, par des politiques monétaire et budgétaire anti-inflationnistes. Par contre lorsque l'inflation moyenne dans le système est redevenue faible, un problème de répartition plus symétrique des charges d'ajustement peut se poser si la croissance globale des économies concernées est insuffisante et si certaines monnaies tendent à s'apprécier excessivement.

1.2 Le bilan

La longévité même du système atteste de son succès et suffit à le différencier de l'ancien "serpent". Aucun pays appartenant au mécanisme de change n'a remis en cause sa participation.

Une asymétrie vertueuse a caractérisé le fonctionnement du SME à ses débuts, tous les pays membres étant conduits par la logique du système à réduire leur écart d'inflation avec celui ou ceux où les prix étaient les plus stables. Le SME a permis d'améliorer de façon spectaculaire la convergence entre les variables nominales (prix, coûts salariaux). Rappelons par exemple que la différence entre les rythmes d'inflation en France et en Allemagne était supérieure à 6% en 1979 au moment où le système a été crée. Elle est d'un demi pour cent aujourd'hui. Les pays où les tensions inflationnistes étaient très vives au début des années 80, ont davantage gagné en termes d'assainissement, consolidant ainsi leurs chances pour l'avenir, qu'ils n'ont perdu en termes de croissance.

Toutefois ce bilan demeure partiel. En effet, la discipline n'est pas encore universellement acceptée, puisqu'elle se limite formellement à la zone d'application du mécanisme de change à marges étroites. Force est de constater que plusieurs pays, en dehors de celle-ci, ont montré en 1988-1989 des signes évidents de surchauffe.

Au surplus, si les taux d'interêt ont été souvent orientés de façon privilégiée par la nécessité de respecter des objectifs de taux de change, les politiques budgétaires n'ont pas bénéficié des mêmes disciplines.

Enfin, au sein du mécanisme de change, d'énormes disparités subsistent dans le domaine des balances des paiements. Leur élimination appelle une coopération plus étroite élargie au-delà des politiques monétaires.

1.3 Le conflit d'objectifs

La plupart des pays européens ont continué à se fixer des objectifs de croissance monétaire en dépit, depuis le milieu des années 80 surtout, de l'affaiblissement de la corrélation entre le stock de monnaie ou de crédit d'une part, le PIB nominal de l'autre. Toutefois la politique monétaire est devenue, d'une application plus délicate. En outre, l'importance prise par la gestion des taux de change, notamment au sein du SME, peut être à l'origine de conflits entre objectifs internes et externes. Cette situation est en apparence d'autant plus difficile à gérer que, dans la plupart des pays (y compris en France où le décloisonnement des marchés et le développement des innovations financières ont entraîné l'abandon de l'encadrement du crédit et du contrôle des changes) les autorités monétaires ne disposent que d'un seul instrument, les taux d'interêt, pour atteindre un objectif monétaire quantitatif interne. L'utilisation prioritaire de cet instrument pour le respect de l'objectif externe peut avoir pour résultat la perte du contrôle de l'objectif interne.

Cependant, le conflit d'objectifs est loin d'être permanent. Dans les pays dont la balance de base reste fragile et dans lesquels la hausse des prix est tendanciellement forte, il constitue même un cas peu fréquent. En effet à moyen terme, il doit être possible de déterminer un sentier de croissance d'un agrégat de monnaie ou de crédit conciliable avec les deux résultats recherchés. Un niveau de taux d'interêt relativement élevé constitue un moyen à la fois de lutter contre les tendances inflationnistes et d'assurer, en attirant les capitaux externes, une bonne tenue de la balance de base et donc du taux de change. C'est d'ailleurs sur de telles bases que la convergence des taux d'inflation, nécessaire au maintien des parités, pourra être assurée.

1.4 Les moyens de surmonter le conflit d'objectifs

C'est dans le court terme que les conflits se manifestent occasionnellement comme on le voit aujourd'hui par exemple en Italie et en Espagne. Un cas typique de conflit apparaît lorsque les besoins de lutte contre une inflation qui est déjà devenue substantielle ou une réelle surchauffe de l'économie conduisent à un niveau de taux d'intérêt qui attire excessivement les capitaux et fait monter les taux de change.

Il existe alors plusieurs moyens de les traiter. D'abord, les autorités monétaires continuent de bénéficier d'un certain degré de liberté dans la conduite des taux d'intérêt. En effet la mobilité des capitaux n'est pas parfaite. Cela résulte moins de la persistance provisoire de quelques entraves réglementaires à leur circulation que d'une localisation de l'épargne caractérisée par une certaine "viscosité". Les mouvements de capitaux ne sont pas seulement fonction des écarts de rendements nets, comme cela se vérifie à l'intérieur des espaces financièrement intégrés que constituent les nations, mais obéissent aussi à d'autres facteurs, tels que la proximité ou la pré-affectation des fonds; les comportements des épargnants et des gestionnaires de trésorerie font preuve d'une certaine inertie. Ensuite, les réserves obligatoires permettent d'influencer sur courte période la liquidité du système bancaire, et donc l'offre de crédit, indépendamment des taux d'intervention sur le marché monétaire. Enfin, la coordination des modifications de taux directeurs des banques centrales du SME multiplie leur capacité d'influer à la fois sur les taux d'intérêt de marché et les taux de change dans le mesure où elle influence les anticipations plus radicalement qu'une action isolée; les décisions conjointes de la Bundesbank et de la Banque de France en novembre 1987 et, plus récemment, en juin 1989, confirment ce propos.

Sur les marchés des changes, les banques centrales ont également certains moyens de faire face à un conflit temporaire d'objectifs. Elles peuvent non seulement utiliser les bandes de fluctuations du mécanisme de change mais aussi procéder à des interventions stérilisées, qui ne sont pas dénuées d'efficacité en très courte période. De telles interventions ont été facilitées, dans le cadre du SME, par les accords de Bâle/Nyborg qui, depuis septembre 1987, ont notamment élargi les possibilités de recours au financement à très court terme.

Notons enfin que les conflits d'objectifs sont souvent liés à un mauvais "policy mix": un poids excessif pèse sur la politique monétaire qui est insuffisamment épaulée par la politique budgétaire, la politique des revenus ou les politiques structurelles. La réduction du conflit d'objectif de la politique monétaire passe alors par le rééquilibrage du "policy mix".

Si le conflit d'objectifs subsiste, les autorités monétaires ne peuvent que privilégier l'un des deux objectifs pour un certain temps. La France n'a guère expérimenté une telle situation ces toutes dernières années, grâce à la réduction de son taux d'inflation qui a contribué à stabiliser la position du franc.

2. LES IMPLICATIONS DU GRAND MARCHE INTERIEUR

2.1 La synergie entre liberté des changes et libre prestation des services financiers

Dans le domaine financier, la mise en oeuvre de l'Acte unique européen repose sur deux volets qui se complètent:
- d'une part, la liberté des mouvements de capitaux, grâce à l'élimination, là où ils subsistent, des derniers vestiges du contrôle des changes, dès juin 1990, sauf pour les quelques pays bénéficiant de prorogations;
- d'autre part, la libre prestation des services financiers qui permettra à tout établissement de la Communauté européenne de s'adresser à des clients dans les autres pays membres sans s'y installer et donc sans contraintes supplémentaires par rapport à celles qu'il subit dans son propre pays.

La libre prestation des services financiers constitue un élément indispensable de l'achèvement d'un marché unique. Elle ne peut guère se concevoir sans liberté des mouvements de capitaux. Toutefois la conjugaison de ces deux principes comporte à côté de leurs immenses avantages, qui sont bien connus et sur lesquels je ne m'étendrai pas, des risques qui doivent être pris en considération par les autorités des pays membres.

2.2 Les risques

Pour sa part, la France a d'ores et déjà éliminé la quasi-totalité des restrictions aux mouvements de capitaux: depuis 1985, des mesures successives de libéralisation ont été prises et à ce jour seule subsiste l'interdiction, pour les particuliers, d'ouvrir des comptes bancaires à l'étranger ou d'en détenir en France en devises autres que l'écu. Il en va de même par exemple en Italie. Ces décisions ont fait écho à la globalisation technique des marchés. Elles ont été rendues possibles par les progrès accomplis dans la lutte contre l'inflation, qui ont calmé les anticipations des marchés. En juin 1990, la liberté des mouvements de capitaux devrait être totale dans la plupart des pays participant au mécanisme de change du SME, sans qu'il y ait à procéder pour cela à une modification substantielle des dispositifs existants. Il n'en reste pas moins que le risque d'importants mouvements de capitaux est ouvert en cas de changement d'appréciation du marché sur les facteurs fondamentaux d'une économie.

Ce risque est accru par la libre prestation des services financiers, qui pourrait inciter une partie de l'épargne à se localiser dans les pays de la Communauté où les contraintes réglementaires et fiscales sont les moins lourdes.

2.3 *Les mesures propres à endiguer les risques*

Il ne faut pas pour autant renoncer à l'achèvement du grand marché intérieur, car celui-ci fera bénéficier les investisseurs de possibilités élargies d'arbitrage entre sources de financements et placements financiers qui sont favorables à l'optimisation de la gestion financière des entreprises et des particuliers. Toutefois, diverses mesures de déréglementation et d'harmonisation devraient permettre d'éviter des tensions trop fortes sur les marchés des changes ou une volatilité excessive des taux d'intérêt.

La déréglementation doit d'abord concerner les marchés eux-mêmes, afin d'éliminer les cloisonnements et particularismes. On contribuera ainsi à une meilleure allocation du capital, à une réduction des coûts de financement et à une plus grande efficacité de la politique monétaire dont les effets pourront mieux se propager dans l'économie. La France a elle-même progressé dans ce sens; elle a abandonné ou supprimé partiellement le recours à certaines procédures administratives telles que l'encadrement du crédit et le contrôle des changes. Avec le soutien des autorités monétaires, de nouveaux instruments de financement, étroitement liés aux conditions de marché, ont été créés. Des étapes devront encore être franchies afin notamment de banaliser les circuits de collecte de l'épargne et de distribution du crédit.

Un effort important d'harmonisation est en outre nécessaire dans le domaine de la fiscalité de l'épargne, afin d'éviter les délocalisations non fondées sur la concurrence normale entre institutions financières. On peut arguer que l'abandon du contrôle des changes *erga omnes* suffit en théorie à rendre cet effort nécessaire à l'échelle mondial; il est encore plus urgent entre des économies intégrées et proches les unes des autres. L'effort d'harmonisation devra s'étendre aux contraintes qui pèsent sur l'activité de ces institutions, liées à la conduite de la politique monétaire. Il en va ainsi par exemple pour les modalités d'application des réserves obligatoires. Ce rapprochement est en bonne voie pour les ratios prudentiels.

2.4 *Un cadre économique favorable*

En situation de complète liberté des mouvements de capitaux, les taux de change seront sans doute encore plus sensibles qu'aujourd'hui aux modifications des anticipations. Au-delà des mesures réglementaires et fiscales que j'ai évoquées, la nécessité de mieux faire converger les données économiques fondamentales revêtira donc un surcroît d'actualité.

3. L'INTEGRATION MONETAIRE EUROPEENNE

3.1 La démarche d'ensemble

Précisément la réalisation d'une union monétaire entre pays membres, loin de nous laisser plus de flexibilité pour accepter la volatilité des taux de change, nous contraint au contraire à éliminer celle-ci. Nous ne devons pas nous en effrayer. Pour affronter des défis supplémentaires, nous devrons en effet aller vers cette étroite union entre européens que les adhérents de la SUERF appellent certainement de leurs voeux. Dans cet esprit, le rapport du Comité pour l'étude de l'union économique et monétaire a dégagé des étapes vers l'union monétaire.

On a soutenu que cette dernière n'était pas une condition indispensable au fonctionnement du grand marché intérieur. Elle en constitue cependant un prolongement logique car un marché unique ne peut fonctionner efficacement qu'avec un système de prix unique, impliquant à terme la fixation irrévocable des taux de change entre les monnaies des pays membres, prélude à l'émission d'une monnaie unique.

Le passage à la monnaie unique ne peut lui-même avoir lieu de manière soudaine; il doit se produire par étapes, pour deux sortes de motifs:
– en premier lieu, les situations économiques doivent d'abord se rapprocher;
– en second lieu, la mise en place d'une monnaie unique appelle d'importantes novations institutionnelles qui ne peuvent intervenir qu'au terme d'une révision du traité de Rome; tel est l'objet de la deuxième étape vers l'union économique et monétaire.

3.2 La première étape

Auparavant, la première étape, dont le Conseil Européen de Madrid a fixé le début au 1er juillet 1990, permettra d'étendre la participation au mécanisme de change à l'ensemble des monnaies de la Communauté et de renforcer les acquis de la convergence économique en dépit de la fluidité accrue des capitaux.

Cette première phase ne constituera pas une véritable rupture pour les pays qui ont déjà atteint un degré élevé de convergence et participent pleinement au mécanisme de change. Elle les obligera cependant à appliquer une coordination plus poussée de leurs politiques monétaires en vue d'atteindre des objectifs définis en commun. Pour ceux qui devront les rejoindre, elle comportera un alourdissement des contraintes qui s'exercent sur la détermination de leurs politiques économiques , en même temps qu'un gain de crédibilité auprès des marchés et une moindre volatilité de leurs taux de change. Elle devra être mise à profit par tous pour développer l'usage de l'écu et améliorer le fonctionnement du SME.

En effet, en dépit de ses imperfections actuelles, liées à sa nature de panier et à l'existence de deux circuits, l'un officiel, l'autre privé, l'écu préfigure la monnaie commune. Il serait donc souhaitable d'en acclimater l'usage et donc de lever les derniers obstacles à sa circulation et son utilisation dans la Communauté et, dès la première étape d'encourager son caractère de monnaie de référence communautaire, par exemple en contribuant à l'essor d'un vaste marché de titres négociables libellés en écu. Il y aura là un pas important de fait dans le renforcement de l'identité monétaire de l'Europe. Les récentes initiatives des Trésors britannique et français vont dans ce sens.

Au cours de la première étape, l'amélioration du fonctionnement du SME devra se faire dans le cadre institutionnel existant mais doit comporter un renforcement significatif de la coordination des politiques monétaires grâce à l'accroissement du rôle du Comité des gouverneurs des banques centrales de la CEE. Celui-ci devrait, selon le rapport Delors, recevoir le soutien de trois sous-comités spécialisés chargés de fonctions d'étude et de surveillance dans les domaines de la politique monétaire, des changes et du contrôle bancaire. Bien que chaque banque centrale demeure seule responsable de la monnaie nationale dont elle régule l'émission, les banques centrales devront collectivement s'accorder sur des diagnostics de la situation monétaire interne et externe de la Communauté. Il serait bon qu'elles débattent de la définition des objectifs nationaux de masse monétaire et de croissance du crédit. Afin de conférer une grande crédibilité au nouveau système, de tenir compte de l'hétérogénéité des situations économiques et de parvenir à un accord à la fois équilibré et incontestable, le choix des objectifs devra tendre vers un taux d'inflation commun, le plus bas possible, comporter des étapes éventuelles pour les économies qui divergent le plus et se prolonger par une procédure de surveillance mutuelle permanente qui nous rende capables de réagir à des chocs et de redresser d'éventuelles déviations.

La coordination des politiques monétaires est en elle-même délicate. Elle sera compliquée au cours de la première étape par l'indépendance des politiques budgétaires, qui sont de la responsabilité des parlements nationaux, et par l'hétérogénéité des concepts et instruments utilisés dans l'analyse monétaire. Toutefois la première difficulté devrait s'atténuer avec la révision de la décision de 1974 du Conseil des Communautés Européennes sur la convergence économique, qui devrait permettre le développement de la coordination des politiques budgétaires, avec des orientations quantitatives précises et à moyen terme. Quant à l'hétérogénéité des définitions monétaires, la mise en place d'un marché unifié des capitaux contribuera sans doute à la réduire, mais un effort d'harmonisation n'en paraît pas moins indispensable.

3.3 *Les étapes suivantes*

Dans la deuxième étape, un système européen de banques centrales serait créé et doté de fonctions opérationnelles mais la responsabilité ultime des décisions de politique monétaire continuerait d'appartenir aux autorités nationales. Il en irait différemment au cours de la troisième étape caractérisée par la fixation irrévocable des parités, le transfert au Système européen de banques centrales de l'ensemble des compétences monétaires et, à terme, l'adoption d'une monnaie unique.

Le transfert progressif des pouvoirs des instances nationales à une institution communautaire s'organisera selon des modalités qu'un traité devra arrêter et en fonction de l'efficacité de la coordination durant la première étape. Sur le plan monétaire, il apparaît souhaitable que, durant la deuxième étape, les réalignements deviennent exceptionnels et d'une amplitude très réduite et que les politiques monétaires nationales se conforment à des orientations générales fixées pour l'ensemble de la Communauté. En outre, l'effort d'harmonisation des réglementations monétaires et bancaires devrait s'intensifier.

Lors de la transition vers la troisième étape, les marchés devraient peu à peu se convaincre de l'irrévocabilité des parités des monnaies européennes et les taux d'intérêt s'aligner progressivement du fait de la parfaite mobilité des capitaux. des écarts pourraient cependant subsister pendant un certain temps, notamment sur les taux longs: ils ne devraient plus refléter des anticipations de change, mais la persistance de déséquilibres entre l'épargne et l'investissement, liés par exemple à des différences dans le poids des dettes publiques. Les monnaies nationales acquérant finalement un caractère de plus en plus substituables, la voie serait ouverte à l'instauration d'une monnaie commune.

CONCLUSION

La SUERF, Société savante européenne, a choisi pour son colloque un thème qui se trouve au coeur de l'actualité en Europe. Puissiez-vous, par vos réflexions, contribuer efficacement aujourd'hui et dans le futur aux développements attendus de l'Europe monétaire.

IIB. Monetary Implications of European Financial Integration

PHILIPPE LAGAYETTE

INTRODUCTION

It is a distinct pleasure to be with you today at this seminar sponsored by SUERF. That society has contributed to the emergence and development of a European spirit in the field of financial research. The process of integration of the markets is now far advanced, even though there are still obstacles to be overcome, and the concept of European monetary unification is approaching a decisive stage. That perspective forms the core of your program and I am glad that you have chosen this time and this country to discuss it.

Although it represents specific objectives and constraints, European financial integration cannot be insulated from the over-all trend of the opening up of the financial markets under the spur of financial innovation and deregulation. That development alone suffices to alter the operating conditions of the financial institutions and the conditions of implementation of monetary policy. The Bank of France has adjusted its instruments to this new situation in recent years by repealing credit ceilings and assigning priority to its money market interventions.

The effects of the globalization of the markets are combined in Europe with the discipline entailed by an increasingly fixed nominal exchange rate system prompted by the determination to make the realignments as infrequent as possible. The EMS, which I will begin with, has prepared us for European integration. But the fact remains that the complete liberalization of capital movements scheduled for July 1990, and the achievement of the single market in 1992, will have serious implications in short order. Finally, the prospect of economic and monetary union, the principal stages of which are outlined in the report of the Committee for study of economic and monetary union and were discussed at the Madrid Summit last June, calls for reconsideration of the role and formulation of national policies.

D. E. Fair and C. de Boissieu (eds), Financial Institutions in Europe Under New Competitive Conditions, 19–26.
© 1990 *Kluwer Academic Publishers, Dordrecht. Printed in the Netherlands.*

1. MONETARY POLICY AFTER TEN YEARS' EXPERIENCE WITH THE EMS

1.1 Principles

The establishment of the EMS in 1979 initially reflected a joint decision by the founding countries to forgo competitive devaluations and excessive overvaluations, a source of inflation in the country whose currency erodes and of distortion of trade. The philosophy basing the EMS goes even farther. It recommends respect for as long as possible of a nominal exchange rate target, leaving it up to the deviating country to reorient its policy. That constraint turned out to be very burdensome, especially in the early years of the EMS, for the comparatively weak currency countries: and while parity realignments concerning one or more currencies had to be made 11 times between 1979 and 1987 (including seven in the first four years), that general philosophy has remained unchanged.

That attempt at convergence would be meaningless and might even have adverse effects were it not coupled with a firm resolve to curb inflation: it is primarily incumbent on the countries the purchasing power of whose currencies has been most impaired by inflation to make the greatest efforts, by anti-inflationary monetary and budgetary policies. But when the average inflation in the system has been brought back down, a problem of more symmetrical distribution of the adjustment burdens may arise if the global growth of the economies concerned is too slow and if certain currencies tend to appreciate excessively.

1.2 The appraisal

The system's life-span alone attests to its success and suffices to distinguish it from the old "snake". No country belonging to the exchange rate mechanism has reconsidered its participation.

The EMS was initially noteworthy for virtuous asymmetry, all of the member countries having been compelled by the system's logic to reduce their inflation gaps with the one(s) whose prices were most stable. The EMS dramatically sharpened the convergence between the nominal variables (prices, wage costs). Thus, the inflation gap between France and Germany exceeded 6 per cent when the EMS was organized in 1979. It is now half of one per cent. The countries in which inflationary pressures were strong in the early 1980s gained more in terms of stabilization, thus improving their prospects, than they lost in terms of growth.

However, this appraisal is partial only. The discipline is not yet universally accepted, since it is expressly confined to the zone of application of the narrow margin exchange rate mechanism. Several countries outside that zone have shown clear signs of overheating in 1988-1989.

Further, while interest rates have often been preferentially affected by the need to respect the exchange rate objectives, budgetary policies have not benefited from the same discipline.

Finally, elimination of the huge subsisting balance of payment disparities in the exchange rate mechanism requires closer cooperation extending beyond monetary policies.

1.3 Conflicts of objectives

Most of the European countries have continued to set money supply growth objectives despite, especially since the mid-1980s, the weakening of the correlation between the stock of money or credit and the nominal GDP. But monetary policy has become harder to implement. And the importance assumed by exchange rate management, particularly in the EMS, may account for conflicts between internal and external goals. That situation seems to be especially difficult to manage since, in most of the countries (including France, in which the desegmentation of the markets and the rise of financial innovation have entailed repeal of credit ceilings and foreign exchange controls), the monetary authorities have a single instrument, interest rates, to attain an internal quantitative money supply objective. Priority use of that instrument to meet the external goal may result in loss of control of the internal objective.

But the conflict of goals is far from permanent; in the countries whose basic balances are still vulnerable and in which underlying inflation is strong, it is even infrequent. In the intermediate term, it should be possible to determine a path of growth of an aggregate of money or credit which is reconcilable with the two results sought. A relatively high interest rate level is a way of both curbing inflation and, by attracting external capital, ensuring a favorable evolution of the basic balance and so of the exchange rate. It is also on such bases that the convergence of inflation rates required for maintenance of the exchange rates can be achieved.

1.4 Ways and means of resolving the conflict of goals

It is in the near term that the conflicts occasionally occur as is now happening in Italy and Spain. A typical conflict appears when the need to curb worrisome inflation or to cool a really overheated economy leads to an interest rate level attracting too much capital and driving up exchange rates.

There are several ways of dealing with them. First, the monetary authorities still have latitude in interest rate management. The mobility of capital is not perfect, less because of the temporary persistence of regulatory restrictions on capital movements than of a localization of savings characterized by a degree of "viscosity". Capital movements are not prompted solely by net yield differentials, as is demonstrated in the financially integrated areas consisting of the nations, but are responsive to other factors such as proximity or preallocation of funds; a degree of inertia is evident in the behavior of savers and money managers. Required reserves also enable the liquidity of the banking system and so the supply of credit to be influenced for short periods, independently of the money market intervention rates. Finally, coordination of the changes in the key rates of the EMS's central banks enhances their ability to influence both the market interest rates and the exchange rates, inasmuch as it affects anticipations more radically than isolated action; the joint decisions by the Bundesbank and the Bank of France in November 1987 and more recently in June 1989 bear this out.

On the foreign exchange markets, the central banks also have ways and means of coping with a temporary goal conflict. They can not only use the fluctuation bands of the exchange rate mechanism but make sterilized interventions, which are effective in very short periods and have been facilitated in the EMS by the Basel/Nyborg agreements which, since September 1987, have expanded the availability of very short term financing.

Finally, goal conflicts are frequently related to a deficient "policy mix" involving excessive use of monetary policy insufficiently backed by budgetary, income or structural policies. In such event, reduction of the goal conflict of monetary policy requires improvement of the "policy mix".

If the goal conflict subsists, the monetary authorities must assign preference to one of the two goals for a given period. France has had little experience with such a situation in very recent years thanks to the decrease of her inflation rate helping to stabilize the franc.

2. THE IMPLICATIONS OF THE SINGLE INTERNAL MARKET

2.1 The synergy between exchange decontrol and freedom to provide financial services

In the financial field, the implementation of the European single act is based on two complementary aspects:
- the liberalization of capital movements by repeal of the last vestiges of exchange controls in June 1990, subject to extension of the deadline in a few countries; and
- the liberalization of financial services which will enable every institution in the European Community to serve customers in the other member countries without qualifying to do business therein and so subject to no restrictions other than those of its home country.

The freedom to provide financial services is an indispensable facet of the achievement of a single market; it can scarcely be conceived without liberalization of capital movements; but the combination of those two principles entails, in addition to their appreciable benefits, which are well known and on which I will not dwell, risks which the member countries' authorities must take into account.

2.2 The risks

France has already repealed practically all restrictions on capital movements: since 1985, successive deregulatory measures have been taken and there now subsists only the prohibition of opening of bank accounts abroad and holding of foreign currencies other than the ECU in France by individuals. The same is true of Italy. Those decisions echo the technical globalization of the markets. They were made possible by the progress in inflation control, which has calmed the markets' apprehensions. In June 1990, the free movement of capital should be total in most of the countries participating in the exchange rate mechanism, without need for any substantial amendment of the existing provisions. But the fact remains that there is a risk of large fund flows in event of a change in the market's assessment of an economy's fundamentals.

That risk is increased by the freedom to provide financial services, which might induce shifts of savings to EEC countries in which the regulatory and tax rules are the least burdensome.

2.3 Steps calculated to contain the risks

This is no reason to forgo achievement of the single internal market because that will afford investors broadened opportunities for switches between sources of financing and financial placements which are favorable to the optimization of financial management by enterprises and individuals. Deregulatory and harmonization measures should, however, enable excessive pressures on the foreign exchange markets or interest rate volatility to be avoided.

Deregulation must start with the markets themselves, in order to eliminate barriers and differences. This will help to improve the allocation of capital, reduce financing costs and enhance the effectiveness of monetary policy by facilitating the spread of its effects in the economy. France has made progress along that line; she has abandoned or partly eliminated certain administrative procedures such as credit ceilings and exchange controls; with the support of the monetary authorities, new financing instruments, closely related to market conditions, have been developed; further steps will have to be taken in order, in particular, to standardize the channels for attracting savings and extending credit.

A significant harmonization effort is also needed in the field of tax treatment of savings to avoid shifts not based on normal competition between financial institutions. It is arguable that the repeal of exchange controls *erga omnes* theoretically suffices to make that effort necessary worldwide; it is even more urgent between integrated economies which are near one another. The harmonization program will have to extend to the restraints on such institutions' operations entailed by the conduct of monetary policy; this is true for instance of the required reserve rules; such reconciliation of the prudential ratios is under way.

2.4 A favourable economic context

In a situation of complete freedom of capital movements, exchange rates will unquestionably be more sensitive than they are now to changes in anticipations. Beyond the regulatory and tax measures that I have mentioned, the need for closer convergence of the economic fundamentals will accordingly be more topical.

3. EUROPEAN MONETARY INTEGRATION

3.1 The joint approach

The achievement of monetary union between member countries, far from giving us greater flexibility to accept exchange rate volatility, requires us to eliminate it. There is no need to panic. To meet these additional challenges, we will have to proceed toward that close union among Europeans that the members of the SUERF surely advocate. In that spirit, the report of the Committee for study of economic and monetary union has outlined the steps toward monetary union.

It has been contended that monetary union was not an indispensable prerequisite for the single internal market. But it is a logical extension thereof since a single market can operate efficiently only with a single price system, entailing in time the irrevocable fixing of exchange rates between the member countries' currencies leading up to a single currency.

The transition to a single currency cannot be a sudden one; it must occur in stages, for two reasons:
– the economic situations must first be converged.
– secondly, establishment of a single currency requires significant institutional innovations which must be preceded by amendment of the treaty of Rome; that is the object of the second step toward economic and monetary union.

3.2 The first stage

To begin with, the first stage, which the European Council in Madrid scheduled to begin on July 1, 1990, will enable the participation in the exchange rate mechanism to be extended to all of the EEC currencies and the economic convergence thus far achieved to be fortified despite the increased fluidity of capital.

This first phase will not be a real break for the countries which have already attained a high degree of convergence and are fully participating in the exchange rate mechanism; but it will require greater coordination of their monetary policies in order to reach jointly fixed goals; for those which will have to catch up with them, it will entail aggravation of the constraints to which the determination of their economic policies is subject as well as greater credibility with the markets and less volatility of their exchange rates. It will have to be turned to account by all to expand the use of the ECU and improve the operations of the EMS.

In spite of its existing imperfections due to its "basket" nature and the existence of two channels, one official and one private, the ECU prefigures the common currency. It would therefore be advisable to accustom people to using it and so to remove the last barriers to its circulation and its use in the EEC and, from the first stage, to encourage its character as an EEC benchmark currency, for instance by contributing to the development of a vast market in negotiable ECU-denominated securities; that will be an important step toward the strengthening of Europe's monetary identity. The recent initiatives of the British Exchequer and the French Treasury Department are conducive to that end.

In the first stage, the improvement of the EMS's operations will have to occur in the existing institutional framework but must include materially increased monetary policy coordination by enhancement of the role of the committee of governors of the EEC's central banks. That committee should, according to the Delors report, be assisted by three specialized subcommittees having study and supervisory functions in the fields of monetary policy, foreign exchange and bank oversight. Although each central bank remains solely responsible for its national currency, all of them will have to agree on diagnoses of the EEC's internal and external monetary situation. It would be advisable for them to discuss the setting of national money supply and credit growth goals. To make the new system very credible, to take the differences of the economic situations into account and to achieve balanced and uncontestable agreement, the agreed goals will have to tend toward a common inflation rate which is as low as possible, involve possible stages for the economies which diverge the most and be supplemented by a standing mutual oversight procedure enabling us to react to shocks and to correct any drifts.

Monetary policy coordination is inherently difficult. It will be complicated in the first stage by the independence of the budgetary policies, for which the national Parliaments are responsible, and by the differences in the concepts and instruments used in monetary analysis. But the former difficulty should be attenuated by the amendment of the 1974 decision of the Council of the European Communities on economic convergence, which should enable budgetary policy coordination to increase, with precise and medium term quantitative guidelines; as for the differences in monetary definitions, the establishment of a unified financial market will unquestionably help to reduce them, but harmonization nonetheless appears to be indispensable.

3.3 The ensuing stages

In the second stage, a European central bank system would be established and assigned operational functions but the final responsibility for monetary policy decisions would continue to be incumbent on the national authorities; matters would be different in the third stage, noteworthy for irrevocable fixing of exchange rates, transfer of all monetary jurisdiction to the European central bank system and, in time, adoption of a single currency.

Progressive transfer of the national authorities' powers to an EEC institution will go forward according to procedures that will have to be formulated by treaty and depending on the efficiency of the coordination in the first stage. From the monetary standpoint, it seems advisable in the second stage for realignments to be infrequent and small and for the national monetary policies to conform to general guidelines for the entirety of the Community. In addition, harmonization of monetary and banking regulations should intensify. When the transition is made to the third stage, the markets should gradually become convinced of the irrevocability of the exchange rates of the European currencies, and interest rates should progressively be brought into line by the perfect mobility of capital. But differences could subsist for some time, especially on the long rates; these should no longer reflect exchange rate anticipations but the persistence of imbalances between saving and investment, due for instance to differences in the weight of public debt. Increasing interchangeability of the national currencies would pave the way for establishment of a common currency.

CONCLUSION

The SUERF, a European learned society, has selected for its seminar a theme which is at the height of topicality in Europe. May you, by your reflections, make an efficient contribution today and hereafter to the expected developments of monetary Europe.

III. The European Regulatory and Supervisory Framework

GEOFFREY E. FITCHEW*

It is clear that as we move towards 1992 in the financial services sector, financial institutions in the Community will be the subject of new competitive conditions. What I want to look at is the present state of development of the regulatory and supervisory framework at the European level (and then how this relates to developments in the Community's competition policy). I then want to look at what else needs to be done if we are to arrive at our destination of a fully liberalized internal market in Europe.

It is perhaps useful just to recapitulate what we mean when we are talking about 1992:

The single market is defined as: 'An area without internal frontiers in which the free movement of goods, persons, services and capital is ensured'.

Two points need to be made about the nature of the 1992 programme in the financial services sector:

First, 1992 certainly does *not* mean an overnight revolution; it does not mean that the Commission or anyone else will pull a switch on 31 December 1992 and the scenery of the promised land will suddenly appear. The programme is a continuous process of change which has already begun and which will no doubt continue beyond 1992. Some of the proposals which I will mention later on have already come into effect or will do before 1992.

Linked with the first point, we will certainly not achieve (even if it were considered desirable, which it is not) complete *uniformity* of market conditions by 1 January 1993. For example, we will still have at least to a considerable extent twelve different laws of contract, twelve different sets of company law, twelve different tax regimes and different consumer protection legislation. Some of these differences will present obstacles to free trade in financial services, which may have to be removed *after* 1992, either by the eroding forces of competition or by actions before the Court of by further harmonization.

* The views expressed by the author are not necessarily those of the Commission of the European Communities.

D. E. Fair and C. de Boissieu (eds), Financial Institutions in Europe Under New Competitive Conditions, 27–37.
© 1990 Kluwer Academic Publishers, Dordrecht. Printed in the Netherlands.

But we are convinced that we are well on the way to achieving three major advances in the financial services sector by the end of 1992:
- freedom of capital movements
- freedom of establishment (the right to open branches)
- freedom for cross-frontier provision of services

The ideal we are aiming at is that any bank, insurance company or investment business should be able to open up a branch in any other Member State as easily as it can in its home Member State; and that similarly any of these financial institutions should be able to market and sell the full range of its financial services and financial products across frontiers to any customer in any other Member States as easily as it can in its home Member State.

This does not of course mean the market can be unregulated. Even in the most liberalized financial centres, all the major types of financial institutions are regulated. (Indeed it is in some of the most liberalized markets that the regulations in force are the most detailed and stringent). Financial markets world-wide are regulated for two reasons; first because the stability of the financial system (in particular the banking system) is a public good, which market forces on their own are not guaranteed to produce; second, in order to protect the investor, depositor and policy-holder against the wide and imaginative variety of frauds and scandals, to which financial markets have always been exposed.

We in the Commission are involved in the business of regulating financial markets for two reasons. First, because we are under an obligation to ensure that the opening up of the Community financial market does not put at risk either the stability of the banking system or the protection of consumers. Second, because all too frequently it is the differences in Member States' national regulatory systems which are the main obstacles to cross-frontier competition. One man's prudential regulation is another man's trade barrier.

So we are drawn into harmonizing regulatory systems as an essential precondition for removing these obstacles. As is well known, we have now moved away from the very detailed comprehensive harmonization of the late 1960s and early 1970s to a three stage approach:

Building on the basic principles of the Treaty and legislation already adopted by the Community, the general method which the White Paper adopts is:
- *the harmonization of essential standards* for prudential supervision of finanical institutions and for the protection of investors, depositors and consumers;
- *mutual recognition* by the supervisory authorities of financial institutions in each Member State of the way in which they apply those standards;
- based on the first two elements, "*home country control and supervision*" (i.e. control and supervision by the Member State in which the financial institution is based) of financial institutions which wish to operate in other

Member States either by establishment or by offering their services directly across frontiers.

We are now well past the halfway stage on the road to our 1992 objective. The Commission had already put forward by the end of last year all the 25 proposals we were scheduled to make in the financial services sector. To date 12 have been adopted by the Council of Ministers and in the case of a further five Common Positions have already been agreed by the Council. I want to look at where we have got to with these proposals.

LIBERALIZATION OF CAPITAL MOVEMENTS

The single most important element in our programme is the liberalization of capital movements – the life-blood of cross-frontier trade in financial services. During most of the 1970s only two Member States (Germany and the Netherlands) allowed unrestricted freedom of capital movements. The rest imposed more or less heavy direct exchange controls or other penalties on outward capital movements. Over the last few years these shackles have been gradually loosened. In 1979 the United Kingdom removed all its exchange controls in a matter of months. In the course of the last few years controls on most capital movements have been dismantled here in France, in Italy and Denmark and loosened in Ireland and the two-tier market is being phased out in Belgium. The Community took the decisive legislative step on this matter on the 24 June 1988, when the Council of Finance Ministers adopted a final Directive liberalizing all capital movements, including for the first time all short-term monetary instruments and transactions, such as the opening of current and deposit accounts.

This Directive will enter into force in June 1990 for eight Member States; four Member States (Ireland, Greece, Portugal and Spain) being given a further derogation until the end of 1992.

The importance of this final step is that the freedom to open bank accounts abroad will enable Community residents and corporations to use these accounts to carry out a wide range of previously forbidden or controlled transactions. Cross-frontier competition should also be enhanced, because those Member States, which have still maintained exchange controls have, as part of the control system, required even permitted transactions to be carried out through domestic intermediaries. That type of discriminatory requirement will also have to disappear. I should mention incidentally that even in those countries which already claim to have liberalized there are still barriers to be removed, notably the exceptionally stringent controls applied to the investment policies of pension funds and insurance companies. We are now examining these and other distortions, such as discriminatory tax incentives to invest in domestic securities, to see what further action is needed.

Freedom of capital movements is, however, only a one-way street. It permits the customer to go to the foreign bank or to transact on the foreign stock exchange but not *vice versa*. To complete it we need freedom of cross-frontier services.

I want now to look in more detail at banking, securities markets and the insurance sector.

BANKING

The First Banking Coordination Directive of 1977 achieved three main goals:
- it cleared away most of the obstacles to freedom of establishment of banks and other credit institutions;
- it laid down common standards for the granting of banking licences;
- it introduced the basic principle of home country control.

But there are still obstacles to be removed before a genuinely unified Community banking market can exist:
- a bank or other credit institution needs authorisations from 11 different supervisors to set up branches in all Member States;
- banking services cannot be provided across frontiers in all Member States;
- banking activities have not been defined.

The Second Banking Coordination Directive aims to remove all of these barriers:
- it lays down the idea of a single banking licence valid throughout the community which will authorize a bank or credit institution to supply its services throughout Europe either by branches or by provision of banking services;
- a list of banking activities (including not only the traditional services of deposit-taking and lending but also new ones for some Member States e.g. trading in securities) is laid down;
- a minimum level of capital (own funds) of 5 m. ECU is laid down for new banks;
- supervisory rules are spelt out in respect of internal management and audit systems. A limit is imposed on equity participation in non-financial companies to less than 10 per cent of own funds;
- control of major shareholders.

Flanking legislation is also designed to guarantee the stability of the market, to ensure equality of competition between banks and credit institutions within the Community and to prevent the migration of banks to countries with less strict supervision. This legislation includes:
- a definition of banks' "own funds", based on an earlier agreement reached

on harmonizing banks' accounting requirements;
- a Directive for a harmonized solvency ratio which will lay down high standards for the solvency of banks and other credit institutions, on the basis of a risk-weighting approach and a comprehensive treatment of all off-balance sheet items. This is closely in line with the Cooke Committee recommendations on capital adequacy;
- rules for the guarantee of depositors and rules on large risks undertaken by credit institutions.

Decisions will be needed soon as to whether to convert the last two from Recommendations into Directives. On all the other legislation good progress is being made. The Own Funds proposal was adopted recently and the Council of Ministers reached "Common positions" on the Second Banking Directive and the Solvency Ratios Directive in July. There is an excellent prospect they will be adopted later this year under the French Presidency.

SECURITIES MARKETS

If our proposals for the banking sector are already largely in place and agreed, there remains much more to be done in relation to *securities markets* and *insurance*.

In the case of securities markets we have to try to secure the necessary freedoms for three categories of players – *investors, issuers* and *intermediaries*. Freedom of action for the *investor* is already assured by the capital movements Directive.

So far as *issuers* are concerned, the objective must be to create a genuine Community-wide market in which companies should be free to raise capital and be admitted to stock exchange trading in other Member States as easily as in their own market, consistently with adequate investor protection and disclosure standards. A number of steps have already been taken towards this goal:
- *Conditions for admission to stock exchange listing* were harmonised by a 1979 Directive.
- *Stock exchange listing particulars* have been harmonized as the result of a Directive adopted by the Council in 1980. Member States have also agreed since 1987 on mutual recognition, i.e. that they will accept listing particulars, which meet the requirements of the 1980 Directive, for the purpose of admission to listing in another Member State without additional authorization.
- An agreement was reached under the Greek Presidency in December 1988 on a *Directive on the first public offer prospectus*, which also provides for "mutual recognition" of the disclosure standards imposed when shares are first offered to the public. This should facilitate simultaneous offerings on more than one exchange.

So far so good, but "mutual recognition" at this stage only extends to the listing and public offer *documents* and not to the decisions to admit companies to listing. Could we not now consider going beyond this to identify criteria under which at least the major issuers are *automatically* eligible for listing on any Community stock exchange? In this context we welcome the recent decision of the European Federation of Stock Exchanges to pursue the so-called "Pipe" project for the real-time transmission of share price and company data of major European firms to their member exchanges.

We also have to be aware of the wider international context. The major international issuers will want to be listed in New York and Tokyo as well as Frankfurt, Paris and London. A major challenge for international regulators is to see if progress can be made to "mutual recognition" of listing and disclosure requirements for all three time-zones. We in the Commission welcome the thought being given to this problem in IOSCO and the IASC and will be cooperating with both of these institutions in their further work.

So far as *intermediaries* are concerned a major achievement is the Directive of 1985 which deals with "open-ended" investment funds or UCITS as they are known in Community jargon (undertakings for collective investment in transferable securities). This Directive, which came into force on 1 October, will allow an investment fund authorized in its home Member State to be sold freely across frontiers into other Member States.

A draft proposal on investment services was adopted by the Commission last December. This is an essential complement to the proposal for the Second Banking Coordination Directive; providing for a similar liberalization of the securities-related services provided by non-banking intermediaries as for banks. It introduces a single licence for both branching and cross-frontier provision of all forms of investment service – broking, dealing, market-making and portfolio management. The Directive will also enable anyone duly authorized by his home country to become a member of a stock exchange or other authorized market in another Member State. I should emphasize, however – because there has been some misunderstanding on this point – we are not seeking to dictate to Member States how their stock exchanges should be organized.

Under this Directive host country rules will still apply to the conduct of business by the investment services with retail clients. Home country rules will, however be needed for minimum initial capital and capital requirements for market risk. These rules will be the subject of a separate Directive early next year, on which we are now consulting Member States. Both the G 10 Recommendation of June 1988 on Capital Adequacy and the Community's Solvency Directive deal only with "credit risk" for banks. But both banks and non-bank securities operations are exposed to a number of other

analytically quite distinct risks. The four most important are:
- interest rate risk;
- foreign exchange risk;
- "position risk" arising from open positions in securities;
- settlement risk.

We are still at a relatively early stage in our discussions with the Member States on these questions. It already seems clear that we will need to find solutions which accommodate two different approaches. On the one hand, the supervisors of non-bank investment firms in the USA, the UK, France and, more recently, Japan have adopted capital adequacy systems, attuned to the rapid changes in size and composition of the investment firm's book. Such systems are based on marking-to-market daily and usually differentiate to a greater or lesser extent between the price volatility and thus the degree of position risk, attaching to different kinds of security. On the other hand there is the "Universal bank" philosophy which is typical of Germany and the Netherlands. In these countries, securities business is largely, though not exclusively, the preserve of the banks. Prudential supervision of the banks' capital adequacy is consolidated. Securities business is usually a relatively small part of the bank's business and accordingly no special account is taken of "position risk" associated with securities trading in calculating capital requirements. The German supervisors have, however, fairly recently decided to introduce a system of quantitative limits on net open positions.

Intuitively, particularly from an economist's point of view, there seems a lot to be said for the more sophisticated mark-to-market approach. But it is very difficult to argue, given the historical strength of the universal bank system, notably in Germany, that the banking supervisors' approach is wrong, still less that it is unsafe. A further point on which views differ is the definition of capital (or "own funds"). Here the banking supervisors prefer to put a greater emphasis on permanent capital (equity and reserves), because of the ongoing need to protect depositors. The securities market supervisors in contrast allow greater use of subordinated debt, but require a strict deduction of all illiquid assets.

We will probably need to find proposals which allow these different systems to live together side-by-side at least in the short-term, and which do not disadvantage European firms vis-à-vis their US and Japanese competitors.

INSURANCE

In the insurance sector last year saw a first major step forward to genuine freedom of services in insurance. After nearly 15 years of negotiation the Second Non-Life Directive was finally adopted by the ECOFIN Council in June under *German Presidency*.

The final phase of negotations on this Directive began immediately after the European Court's judgements of 4 December 1986. The result is the Second Non-Life Insurance Coordination Directive, which was adopted on 22 June 1988 and will come into force in July 1990.

In accordance with the philosophy of the Court's judgement the Directive recognizes that "mass risks" (the smaller policyholders) require more protection than "large risks" (commercial policyholders). For "large risks", regulation will be carried out for the most part in the state where the insurer is established. There is thus no prior harmonization of either technical reserves or of policy conditions. For "mass risks", the state where the risk is situated may, subject to certain conditions, apply the authorization requirements and controls which the Court permitted.

This Second Non-Life Directive does nevertheless constitute a major breakthrough because it establishes the Community-wide internal market in non-life insurance.

Admittedly, at this stage, it only does so for the so-called "large risks". One important benefit is that industrial and commercial concerns having risks situated throughout the Community will now be able to insure them under a single contract, if they wish, without having to resort to complicated and expensive fronting operations.

Since the adoption of the Second Non-Life Directive on 22 June 1988, we have continued to follow the logic of the Court's judgement and to seek to identify cases where we can persuade the Council and Parliament that the policy-holder does not stand in special need of protection. This is the approach we have followed in two new draft Directives adopted by the Commission in December last year. The first of these is a Directive providing for cross-frontier freedom of services for motor insurance. Here we have extended the distinction between *large risks* and *mass risks* in the Second Non-Life Directive to motor insurance (both civil liability and vehicle damage); if the Directive is adopted, the larger car fleet or commercial vehicle owner will be able to buy insurance wherever he wants within the Community.

To safeguard the interests of accident victims in a freedom-of-services context the proposal allows Member States to require an on-the-spot claims settlement representative, without this constituting the opening of a branch or agency.

The second of these proposals, the *Second Life Directive*, also adopted by the Commission in December last, is a modest first step towards achieving genuine cross-frontier competition in the life sector. In it we have drawn a distinction between the "active" and "passive" selling of insurance, by introducing specially liberalized rules in order to remove the barriers to cross-frontier "own initiative" insurance i.e. where the customer takes the initiative (which in some Member States is still a criminal offence).

We have proposed this first step for two reasons:
- first, any restrictions on own initiative insurance will become increasingly meaningless and unenforceable with complete freedom on capital movements;
- second, to keep the momentum going after *the Second Non-Life Directive* and prepare the way for work on "mass risks".

Although I have described this proposal as modest it contains some elements which are regarded as controversial in some quarters. In particular, we are proposing that "own initiative" insurance should include the case where the customer does business with an insurance company in another Member State through a broker whether in his own Member State or elsewhere.

Own initiative insurance *must* in our view include the freedom of the client to approach a broker and we in the Commission cannot discriminate between brokers in the client's own Member State and elsewhere. Nevertheless, we have made this liberalization conditional on a number of safeguards, in particular the signing of a declaration by the customer to demonstrate that he is shopping abroad of his own free choice.

We are also planning to come forward with a proposal to liberalize the provision of group insurance, in particular pension schemes. Here again we are trying to identify a category of "larger risks" where the purchasers of insurance can be regarded as strong enough to take care of themselves.

But the heart of our future work – and the most difficult problems – lie in the area of *mass risks* for both life and non-life. We are aiming to produce proposals on non-life by the end of 1989 and on life in 1990. In its judgement of December 1986 the European Court said that in order to liberalize the "mass risks" market, harmonization may need to extend both to technical reserves and to general and special policy conditions. As far as technical reserves are concerned, it will be necessary to examine not only the question of the nature and valuation of the reserves (where the most controversial point is undoubtedly equalization reserves, since there is an agreement neither on when they are needed nor on how they should be calculated), but also on the nature, spread and valuation for supervisory purposes of the assets representing those reserves. (The admissibility or not of claims against reinsurers is perhaps the single most difficult issue). As regards the representation of assets we have to look at how far it is really necessary or justified in an era of global securities markets, to require insurance companies, on grounds of consumer protection, to hold x per cent of their assets in government securities or y per cent in real estate in the country where the risk is situated. I am bound to say that I am sceptical of the validity of such requirements.

We have already (end 1986) put forward a Directive on the annual and consolidated accounts of insurance companies which contains rules on how technical reserves should be shown in the accounts. We are now considering whether we need to go beyond the harmonizing implicit in the Accounts Directive for prudential purposes. The answer may well be that the Accounts Directive will largely suffice.

We have also to look critically at the question as to how far there is really a need to harmonize general and special policy conditions for both life and non-life insurance as a means of protecting the consumer.

The danger is that detailed control of policy conditions will simply stifle innovation.

The relative lack of progress in insurance creates difficulties not only for the Commission but also for the insurance industry in the Community. The consumer is now presented by banks and other financial institutions with a wide range of *investment products* some of which are increasingly difficult to distinguish from insurance products. If the insurance industry does not adapt, it will lose market share to these competitors.

If the insurance industry does not adapt, it will also miss out on the great opportunities offered by the single market. Insurance is likely to be a growth sector in the next two decades. As Europe grows richer, its citizens will be ready to spend more on insurance (per capita expenditure on insurance premiums is only half that in USA). Provision of group and personal pensions is particularly likely to offer new opportunities given the demographic changes which are taking place in the Community as in other industrialized countries.

THE FRONTIER BETWEEN HOME COUNTRY CONTROL AND HOST COUNTRY CONTROL

As I have already mentioned, a central characteristic of the regulating approach we have adopted is the concept of "home country control" of banks and other financial institutions. But "home country control" is an ideal which we do not yet believe can be applied to all aspects of supervision and consumer protection. Our main aim is to apply the "home country control" to the process of authorization and the supervision of solvency and financial soundness. The proposal in which the "home country control" Directive has been most fully developed is the UCITS Directive adopted in 1985 which comes into force this year. This leaves only "marketing and advertising" under "host country" control. Even this has been criticised in some countries as not going far enough. Elsewhere, as in the Investment Services Directive, we have felt obliged to leave "conduct of business rules" fully in the hands of host countries.

I am bound to say the division between home and host country is a cause of some concern to us. There is clearly a risk that host country regulation of the conduct of business or even of marketing and advertising can lead to the creation of serious obstacles to cross-frontier trade. We will have to keep a watchful eye open for this. In some cases further legislation may be needed. For example we shall make it clear in an amendment to the Second Banking Directive that any authorized bank must have access to all the normal advertising media. We will probably also in the due course seek some further harmonization of deposit guarantee and investor compensation schemes.

On the whole the approach we have adopted in this area is to wait until the problems are thrown up and hopefully solved by the market itself. It is clear though that further litigation before the European Court and perhaps also some further harmonization may be necessary to remove "host country" rules which constitute serious obstacles.

Since this is a Conference about the regulation of financial markets, let me emphasise three further points. First, regulation is costly – ultimately to the consumer. So we try to keep our efforts at harmonization to the minimum necessary. Second, regulators need to practice caution and humility in interfering with markets. Again a powerful argument for minimum harmonization and a large degree of 'competition between rules'. Third, none of us in the Commission believes that regulation is achieved by writing Directives on pieces of paper. That is no more than a starting point. In today's markets effective regulation also requires effective and close cooperation between supervisors. That cooperation is already well advanced within the Community. We in the Commission will also do everything we can to promote such cooperation world-wide.

IV. Banking Strategies for the 1990s

ANDRÉ LEVY-LANG

I feel as though I am a rather non-traditional, slightly peripheral banker, compared to the main trend noted in universal banks. I am going to assume that your choice was a deliberate one, and not merely the outcome of chance or coincidence, and I shall therefore take the viewpoint of Compagnie Bancaire and not that of universal banks. In other words, the viewpoint of a group of institutions specialized in financial services, which does not exercise the basic profession of collecting bank deposits as commercial banks do, but which has recently become European enough to reflect an outlook not exclusively French.

What is Europe's situation now, at the end of 1989? And to what extent will the advent of "1992" change this situation? How will other factors of change come into play independently of 1992? Such are the three points which I shall discuss with you before broaching the topic of possible banking strategies in the coming years.

TODAY'S SITUATION

Today, Europe's banking markets are characterized by a rather strong concentration in each country. The four or five principal banks currently enjoy a dominant share in each national market – with a relatively low foreign penetration, falling short of 20 per cent – with the noteworthy exceptions of Great Britain, Belgium and Luxembourg. The consequence of this situation in each country is that no major European bank exists, and each of the leading banks on its national market holds only a few per cent of the European market – in this respect, the March 1989 issue of the EIB Notebooks (N°. 8) is a good reference.

Another characteristic of European national markets is the broad development of banking services and of physical banking equipment – with considerable variations but generally speaking a high density of bank branches. This situation can be explained by the regulated nature of banking activity – here again with noteworthy differences from one country to another –

D. E. Fair and C. de Boissieu (eds), Financial Institutions in Europe Under New Competitive Conditions, 39–46.
© 1990 *Kluwer Academic Publishers, Dordrecht. Printed in the Netherlands.*

and notably by the regulation of the prices of banking activities.

Regulations, or the restrictive practices which replace them in certain countries, have reduced price competition and encouraged service competition notably in the collection of deposits, whence the development of payment services, through neighborhood branches and automatic tellers.

These characteristics, which are common to national markets, must not make us lose sight of the considerable environmental differences which will disappear only progressively:

- *Technical Environment*: means of communication (telephone and mail, Transpac type data transmission systems), interbank payment systems (clearing, automatic withdrawal), cash distribution systems (ATM networks), card payment systems (interbank operations) – the differences in the technical equipment available from country to country affect both the productivity of the national banking system and the penetration possibilities available to foreign banks. Both grow as the environment is modernized and as interbanking systems develop.
- *Taxation*: savings taxation, taxation on borrowings and on real estate (deductibility of interest), taxation on transactions (for example stock market tax), taxation of financial businesses (specific taxes, VAT). One might say that the rule in tax matters is the differences, and that harmonizing will be the exception. It is difficult however to estimate the consequences of these differences other than in general terms.
- *Activity regulation and operator regulation*: in the domain of activity regulation, the differences involve protection of the public (borrowers and savers). For operations, there are fewer regulation differences: the universal bank is the accepted model throughout. The boundaries of this all-purposeness vary however, particularly with respect to stock market and insurance brokerage. In the field of stock market brokerage, regulations and above all practices, vary a great deal from one country to another regarding the protection of savers, and as of today Great Britain is the only country in which "Chinese walls" exist and are effectively controlled. This has consequences primarily for bank-related activities engaged in by commercial banks, as well as for shares which banks may take in other activities – in other words consequences for their diversification and partnership strategies.
- *Difference of Commercial Environment*: lastly, with varying development, depending on the country, of nonbanking distribution channels: insurance brokers and agents (with rules which may vary from one country to another), commodity distribution networks (mailorder houses, large retail stores).

In short and very schematically, one might say that EEC domestic markets are all in a situation of limited competition, to varying degrees, but that factors of evolution, beginning with this situation, vary greatly from one country to another. A study published by Peat Marwick in 1988 attempted to quantify this situation by providing figures, country by country and activity by activity, corresponding to the potential for reducing financial gross margins due to future competition. The figures are questionable, but the methodology and general conclusions appear to me to indicate a probable evolution toward a reduction of financial intermediation margins in Europe.

WHAT WILL CHANGE WITH THE UNIFIED MARKET?

It seems to me that each of the three liberties brought about by the unified market, liberalization of capital movements, liberalization of services and free establishment, contributes in a different manner to the evolution which banking strategies must take into account.

Free capital circulation appears to me to be the most important in its consequences. It alters the demand for financial services, at least for the major financial actors. The evolution in the demand by major corporations, for which the free circulation of capital has in fact existed for a long time, is the best illustration of this. Today, the market constituted by large corporations has become a quasi-perfect competitive market from the stand-point of financial services.

By reaching out to encompass smaller businesses and a portion of households, the free circulation of capital will provoke an evolution in its demand for financial services, as it did for large corporations. Of course the free circulation of capital has monetary and macro-economic implications, which I shall not discuss here.

Free services supply is the topic of a great deal of regulation and legal debate. This appears to me to be of relatively less importance. However, it will have an indirect effect, by allowing the appearance of a marginal offer on each market which may result in an evolution of national regulation frameworks. For example, in matters of mortgage credit or credit granted to individuals, it will become more difficult to maintain certain forms of pseudo-protection of borrowers in France, when each person is able to see that our most civilized neighbours do not deem them necessary and are therefore able to offer less expensive credit.

Free establishment already exists to a great extent. The existing obstacles are not all apparent, and their disappearance depends more on the will of the national authorities responsible for approving banks and insurance companies than on guidelines from Brussels.

Today, after having created or purchased approximately twenty establishments outside France, in various fields of finance, including insurance, we can testify to the major discrepancies which, in practice, remain among EEC countries in matters of free establishment.

The test of this freedom will come about the day, if that day ever comes, on which the merger of two major banks, located in two EEC countries, comes up. Theoretically, nothing stands in the way of a project such as this. But will it be accepted by the public authorities?

Free establishment leads me to the topic of the *behavioural effects* induced by the prospect of the unified market, which appear to me to be at least as important as those of the regulated changes. The behaviour of clients who have become aware of the potential existence of an offer beyond their borders, thanks to the media and their politicians who have explained to them at length that July 1st, 1990 was the fateful date in financial matters. The behaviour above all of financial enterprises which all seem to have adopted the following attitude: "I don't exactly know what will change in 1993, but I am taking all the necessary measures to be prepared for it..." Whence the wave of agreements, of new subsidiaries, and acquisitions, which will necessarily have an effect on supply and accelerate the evolution which has already begun in each country.

WHAT WILL CHANGE REGARDLESS OF 1993?

The advent of the unified financial market is occurring along with other changes in the environment of financial professions – changes with effects just as important on banks' strategies. These other changes involve all banks in developed economies and not only those within the EEC. They involve on the one hand client behaviour, and that of banks, on the other hand.

The change in client behaviour is induced by the development of data and communication means combined with the durable maintenance of high interest rates. Economic agents, households, businesses and institutions enjoy rapid, convenient access to a mass of economic and financial data.

In the instance of market data (exchange rates, price of securities, etc...), the networks distributing these data (Reuter, Telerate), are increasingly providing means for transmission and the carrying out of transactions. Lastly, the persistence of high interest rates – regardless of the causes – is inciting economic agents to manage their finances – excess liquidities or financing needs – more closely.

Bank intermediation, which relies in particular on data management by the bank and on a transaction service, is confronting a drop in data access costs, a drop in transaction costs and a rise in opportunity costs for clients who do not manage their finances in the best manner possible.

The consequences for bank strategy appear to me to be numerous and deep:

- a development in the purchasing of specialized financial products or services, to the detriment of the overall relationship between the client and his bank: more easy access to numerous offers, high opportunity costs, make the bundling of products implied by the global relationship become precarious. This is the transition from relationship banking to transaction banking.
- a loosening of proximity constraints in the financial service supply relation: the trade off between transport time and service cost which justified the development of a local supply of services is taking place under different conditions: transport costs less or is replaced by economical transmission means, while the price of the failure to optimize the product increases – clients have every reason to go farther to find a better product.
- a change in behaviour in the domain of clients' management of assets and liabilities. Not so long ago, clients had to go out to seek credits, but managed their liquidities and their savings passsively. Today, savings management has become an active matter, while credit, which is broadly available, has become automatic through plastic cards.

This means that bankers' precepts of conventional wisdom, the foundation of their traditional strategy, are in the process of becoming outdated – examples of such precepts: "one changes banks less often than one does spouses" – "cash deposits displaced toward long products always replenish themselves" – "a borrower with a home mortgage is a client for life".

These evolutions can be observed throughout – and the banks who have understood this are those which are already experiencing greater success. These are often banks outside the EEC, in particular American banks which were the first to experience deregulation and derive its benefits.

The change in banks' behaviour is a consequence of the rule fixing solvency ratios following the "Cooke" report. By establishing a uniform rule for all international banks, this report created a minimum profitability constraint for banking assets, because the capital stock necessary for covering these assets must indeed be remunerated. By placing the accent on asset profitability, the Cooke report opened the door for cost accounting and economic analysis in banks and slowly led them to review their development strategy in the same terms as any commercial enterprise which must analyze the profitability of its activities and investments. This has already been developed – I merely wanted to emphasize that this change affects all banks, independently of the unified European market.

THE STRATEGIC ISSUES FOR BANKS

As it confronts these changes, each bank must choose its strategies according to its own situation. There are therefore as many strategies as there are banks and it would be useless to attempt to formulate general rules.

There are however several questions which must be asked and to which the economists studying the sector can perhaps provide elements of reply. Indeed, one often hears statements justifying such or such strategy with advantages which are thought to be obvious: economies of scale, critical size, globalization, complete range of services. Are these truly strategic advantages? Without replying, I would like to enumerate a few questions:

- economies of scale: are yields increasing in financial professions and, if so, up to what size? Just asking the question suffices to show that it is poorly formulated and that a distinction must be made between the professions and the factors of economies of scale for each profession – administrative processing costs, costs of funds, distribution costs (notably brand and image effects and advertising costs), effectiveness of fund management.

- For each of these cost factors, I am tempted to say that there are economies of scale, but that they saturate at relatively low levels – which vary depending on the case – and to add that, when dealing with services, and therefore activities which depend greatly on the quality of men and organizations, diseconomies of scale also exist and decreasing yields in enterprises beyond a certain size.

- globalization: very fashionable several years ago, with the image of markets which never close, but less so since October 1987. Is it absolutely necessary and, if so, for which professions and at what price? In this respect there has been a tendency to reduce the banking profession to that of a dealing room.

- the complete range of services or scope economies: the underlying idea is that the clientele relation has a (distribution) cost and a value (that of the client's loyalty or inertia) and therefore that the broadening of the range of services offered to each client is more advantageous (more profitable) than the separate offer of each service. This idea is at the root of the universal bank, at the root also of numerous partnerships, insurance-banks, etc... It obviously comprises a strong dose of truth. Should we perhaps specify its limits and calculate its impact in figures? I have already mentioned the drop in distribution costs, and the increasing mobility of clients which weaken the value of the personal relation. We must add the costs of training sales personnel when broadening product range, the absolute limits on the number of products which a given individual can become familiar with and sell. We must also take into account the possible conflicts between products (management consulting and business credit for example), the desire on the part of clients for privacy and independence. In short, economies of scope are not automatic and there is an entire field of reflection and analysis to be explored in order to enlighten the strategic choices made by banks.

Without concluding, following these remarks and questions, I shall make several comments on the strategies adopted by the financial actors as they have been noted in past years.

We must first of all note that few European banks express their development strategies publicly – this is particularly true of the large universal banks. This is undoubtedly due to the discretion they prefer to maintain regarding their strategies. We must therefore judge from their actions and comment on the rare explicit strategies made known – because there are a few.

Development by acquisition of existing universal banking networks is hardly frequent. We can quote the acquisitions by the Deutsche Bank in Italy (Banca d'America et d'Italia) and in Spain, those by the Crédit Lyonnais in the Netherlands and in Italy. The other cases involve very modest networks and a few branch offices. The scarcity of network acquisitions can be explained of course by the absence of offers – but one might think that this is an evolving situation and that in the coming years sellers of such networks will exist or at least candidates for regrouping. When this does occur, national banking authorities will perhaps have a difficult choice to make between European solutions – accepting foreign shareholders for relatively major banks – and national solutions – which can comprise a high social cost if there is a subsequent rationalization of networks.

A certain number of universal banks have adopted a different strategy, which is that of specialization outside their borders in bank-related professions: leasing, consumer lending, fund management. This is a strategy which has already been successfully implemented for a long time by Société Générale in the domain of leasing. Certain British and Spanish banks appear to have adopted the same strategy without saying so. This reminds us of what was observed in the United States at the end of the 1970s: as they could not open branches outside their home state, many major American banks purchased finance companies specializing in consumer loans or in leasing activities, in order to "be present" when legislative borders would fall. None of them succeeded – neither the synergy with its own activities, nor the extension of the businesses purchased. The latter were often resold to recover capital stock invested (this was the case with the Bank of America and Manufacturers Hanover) or, at best, remained autonomous subsidiaries, distinct from the bank. Without exaggerating the parallel between the United States and Europe, one might think that the transitions from the profession of universal bank to that of specialized banker, and vice versa, are not easy exercises to accomplish.

Another type of strategy, for a universal bank, is that of crossed holdings of minority shares, or more generally speaking, that of "clubs". These clubs, which were very much in vogue during the 1970s, are apparently experiencing a comeback – in particular the Euro-Partners (Crédit-Lyonnais, Commerz-bank, Banco di Roma, Banco Hispano Americano, ...). It is impossible to judge the impact and effectiveness of this type of club from the outside – or of the closer bilateral relations to which they may give rise – and I shall certainly not attempt to do so. In theory, they nonetheless constitute an attractive formula the evolution of which it will be interesting to observe.

This inventory, and the preceding analyses have perhaps convinced you that a group of specialized establishments, such as the Compagnie Bancaire for example, is the best structure for tackling the unified financial market. If this is the case, you can understand that I am overjoyed. Despite appearances, I would not like to give you the impression that we are convinced that we hold the truth. I do not believe that there is a dominant strategy for banking markets for the coming years – ours any more than that of the universal banks. I merely wanted to put forth a number of questions which will I hope help to launch your work, which I am sure will be fruitful and interesting.

Part B
Competition in Banking Services
and Its Implications

V. Financial Innovation, Internationalization, Deregulation and Market Integration in Europe: Why Does It All Happen Now?

ALFRED STEINHERR*

I. INTRODUCTION

A 15th century Venetian or Florentine could have asked a very similar question to the one in the title of this paper although his notion of the world would have been much more restricted. And one speculates that his final explanation also would have been similar to one I arrive at in this paper: the world around him in terms of technology, trade intensity, trade channels and the associated risks required financial adaptation.

I shall argue that financial adjustments in the 1980s were driven by the evolution of the "real" world economy. Although world trade and payments have grown at a rapid rate during the entire postwar period, adjustment of the financial sector had been lagging behind. What is happening now around the globe is to catch up.

My hypothesis that the financial sector lagged behind the evolution of a changing international structure of production and trade is certainly not going unchallenged and therefore requires some demonstration and an explanation of the cause for retarded adaptation.

The business of banks did not change significantly from the late 1940s to the 1970s in most countries. The products offered, the management and sales techniques applied showed great constancy. Whilst industry increasingly became international and sold its products on world markets, banking remained confined to national markets in most countries and still is in many. The European Community started in 1958 to set up a customs union and since then has steadily moved forward to the ultimate goal of a single market. Financial services did not follow that trend. Some of the most trade-intensive economies in Europe and elsewhere still have a virtually closed domestically oriented financial sector. Innovation, the driving force in most of industry, had not changed the financial landscape significantly until recently. Whilst an Italian car of the 1980s has little in common with its predecessor of the

---

* Views expressed in this paper are purely personal and in no way reflect those of the institutions to which the author is attached.

D. E. Fair and C. de Boissieu (eds), Financial Institutions in Europe Under New Competitive Conditions, 49–63.
© 1990 Kluwer Academic Publishers, Dordrecht. Printed in the Netherlands.

1940s and whilst Taiwanese electronics did not even exist 20 years ago, fund collection, lending and enterprise financing more generally are only marginally different in these countries now compared to 40 years ago.

Why? The most important explanation certainly relates to regulation. The interwar depression has left a big mark on financial institutions and their regulators. Regulatory systems were therefore set up to prevent a repeat of the banking crisis of the 1930s. Even more damaging was the furnished evidence that the financial sector is exposed to risks that ultimately put the whole economy at danger. This sector needed therefore to be supervised more closely than others. Add to this the obvious interests of governments to collect seigniorage and to assure priority access to privileged borrowing conditions and government involvement as regulator, as protector from foreign influences and sometimes as owner of major banks is quite understandable. As a result all countries in the world have national banks more often than not protected from foreign competition. Thus, it is not just the regulatory aspect, to preserve stability, avoid negative spill-over effects and protect savers, but also the key intermediary role of financial institutions in the economic system that has led governments to intervene and tightly control this sector. Entry as well as exit is also controlled and this protects the sector not only from foreign but often even from domestic competition. Product innovation is regulated and particularly the role played by banking in the monetary system of a country has rendered monetary authorities very prudent and reluctant in authorizing innovations such as money market funds, free deposit rates, elimination of credit ceilings and so on.

Controllability of monetary aggregates is only one macroeconomic issue directly linked with banking operations. Another one of equal importance is controllability of the external accounts. Capital controls have been seen as necessary to keep savings at home and to prevent speculative crises, i.e., the market's judgement of domestic policy management.

In this tightly regulated and circumscribed environment internationalization and innovation had only little scope and lacked strong incentives. To this it may be added that strong competitive forces are quintessential for innovation in finance. Financial institutions need to be forced to innovate otherwise there is not enough incentive to do it. The major reason is that any financial innovation can easily be copied as there is no way to keep the process or product technology inaccessible to competitors for extended periods of time, nor is there scope for intellectual ownership protection.

Finally, it is economies of scale that make it acceptable to leave world-wide production of airplanes to a handful of companies. If the same were true in banking, it would have been very costly and in the end impossible not to internationalize. But economies of scale are too limited to justify giving up banking even in very small countries. For a survey of the empirical literature see Clark (1988); the difficulty of determining an optimal size for banks is discussed in Artus and Pollin (1989).

Only recently has a global reach become technologically and hence economically feasible. Developments in computer technology and telecommunications reduced the cost of information processing and transmission. Such cost reductions enlarged the markets in which financial institutions could provide services. Advanced computer technology and statistical information systems made possible pricing of new instruments including options and their derivative products. 24-hour trading, linking exchanges in different time zones, is the visible result of globally linked financial markets through technological advances.

Thus, there is a number of reasons why the financial sector has been lagging behind industry in innovation and internationalization for a very long time. But in the 1980s and even more pronounced in the late 1980s there is a remarkable renaissance of finance. Section II sketches the phenomenon and provides a hopefully coherent story.[1] Section III discusses the trend towards despecialization and Section IV puts the European financial integration into perspective.

II WHY IN THE 1980s?[2]

It is of course not correct to limit the financial renaissance to the 1980s. American and some European banks set up foreign operations during most of this century, the euromarkets started in the 1960s. Regulation Q was phased out gradually up to 1986, some countries achieved convertibility of their currency without capital controls in the 1950s, etc.[3] What happens now is both a quantitative and a qualitative jump with deregulation proceeding in many countries at a sharply accelerated pace, capital controls being reduced in many parts of the globe, innovation becoming a driving force and finance rapidly internationalizing. It is the simultaneous occurrence of these factors, in many parts of the world, at a rapid pace which is the new phenomenon. Nevertheless, 1980 is clearly a major watershed for financial innovations such as variable rate loans, money market accounts, options, futures and derivative products.

How can this be explained? I think there are two major forces at work mutually reinforcing each other. One is the increasing internationalization of the non-financial sector. The other is that existing regulations were largely set up for needs of the past and are therefore not well suited for present needs. Innovative ingenuity of bankers was therefore for a long time concentrated on the question how to circumvent regulations. This search often drove them outside national boundaries and contributed to internationalization. Pressure was thereby put on regulators to rethink their approach and thereby to repatriate financial business moved abroad or even to attract foreign business.

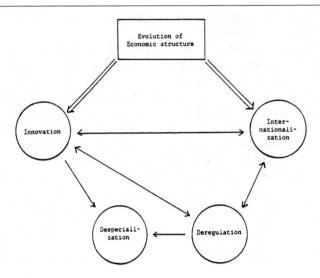

Evolution of economic structures

1. *International trade*
   Becoming more global, entry of new key actors (Asian NIC's), European integration, growth in excess of GDP growth.
2. *Trade imbalances*
   Rising current account imbalances, major shocks (e.g. oil, slack of Latin American demand).
3. *World monetary order*
   Increased exchange rate volatility and medium-term overshooting, higher volatility of interest rate diffentials Major shifts among world net creditors from US to Japan and other Asian countries. Absolute change for US, relative change for Europe.
4. *Shifting growth centers*
   During the 80s slow growth in Europe, higher growth in the US, new 'pôle de croissance' in East Asia. Business becomes global.

Major features of:

1. *Financial innovations*
   - Rapid growth of Euromarkets
   - Syndicated loans
   - Securization and disintermediation
   - Futures, options and derived products
   - Swaps.
2. *Internationalization*
   - Above-trend growth of trade finance
   - International issuing, placing and trading of securities
   - Fund management growingly international
   - Internationalization of payments systems (credit cards)
   - International acquisitions and mergers.
3. *Despecialization*
   - Universal bank model spreads
   - Banking and insurance are being combined
   - Securities trading and broking tend to combine
   - But: new specialized competitors merge from non-financial sector: credit cards, consumer financing
   - Within financial sector rapid growth of specialized boutiques (fund management, M & A).
4. *Deregulation*
   - Limited branch banking and separation between commercial and investment banking in decline (US and Japan)
   - Capital controls in retreat (France, Italy, UK)
   - Deposits rates liberalized
   - Credit ceilings eliminated or reduced (France)
   - New products admitted (futures, options, money market instruments)
   - Fixed commissions and fixed (national) membership of management syndicates for bond issues revised (Germany, Switzerland)
   - Stock exchange regulations revised (big bang).

Increasingly it also becomes evident that some regulations, designed to avoid 1930s-type problems, now may be responsible for other and equally serious difficulties. Thereby the whole regulatory approach has become exposed to increasing criticism. It is frequently argued that one major reason for high involvement of US money centre banks in Latin America is that growth in their traditional domestic markets was limited and regulation prevented them from moving into other domestic areas. Similarly, savings and loan associations ran into major difficulties in the early 1980s when yield curves became inverted. Desperate to get out of this difficulty and to diversify their assets they moved with the approval of regulators into non-traditional but *high-risk businesses* (oil, real estate, securities) and then definitely broke their neck. Regulations are seen doubly responsible; first, by quasi forcing S&Ls to finance long-term mortgages with deposits without adequate sectorial risk diversification and second by guaranteeing deposits with the effect of providing subsidized short-term funding.

One particular feature of the main product of banking, that is money, makes national regulation of the banking industry extremely difficult: unlike goods, money can be transported virtually costlessly and to some extent invisibly. Hence, border controls are not very effective and low transport costs (in terms of time and freight) represent no cost barriers. As long as all countries regulate tightly and control capital movements this potential mobility may not be exploited. But as soon as some countries open their financial markets or as uncontrolled markets exist outside of sovereign control (euromarkets) actual international competition occurs and this eventually implies competition among regulators. Quite often innovations start in the euromarkets where no regulatory constraints exist and then find their way into national markets through deregulation under competitive pressure. If German authorities do not allow their residents ECU holdings they will have them in Luxembourg; if they cannot obtain money market funds they will also obtain them in Luxembourg. Some regulators see the danger of losing certain business to outside financial centres and of not being able to bring these funds back home even when regulation catches up. Quick regulatory adaptation is therefore necessary.

Regulatory reaction was felt necessary not only on the national level. Internationalization of financial transactions made it necessary to establish comprehensive prudential practices to ensure that banks' foreign operations did not escape supervision. The problems created by the failures of Bankhaus Herstatt and of Franklin National Bank in 1974 led to the formation of the Cooke Committee which in 1975 endorsed a concordat on international bank supervisory cooperation. The proposal that banks' capital adequacy should be monitored on a consolidated basis was endorsed in 1978 by BIS governors. Problems of Banco Ambrosiano Holding, Luxembourg, in 1982 revealed that there were still gaps in the supervisory framework and that revision of the concordat was necessary.

By 1986 consolidated supervision for purposes of capital adequacy of foreign branches and majority-owned subsidiaries had been established among the G-5 and Switzerland. The ulterior approach to capital adequacy in an integrated financial market was greatly inspired and facilitated by the work of the Cooke Committee.

Parallel to the search for circumventing regulations and to escape national controls, occurred an increasing internationalization of the world economy accompanied by deep structural changes.

The major features can be summarized as follows. For the last 30 years the growth of international trade has outpaced the growth of production. Over time most economies have therefore become more trade dependent. This evolution has stimulated trade finance, foreign currency hedging operations and management of foreign currency holdings. Over the years the US dollar has somewhat lost its dominating vehicle currency role so that foreign currency management has become more diversified and complex.

This complexity has been further enhanced by high volatility and, during the late 1970s and 1980s, extreme medium-term exchange rate movements. These movements can be more significant for producers than variations in costs and prices. Unhedged positions generate large gains or large losses, at times pushing some otherwise healthy firms to the brink of bankrupcy. Direct and indirect hedging has thus become a standard for sophisticated trading firms.

A double impetus influenced the growth of international financial transactions. Current account imbalances reached record dimensions in the 1980s, promoting Japan and Taiwan to the top of the world's net lenders and, inversely, turning the US from top lender to top borrower. Most of this financing was done by private capital. Unlike in the 1960s and 1970s when Europe lent short-term to the US and the US invested long-term in Europe with only limited net flows, the net flows are now huge. Because they are so large investors are keen on diversification. Funding of the US current account occurs through securities purchases of all types of borrowers and not only treasury bills, investment funds, stocks, direct investments, real estate acquisitions and takeovers of companies.

Not only industry is moving into a global role, also investors turn global. They take advantage of differences in business cycles, hence differences in growth performance, interest rate differentials and hedging possibilities. Until the 1970s individual investors focused mainly on domestic markets. Three developments have contributed to internationalization. First, to take advantage of international differences in performance freedom to exit and to enter home and foreign currency markets is required. Reduced capital controls made this possible. Second, modern portfolio theory stresses the benefit of diversification and the fact that even a more volatile asset can reduce aggregate risk through less than perfect positive correlation. A foreign asset is always intrinsically riskier for returns measured in domestic currency but still may serve to reduce overall portfolio risk. This also shows up in the search for investment possibilities in LDCs with high expected returns but also high risk. Only through diversification can those risks be handled. Third, increasing shares of private wealth are managed by institutional investors (investment funds, pension funds, insurance companies) which have the sophistication to apply modern portfolio management techniques, to use hedging products and which have the resources to collect and treat information of the major markets. There is therefore not only net foreign investment to channel current account surpluses but, more importantly, there is two-way trade as each institutional investor seeks international portfolio diversification.

From Table 1(A) it can be seen that between 1981 and 1988 privately-owned foreign assets by US residents nearly doubled and US assets held by non-residents more than trebled. The increase in foreign official reserves was much less pronounced. Table 1(B) shows that banks in major countries on average trebled their gross foreign assets since 1980. Exceptions are Japan and other Asian economies whose banks have increased their foreign assets by more than 10 times over the same time period and in 1988 surpassed US banks. However, these huge foreign assets are in most countries matched by foreign liabilities so that banks do not contribute the largest share to

Table 1A. The United States debtor/creditor position.[1]

$ billion	1981	1984	1986	1988
Net international investment position	141.1	3.6	−263.6	−551
U.S. assets abroad, of which	719.8	896.1	1 067.9	1 237
U.S. official reserves	30.1	34.9	48.5	132
Other U.S. govt. assets	68.7	84.9	89.4	
Private assets, of which	621.1	776.3	929.9	1 105
direct investment	228.3	211.5	259.9	325
securities	63.4	89.1	131.1	143
other private	329.4	475.7	539.0	637
Foreign assets in U.S.	578.7	892.5	1 331.5	1 788
Foreign official reserves	180.4	199.2	240.8	329
Other foreign assets, of which	398.2	693.3	1 090.7	1 459
direct investment	108.7	164.6	209.3	294
securities	93.6	185.5	405.6	522[1]
other assets	196.0	343.2	475.8	643

[1] Including unidentified capitel.
Sources: Morgan Guaranty Trust 'World Financial Markets'; B.I.S.

Table 1B. External positions of banks in the following countries (excluding exchange rate effects.)

$ billions	Gross asset values				Net asset values			
	1975	1980	1985	1988	1975	1980	1985	1988
United Kingdom	120	356	673	884	−17.5	−17.9	−50.7	−78.4
France	40	143	200	276	−2.3	+12.8	−9.1	−16.3
Germany	32	73	133	206	+8.7	−0.9	+35.6	+76.2
Luxembourg	41 {	89	135	189		+4.0	+12.8	+17.1
Belgium		56	106	143	+0.2	−10.3	−18.3	−24.7
Netherlands	21	62	88	122	+2.3	−2.4	+8.2	+8.2
Italy	15	31	58	63	−1.2	−15.8	−17.9	−35.2
Spain	n.a.	n.a.	22	24	n.a.	n.a.	+1.1	−11.0
Denmark	n.a.	4	13	20	n.a.	−0.1	−0.2	+1.0
Ireland	n.a.	2	4	5	n.a.	−3.1	−4.7	−6.0
U.S.A.	60	177	428	556	+0.9	+38.7	+50.6	−34.5
Japan	20	66	273	734	−6.4	−14.4	+30.1	−38.7
Asian market centres	n.a.	n.a.	287	598	n.a.	n.a.	+13.9	+43.1

Source: B.I.S.

current account financing. For example, in 1988 Japanese banks had gross foreign assets of US$ 556 bn but net foreign assets of US$ −38.7 bn. This means that large current account balances are mostly financed by the non-banking sector through acquisition of securities. Only Germany differs from this pattern: about one third of banks' gross foreign assets represent a net investment.[4]

Table 2 confirms this view from a different perspective. Although total international financing nearly doubled between 1981 and 1988, bank financing actually declined. Issues of securities in foreign and international markets quintupled over the same time period.

This suggests that internationalization in securities markets has proceeded more rapidly than in other banking markets. Not captured by those data is banking business in foreign markets carried out by branches or subsidiaries which, as attested by Table 3, expanded rapidly in the (late) 1970s and 1980s. In the late 1980s traditional banking is still lagging behind other activities (securities industry, manufacturing) in internationalization.

Internationalization of financial markets clearly was stimulated by the macroeconomic events sketched out. The search for escaping regulations initially helped further. Successful escapes in combination with more market-oriented macroeconomic policies made reduced controls and regulation both necessary and acceptable. The efficiency gains for resource allocation provided these policy changes with a further rationality.

Once euromarkets developed and national markets opened up, the possibilities for innovations lost their predominantly defensive character to escape

Table 2. Total international financing through public issues of securities, short-term issuance facilities, merger facilities and internationally syndicated and foreign bank loans (billion ECUs)

	1981	1982	1983	1984	1985	1986	1987	1988
Security issues total (International securities Foreign securities)	30.5	58.0	64.7	115.4	200.5	202.5	140.0	162.9
(% of grand total)	19.3	35.7	42.2	44.3	57.7	67.6	56.1	57.8
Total bank and bank guaranteed finance (Internationally syndicated and foreign bank loans; other international facilities)	127.3	104.3	88.5	145.2	146.8	97.3	109.7	118.7
(% of grand total)	80.7	64.3	57.8	55.7	42.3	32.4	43.9	42.2
Grand total	157.8	162.3	153.3	260.6	347.4	299.8	249.7	281.7

Source: 'International Capital Markets', *European Investment Bank Papers*, various issues.

regulations. Swaps are the typical example of exploiting comparative advantages across market segments and they contribute to reducing market (and not only regulatory) imperfections. Similarly, leveraged buy-outs is a type of financial engineering that exploits fiscal distortions and completes the market's control over management.

Innovations directly affect regulations either by posing new problems or providing escapes from existing regulations. They also feed back on internationalization. A swap desk is like a telephone system: the more telephone owners there are the more efficient and useful is the system. A profitable swap-desk is therefore necessarily international and as close to global as possible. M&A requires tremendous experience and skill which clearly is not usefully bottled up in one national market. Any citizen or institution of this world, eager to acquire liquid, high-value securities in a diversified portfolio cannot neglect the securities markets of the handful of major currencies.

III THE TREND TOWARDS GLOBAL BANKING

I hope to have shown the tight interrelationship and mutual reinforcement between deregulation, innovation and internationalization, all made necessary by the evolution and structural changes in the world economy.

It would be amazing if the banking industry itself had not been profoundly affected by this turbulent evolution. Although in many countries adaptation has been slowed down by regulatory barriers deep changes have occurred

Table 3. Expansion of international banking networks 1960–1986 (at end-period).

	1960	1970	1980	1984	1985	1986
			1. *Foreign Banking Presence in OECD Countries*[1]			
Host country						
Australia	3	3	2	2	10	18[2]
Austria	–	–	17	22	22	22
Belgium	14[3]	26	51	56	57[4]	–
Canada	0	0	0	–	57[4]	–
Denmark	0	0	5	8	8	8
Finland	0	0	0	3	–	–
France	33	58	122	147	148	152
Germany	24	77	213	–	283[4]	–
Greece	2	3	18	–	19	–
Italy	1	4	25	34	36	36
Japan: banks	34	38	85	108	114	115
Japan: securities firms	–	–	5	11	22	38
Luxembourg	3	23	99	103	106	110
Netherlands	1	23	39	42	41	42
New Zealand	3	3	3	3	3	3[5]
Norway	–	–	–	–	7	7
Spain	4	4	25	45	47	49
Sweden	0	0	0	0	0	12
Switzerland	8	97	99	119	120	125
United Kingdom	51[6]	95	114	–	293[4]	–
United States	–	79[8]	153	233	234	243
			2. *Presence of Domestic Banks Abroad*[1]			
Home country						
Australia	–	–	–	–	–	85
Austria[9]	0	0	1	3	5	5
Belgium[10]	5	6	14	27	–	–
Denmark	0	0	18	41	50	56
France	–	–	–	351	385	455
Germany	3	8	126	–	164	–
Ireland	60	84	224	–	276	–
Italy[9]	17	22	44	69	74	75
Japan: banks	37	67	213	294	346	380
Japan: securities firms	–	–	39	56	62	82
Netherlands	3	55	145	171	171	170
New Zealand	1	1	1	1	1	1
Norway	1	6	16	18	23	27
Spain[9]	5	25	82	135	133	136
Sweden	0	0	7	21	19	17
Switzerland	–	–	71	76	79	79
United States[11]	8	79	159	163	162	151
	(131)	(532)	(787)	(917)	(916)	(899)

[1] Number of branches and subsidiaries if not otherwise indicated; subsidiaries and branches of overseas subsidiaries are generally excluded.
[2] End-June 1988; does not include savings bank subsidiaries.
[3] End-1958.
[4] End-June 1985.
[5] 1987: 12.
[6] End-1962.
[7] United States branches and agencies of foreign banks.
[8] 1975.
[9] Branches only.
[10] Three large banks.
[11] Number of Federal Reserve member banks with foreign branches; figures in brackets: number of foreign branches of these banks.
Source: Bröker, 1989.

in all major markets. Not only have international operations augmented more than domestic business but financial institutions, particularly in the 1980s, have set up operations abroad at a very accelerated pace. Most larger European banks have subsidiaries or branches in London, New York and in Asia. Their product range has been substantially enriched through innovation in their traditional product markets and through expansion into new product markets. One trend observable world-wide is for banks to "despecialize". In the United States, Japan and the United Kingdom this means the legal or traditional separation of commercial banking from investment banking is increasingly considered as outlived. UK commercial banks have already expanded into investment banking, US banks have done so abroad and are pressing for legislative changes at home, as do, Japanese banks. On the continent where universal banking has been the norm in many countries the model spreads and the Second Banking Directive accepts the universal banks as a basic model. It hardly could have done otherwise as creation of an integrated financial market is considerably easier through provision of extended freedom in choice of banking organization rather than through splitting up existing banking structures. In countries where universal banking was legally ruled out, as in Italy, legislation is being adapted ("polyfunctional banking"). Existing universal banks even reinforce their reach by moving massively into insurance business, business consulting, and by stepping up investments in investment banking.

There are several economic trends underlying this quest for "Allfinanz". First, I have argued elsewhere that a universal bank system slows down the development of securities markets (Steinherr and Huveneers, 1989). In countries where universal banking is dominant, securities markets are underdeveloped, the prime example being Germany. The Single Market will, however, emphasize "Europeanization" of non-financial firms, lead through M&A to larger firm size and thereby diminish exclusive firm-bank relationships. Such firms with greater sophistication in financial management will increasingly use the securities markets for their financial needs and for their investments. In addition, with stock exchange liberalization and increasing institutional wealth to be invested securities markets will gain in cost effectiveness and depth.

The effects of this trend (called disintermediation) on securities markets is reinforced by banks themselves through securitization. Increased capital requirements and the greater need for risk management induce banks to securitize increasingly their assets. Competition on the funding side (deposits vs short-term securities) will also shift a larger share of funding into securities.

Both disintermediation and securitization displace business opportunities from deposit-taking/lending to advisory services and securities business. Advisory services include global financing and investment services and contribute to breaking up traditional lending activities into their components (loan initiation, financing, monitoring, insurance, etc). This shift in activity takes place within the reach of the universal bank whilst the specialized commercial bank risks losing part of the traditional business.

The recent tendency to merge banking and insurance activities is motivated by the general quest for global finance. Banking and insurance products are either close substitutes or direct complements. Both products deal with risk and, in the case of life insurance, are placements for savings. Other insurance products are complements to banking products (e.g. real estate or car finance and insurance). Bank distribution systems also serve to market insurance products at low fixed costs to captive clients whilst bank products can be marketed more aggressively to individuals through the insurance sales force.

To offer both types of products is therefore natural for both banks and insurance companies. Recently, the incentive for banks to move into insurance increased dramatically: on the continent, a rapidly aging population requires insurance-based old age provisions to unload an otherwise overburdened state social security system financed out of current tax receipts. During recent years in the major countries of the continent the share of savings invested in insurance and pension fund products has been increasing to the detriment of the share in banking products.[5] See Bröker (1989), p. 125.

This general trend in favour of "despecialization" is not unchallenged. The major challenge is certainly going to be cost-effectiveness and not regulation.[6] But, at least in the longer run, when regulatory generosity will have generated its own problems there may be corrective regulatory constraint. On the way to the European integrated financial market there are several potential hurdles which are relegated to the next Section.

IV. OUTLOOK FOR THE INTEGRATED EUROPEAN FINANCIAL MARKET

In the late 1980s Europe is in "Aufbruchsstimmung" and ready to move toward a single market. At the basis of this fundamental break-through is a remarkable convergence of national views in the domain of economic policy. Protectionism, national economic policy choices, private ownership are all issues that do not raise ideological debates anymore. Since 1983 when France abandoned its policy course adopted in 1981, this basic convergence of economic policy has resulted in a more stable and better functioning EMS. It also made it possible to gradually eliminate capital controls in some member countries. The Community finally reached a macroeconomic balance and found general political readiness to embark on integration of its financial markets.

It certainly has not been easy to reach overall support for liberalising trade, capital flows and more generally a largely market-oriented economy. The latter in turn was a precondition for the wave of privatization of publicly owned firms (including banks) in preparation for more open competition in the integrated market. Privatization and other strategies to prepare for the integrated market through M&A give securities markets a substantial boost and will reinforce development of capital markets which only recently started to be deregulated and liberalised![7]

Stock exchanges around the world, in reaction to London's "big bang" (which occurred only in 1987!) and in preparation of their more complex tasks in terms of volumes, products, costs and international role are completely revising their rules, procedures and technological support.

There is of course a long and difficult way from the general willingness and the macroeconomic preconditions to a practical legal, fiscal and regulatory framework. The Communities' approach has been pragmatic and therefore successful. It has not attempted to set up a fully harmonized regulatory and fiscal framework. Much is therefore left to regulatory and fiscal "competition". In order to accept and englobe the banking systems of all member countries the approach is in no sense restrictive. And through the principle of "home regulatory control" no national system or product can be prevented from being exported to other member countries. One can therefore witness a regulatory flexibility and permissiveness that is unique in this century.

The conditions that made this progress possible and the approach adopted both suggest that there is a considerable risk that the integrated financial market may still encounter delays and difficulties that are perhaps under-estimated in the current euphoria.

Politics and economics tend to be cyclical. A shift to the political left, a prolonged recession, difficult adjustment to completely open frontiers in some countries, and massive acquisition of national enterprises by foreigners may all contribute to slow down market integration and to revert to what is now considered "old-fashioned" nationalistic policy-making.

On the more technical level there are still many unresolved, important issues. Recent attempts to harmonize withholding taxes on capital income failed and are unlikely to be successful in the near future. Hence competition will remain tax-biased. The only economically rational solution would at any rate be elimination of withholding taxes. At any other level European tax-shy funds would find their way out of the Community rather than to Luxembourg. But even if withholding taxes were eliminated in the Community there would still be the problem of very different corporate and income tax structures. They distort competition because in the integrated market com-petition is not limited to domestic and foreign firms established in a national market.

Another serious difficulty for a European regulatory approach is that accounting systems are not uniform across member countries. This seriously limits and distorts regulations. For example, in the Second Banking Directive the proposed restrictions on bank holdings of participations in non-financial sector firms crucially depend on how share holdings are to be valued.

Community acceptance of the universal bank model also implies potential distortions and unresolved questions. In some countries proxy-voting is admitted, in others not. In Germany, for example, proxy-votes provide banks with more votes than owned shares. The risk of conflicts of interest, which is present in all banking systems, is certainly more acute for universal banks.[8] Again it is unlikely that much progress is going to be achieved in this domain.

Finally, there is the question of "excessive" economic power of large diversified banks. The restrictions on their share holdings are too easily circumvented to ease the critical observer's mind. If the largest European banks team up with large insurance companies and have effective control over industrial enterprises in their home markets, plus a market presence throughout Europe all traditional concepts of anti-trust would be seriously boggled. What is lacking is a European anti-trust policy, one that gets away from concentrating on traditional market-share analysis restricted to the home market or to trade flows.[9] The difficulties in this field are, however, such that significant progress is unlikely to the seen. In the US, where preservation of competitive conditions is perhaps most fully supported politically, the only feasible, even if not in all instances optimal, approach was chosen: prohibition for commercial banks to hold investments in non-financial firms.

To conclude, it seems to me that the integration approach chosen was the only feasible one and that Europe seized a chance offered through political and economic convergence. It was not possible to reach for an integrated financial market earlier. The current euphoric fashion may, however, overlook a number of essential unresolved (unresolvable?) issues and some quite serious implications. One can also foresee with confidence an explosion of innovations in European markets hitherto lagging behind. However, because this lag is due to regulations and restrictions to international competition a substantial part of this innovatory bout represents a catch-up effect and not a new trend. Beyond 1993, when most of this catch-up will be realized, innovatory progress will return to a level that is unlikely to be in excess of the macroeconomic average.

NOTES

1. Papers on this topic are abundant. I like Folkerts-Landau (1989).
2. See Box 1 for a structure of the discussion of this Section.
3. However, the UK placed restrictions on the use of sterling for financing third country trade

in 1957, the US imposed the interest rate equalization tax in 1963 (discouraging foreign borrowers from issuing securities in the US) and a voluntary Foreign Credit Restraint Program inhibited lending to foreign entities. Only by 1974 were these measures and administrative guidelines removed and the withholding tax levied on non-resident bond holders was abolished in 1984. In the UK exchange controls were removed only in 1979. In Germany, restrictions on capital inflows i.e., authorization requirements, were gradually removed in the 1980s.

4. It would probably be fair to claim that if the Bretton Woods system was still in place, with rather stable exchange rates, no capital controls and therefore more converging interest rates, financial markets would be less internationalized than they are now because there would be less of an incentive to invest internationally.

5. Mutual penetration is also facilitated by the fact that regulatory restrictions of capital participations by banks only apply to the non-financial industry. Whether a concentration of banking and insurance is desirable from an anti-trust point of view remains an open question.

6. The advantages of specialized financial firms are extensively discussed in Steinherr and Gilibert (1989).

7. This is discussed at greater length by Walter and Smith (1989).

8. For extensive discussion of these problems see Steinherr and Huveneers (1989).

9. In principle, Art. 85 and 86 of the Rome Treaty could be applied to banking. However, market dominance, abuse of a dominant position, and trade restrictive behaviour are concepts that are particularly difficult to apply empirically to banking.

REFERENCES

Artus, P. and J. P. Pollin, (1989). "Les effets de la règlementation et le comportement des banques", *SUERF*, October.

Bröker, G., (1989). *Competition in Banking*, OECD.

Clark, A. (1988). "Economies of scale and scope at depository financial institutions: A review of the literature", *Economic Review Federal Reserve Bank of Kansas City*, September/October.

Folkerts-Landau, D., (1989). "The Internationalization of Financial Markets and the Regulatory Response", in: Vosgerau (ed.), *New Institutional Arrangements for the World Economy*, Heidelberg: Springer.

Steinherr, A. and P. L. Gilibert, (1989). "The Impact of Financial Market Integration on the European Banking Industry", *Centre for European Policy Studies*, no 1.

Steinherr, A. and Ch. Huveneers, (1989). "Universal banks: The Prototype of Successful Banks in The Integrated European market? A view Inspired by German Experience".

Walter, I. and R.C. Smith, (1989). "European Investment Banking; Structure, Transactions-Flow, and Regulation".

VI. La Banque à Géométrie Variable: Un Nouveau Facteur de Compétitivité

CATHERINE LUBOCHINSKY et JOËL METAIS

INTRODUCTION

Les bouleversements de l'environnement macroéconomique et financier de ces dix dernières années ont vu leurs effets relayés et amplifiés par un foisonnement d'innovations financières et une érosion des réglementations existantes pour transformer radicalement les modes de financement de l'économie. Les conditions d'exercice et la nature de l'activité bancaire en sont durablement et profondément modifiées. Deux faits sont particulièrement importants à cet égard:
- le caractère extrêmement mouvant des "marchés porteurs" par catégorie de clientèle, nature de l'activité, zone géographique...[1]
- l'importance retrouvée des forces de la concurrence dans la transformation structurelle de la branche bancaire qui acquiert le statut d'une branche d'industrie ordinaire.

Ces évolutions ont au moins deux conséquences sur le plan analytique:
- Il faut reconsidérer la nature et le statut des intermédiaires financiers et leurs rapports avec les marchés. Le cadre théorique de référence inauguré il y a trente ans par J. Gurley et E. Shaw (1960) doit être réexaminé.
- Le recours aux concepts de l'économie industrielle devient indispensable pour analyser les transformations des systèmes financiers et les comportements des banques.

Cet article s'inspire de ce double postulat théorique pour étudier les fondements de la compétitivité bancaire au cours des prochaines années. Celle-ci devient en effet une préoccupation majeure des banquiers à un moment où ses déterminants habituels semblent largement remis en cause par l'avènement d'un environnement instable, concurrentiel et déréglementé.

La première partie procède d'abord à un rappel des principaux facteurs qui façonnent l'évolution structurelle de la branche bancaire et sont susceptibles de l'influencer lors des prochaines années. L'industrie bancaire, désormais parvenue au stade de la globalisation, ne pourra sûrement pas faire l'économie d'une restructuration à l'échelle mondiale. Une telle perspective alimente depuis quelque temps la réflexion sur les options stratégiques des banques et les sources de leur compétitivité. Certains auteurs formulent des propositions radicales comme celles préconisant la "banque sans actifs" ou

D. E. Fair and C. de Boissieu (eds), Financial Institutions in Europe Under New Competitive Conditions, 65–81.
© 1990 *Kluwer Academic Publishers, Dordrecht. Printed in the Netherlands.*

la "banque éclatée". La première privilégie les activités de service et de courtage des banques qui laissent alors aux marchés le soin d'assumer la plupart des risques habituels de l'intermédiation financière. La seconde, assez voisine, prône la séparation complète de diverses fonctions normalement combinées au sein d'une banque: gestion des moyens de paiement, octroi de crédit, etc... Ces diverses activités seraient conduites par des entités juridiques distinctes et règlementées par des autorités différentes.

Après avoir montré la nécessité de renouveler le cadre d'analyse de la compétitivité, la seconde partie de cet article en examine plus particulièrement une des dimensions essentielles: la flexibilité dans les rapports qu'établissent les banques avec les marchés pour diversifier leurs activités, moduler la structure et la taille de leur bilan et gérer leurs risques. Cette flexibilité est l'attribut premier de la banque à géométrie variable (présentée ici comme alternative à la banque éclatée). Une telle institution continue à intégrer la plupart des activités traditionelles qui fondent la spécificité des banques. Toutefois les innovations financières engendrent de nouveaux services et surtout des formes d'intermédiation qui remettent en question le partage traditionnel des activités entre intermédiaires financiers et marchés au gré des évolutions de leurs avantages comparatifs dans le financement de l'économie. Si on considère les intermédiaires financiers comme des variétés internalisées de marchés financiers, on assiste aujourd'hui à une certaine dilution de ces intermédiaires au sein des marchés consécutive à l'érosion de leur frontière traditionnelle sous l'effet des innovations et du progrès technique. Ce caractère désormais mouvant des contours des banques fonde la notion de banque à géométrie variable.

I. VERS UNE INELUCTABLE RESTRUCTURATION DU SECTEUR BANCAIRE

Les transformations de la structure d'une branche d'industrie obéissent principalement aux évolutions de trois catégories de facteurs: les conditions de la demande, la technologie et la réglementation publique.

La branche financière et bancaire ne déroge pas à ces principes élémentaires de l'économie industrielle. Tout au plus sa réglementation plus stricte joue-t-elle un rôle plus important dans son évolution structurelle.

L'examen des conditions de ses récentes mutations permet d'émettre l'hypothèse selon laquelle elle entrerait actuellement dans une phase de restructuration à l'échelle planétaire.

1. Les facteurs de transformation du système financier international

1.1 Les évolutions de *la demande* de produits et services financiers sont essentiellement commandées par les changements dans l'environnement économique et financier à travers leur influence – via des effets de substitution et de richesse, notamment – sur les comportements patrimoniaux des agents économiques. Par ce biais, elles sont souvent génératrices d'innovations financières de produits (Greenbaum et Haywood, 1971).

Les dix dernières années sont, à cet égard, caractéristiques:
– Si d'importants déséquilibres des paiements courants se sont perpétués depuis quinze ans, leur répartition entre les grandes zones géographiques a subi de profondes transformations. Celles-ci ont été largement responsables du passage, après 1982, d'un financement international reposant essentiellement sur l'intermédiation des grandes banques de dépôts à celui faisant appel aux marchés d'actifs financiers négociables.

Au sein des économies des principaux pays industrialisés, la répartition des capacités et des déficits de financement des principales catégories d'agents économiques a connu des évolutions similaires. Ainsi, les déficits publics ont-ils largement stimulé le développement des marchés obligataires et de ceux des nouveaux actifs financiers destinés à réduire les risques d'éviction des emprunteurs du secteur privé. Ce recours accru aux marchés s'est trouvé renforcé, jusqu'à mi 1987, par la lente décrue des taux d'intérêt nominaux, génératrice de plus-values rapides pour les opérations d'achat/vente des obligations.
– Après l'introduction des nouvelles procédures de mise en oeuvre de la politique monétaire américaine en octobre 1979, la variabilité des taux de change et des taux d'intérêt a fortement augmenté. Cette dernière est à l'origine d'une demande croissante d'instruments de couverture ou de gestion des risques, entraînant la création de marchés dits "dérivés" ("futures", options etc.) et la diversification des contrats négociés.

1.2 Les *progrès technologiques* considérables dans les secteurs de l'informatique et des télécommunications ont trouvé un champ d'application privilégié dans la branche financière dont l'activité repose largement sur la collecte, l'analyse et l'accumulation de l'information indispensable à l'évaluation des risques. Leur incorporation massive et rapide dans le cadre d'innovations de processus a permis de réduire considérablement les coûts opératoires des banques et les coûts de transaction associés aux divers types d'opérations financières. Ils ont aussi stimulé l'élaboration de nouveaux produits financiers sophistiqués. Plus généralement, ils ont contribué à une redistribution des avantages comparatifs entre les diverses variétés d'acteurs financiers et entre ceux-ci et les agents non financiers qui entrent parfois eux mêmes directement sur certains segments de l'activité financière.

1.3 *La réglementation*, souvent historiquement marquée dans son contenu par la crise des années trente, s'est alors trouvée de plus en plus en porte à faux vis-à-vis des évolutions décrites ci-dessus. La pression des innovations financières, parfois induites par des contraintes règlementaires (Silber, 1975), n'a pourtant constitué qu'un des motifs de la vague de dérèglementation financière. Un second motif est lié au souci des autorités de nombreux pays d'augmenter l'efficacité et la flexibilité du système financier afin d'accroître sa contribution à l'amélioration des performances macroéconomiques.[2] Enfin, un troisième motif traduit la nécessité pour ces pays de renforcer, sinon de préserver, la compétitivité internationale de leurs intermédiaires financiers ou de leur place financière nationale.

Dans ce dernier cas, les possibilités d'arbitrage par les multinationales financières[3] entre les différentes degrés de réglementation au gré de la localisation de leurs activités ont enfermé les autorités de tutelle de nombreux pays dans le jeu d'un véritable processus de dérèglementations compétitives (Giddy et Allen, 1979). L'abolition des contrôles des changes qui s'est répandue au sein des pays industrialisés depuis 1979 a indéniablement constitué un cadre propice autant qu'un relais pour ce processus.

2. Vers la globalisation de l'industrie bancaire mondiale[4]

La branche d'industrie financière, dont les structures ont longtemps été maintenues figées et le développement biaisé par des règlementations parfois contraignantes, fait preuve depuis dix ans d'une dynamique structurelle qui la rapproche considérablement des autres branches d'industrie. Deux grandes évolutions peuvent être dégagées: l'apparition d'une surcapacité d'intermédiation financière et l'avènement de banques multiproductrices alors que s'estompent les frontières traditionnelles entre intermédiation financière et finance directe.

2.1 L'émergence d'une *surcapacité* d'intermédiation financière

Pendant les années soixante-dix, la domination de l'intermédiation financière internationale par les grandes banques de dépôts multinationales s'est inscrite dans un cadre au sein duquel coexistaient un espace financier très concurrentiel, correspondant aux euro-marchés, et des systèmes bancaires domestiques aux structures oligopolistiques, fortement réglementés et protégés par les contrôles des changes.

Les interdépendances oligopolistiques ont d'ailleurs largement marqué les stratégies et les activités internationales des grandes banques des principaux pays: les banques ayant été incitées à soutenir l'expansion des activités en euro-devises grâce aux subventions implicites inhérentes à l'existence d'un prêteur en dernier ressort au niveau domestique, et parfois à celle d'un système public d'assurance des dépôts, ces interdépendances ont finalement conduit à l'émergence d'une surcapacité d'intermédiation financière internationale

(Bond et Briault, 1983; Penato et Protopapadakis, 1986). Difficile à mesurer, celle-ci s'apprécie essentiellement à partir de ses effets, notamment la "guerre" des marges et des commissions afin de conquérir des parts de marché.

La persistance de cette surcapacité dans un contexte d'innovations permanentes et de croissance de la demande gobale de produits financiers peut surprendre. Elle est attribuée par certains aux désajustements passagers entre offre et demande, consécutifs à des surinvestissements dans des segments particuliers de l'industrie des services financiers.

2.2 Répartition de l'intermédiation entre banques et marchés

Depuis le milieu des années quatre-vingt, les frontières entre opérations en eurodevises, étrangères et domestiques, s'estompent au gré des mesures de déréglementation. Le champ de la concurrence directe entre les systèmes financiers nationaux s'élargit, comme en témoigne leur degré croissant d'interpénétration. Dans le même temps, s'engage un double redéploiement des banques internationales confrontées aux conséquences de la crise de l'endettement après 1982: les banques moyennes de certains pays privilégient de nouveau le développement des activités domestiques.[5] Les plus grandes reportent leur surcapacité dans les activités de marché et d'"investment banking" suivant des mouvements stratégiques discrétionnaires prévus par la théorie de la surcapacité d'intermédiation financière.[6]

En effet, à partir de 1982, les marchés d'actifs financiers supplantent l'intermédiation des banques de dépôts. Leur dynamisme soutient désormais l'expansion internationale des 'investment banks" et des maisons de titres, autant qu'il en bénéficie. Il témoigne en contrepartie de l'érosion de l'avantage comparatif des banques de dépôts dans l'allocation des capitaux consécutive notamment à la détérioration de la qualité de leur signature ("rating"), du fait de leurs créances douteuses sur les pays en voie de développement. De plus, ce dynamisme est renforcé par la croissance régulière de l'épargne gérée par les investisseurs institutionnels des grands pays industrialisés et la progression de la diversification internationale de leurs portefeuilles.

La crise d'octobre 1987 a certes quelque peu infléchi ce mouvement et désormais les deux composantes de l'intermédiation financière, c'est-à-dire les marchés d'actifs et l'intermédiation des banques de dépôts, évoluent de manière plus équilibrée dans les principaux pays industrialisés comme sur le marché international des capitaux.

2.3 Une restructuration inéluctable

L'analyse des transformations de l'industrie financière internationale permet de montrer leur interaction avec certains facteurs économiques fondamentaux malgré quelques effets de "mode" qui se sont succédés au cours de ces dernières années.

Un raisonnement similaire permet de dégager les grandes lignes des évolutions futures tout en relativisant ces pronostics:

- Les parts respectives des financements intermédiés par les banques et de ceux réalisés par le canal des marchés, le développement quantitatif et qualitatif de produits dérivés, et le rythme des innovations financières n'ont pas de raison de voir s'atténuer leur dépendance vis-à-vis des évolutions des facteurs macro-économiques analysés précédemment. En revanche, essayer de discerner ces évolutions n'est que pure conjecture sans la formulation de scénarii macro-économiques à moyen terme qui comporte elle-même ses propres limites.

- La poursuite des progrès technologiques et de leur application massive au sein de la branche financière est plus facile à prévoir. Le coût et l'irréversibilité de certains investissements pèseront sûrement de plus en plus lourdement sur les décisions stratégiques des institutions financières.

- Enfin, et surtout, la réglementation publique continuera d'exercer une influence considérable:

  - Les premières conclusions des travaux du comité Cooke semblent révéler un revirement de tendance du mouvement international de dérèglementation et prennent acte du caractère désormais global de la branche bancaire pour instaurer un début d'harmonisation internationale des normes prudentielles et une coordination des activités de contrôle-surveillance.

  - Parallèlement, les autorités de tutelle des marchés financiers et des produits dérivés prennent aussi conscience de la nécessité d'une coordination nationale et internationale. Cependant, dans la plupart des pays, l'approche institutionnelle de la réglementation freine une action cohérente et coordonnée de surveillance et de contrôle des activités respectives des banques et des marchés.

  - L'avènement du marché unique alimentera pendant encore un certain temps le processus de dérèglementation au sein de la Communauté Economique Européenne. En effet, l'abolition du contrôle des changes à partir de juillet 1990 et la mise en concurrence des système règlementaires nationaux qu'implique le principe de reconnaissance mutuelle des règlementations nationales risquent de provoquer un alignement sur les pays les moins réglementés. C'est pourquoi la Commission de Bruxelles a introduit une harmonisation minimale en matière de couverture de risques bancaires et de ratios de solvabilité et de fonds propres.

Les forces du marché devraient continuer de façonner le processus de restructuration de la branche bancaire en cours de globalisation.[7] Cette restructuration apparaît comme l'issue la plus probable à la situation de surcapacité qui a successivement affecté divers compartiments de l'activité financière internationale (J. Metais, 1989). Toutefois, la rationalisation des structures de l'industrie des services financiers n'empruntera sûrement pas les mêmes voies que celle des autres branches d'industrie qui ont vu, à cette occasion, émerger un oligopole international. Les faillites pures et simples ou les prises de contrôle hostiles ne peuvent jouer le même rôle régulateur en raison des externalités associées aux faillites et des questions d'indépendance économique nationale que soulèvent les prises de contrôle.

De nombreuses banques, désormais privées du rempart de la réglementation publique et confrontées à un environnement plus concurrentiel, vont pourtant voir leur survie menacée. La notion de compétitivité va acquérir une importance accrue dans une branche d'activité pour laquelle elle ne représentait pas une priorité essentielle.

II LA FLEXIBILITE SOURCE DE COMPETITIVITE DES BANQUES

Dans un contexte caractérisé par un environnement instable et des contraintes réglementaires en mutation, un des facteurs importants de la compétitivité des banques semble résider dans la capacité d'adaptation de leur production à ces deux paramètres fondamentaux et dans la flexibilité des différents types de relations qu'elles établissent désormais avec les marchés. L'analyse des déterminants de cette flexibilité soulève quelques problèmes théoriques qui invitent à une reformulation de certains aspects de la théorie des intermédiaires financiers.

1. Les rapports banques/marchés: quelques éléments théoriques

1.1 Renouvellement du cadre d'analyse de la compétitivité bancaire.
Les premières analyses de la compétitivité bancaire reposaient essentiellement sur le modèle de référence traditionnel de l'économie industrielle: Structure de marché – Comportement – Performance. Imprégnées par les particularismes des marchés bancaires américains, elles privilégiaient la relation Structure-Performance marquée par l'influence des structures contraignantes et figées issues d'une réglementation alors très stricte.

Depuis le début de l'actuelle décennie, le décalage croît entre cette approche statique (et à court terme) et les nouvelles données de la compétitivité bancaire dans un univers déréglementé (J. M. Parly et M. Poix, 1987). A cela il y a au moins trois raisons essentielles:
- Les banques sont désormais des entreprises pluriproductrices au sein desquelles coexistent deux catégories de fonctions: l'intermédiation financière au sens traditionnel et les services liés aux différentes formes d'intervention des banques sur les marchés d'actifs et de produits dérivés.

– Les marges d'intérêt et les revenus issus des activités de services obéissent de plus en plus aux forces de la concurrence depuis l'abolition de divers taux d'intérêt et commissions fixés réglementairement. Cette évolution est souvent qualifiée de marchéisation des activités bancaires.

– L'incertitude et le risque dus à l'instabilité de l'environnement macroéconomique et à celle des conditions de concurrence accroissent la vulnérabilité des profits et de la rentabilité des banques. Aussi ces deux paramètres vont-ils influencer à la fois leurs stratégies et leur gestion quotidienne.

Ces prémisses sont à l'origine d'un renouvellement des études de la compétitivité bancaire. Celles-ci s'inspirent désormais de deux grands courants d'analyse: la théorie des marchés contestables (Baumol W. C., Panzar J. C. et Willig R. D., 1982) et l'analyse stratégique. Les travaux théoriques et empiriques sont certes encore peu nombreux mais on peut déjà mentionner leurs apports à l'analyse de la compétitivité bancaire (Szymczak P., 1988):

– Alors que la maîtrise des coûts devient fondamentale, les économies d'envergure sont certainement aussi importantes que les économies d'échelle. Mais les travaux économétriques ne sont pas encore parvenues à l'établir de manière claire.

– Nombre de segments de l'activité financière ont vu s'accroître leur degré de contestabilité en raison des progrès technologiques et de l'érosion des barrières réglementaires qui en ont considérablement réduit les coûts nets de sortie ("sunk costs"). Toutefois, l'importance des relations de clientèle et de la réputation réduit parfois la portée de cette proposition.

– De nouveaux entrants peuvent être tentés de se livrer à des mouvements d'aller-retour destinés à écrémer les segments de marché les plus lucratifs.

– Ces mouvements sont souvent financés par le biais de subventions croisées entre les diverses activités d'une même banque. Ils font partie des actions discrétionnaires visant à la conquête de nouveaux marchés ou à la dissuasion de nouveaux entrants sur des marchés où les producteurs en place recherchent une position dominante. Parmi ces actions, on trouve également la pratique de prix de prédation, la surcapitalisation, des dépenses élevées de recherche-développement ou de publicité, la différenciation excessive des produits, la multiplication des innovations mineures, etc.

Dès lors, certains facteurs traditionnels de la compétitivité bancaire ont sûrement perdu de leur importance, comme la taille du bilan ou la densité du réseau. D'autres voient leur rôle renforcé, comme la capacité d'innovation.

En revanche, malgré l'étendue et la complexité croissantes des relations entre banques et marchés, la flexibilité en matière d'articulation des activités d'intermédiation et des activités de marché ne semble guère avoir retenu l'attention. On se propose de montrer ici que la "banque à géométrie variable" pourrait bien être une source majeure de compétitivité au cours des prochaines années.

L'analyse des formes contemporaines de cette articulation fluctuante entre les deux grandes composantes de l'activité bancaire en confirme les principales justifications théoriques.

1.2 Les apports récents de la théorie des intermédiaires financiers

Les intermédiaires financiers existent pour réduire certains coûts de transaction et surmonter diverses imperfections et externalités associées au fonctionnement des marchés d'actifs financiers.[8] Leurs attributs sont de ce fait variables, allant d'un simple rôle de courtier sur des marchés d'actifs à celui de producteur d'actifs financiers spécifiques dans le cadre du processus de transformation étudié notamment par Gurley et Shaw.[9] Cette théorie permet de situer les divers types d'intermédiaires financiers par rapport aux marchés d'actifs selon une voie qui rappelle celle utilisée pas Ronald H. Coase (1952) pour expliquer l'existence des entreprises. Celui-ci l'attribuait à un processus d'internalisation destiné à surmonter les défaillances, imperfections et externalités associées aux marchés.

La répartition des rôles entre intermédiaires financiers et marchés s'effectue alors en fonction de leurs avantages comparatifs dans la collecte et le traitement de l'information et dans la diversification des risques lorsqu'il y a production effective d'actifs financiers nouveaux, comme c'est le cas pour les banques.

Ces propositions ont un corollaire simple: toute innovation financière, progrès technologique ou modification de la réglementation qui réduit (ou augmente) les coûts de transaction et imperfections sur les marchés est susceptible de déplacer les frontières initiales entre ceux-ci et les formes plus ou moins complètes d'intermédiation. Ceci s'accompagne d'une évolution du degré d'intégration verticale et/ou horizontale de certaines fonctions, rendue désormais possible par les actifs dérivés et les actifs synthétiques.[10] L'émergence de la banque sans actifs – au fur et à mesure du développement des activités hors bilan (Ian Giddy, 1985) et celle de la "banque éclatée" s'expliquent alors aisément sans avoir à remettre en cause la théorie de l'intermédiation financière. En effet, comme le note Ian Giddy[11]: "l'essence de l'activité de banque sans bilan est de traiter les avoirs et engagements – actifs financiers – tout simplement comme des assemblages de caratéristiques. Ces dernières comportent des droits de propriété, des risques de défaut, de transformation, de taux d'intérêt, de devise et de juridiction. Chaque caractéristique, dès lors qu'elle est correctement identifiée, peut être découplée de l'ensemble et achetée, vendue ou échangée de manière séparée. Lorsque des assemblages particuliers de caractéristiques font l'objet d'une tarification inappropriée en raison d'imperfections de marché ou sont interdits par la réglementation, des banquiers astucieux les démembreront et échangeront ces caractéristiques séparément".

Au cours de ces dernières années, les rapports entre banques et marchés ont subi de profondes modifications qui illustrent parfaitement ces principes théoriques et rien ne permet de penser qu'elles soient achevées. Bien au contraire, les banques doivent être prêtes à moduler et adapter en permanence leurs rapports avec les marchés en fonction de l'évolution de l'environnement.

2. Approche fonctionnelle des relations banques/marchés

La banque n'a plus seulement un rôle de transformation de ressources à court terme liquides et non risquées (du fait de l'assurance implicite ou explicite des dépôts) en actifs à long terme, non négociables et risqués pour lesquels la diversification et la mutualisation des risques conféraient aux établissements financiers un avantage comparatif indéniable.

La banque est maintenant une firme multiproduits: le développement des marchés conjugué aux progrès technologiques a permis une diversification des activités, avec un essor important des activités de services, et surtout, a donné la possibilité de désagréger des fonctions et des risques bancaires qui étaient indissociables auparavant.

2.1 Diversification des activités

Les banques ont développé des activités qui ne relèvent plus du seul financement de la clientèle mais sont aussi largement liées à l'essor des marchés financiers et à la déréglementation concomitante des activités financières. Celles-ci peuvent être regroupées en deux grandes catégories: des services plus ou moins sophistiqués et les interventions directes d'achat/vente d'instruments cotés sur les marchés.

Les activités de service

Les formes les plus récentes du financement direct des agents économiques n'évincent pas pour autant les banques mais modifient leur rôle: ces dernières interviennent à divers stades d'une opération de financement et sont rémunérées par des commissions.[12]

Les Facilités à Options Multiples (M.O.F.) illustrent parfaitement ces principes. Dans ce type d'opérations, la banque garantit pendant une période donnée et à hauteur d'un montant prédéterminé la disponibilité des fonds pour un emprunteur. Ceux-ci lui seront effectivement procurés par émissions renouvellées de titres (ex: des billets de trésorerie) ou par octrois de crédit bancaire dans la (les) devise(s) de son choix pendant une durée décidée au moment de l'emprunt. Cette formule permet donc de dissocier diverses caractéristiques normalement liées au sein d'un eurocrédit syndiqué (qui en est l'ancêtre). En particulier les risques de liquidité et de défaut sont répartis entre divers intervenants selon la nature de leur participation à l'opération.

L'expérience des dernières années révèle, à ce titre, une redistribution des rôles entre types de banques: alors que seules les banques de dépôts dirigeaient et participaient à des eurocrédits syndiqués, les banques d'investissement interviennent à leur côté lors de la mise en place des M.O.F.. Or les M.O.F. constituent un marché à fort potentiel puisque, apparues par exemple en France seulement en 1986, elles étaient au nombre de 37 dès mars 1988 pour un encours de 50 milliards de francs.

Les innovations permettent une sophistication croissante des opérations de financement. C'est ainsi que les émissions obligataires "à la vanille" ont vu leur part diminuer au profit d'émissions convertibles, avec warrants, à taux variable mais avec un "cap" (taux plafond), avec option de remboursement anticipé et surtout, pour les euro-obligations des émissions avec un swap simultané.[13] Pour être chef de file, activité la plus lucrative étant donné les commissions plus élevées, les établissements financiers rivalisent d'imagination.

Les banques développent également "l'ingénierie financière", c'est-à-dire le conseil en financement "haut de bilan" des entreprises: émissions d'actions souvent assorties de gadgets; opérations de R.E.S. (reprise de l'entreprise par les salariés); montages d'opérations de fusions et d'acquisitions.

Enfin, la gestion globale du patrimoine de la clientèle et celle de la trésorerie des entreprises se généralisent, essentiellement par le biais des O.P.C.V.M. (organismes de placement collectif en valeurs mobilières). Leur développement extraordinaire a permis aux banques qui ont créé les leurs de bénéficier d'importantes commissions sous forme de prélèvements de frais de gestion et de droits d'entrée ou de sortie.

Les activités de marchés

L'une des caractéristiques récentes des marchés financiers, plus particulièrement ceux liés aux taux d'intérêt, est l'explosion des volumes de transactions: de 50 milliards de dollars par trimestre en 1980, celui sur les euro-obligations est passé à 1.200 milliards de dollars au 4ème trimestre 1988. Autre exemple, le volume de transactions sur les contrats à terme de taux d'intérêt, exprimé en nombre de contrats, a crû d'environ 15 millions en 1980 à plus de 150 millions en 1988.

Si la baisse des coûts de transactions due aux progrès technologiques a facilité cet essor, l'intervention croissante des banques sur ces marchés a également joué un rôle fondamental. En effet, confrontées au recul des financements intermédiés, les banques de l'OCDE ont réagi en redéployant leur présence sur les marchés financiers. Ce redéploiement a nécessité des investissements d'infrastructure colossaux (un poste d'opérateur coûte en moyenne un million de francs) qu'il a fallu rentabiliser. De ce fait, les banques, outre leur participation sur le marché primaire en tant que prestataires de services, se sont engagées sur les marchés secondaires à la fois pour soutenir les cours des émissions de certains emprunteurs et surtout pour assurer la liquidité des marchés en intervenant comme teneurs de marché ("market makers").

La rentabilité de ces activités est pourtant loin d'être assurée en raison d'une concurrence effrénée qui réduit très rapidement l'écart cours acheteur / cours vendeur à des niveaux insuffisants pour permettre une rémunération adéquate des risques. Fréquemment, à la suite de pertes, de nombreux acteurs décident de se retirer, comme l'ont récemment fait à Londres certains "market makers" des "Gilts"[14]: d'une trentaine à la suite du Big Bang d'octobre 1986, seule une vingtaine subsistait en août 1989.

Cet exemple illustre bien la nécessité de pouvoir opérer rapidement des mouvements stratégiques d'un secteur d'activité à un autre. Pour améliorer les profits tirés de leurs activités de marché, les banques sont tentées d'accroître leurs opérations de spéculation par des prises de position dont la profitabilité dépend uniquement de la réalisation des anticipations. Afin de minimiser le volume de capitaux engagés, elles s'orientent naturellement vers les marchés à terme dont les effets de levier sont importants.[15]

Bien que ces activités soient très risquées et génèrent des profits non récurrents, presque toutes les grandes institutions financières les jugent indispensables non seulement pour tenter de rentabiliser leurs investissements mais aussi en tant qu'adjuvants de leurs activités de conseil et pour renforcer leur réputation dans la maîtrise d'instruments financiers de plus en plus complexes. A ce titre, les services et les opérations de marchés sont étroitement imbriqués. Dès qu'une institution financière a une stratégie internationale "multi-services", son omniprésence n'est alors souvent possible qu'au prix du recours à un système de subventions croisées dont la fragilité augmente pourtant avec la contestabilité accrue de certains marchés. Tel est le cas des activités des banques sur le marché euro-obligataire: dans leur participation aux syndicats d'émission, les banques enregistrent fréquemment des pertes mais maintiennent ce type d'activité en espérant capter la clientèle pour d'autres services plus lucratifs en raison d'une moindre concurrence.

2.2 Marchés et gestion du bilan et des risques

Les innovations financières se sont traduites, en particulier, par une mobilièrisation et une marchéisation accrues des bilans des banques (augmentation de la part des instruments négociables et des opérations rémunérées à des taux de marché) et un gonflement du hors bilan. La gestion de ces bilans devient véritablement active, en termes tant de volume que de structure (composition). Ces innovations ont corrélativement donné une nouvelle dimension à la gestion des risques.

Gestion active du bilan (et du hors bilan)

La mobiliérisation du bilan des banques concerne aussi bien l'actif que le passif. Pour les banques françaises, le pourcentage des produits négociables passe de 3,3% de l'actif en 1980 à 7,9% en 1987 et de 2,5% à 12,8% du passif.[16] Cette évolution s'explique, à l'actif par l'augmentation des titres de créances négociables et de placements détenus, au passif par la forte hausse du financement des banques sur les marchés par émission de certificats de dépôt et d'obligations.

Un des corrolaires de cette évolution réside dans la négociabilité des composantes des bilans qui permet aux banques de maîtriser plus facilement la taille de ces derniers.

Plusieurs techniques plus ou moins souples sont envisageables. Les banques peuvent, par exemple, procéder à des émissions croisées de certificats de dépôt. Cette pratique a parfois été utilisée en France pour gonfler les bilans lors de la clôture d'exercice. En revanche, la réduction de la taille du bilan peut s'avérer difficile à réaliser quand la part des titres publics négociables détenus est faible.

La titrisation des créances constitue une méthode plus souple et plus élaborée de gestion du bilan. En effet, non seulement elle permet d'en moduler la taille mais de plus elle autorise la dissociation des activités de financement, placement et gestion des prêts. Après l'introduction en France, en 1989, des fonds communs de créances, les institutions financières, selon leurs avantages comparatifs, pourront, comme aux Etats-Unis depuis les années soixante dix, se spécialiser dans l'une ou plusieurs de ces activités et ne seront plus contraintes de considérer l'octroi de prêts comme une production jointe englobant la collecte de l'information, la distribution des prêts, le refinancement, la gestion des paiements et des contentieux.

Ainsi la gestion bancaire ne se résume-t-elle plus uniquement à la gestion de l'actif et du passif ("asset and liability management") afin de dégager une marge nette d'intérêt positive en minimisant les risques (cf infra). La taille du bilan est une variable de décision stratégique et l'arbitrage s'effectue entre activités de bilan et activités de hors bilan. Comme le suggère Ian Giddy (1985), les deux stratégies principales pour "perdre des actifs" consistent soit à vendre des services financiers sans prendre de position (activité de courtier) ou des informations (conseil), soit à prendre des risques de marché et/ou de défaut du débiteur par le biais d'instruments hors bilan (contrats à terme, options, swaps, hybrides, caps, floors, etc) ou à l'occasion de prises fermes lors d'émissions d'instruments négociables.

Si le développement des marchés financiers a constitué un élément permissif de la mobiliérisation des bilans bancaires, la déréglementation et les innovations financières ont induit une diversification des productions bancaires à l'origine d'un nouveau comportement vis-à-vis de la taille et de la structure des bilans bancaires, désormais beaucoup plus "malléables". Ceci offre un degré de liberté supplémentaire aux banques dans la conduite de leur stratégie.

Gestion externalisée des risques

Simultanément, les banques adoptent également une nouvelle attitude vis-à-vis des risques liés à leurs opérations. Outre les risques systématiques – de plus en plus importants – de compensation et de réglement liés aux activités de marché, les risques microéconomiques d'une banque, par devise, relèvent de trois catégories: risque de défaut, risque de liquidité et risque de taux.

Dans les activités d'intermédiation financière classique, les risques étaient mutualisés et agrégés. Les banques pouvaient ainsi réaliser des économies d'échelle, en particulier vis-à-vis des coûts de collecte de l'information, et des économies d'envergure dues à l'existence de produits à coûts joints. Par contre la gestion des risques était lourde car internalisée: seule la diversification des opérations permettait de réduire le niveau global des risques. Le risque de défaut était géré en diversifiant les emprunteurs par secteurs d'activité, par zones géographiques, etc; le risque de liquidité dépendait du comportement de la banque quant à la maturité de ses actifs comparée à celle de ses ressources. Et le risque de taux, moins bien évalué, n'apparaissait pas fondamental étant donné l'ampleur des marges d'intérêt et la relative stabilité des taux, ou du moins de leur structure par terme (C. Lubochinsky, 1988). Gérer le risque de taux se limitait à agir sur le taux de transformation et à recourir aux opérations à taux variable.

La marchéisation du financement des économies et le décloisonnement des circuits financiers ont eu comme effets un renchérissement des ressources bancaires, une baisse de la rémunération tirée des crédits distribués (renforcée par la concurrence accrue) et donc une réduction des marges d'intérêt. Les banques ont été tentées de réagir en augmentant le degré de transformation afin de profiter de la structure "normalement" ascendante des taux. Or la décennie 1980 est marquée par une augmentation de la variabilité des taux et de leur structure et par la crise de l'endettement. Ceci s'est traduit par une élévation du niveau global des risques de défaut (les signatures de meilleure qualité se finançant directement sur les marchés), de liquidité et de taux. Ce dernier s'est aussi trouvé accru par la taille des positions spéculatives sur les marchés à fort effet de levier.

Toutefois, la mobiliérisation des bilans bancaires et les innovations de produits ont simultanément permis aux banques d'externaliser la gestion des risques qu'elles ne désirent pas assumer. Il est en effet maintenant possible de décomposer les différents risques contenus dans une opération et de les transférer à d'autres agents par le biais de marchés de produits dérivés. Ainsi dans un crédit classique, les trois risques sont-ils agréges pour la banque mais celle-ci peut par différentes méthodes externaliser la gestion de l'un d'entre eux ou de tous:

- La titrisation des créances permet, outre la réduction de la taille du bilan, d'évacuer simultanément ces trois risques, la banque ne jouant plus alors qu'un rôle de courtier.[17] De plus, la faculté seule de titriser facilement ces créances réduit automatiquement le risque de liquidité. En fait, tout produit négociable détenu à l'actif d'une banque est utilisable pour gérer la liquidité (sauf en cas de crise affectant l'ensemble des marchés), mais le risque en capital subsiste.
- La gestion active et externalisée des risques – dont l'objectif n'est pas toujours leur réduction – fait aussi largement appel aux contrats à terme, aux options et aux swaps. A l'origine, ces produits, qui lui ont donné son véritable essor, ont été conçus en tant qu'instruments de gestion du risque de variation des taux de change et d'intérêt, risque qui est alors dissocié du risque de liquidité. Selon qu'ils s'échangent sur des marchés organisés ou des marchés de gré à gré, ces produits confèrent aux intervenants – dont les institutions financières – la possibilité de modifier leur degré d'exposition au risque de taux avec plus ou moins d'avantages en termes de liquidité, de risque de défaut, d'utilisation des lignes de crédit, de coûts de transaction etc.
- Les progrès technologiques ont également facilité la création de produits synthétiques, c'est-à-dire reconstitués à partir de plusieurs actifs afin d'obtenir exactement le profil de risque souhaité.[18] En ce domaine, la sophistication croissante des opérations ne cesse d'offrir de nouvelles possibilités de gestion des risques.

Ainsi tant les marchés de produits dérivés et la titrisation des crédits que les progrès technologiques procurent-ils aux banques la possibilité de mener une gestion externalisée et active de leurs risques. Toutefois, celle-ci suppose l'existence de marchés liquides et efficaces. Ceci se traduit par une nécessaire interdépendance entre la compétitivité des institutions financières et celle des places financières sur lesquelles elles opèrent habituellement. Les premières ne peuvent atteindre leurs objectifs quant à leur degré d'exposition au risque que s'il existe une gamme suffisamment large et diversifiée de produits dérivés.

Finalement, certaines formes d'organisation des banques – conglomérat, banque universelle, etc. – sont peut-être plus aptes que d'autres à assurer cette flexibilité. Il est indéniable que les réorientations rapides que cette flexibilité suppose soulèvent d'énormes difficultés. Celles-ci tiennent à l'adaptabilité et à la qualification du personnel, à l'irréversibilité et aux coûts d'amortissement élevés de certains investissements ou à la mise au point d'une comptabilité analytique élaborée. Mais il est clair que, dans le contexte actuel d'interne concurrence, la "banque à géométrie variable" constitue l'une des stratégies possibles.

NOTES

1. Une analyse des suppléments annuels de ces dix dernières années de l'hebdomadaire *The Economist*, consacrés aux activités bancaires internationales, suffit pour s'en convaincre.
2. Les développements désormais consacrés à l'analyse de cette contribution par l'O.C.D.E. dans ses monographies relatives aux economies des pays membres sont révélateurs de ces préoccupations.
3. Les opérations de swaps de devises correspondent parfois à de tels arbitrages entre différentes règlementations des marchés de capitaux, comme par exemple lorsqu'un marché domestique est "fermé" aux emprunteurs étrangers.
4. La notion de globalisation utilisée ici est celle retenue par les économistes industriels – par exemple, Porter – pour analyser les transformations structurelles de diverses branches d'industrie en cours de mondialisation – par exemple, la construction automobile. Elle ne recouvre donc pas totalement celle de globalisation des activités financières souvent employée dans l'analyse de l'évolution des systèmes financiers.
5. Ce mouvement a été très net pour les banques régionales américaines attirées par les perspectives offertes par la déréglementation domestique, en particulier les possibilités d'implantation – sous certaines conditions – dans plusieurs Etats.
6. Les mesures de déréglementation des marchés de valeurs mobilières dans plusieurs pays – à l'instar du "Big Bang" londonien d'octobre 1986 – ont évidemment facilité la mise en oeuvre de telles stratégies par les banques de dépôts auparavant exclues de ce secteur.
7. Ce mouvement pourrait passer par une phase initiale de consolidation régionale au niveau des grandes zones: Etats-Unis, Communauté Economique Européenne, Japon. Elle semble en effet bien engagée aux Etats-Unis où le besoin de rationalisation du système était le plus grand. A noter que les transformations en cours dans ce pays peuvent être riches d'enseignement pour les banques européennes confrontées au Marché Unique (ce point de vue est à juste titre défendu par A. Levy-Lang dans sa préface du livre *La banque éclatée* de Lowell L. Bryan).
8. Ces actifs financiers existent pour assurer les transferts de consommation entre différents biens et services ou les transferts intertemporels (approche microéconomique des intermédiaires financiers, cf George J. Benston et Clifford W. Smith Jr, 1976).
9. Dans ce cas précis, les imperfections de marché que réduit l'intermédiaire financier procèdent surtout de l'illiquidité et de l'indivisibilité de certains prêts aux agents á déficit de financement.
10. Ces mouvements ont toutes chances de s'accompagner de mutations dans les formes organisationnelles adoptées par les intermédiaires financiers, par exemple l'émergence de conglomérats.
11. Ian H. Giddy, op. cit.
12. Ainsi la part des commissions dans le produit net bancaire a-t-elle augmenté régulièrement et rapidement pour les grandes banques françaises, passant de 10–15% au début de cette décennie à près de 25% en 1988. Cette part est plus élevée pour leurs homologues américaines. Par exemple, le total des commissions a représenté 40% du profit (1,7 milliards de dollars) réalisé par Bankers Trust en 1988.
13. On estime à 80% la part actuelle des émission euro-obligataires immédiatement swappées.
14. Ce phénomène est toutefois renforcé par la diminution de l'encours des titres publics en circulation due à l'excédent budgétaire britannique et la politique de remboursement anticipé de la dette.
15. C'est ainsi qu'il s'échange quotidiennement, sur le Chicago Mercantile Exchange, l'équivalent de 180 à 190 milliards de dollars sur le seul contrat "Eurodollar 3 mois", dont l'essentiel correspond à des opérations de spéculation.
16. Source: Rapports annuels de la Commission Bancaire.

17. Toutefois, comme seules les "meilleures" créances sont titrisées, le risque de défaut de la banque sur les opérations de credits conservées au bilan s'élève (problème de démutualisation du risque de défaut).
18. Un exemple simple est celui de la vente d'une série de quatre contrats de taux à 3 mois qui garantit ainsi un taux synthétique à 1 an – mais qui ne garantit pas la disponibilité des fonds.

BIBLIOGRAPHIE

Baumol, W. C., Panzar, J. C. & Willig, R. D.: *Contestable Markets and the Theory of Industry Structure*, Harcourt, Brace, Jovanovich Eds, San Diego, Cal., 1982.

Benston, J. & Smith, Clifford W.: "A transaction cost approach to the theory of financial intermediation", *The Journal of Finance*, Mai 1976.

Bond, I. D. & Briault, C. B.: "The Commercial Banks' Contribution to Current Debt Difficulties", Discussion Paper, Bank of England, 1983.

Bryan, Lowell L.: *Breaking up the bank*, Dow Jones Irwin Homewood Ill. 1988 (traduction française: La Banque Eclatée).

Coase, Ronald H.: "The Nature of the Firm" *Economica* NS N° 4 1937 reproduit dans *Readings in Price Theory*, édité par Georges J. Stigler et Kenneth E. Boulding Richard D. Irwin, Chicago 1952.

Giddy, Ian H.: "Assetless Banking" in *Strategic Planning in International Banking*, P. Savona & G. Sutija, Eds. Macmillan, London 1985.

Giddy, Ian H. & Allen, Deborah L.: "International Competition in Bank Regulation", *Quarterly Review Banca nazionale del Lavoro*, sept. 1979.

Greenbaum, Stuart I. & Haywood, Charles F.: "Secular change in the Financial Services Industry", *Journal of Money, Credit and Banking*, May 1971.

Gurley, John G. & Shaw, Edwards S.: *Money in a Theory of Finance*, The Brookings Institution, Washington D.C. 1960.

Lubochinsky, Catherine C.: "Analyse du risque de taux des établissements bancaires', *Repères* N° 15, Luxembourg, 1988.

Metais, Joël P.: "Towards a Restructuring of the International Financial Industry" in Gardener E.P.M. ed. *The future of Financial Systems and Services*, Macmillan (à paraître) 1989.

Parly, J. M. & Poix, M.: "La compétitivité bancaire: une revue critique de la littérature", Etude pour le Commissariat Général du Plan Mimeo, Paris juin 1987.

Penato, A. & Protopapadakis, A.: "Implicit Deposit Insurance and Banks Portfolio Choices: a Positive Theory of International Over Exposure", papier présenté au Colloque H.E.C.-I.S.A. "Recent Developments in International Finance' Jouy en Josas, 1986.

Silber, William L.: "Towards a Theory of Financial Innovation" in *Financial Innovation*, édité par W. L. Silber, D. C. Heath, Lexington, Mass, 1975.

Szymczak, Philippe J. P.: "Essai sur la rentabilité bancaire" Thèse pour le Doctorat en Science Economique Université de Paris I (Panthéon – Sorbonne) Paris, 1988.

VII. Les Pouvoirs Publics Français et Les Résistances à la Création d'un Marché Bancaire Intérieur Unifié

FRANÇOIS LEONARD DE JUVIGNY

Pendant plusieurs décennies, le problème de l'égalité de concurrence entre les établissements de crédit n'a pas constitué une priorité pour les pouvoirs publics français.

Les priorités concernaient les besoins de financement sociaux, collectifs ou d'investissements productifs qui étaient jugés ne pas pouvoir être satisfaits par le marché et justifier, soit l'orientation, à leur profit exclusif de flux de ressources – ce système impliquant une réglementation très précise des conditions de rémunération des ressources – soit des bonifications financées sur le budget de l'Etat, soit des procédures particulières de refinancement ou de mobilisation à des conditions avantageuses. En outre, des avantages fiscaux, réglementaires et de toutes sortes étaient consentis à des établissements, en principe spécialisés dans telle ou telle activité, mais dont certains étendaient progressivement leur champ d'action tout en conservant leurs monopoles, et les capitaux que ceux-ci leur avaient permis d'amasser pour leur compte propre. Il faut dire qu'en ce qui la concerne, la technique de cloisonnement des processus d'affectation des ressources à des emplois déterminés était facilitée par l'existence de structures "bancaires" très diversifiées juridiquement et économiquement.

Par la suite, à ces dispositions très diverses mais très importantes, en volume, s'est superposé l'encadrement du crédit, avec tout un cortège d'exonérations particulières en faveur d'affectations jugées prioritaires.

En outre, le taux de base bancaire est demeuré pendant fort longtemps fixé par la Direction du Trésor du Ministère des Finances.

Telles sont les raisons pour lesquelles on ne saurait expliquer la situation actuelle de la concurrence interbancaire en France sans évoquer le rôle des pouvoirs publics, d'abord parce qu'il a été considérable, ensuite parce que, en dépit de récentes et appréciables remises en cause, il s'est exercé dans un sens si peu favorable à une véritable concurrence qu'il en reste aujourd'hui des pans entiers encore trop importants; en outre, les conséquences du passé sont loin d'être résorbées. D'ailleurs, il n'est pas absolument certain qu'en matière bancaire, les pouvoirs publics soient, aujourd'hui encore, tellement partisans d'une véritable concurrence, du moins lorsqu'il s'agit de leur propre rôle.

D. E. Fair and C. de Boissieu (eds), Financial Institutions in Europe Under New Competitive Conditions, 83–94.
© 1990 *Kluwer Academic Publishers, Dordrecht. Printed in the Netherlands.*

Certes, il ne saurait être question de mettre ici en cause la surveillance bancaire ni dans son principe ni dans ses modalités.

En effet, le bien-fondé de la réglementation prudentielle est indiscutable. Serait-il raisonnable de fonder une banque sans s'être, au prèalable, assuré d'un capital minimum et des compétences voulues? Serait-il raisonnable de la faire fonctionner sans se préoccuper de sa liquidité, de sa solvabilité et d'une saine division des risques? Il ne s'agit donc pas, à proprement parler, d'entraves à la concurrence, mais de règles tenant à l'exercice même du métier et conditionnant son succès. Il s'y ajoute que la loi bancaire en étendant le contrôle bancaire à l'ensemble des établissements de crédit a fait oeuvre utile.

Il ne s'agit pas non plus de contester la politique monétaire, au moins dans son principe, la création monétaire tout comme la sécurité des dépôts devant faire l'objet d'une attention vigilante des pouvoirs publics. Il s'agit plutôt de savoir si certains moyens ou certaines modalités des politiques économique, financière et monétaire n'ont pas constitué des entraves inutiles ou fâcheuses à la concurrence interbancaire.

Dans une première partie, nous examinerons les obstacles à la concurrence dûs à l'action des pouvoirs publics, dans une seconde, la lutte des pouvoirs publics contre les entraves à la concurrence dues aux établissements.

PREMIERE PARTIE:

LES OBSTACLES A LA CONCURRENCE DUS AUX POUVOIRS PUBLICS

Nous aborderons successivement le cadre institutionnel, la collecte des dépôts, la gestion de moyens de paiement, l'octroi des crédits et la réglementation des guichets. En revanche, et en dépit de leur importance, nous n'aborderons pas les inégalités de fiscalité des établissements – sujet très technique que nous ne mentionnerons que pour mémoire dans la conclusion à propos des fonds propres.

LE CADRE INSTITUTIONNEL

Aux termes des premières "lois bancaires" françaises, celles de 1941 et 1945, il y avait, d'une part, une législation s'appliquant à un secteur pleinement concurrentiel, c'est-à-dire aux banques et aux établissements financiers ne bénéficiant d'aucun avantage ou monopole et subissant de plein fouet les contraintes de la politique monétaire et, d'autre part, des législations très spécifiques accordant à des ensembles ou des unités, en principe, spécialisées, des monopoles et des avantages particuliers et restreignant en contrepartie leur champ d'activités, ce qui n'empêchait pas certains, sortant des limites de leur statut – soit en prenant des libertés qu'ils faisaient avaliser, par la suite, par les pouvoirs publics, soit par le biais de structures bancaires de droit commun qu'ils contrôlaient intégralement –, d'étendre progressivement – et parfois avec un dynamisme tout-à-fait remarquable – leur domaine à l'ensemble des opérations bancaires et des clientèles et de gagner, ainsi, globalement, des parts de marché.

Le système bancaire français était, en effet, composé d'une part de banques commerciales – nationalisées ou privées – et d'établissements financiers privés, et, d'autre part, de toute une mosaïque de réseaux ou d'organismes dits "à statut légal spécial". En effet, l'une des caractéristiques de l'esprit cartésien, qui a particulièrement prévalu dans la haute administration, aboutit chaque fois qu'il y a un problème général de financement qui ne se résout pas à la satisfaction des pouvoirs publics, c'est-à-dire suivant l'idée qu'ils se font de l'intérêt général, à créer un organisme financier ad hoc qui a pour vocation initiale de répondre à un besoin financier déterminé et qui bénéficie à cette fin d'avantages ou de monopoles particuliers. D'où toute une constellation d'établissements et de réseaux spécialisés.

Par la suite, une évolution se faisant jour, les problèmes changent d'importance, sinon de nature; mais les organismes ainsi créés sont là et cherchent à perdurer en développant et en étendant à d'autres domaines leur activité. Souvent, le monopole dont ils bénéficient constitue un produit d'appel, du moins dans la mesure où ils tendent progressivement à effectuer les mêmes opérations et à rendre les mêmes gammes de services que les établissements qui ne disposent pas d'un monopole.

La tendance spontanée était donc celle d'une attaque des contraintes imposées initialement et d'une banalisation des champs d'activité avec, cependant, maintien des législations spécifiques, et des monopoles, aboutissant à une réduction progressive des parts de marché des structures bancaires qui ne pouvaient lutter à armes égales (banques commerciales, trésor public, P.T.T.).

A cet égard, la loi bancaire de 1984 a marqué une étape décisive. En effet, l'internationalisation croissante des activités financières, le progrès de la technologie dans le domaine de la télématique, l'extension de la bancarisation, l'accession du public à une information financière développée, appelaient la sortie d'un cadre juridique marqué par la multiplication des privilèges, des frontières et des octrois. Cette levée des barrières et des particularismes s'imposait d'autant plus qu'ils avaient été conçus en fonction de priorités qui avaient évolué. C'était précisément le défaut du système qui consistait à répondre à des besoins précis par la création d'organismes ad hoc, que de figer l'échelle des priorités et de continuer de diriger, à des taux de faveur, les flux de ressources vers des emplois devenus moins prioritaires ou qui, en tout cas, pouvaient être largement satisfaits par l'ensemble des établissements de crédit et non plus seulement par les établissements à statut légal spécial.

Néanmoins, la loi bancaire de 1984 n'est pas allée jusqu'au bout de la tâche dans l'application de l'universalité et dans le rétablissement de la concurrence. Sans doute était-ce difficile de le faire d'un seul coup.

Elle s'applique intégralement à l'ensemble des établissements de crédit, mais dont elle reconnaît la diversité, créant six catégories: banques, banques mutualistes ou coopératives, caisses d'épargne, caisses de crédit municipal, sociétés financières et institutions financières spécialisées.

Elle s'applique partiellement aux compagnies financières, aux intermédiaires en opérations de banque, aux agents du marché interbancaire et aux établissements de gestion de portefeuille de valeurs mobilières (maisons de titres).

Mais elle ne s'applique ni à la Caisse des dépôts, en dépit de l'importance considérable de cet organisme dans le système financier français, ni aux services financiers des postes. Cette dernière disposition qui a été violemment critiquée par les parlementaires et par le conseil économique et social lors de l'examen du projet de loi a été validée par le Conseil constitutionnel au motif que les services postaux sont des "services de l'Etat".

Le même principe d'universalité tempérée se retrouve dans la compétence de la tutelle: tous les établissements de crédit se trouvent désormais soumis aux mêmes instances mais dans des conditions qui ne sont pas homogènes. D'une part, le Comité de la réglementation bancaire n'a pas compétence sur les conditions d'accès au sociétariat des banques mutualistes ou coopératives, sur la définition des compétences des institutions financières spécialisées, des caisses d'épargne et des caisses de crédit municipal. D'autre part, un rôle particulier est dévolu par la loi aux organes centraux chargés de représenter leurs affiliés auprès des autorités de tutelle qui leur délèguent une partie de leurs pouvoirs.

LA COLLECTE DES DEPOTS

A l'heure actuelle, les dépôts (sauf les dépôts à terme de 3 mois et plus), font encore, dans leur quasi-totalité, l'objet d'une réglementation de leur rémunération: interdiction pour les dépôts à vue, plafonnement spécifique pour les diverses autres catégories.

D'autre part, la plupart des catégories de livret bénéficient d'avantages fiscaux et sont, de ce fait, soumis à des règles d'emploi particulières.

Les livrets les plus répandus – les livrets dits "A" et les livrets dits "bleus" – cumulent trois avantages: rémunération égale à celle des livrets ordinaires, défiscalisation des revenus et disponibilité totale pour le déposant. Or, ils représentent, à eux seuls, le cinquième de l'ensemble des liquidités de l'économie. L'importance commerciale de tels produits est considérable, comme le confirme la toute récente grande campagne publicitaire des caisses d'épargne essentiellement axée sur le livret A. Ajoutons que le livret A est exonéré des réserves obligatoires et qu'en ce qui concerne les règles d'emploi, celles concernant les livrets bleus ne sont pas particulièrement contraignantes pour le seul réseau qui peut les proposer à sa clientèle.

Depuis 1975, époque à partir de laquelle on peut considérer que la bancarisation de la population française s'est trouvée achevée, les deux réseaux qui se partagent le monopole de ces produits, tout en pratiquant désormais les autres opérations bancaires (caisses d'Epargne et Crédit mutuel) ont doublé leurs effectifs alors que les banques stabilisaient les leurs et que ceux du Crédit agricole voyaient la progression des siens se réduire sensiblement. Comme chacun sait, l'essor extraordinaire des deux premiers réseaux ne peut s'expliquer par le seul dynamisme de leur personnel mais bien plutôt par le monopole dont ils bénéficient.

D'autres entorses à la concurrence continuent d'exister: les dépôts des notaires sont placés obligatoirement, soit à la Caisse des dépôts et consignations, soit aussi, mais uniquement pour les notaires résidant dans des communes de 30.000 habitants ou moins, dans les Caisses de crédit agricole. La rémunération de ces dépôts étant plafonnée à 1% et leur encours étant de l'ordre de 50 Mds de F. l'avantage, pour les réseaux à qui cette collecte est réservée, est évident.

Par ailleurs, depuis la loi du 25 janvier 1985, en cas de redressement judiciaire d'une entreprise, toutes les sommes qui ne sont pas nécessaires à la poursuite de l'activité doivent être versées immédiatement à la Caisse des Dépôts. En cas de liquidation, toutes les sommes reçues par le liquidateur doivent être versées à la Caisse des Dépôts.

Enfin, la trésorerie des collectivités locales est obligatoirement déposée chez les comptables publics ou dans le groupe de la Caisse des dépôts.

Telle est la situation actuelle en matière de collecte des dépôts.

Cette vue instantanée doit être complétée par un rappel de l'évolution de la réglementation et de la fiscalité. En 1945, les billets réprésentaient le quart de la masse monétaire au sens le plus large (L). Ils n'en forment aujourd'hui que le vingtième. Même si l'on fait la part de l'excès de liquidité dû aux circonstances de l'époque, force est de constater qu'en dépit d'une forte inflation, la circulation fiduciaire jouait alors (plutôt mal que bien, certes) un rôle de conservation de l'épargne qu'elle n'assume plus aujourd'hui. D'ailleurs, si cela n'avait pas été le cas, le retrait des billets de 5.000 Frs opéré en 1948 n'aurait pu avoir lieu.

Le plafonnement, intervenu en 1956, puis l'interdiction, qui date de 1967, de la rémunération des dépôts à vue, se sont traduits par un gonflement des dépôts à terme: il s'agissait, pour les pouvoirs publics, d'accroître la part de l'épargne liquide dans l'ensemble des liquidités.

En 1981, pour favoriser le marché financier, on a pénalisé fiscalement les dépôts à terme et les bons de caisse: 20 points d'écart entre le prélèvement forfaitaire d'impôts sur le revenu applicable aux intérêts de l'épargne liquide et celui applicable aux intérêts de l'épargne obligataire. Il en est résulté un important transfert de fonds au détriment des dépôts à terme et au profit des SICAV court terme, notamment monétaires, dont les performances font l'objet d'une vive concurrence.

On peut présenter schématiquement la politique des pouvoirs publics ainsi: la détention de monnaie a été jugée, a priori, inflationniste, malsaine, néfaste à l'économie. Au contraire, la détention d'actifs financiers apparemment plus stables a été jugée favorable à l'économie (on a parlé d'épargne "saine"). De ce fait, les banques ont été contraintes d'offrir à leur clientèle les produits que les pouvoirs publics souhaitaient qu'elles offrent. Politique arbitraire, coûteuse pour les emplois et l'économie et sans doute assez vaine dans la mesure où elle n'a pas, en fin de compte, modifié fondamentalement les comportements. On ne discutera pas le principe selon lequel l'épargne longue doit être mieux rémunérée, encore faut-il qu'il s'agisse d'une épargne véritablement longue et stable.

Ainsi, en une génération, la même réalité aura changé plusieurs fois d'étiquette, sans changer de nature, la seule différence réelle aura été un alourdissement sensible du coût de la ressource pour l'économie et une amélioration considérable de la rémunération d'une épargne liquide.

De ce fait, la concurrence que l'on interdisait ici est apparue là et ce, avec une intensité sensiblement accrue et l'on est parvenu à des excès que l'on aurait pu éviter et si les banques n'étaient, en quelque sorte, contraintes de proposer les mêmes produits ou les mêmes types de produits. Il est devenu difficile de revenir en arrière, dans la mesure où le volume des dépôts à vue fait qu'ils ne représentent plus, pour leurs détenteurs, que des stock-outils.

S'agissant de certains produits à régimes spéciaux tels l'épargne-logement, les CODEVI, les PER ... on peut admettre la nécessité de les maintenir. Mais une égalité de concurrence n'est assurée que si les établissements qui les distribuent ne disposent, par ailleurs, d'aucun monopole leur permettant d'offrir un produit d'appel.

Merite également d'etre citée une entrave non à la concurrence bancaire, mais à la concurrence entre banques et non banques, avec l'autorisation donnée aux entreprises d'émettre des billets de trésorerie qui ne sont pas assujettis aux réserves obligatoires, comme le sont les dépôts bancaires et notamment les certificats de dépôts.

De ce fait, l'intermédiation bancaire est considérée comme inefficace, et devant être pénalisée.

LA GESTION DES MOYENS DE PAIEMENT

Il ne saurait y avoir de véritable concurrence sans vérité des prix, même si celle-ci ne peut être absolue. Or, le dernier rapport de la Commission bancaire précise que le déficit qui résulte, pour les banques de la gestion des moyens de paiement, a représenté, en 1987, près de la moitié (45,2%) de leur marge bénéficiaire brute.

Autrement dit, la gestion des moyens de paiement n'est pas, en France, rémunérée, ou en tout cas loin de l'être à son prix. Une tentative de mise en place d'une facturation des écritures de débit relatives aux chèques et ce, d'une façon généralisée, a eu lieu, en 86–87, dans le cadre d'une concertation entre les banques et les organisations de consommateurs. Alors qu'elle était fort près du but, cette négociation a achoppé, à la suite de positions inattendues prises au dernier moment par les pouvoirs publics.

Néanmoins, quelques banques ont pu, soit fermer des comptes présentant une forte disproportion entre leur solde – quelle que soit l'importance de celui-ci – et le nombre de leurs opérations gratuites, soit mettre en place des commissions dont le montant effectivement perçu tient compte de l'importance du solde. Mais ces comportements bancaires sont récents et il va de soi que, s'agissant de services rendus en principe gratuitement, la concurrence est limitée.

Cependant, certains moyens de paiement, telles les cartes, font l'objet d'une rémunération. Mais, comme le notait récemment le professeur Denis Kessler, Président du Comité consultatif (cf. infra) "pour des raisons notamment de mauvaise facturation des services financiers et plus particulièrement des chèques, nous n'avons pas une situation tout à fait satisfaisante ... tant que nous n'aurons pas, en France, une facturation généralisée de l'ensemble des services financiers, une facturation qui soit économique ... c'est-à-dire qui induise chacun des agents à minimiser le coût d'utilisation des moyens de paiement, le coût global de la gestion des moyens de paiement restera trop élevé."

Il va de soi que cette situation est non seulement regrettable en termes de productivité, mais au surplus, pénalise les établissements en fonction de l'importance relative de la collecte des dépôts.

L'OCTROI DES CREDITS ET LA POLITIQUE MONETAIRE

C'est le domaine dans lequel la levée des entraves à la libre concurrence a été la plus forte.

D'une part, après plus d'une decennie, l'encadrement du crédit, avec tout son cortège de dérogations, a été levé. D'autre part, les pouvoirs publics se sont engagés progressivement dans une réduction du champ des prêts bonifiés dont l'octroi, en France, fait traditionnellement l'objet d'un monopole. Ce dernier a connu, lui aussi, un début de réduction, avec la banalisation des prêts bonifiés à l'artisanat.

Si à l'heure actuelle, le Crédit agricole conserve le monopole des prêts bonifiés à l'agriculture, aux SAFER (Société de droit privé, d'aménagement foncier et d'établissement rural), aux coopératives céréalières pour les financements de récoltes avec aval de l'ONIC, il est sérieusement envisagé de procéder par étapes à une certaine banalisation.

Cependant, le poids du passé demeure bien lourd puisque pendant l'encadrement du crédit, le Crédit agricole a souvent bénéficié de dérogations dont l'impact commercial était d'autant plus décisif que ce réseau bénéficiait du monopole des prêts bonifiés à l'agriculture et qu'il n'hésitait pas à s'en servir pour faire souscrire à des emprunteurs, même non mutualistes, des engagements de fidélité. Cela n'enlève rien aux mérites de cette institution qui a su mettre à profit des circonstances favorables pour accroître sa part de marché mais on ne saurait nier cependant que les pouvoirs publics ont faussé le jeu de la concurrence.

Maintenant que l'encadrement du crédit n'existe plus, et est remplacé principalement par une politique de taux d'intérêt, il convient de s'interroger sur l'incidence que peut exercer sur cette politique la réglementation de la rémunération des dépôts. Il va de soi qu'une politique monétaire s'exerçant par les taux a d'autant plus d'impact que son assiette est large. A cet égard, le plafonnement de la rémunération des dépôts et, davantage encore, la détermination a priori des emplois de certaines ressources – même si cela est justifié par les avantages fiscaux dont elles bénéficient – limitent artificiellement le champ et la portée d'une politique par les taux.

Or, nous avons vu qu'il ne s'agissait pas du tout de quelque chose de marginal, mais au contraire d'une masse fort importante de capitaux. Aussi, l'arme des taux d'intérêt ne s'appliquant qu'à une partie des financements ne peut, en conséquence, qu'être maniée plus brutalement. Et comme la collecte des ressources pré-affectées fait l'objet, nous l'avons dit, pour sa plus grande part, de monopoles, il ne peut en résulter qu'une entrave à la concurrence.

LA REGLEMENTATION DES GUICHETS

La création des guichets par les banques commerciales a été soumise á autorisation à partir de 1945. Cette règle ne s'appliquait pas aux réseaux mutualistes, et notamment au crédit agricole qui a acquis ainsi un quasi-monopole dans la plupart des zones rurales.

Lorsque la liberté de création des guichets a été rendue brutalement en 1966, les banques ont développé hardiment leurs réseaux de guichets qui, en nombre, ont doublé en dix ans.

En 82, les pouvoirs publics ont remis en place une procédure d'autorisation avec contingentement. En 86, la liberté a été de nouveau rendue aux seuls établissements qui ne disposaient pas de privilège; pour les autres, l'ouverture de nouveaux guichets demeure soumise à autorisation. Cette situation peut être considérée comme relativement justifiée, dans la mesure où il est normal que le développement des guichets ne repose pas sur une distorsion de concurrence d'origine légale ou réglementaire en matière de services rendus à la clientèle.

La situation est beaucoup moins satisfaisante s'agissant des possibilités d'ouverture horaire des guichets.

En effet, le décret du 31 mars 1937 contraint les banques à une répartition uniforme du temps de travail hebdomadaire sur 5 jours ouvrables avec 2 jours de repos consécutifs (dont un dimanche). Il interdit le travail par roulement (dans un même établissement, les jours de repos doivent être les mêmes pour tous).

Ces dispositions auxquelles il ne peut être dérogé qu'avec l'accord de l'ensemble des salariés de l'établissement, ne s'appliquent pas au crédit agricole – régi par le Code rural – ni aux sociétés financières – non visées par le décret –.

DEUXIEME PARTIE

LES POUVOIRS PUBLICS ET LES OBSTACLES A LA CONCURRENCE DUS AUX
ETABLISSEMENTS

Si, en ce qui les concerne, les pouvoirs publics ont encore beaucoup à faire pour réaliser l'égalité dans la concurrence, ils se sont, en revanche, montrés beaucoup plus vigilants et ardents dans la suppression des obstacles à la concurrence, dans la mesure où ces obstacles relèvent du comportement des établissements eux-mêmes.

D'une part, il y a en France une réglementation très précise du crédit à la consommation et du crédit à l'habitat qui vise à protéger les emprunteurs.

Les lois correspondantes canalisent la concurrence, notamment lors de l'octroi des prêts.

De son côté, l'ordonnance du 1er décembre 1986 règlementant la concurrence, qui s'applique à tous les agents économiques et aux activités de production, de distribution et de services, vise à réprimer les pratiques anticoncurrentielles qu'elle redéfinit et institue un contrôle des projets de concentration économique. En outre, elle crée une autorité administrative indépendante: le Conseil de la concurrence. L'interdiction des pratiques anticoncurrentielles s'applique aux opérations de banque. Les infractions éventuelles des établissements de crédit doivent être constatées, poursuivies et sanctionnées par le Conseil de la concurrence, la Commission bancaire n'étant saisie que pour avis (cette situation est exceptionnelle dans les pays industrialisés).

Par ailleurs, la loi bancaire de 1984 a prévu la création d'un comité consultatif, dit "des usagers", "chargé d'étudier les problèmes liés aux relations entre les établissements de crédit et leur clientèle et de proposer toutes mesures appropriées dans ce domaine, notamment sous forme d'avis ou de recommandations d'ordre général".

Enfin, la Commission des opérations de bourse doit, aux termes de la loi du 11 juillet 1985, "veiller à la protection de l'épargne investie en valeurs mobilières ou tous autres placements donnant lieu à appel public à l'épargne" et â "l'information des investisseurs" et la loi du 14 décembre 1985 lui a reconnu la faculté d'édicter à l'attention des professionnels des règles de conduite.

Aucun de ces organismes n'est resté inactif.

S'agissant du Conseil de la concurrence, celui-ci est intervenu à plusieurs reprises, notamment à propos de décisions précises par le Groupement des cartes bancaires.

Rappelons que sous la pression des pouvoirs publics, a été réalisée en France, fin 84, pour la première fois au monde, la création d'un organisme unique couvrant l'émission, sur le territoire national, de toutes les cartes bancaires et assurant la réciprocité des services, ce qu'il est convenu d'appeler l'interbancarité.

Or, précisément, le Conseil a enjoint au groupement de modifier certaines de ses décisions parce qu'elles lui paraissaient de nature à limiter la concurrence. Ce qui fut fait. Dans un cas, cependant, la solution apportée par le groupement ayant été contestée, celui-ci a fait appel devant la Cour de Paris. D'autres modifications sont intervenues sans intervention du Conseil pour satisfaire des demandes émanant d'associations de commerçants.

Par ailleurs, lorsque les 3 plus grandes banques commerciales annoncèrent, à quelques jours ou semaines d'intervalle, des relèvements des prix aux porteurs des cartes bancaires – qui n'avaient pas été relevés depuis trois ans et dont les majorations étaient différentes d'un établissement à l'autre et n'intervenaient pas aux mêmes dates – non seulement le ministre est intervenu pour faire rapporter par certains établissements la décision, mais une enquête, la première du genre, a été immédiatement diligentée par ses services.

S'agissant du Comité consultatif, ses travaux couvrent un champ très vaste "allant des contrats de location de coffres-forts aux incidents de paiement par chèque, de la révision des modalités de la loi sur l'usure à l'opportunité d'introduire la titrisation des crédits aux personnes, du rapprochement des dispositions gouvernant le crédit à la consommation en France avec celles de nos partenaires européens, aux clauses de remboursement anticipé", de l'endettement des ménages à la qualité des services bancaires.

Le Comité consultatif a notamment, dans le but de développer la concurrence entre les banques, accepté d'enteriner la normalisation de la présentation des conditions tarifaires générales des principales opérations, telle que la profession bancaire l'avait proposée. Une enquête effectuée auprès de 1300 guichets a montré que le Conseil consultatif avait eu satisfaction dans 98% des guichets.

Les travaux du Comité consultatif, comme d'ailleurs, et d'une manière plus générale, ceux du Conseil national du crédit auquel il est rattaché, donnent lieu à des enquêtes extrêmement lourdes et précises sur divers aspects du comportements des banques.

Autrement dit, on a l'impression qu'au contrôle par les financements (admission au réescompte, examen des dossiers individuels, encadrement du crédit), se substitue non seulement une action par les taux d'intérêt et les réserves obligatoires mais, en outre, un examen permanent des divers aspects de l'activité des banques qui, dans des groupes de travail variés, doivent rendre compte des aspects les plus divers de leurs comportements. Ceux-ci font l'objet d'une discussion serrée avec les représentants des pouvoirs publics et parfois avec ceux des organisations de consommateurs et de divers types de clientèles. Si, d'une certaine manière, ces initiatives des pouvoirs publics constituent un indéniable progrès, encore faut-il raison garder et laisser les banques responsables de leur gestion. Autrement dit, si des contacts approfondis avec les usagers et une réflexion commune sur leurs relations avec les banques peuvent constituer une source certaine de progrès, encore faut-il laisser aux établissements de crédit la maîtrise de leurs décisions.

Ajoutons qu'en province, le plus souvent à l'instigation des directions de la concurrence, les représentants des banques consacrent parfois un temps non négligeable à dialoguer avec les organisations de consommateurs. C'est ainsi qu'à STRASBOURG, à l'initiative conjointe de la profession et de la direction des relations avec le public du Ministère des finances, le Comité régional des banques a tenu récemment un colloque important sur le thème "Banques et consommateurs: concurrence et transparence" avec les organisations de consommateurs: des groupes de travail qui se réunissaient régulièrement avaient préparé d'importants rapports sur le sujet.

Au terme de cette analyse, il apparaît que les pouvoirs publics sont encore assez loin d'être parvenus à créer sur le territoire français un véritable marché intérieur unifié, c'est-à-dire un marché dans lequel toutes les dispositions sont prises pour que la concurrence puisse s'y exercer dans des conditions saines et loyales, conformément aux exigences du "level playing field". A cet égard, il convient de rappeler que les associations bancaires des Etats membres du marché commun, regroupées au sein de la Fédération bancaire européenne, ont toutes été d'accord pour faire savoir à la Commission des communautés européennes que des aides à l'épargne "populaire" ne devaient, en aucun cas et sous aucun prétexte, constituer le monopole de certains réseaux.

Ce ne sera pas un des moindres mérites de la construction européenne que de contraindre la France à créer ce marché unifié. Mais il faut s'interroger sur les causes de la lenteur mise à la création de ce marché. On peut considérer qu'elle résulte de trois forces: l'attachement de certains réseaux, très puissants économiquement, à leurs privilèges, l'assise politique dont ils bénéficient et surtout l'attachement de la haute administration à un système qui lui donnait de singuliers pouvoirs. Il aura fallu attendre le rapport Marjolin-Sadrin-Wormser pour observer une évolution des meilleurs esprits. Mais combien d'années ensuite pour qu'elle s'inscrive dans les faits!

Mais, il ne faut pas se leurrer: quels que soient les progrès qui seront réalisés dans la voie vers l'égalité de concurrence, le poids du passé demeurera très lourd: qu'il s'agisse des parts du marché, ou des fonds propres constitués par certains établissements dans des conditions exorbitantes du droit commun et, pour certains, pendant des décennies, en franchise d'impôt dont l'effet cumulatif a été fantastique. Les inégalités demeureront longtemps considérables. C'est dire l'ampleur de l'effort à accomplir pour les faire disparaître.

VIII. Competition in Banking Services and Its Implications: The Italian Case

MARCO ONADO

I. FOREWORD

During the 1980s deregulation and increased competition have been the new doctrine for regulators, economists and market participants. The structural characteristics of intermediation have changed (the more common adverb is "dramatically"), blurring in a few years traditional barriers between intermediaries and markets, which had taken regulators many years to build and defend.

These changes do not seem to have curbed the overall profitability of the financial services industry. With the notable exception of US Saving and Loans Associations, in every country all sectors of financial intermediation have shown satisfactory profits, normally not far from the peaks of late 1970s and early 1980s. After many worries raised in the mid-1980s (Bennet, 1986), the performance looks generally rather satisfactory even looking at individual cases.

All that does not fit perfectly into the traditional structure-conduct-performance models of banking markets, especially in their strictest version, which maintains that in less concentrated and more competitive markets profits should be lower. In a sense, in many countries, the 1980s have been the strongest challenge to this approach to banking markets, which inspired so many empirical researches and even regulatory policy in recent decades.

Although in the Italian experience the move towards competition began late in comparison to other countries, the changes seem already quite clear and can be an interesting (and in some ways typical) example of the new conditions of European credit markets.

This paper will examine the competitive environment of the Italian banking system, with particular reference to the present situation and the aftermath of the new competitive thrust of the 1980s. Cross-section data will be used to examine the different performance in terms of costs, margins and risk of a sample of Italian banks.[1] After a brief description of the main characteristics of bank competition in Italy (Section II), we shall examine the available evidence to test whether traditional models of structure-conduct-

D. E. Fair and C. de Boissieu (eds), Financial Institutions in Europe Under New Competitive Conditions, 95–106.
© 1990 Kluwer Academic Publishers, Dordrecht. Printed in the Netherlands.

performance can explain the present Italian situation (Section III). The final Section will try to point out the main problems that Italain authorities have to face and to draw some general conclusion from the Italian experience.

II. BANK COMPETITION IN ITALY: THE MAIN CHARACTERISTICS

A few characteristics of the Italian financial system must be remembered to understand the present situation:
i)   competition among banks has been traditionally limited by two factors:
  – the division of banks into institutional categories; the idea of the Italian banking law (approved in 1936) was to assign each category a specified market: national in scope for a few banks and local for the others (Cassese, 1983). This principle was observed up to the early 1970s, creating a geographic segmentation stronger than in other countries.
  – controls on entry, were applied by the Bank of Italy very strictly, using an "economic need" approach.
ii) the priority given to monetary policy objectives in a system characterised by an unusually high level of bank intermediation, forced the Bank of Italy to use administrative controls (credit ceilings and compulsory investment in securities) which limited competition throughout the 1970s.

Both these factors, and particularly the former, tended to concentrate banks on their historical markets of origin, limiting their mobility into new markets and letting survive old elements of segmentation. Individual banks' growth rates were mainly determined by geographical differences in economic development. In a situation characterised by strong segmentation, market shares grew (or diminished) reflecting the higher (or lower) rate of growth of each segment rather than the actual competitiveness of each bank in terms of prices and other conditions.

Unlike other countries' authorities (and more like the policy of the Federal Reserve Board) the Bank of Italy has had a strong preference for keeping rather low the degree of concentration in the banking system. A sort of bias against mergers has been a constant of the Bank of Italy's policy since the 1960s. Small banks with high growth potential have been the fulcrum of Bank of Italy's competitive policy (Onado, 1988). These banks were in many ways favoured in their ambition to enter national markets. Competition in the Italian case has been a "bottom-up" process, with local banks progressively eroding traditional big banks' markets. This group of banks has certainly been successful as demonstrated by the increase in market share of savings and people's banks. Their competitive advantage came from high profitability in local markets, strong capital position, and excess capacity of financial resources.

In this sense, small banks played the role of non-bank financial intermediaries in other countries. The difference in the Italian case has been the
lack (or the delay) of big banks' response. This has normally been explained
by administrative controls on lending; the desire to maintain traditional
customer relationships, particularly with big firms (Brandolini-Noera, 1988);
and even a strategic underestimation of the structural changes under way.

Unlike other countries, competition did not follow an external shock due
to the entry of new subjects in the banking market or from a fundamental
change in regulation.

This bottom-up approach to competition changed only slightly the degree
of concentration and no significant merger between large banks has been
recorded. Actual mergers followed a growth strategy, with a few local banks
gradually growing in size and scope with successive acquisitions of smaller
banks (Prometeia, 1989). While in other cases, winning banks can reconcile
both the efficiency and stability objectives of regulators, because they can
eliminate, without trauma, less inefficient banks through mergers, in the case
of Italy this happened only to a limited extent because of the relatively small
size of growing banks. It is normally argued that from the early 1980s
competitive conditions began to change. The pressure of a public debt
continuously growing in size forced the Treasury to offer high yields and
high liquidity to its securities, so that the process of disintermediation was
more acute than in any other country (De Felice et al, 1988). Later on,
administrative controls were lifted and entry controls gradually changed to
widen degrees of freedom for the banks.

This firm move of the Bank of Italy towards competition marked the
beginning of important changes in the characteristics of bank intermediation.
All categories of banks restructured the composition of their deposits, showing
closer attention to payment services on the one hand and creating a CDs
market on the other. Moreover their propensity to lend increased sharply,
particularly in the retail markets (small- and medium-size firms; households).

In a rather short period of time. Italian banks had to face the two kinds
of shocks experienced earlier in other countries: one from outside (in our
case, the pressure from the public debt and the ensuing disintermediation);
the other from within the banking system, particularly in the loan market.

Overall profitability remains however quite high. Both margins and even
differences between loan and deposit rates (Onado, 1986; Banca d'Italia, 1988)
have been high (and well above the average levels of the previous decade)
throughout the 1980s. This is not *prima facie* incompatible with theoretical
models, but needs to be verified looking at the individual data.

III. A CROSS-SECTION ANALYSIS OF COMPETITIVE CONDITIONS AND PERFORMANCE OF ITALIAN BANKS

The evolution briefly described in the preceding section could be particularly favourable for rapid changes in the conditions of banks. In a sense, this should be an ideal situation to see more efficient banks overcome less efficient banks.

Although our data do not permit examination of different growth patterns of banks, it is worth remembering that other researches have demonstrated that over the years changes in market shares have mainly followed the historical trend and that only slight changes can be seen in recent experience. Taking into account the strength of customer relationships in banking, a stickiness in market shares should not surprise. This however means that the effects of a more competitive environment should be traced even more easily in performance indicators.

According to traditional models, particularly structure-conduct-performance (s-c-p) models, the relationship between competition and operating efficiency is particularly important. The higher the competitive level, as measured by concentration ratios, the stronger the pressure from more efficient banks, which can use their competitive advantage forcing out of the market less efficient banks.

As a matter of fact, operating efficiency conditions have traditionally showed a remarkable variability across Italian banks. All empirical evidence (Ciocca-Giussani-Lanciotti, 1975; Conigliani, 1981) came to the conclusion that in the Italian banking system economies of scale exist and therefore that big banks have a competitive advantage over small banks. A caveat of this body of research has been that economies of scale disappear when the dimensional increase is obtained through an increase in the number of branches.[2] This somehow gave further support to controls to bank entry, whose objective became to avoid over-branching and inefficient growth of banks. A finding which could give support to a regulatory policy favourable to big banks led the Bank of Italy to be even more careful in the authorization of new branches.

Further research (Lanciotti-Raganelli, 1988; Prometeia, 1989; Landi, 1989; Baldini-Landi, 1989) confirms the existence of economies of scale but gives even more importance to the problem of the optimal size of bank branches. Which is tantamount to saying that plant economies are more important than scale economies *per se*. In other words, conditions of efficiency are found over a wide range of dimensions. Moreover, the research demonstrated that many banks suffered from a sub-optimal size of each branch, which means that entry controls limited the total number of branches but could not prevent (and in a sense encouraged) banks from having branches with high average size, as measured by the capital investment and the number of staff required.

For the sake of our analysis the efficiency of each bank can be measured by the distance of every observation from the estimated cost curve. We use a traditional specification, which is consistent with the cited research, such as:

$$\ln TC = a_0 + a_1 \ln TA + a_2 \ln BR + a_3 \ln W + a_4 \ln LTA \qquad [1]$$

where: TC = total costs; TA = total assets; BR = number of branches; W = staff costs per employee; LTA = ratio of loans to total assets.

Table 1. Results of regression (1).

Dep. var. ln TC	Cost	TA	BR	W	LTA
coeff.	−5.103	0.713	0.258	0.922	0.281
t test	−7.072	21.519	6.156	6.324	3.336
R2 adj.	0.984				
F stat	1722.971				

The results in Table 1 confirm the existence of economies of scale; the analysis of residuals confirms the high variability of conditions of efficiency all along the cost function. More efficient (or less efficient) banks can be found in every size class. While the competitive struggle has always been between large (national) banks on one side and medium and small (local) banks on the other, one cannot pinpoint a competitive advantage to a single size class.

Moreover, in the Italian situation small (local) banks have always shown a substantial propensity to risk, as measured by the ratio of loans to earning assets or the ratio of loans to deposits. The quiet-life hypothesis in its simplest form does not hold. While it is certainly true that many banks apparently behave according to a quiet-life hypothesis (banking has never been the realm of adventure) it also seems that many banks operating in local markets have historically been more risk-oriented than some big banks. Lending to the local community and local firms (which played so big a part in the industrial development of Italy) was a vital point of the mission of local banks and has been a fundamental cause of their extraordinary growth in past decades and therefore of what has been defined the "bottom-up" approach to competition.

In the controversy about the definition of the object of banks' production, deposits and other financial resources are not treated as an input on the grounds that the markets are competitive enough to assume that costs are equal for all firms, so that only differences in operating costs matter.

In the Italian situation, where the public debt is so huge, common and easily accessible, it should be quite obvious to have homogeneous financial costs. Although there is a widespread belief that interest differences tend to narrow, especially in the past few years, the evidence shows that the variability is quite high. Even the cost of deposits, which should be equalized by the effects of competition coming from the public debt has a great variance. The actual cost which takes into account also non-price conditions varies from one bank to the other.[3]

While banks operating in local markets are neither inefficient nor less risk-oriented, it is true that they normally benefit from better rate conditions. In our sample, conditions of inefficiency are neither linked with lower deposit rates, nor with higher lending rates, but generally speaking with better intermediation conditions as expressed by the spread between these two rates.

The monopoly privilege of local banks cannot be linked to one specific market but, according to each local situation takes one form or the other. The variability of rate of return is quite high and according to expectations is lower in the deposit market (coefficient of variation 12 per cent) than in the loan market (16 per cent). The correlation between the two series is 0,324.

This finding can be considered as good evidence of a mark-up (or mark-down) pricing based on deposit and operating costs. These two variables explain 23 per cent of the variability of loan rates.[4]

The reason why inefficient banks can still survive is mainly the fact that there is still a strong capacity to translate higher costs on to banks' customers, as demonstrated by a rather strict correlation between the level of costs and the level of gross margins (interest margin plus net non-interest income).

$$\ln GRIN = b_0 + b_1 \ln OPCT \qquad [2]$$
where GRIN = gross income; OPCT = operating costs

Table 2. Results of regression (2).

Dep. var. GRIN	Cost	OPCT
coeff.	0.844	0.692
t test	12.129	10.838
R2 adj.	0.521	
F test	117.471	

The elasticity of translation is almost 70 per cent, and more than 50 per cent of the variability of gross income is explained by the level of operating costs.

This situation is very far from a competitive market where higher (lower) operating costs should result in lower (higher) profits, not in higher (lower) margins.

One can argue that monopolistic power is still strong, given that similar researches have always found a strong correlation between costs and margins. It must be remembered however that the composition of banks' assets and liabilities has completely changed in the last few years.

To compare simply margins over time requires a *ceteris paribus* assumption on the structure of intermediation and therefore of the risks involved. From this point of view two points must be remembered:

a) the composition of deposits has changed. The disintermediation and the creation of a market for certificates of deposit has increased the monetary nature of current accounts (which used to perform an investment function) and has insulated the segment of the deposit market which follows more closely market interest rates. Accepting disintermediation, banks could increase their ability to differentiate products and to segment markets. The consequence has been a decrease of the average cost of deposits (in comparison to market interest rates).

As a matter of fact, the deposit rate shows a higher and higher velocity of response to market interest rates, which is positive evidence of increasing competition in the deposit market (Lusignani, 1989). This is difficult to reconcile with the stickiness of the average cost of deposits (which is clear also in our cross-section analysis). One possible explanation is that better segmentation allows banks to differentiate more in non-price terms; another hinges on the different composition of deposits and the decrease of the relative share of high-interest accounts. Competition has therefore increased, but it has shifted to a less costly segment of the deposit demand.

Competition is there, but has weaker effects than expected and it is difficult to be detected in banks' margins.

From the point of view of the performance of the banking system as a whole, qualitative changes are more important than the variations of the level of profits. Qualitative changes mean first of all a different pattern of risk; as a matter of fact, dynamic analysis confirms that in the last few years banks changed completely the structure of their financial management, greatly increasing their exposure to interest risk (Lusignani, 1989). Therefore risk is the point where attention has to be focused.

b) From this point of view the changes regarding the asset side of bank management are even more important. As already mentioned, the substitution of loans for Government securities has been the most remarkable trend for all banks since the early 1980s.

An analysis of the performance of banks has to take into account the credit risk, which is a typical component of financial activity, and therefore of all the performance indicators. S-c-p models were developed with reference to industrial sectors, where the concentration-price relationship can be considered a good synthesis of the characteristics of the market and the profitability of the firms. In the case of the banking industry, however, the behaviour of firms must be judged in terms of the return-risk relationship.

One possible way to include risk in s-c-p models is offered by the so-called quiet-life hypothesis. If such a model is true, banks with high monopoly power (both in the deposit and lending market) should be characterised by higher operating costs (assuming the form of expense preference behaviour) and/or lower deposits costs and lower risk (as measured by the ratio of risky assets to total assets). The net result of these three components could be to equalize gross profits or at least to narrow differences across banks. As we have already seen, quiet-life hypothesis in the simplest form does not reflect the situation of the Italian banking system. A more similar approach to the portfolio theory can be used calculating the relationship between return on loans and risk (as expressed by the ratio of non-performing loans to outstanding loans).

This means estimating the following relation:

$$LRR = c_0 + c_1 \, RISK \tag{3}$$

where LRR = rate of return of the loan portfolio; RISK = ratio of non-performing loans to outstanding loans.

Table 3. Results of regression (3).

Dep. var. LRR	Cost	RISK
coeff.	12.587	0.183
t test	28.967	2.967
R2 adj.	0.077	
F test	8.803	

The results are mixed. Looking at the coefficients (which are statistically significant) one can deduce that banks are rather rational: the intercept is reasonably close to the risk-free rate and the rate is positively related to risk. The degree of correlation is however very poor, meaning that many banks are far from an ideal risk-return relationship. Analysis of individual data shows that local banks do not appear to have a higher marginal rate of substitution than big banks, implying that even this sort of quiet-life hypothesis does not hold for the Italian banking system.

Even from this point of view, one can gather that competition led to an increase of risks, determining many sub-optimal conditions.

Another way to confirm this relative inefficiency in the pricing of risk is to estimate the main determinants of bank gross profit (gross margins net of operating costs). If we assume that they should be related mainly to the capitalization ratio (which increases net working capital, thereby contributing to nominal interest margins), the level of spread (i.e. a price factor) and the level of risk, the following relation can be estimated.

$$GRPR = d_0 + d_1 CAP + d_2 SPR + d_3 RISK \qquad [4]$$

where GRPR = gross profits; CAP = ratio of capital to total assets; RISK = ratio of non-performing loans to outstanding loans.

Table 4. Results of regression (4).

Dep. var. GRPR	Cost	CAP	SPR	RISK
coeff.	0.027	0.112	0.327	−0.028
t test	7.072	9.914	11.040	−2.751
R2 adj.	0.714			
F stat	134.748			

The results confirm that capitalization and the level of spread have a great explanatory power of banks' gross profits. The relationship of risk is however weak and contrary to expectations. This means that in many cases operating inefficiency and pricing inefficiency are mingled together. Once more, sub-optimal conditions do not belong to a single size class or a single institutional category. It is however worth stressing that some big banks (very limited in number but by no means less important) appear in a rather weak condition both in terms of the average level of profit and of the distance from the estimated function.

IV. CONCLUSIONS

Competition has certainly increased in the last decade in the Italian banking system, but the results are not clearcut. Neither market shares, nor performance indicators seem to fully reflect a strongly competitive environment.

In a sense, the evidence of competition is to be seen in the way banks reacted to the stimuli coming from the market conditions of the 1980s. Trying to maintain their market shares, all banks changed their asset and liability structure following the general trend for the banking system as a whole. Particularly, they greatly increased the weight of loans on total assets.

The process of disintermediation has been stronger in Italy than in other countries, but paradoxically the consequences for profitability have been more favourable for Italian banks than for banks of other countries which suffered competition from other intermediaries or new agents of the financial market. Like Italian financial innovation, Italian disintermediation has also been a sort of lop-sided process. It implied only a transformation of bank revenues from direct intermediation (an interest margin) to placement fees. Alternatively stated, banks have not lost their relationship with the customer and that certainly helped to maintain segmentation (by location, type of deposit, class of customer, size of accounts, etc). This shows that competitive conditions change more quickly when the pressure comes from outside the banking system, and when it can really break existing customer relationships.

Moreover, in the previous decades as well as in the 1980s only a few inefficient banks have been pushed out of the market through mergers or other less rigorous measures. The pressure of competition came upon a banking system not homogeneous, contributing to increase differences.

The "bottom-up" process of competition has accomplished its objectives (or the objectives of regulators) but now it is not clear who shall take the leadership in the competitive arena, both in the deposit and the lending services. There is no longer a group of banks with very high growth potential nor are cost differences so strong as to allow more efficient banks to change the structural characteristics of the markets just using their competitive pressure. The market cannot be pushed on a string.

It is difficult to imagine that new doses of competition (coming from regulators, foreign banks or whatever) will progressively decrease segmentation and force down spreads and profits, as s-c-p models would imply. Moreover, the s-c-p paradigm when applied to banking must allow for the peculiar nature of financial services. Most empirical research in this subject fails to take into account the risks that banks have to face or is based on the assumption that risks are equal for all banks.

The experience of the 1980s has shown that in a very dishomogeneous banking system, competition has had the effect of increasing risk (probably enlarging existing differences) and forcing many banks to sub-optimal risk-profitability conditions. In a competitive environment, banks are pushed out of the market not only because of their poor performance in terms of operating costs, but also because of their higher level of risk, which normally comes to the light all of a sudden.

Given the low concentration ratio of the Italian banking system and the diffusion of sub-optimal conditions to the whole size range, it is also difficult to imagine that more efficient banks (as far as costs and risks are concerned) can engage in painless mergers with less efficient banks.

The reasons that in the past led the Italian authorities to minimize structural changes (in comparison to other countries) were by no means compelling, but now risk creating a sort of vicious circle. The approach to the problem of less efficient banks will be the real trial of regulators' policy in the coming years. If barriers to exit continued to be rather strong, the effects of competition could be perverse.

Competition cannot be separated from market discipline. As risk is the missing link of s-c-p models, a rigorous approach to problem-banks can be the missing link of a policy aiming at achieving higher levels of efficiency.

More generally the Italian experience has shown that competition has tangled effects, because it impacted on a banking system with structural and strong differences. The heritage of past conditions is very heavy and tends to drive the actual path of the market away from those predicted by many theoretical models. From this point of view, one can suppose that the effects of European competition, involving different regulatory frameworks, different economic and financial situations of individual banks can be even more complex and not so close to the sort of promised land the European markets of the 1990s are expected to be.

NOTES

1. The sample is formed by 108 banks communicating accounting and other data to "Centrale dei bilanci"; data for non-performing loans were directly collected from individual published accounts (the help of Dr. Stefano Cenni is gratefully acknowledged). All big and medium banks are contained in the sample; the remainder can be considered highly representative of smaller banks, while banks operating in northern regions are over-represented.
2. In the estimated cost function, the elasticities of size (total assets) and number of branches add to one.
3. Although this measure suffers from the lack of reliable measures of the average amount outstanding, it is worth remembering that in a sample of 60 banks submitting bi-annual data, the average cost of deposit for 1988 ranges from a minimum of 5,61 per cent to a maximum of 7.44 per cent.
4. Further analysis is needed in this regard, looking at a more homogenous group of banks and using data for rates of return based on average amounts and, what is more important, separating the rate of return on loans denominated in lire from loans denominated in foreign currency.

BIBLIOGRAPHY

Banca d'Italia, (1989) *Relazione per l'anno 1988*, Roma.
P. Bennet, (1986) *Weaker Bank Earnings: Trend or Cycle?*, in Federal Reserve Bank of New York, *Recent Trends in Commercial Bank Profitability*, New York.

106

D. Brandolini & M. Noera, (1988) *Ristrutturazione industriale e riallocazione della domanda di credito in Italia*, in F. Cesarini, M. Grillo, M. Monti & M. Onado, *Banca e Mercato*, Bologna, Il Mulino.

S. Cassese, (1983) *Le banche d'interesse nazionale e i cambiamenti dei sistemi bancari*, in "Economia Italiana".

P. Ciocca, C. Giussani, G. Lanciotti, (1971) *Sportelli, dimensioni e costi: uno studio sulla struttura del sistema bancario*, Quaderni di Ricerche Ente Einaudi, Roma.

C. Conigliani, (1983) *Dimensioni aziendali, costi ed efficienza nel sistema bancario italiano*, in "Bancaria".

G. De Felice, D. Masciandaro, A. Porta, (1988) *Evoluzione del sistema bancario nella struttura finanziaria e problemi di regolamentazione: un'analisi comparata*, in F. Cesarini, M. Grillo, M. Monti & M. Onado, *Banca e Mercato*, Bologna, Il Mulino.

G. Lanciotti & T. Raganelli, (1988) *Funzioni di costo e obiettivi di efficienza nella produzione bancaria*, in "Banca d'Italia Temi di Discussione del Servizio Studi".

A. Landi, *Dimensioni costi e profitti delle banche italiane*, forthcoming.

G. Lusignani, (1989) *Il rischio di interesse nelle banche italiane: un'analisi empirica*, Bologna, mimeo.

M. Onado, (1986) *Venti anni di margini bancari*, "Banca d'Italia Temi di Discussione del Servizio Studi", Roma.

M. Onado, (1988) *La specializzazione per categorie giuridiche*, in F. Cesarini, M. Grillo, M. Monti & M. Onado, *Banca e Mercato*, Bologna, Il Mulino.

Prometeia, (1989a) *Analisi dei bilanci bancari*, Bologna, maggio, mimeo.

Prometeia, (1989b) *La dimensione e l'articolazione delle aziende di credito ordinario: gli effetti sulla produttività e sulla redditività*, Milano, Assbank.

IX. Le Secteur Bancaire Espagnol et le Problème des Fusions

JOSÉ LUIS LEAL MALDONADO

1. INTRODUCTION

Le système bancaire espagnol comprend les banques, les caisses d'épargne et les coopératives de crédit, qui répresentent, respectivement, 52, 32 et 6% du passif du secteur privé dans l'ensemble du système. Aux côtés du système bancaire opère le crédit officiel, qui, actuellement, modifie la structure de son financement, très dépendante encore du secteur public et du système bancaire lui-même, au moyen du développement d'émissions de bons et de titres hypothécaires. Le crédit officiel pourvoit le secteur privé d'un financement équivalent à 10% de celui fourni par le système bancaire. Il existe, autour des intermédiaires de base, toute une gamme d'intermédiaires non-bancaires, de caractère très divers, et dont beaucoup sont directement liés aux banques ou aux caisses d'épargne.

Il existe 98 banques possédant le statut de banque espagnole, et 44 ayant le statut de banque étrangère. Les 6 grandes banques privées et le Banco Exterior de España représentent 62% du bilan total des banques espagnoles et 57% du bilan total du secteur bancaire. Il s'agit de chiffres semblables à ceux d'autres systèmes bancaires. Le degré de concentration en Espagne est inférieur à celui de la France, de la Belgique ou de la Hollande, et supérieur à celui du Royaume-Uni ou de l'Allemagne. Malgré cela, la dimension unitaire des banques espagnoles, à l'exception du BBV, est relativement modeste si l'on compare l'importance de leurs bilans avec celle des grandes banques européennes ou américaines. La situation change en faveur des banques espagnoles lorsqu'on considère les ressources propres ou les bénéfices. La raison repose sur le fait que, traditionnellement, les banques espagnoles n'ont exercé qu'une activité internationale relativement faible, ce qui, comparativement, réduit leurs bilans.

Les banques espagnoles se trouvent, dans leurs opérations quitodiennes, face à d'importantes limitations quant à la disposition de leurs ressources; elles doivent respecter un coefficient de caisse de 19%, dont 11,5% est rénumeré à des prix inférieurs à ceux du marché. Outre ce coefficient, elles respectent encore un autre coefficient dénommé "d'investissement", qui correspond actuellement à 10,25% de leurs ressources et qui est destiné, dans sa quasi totalité, à l'acquisition de dette publique.

D. E. Fair and C. de Boissieu (eds), Financial Institutions in Europe Under New Competitive Conditions, 107–113.
© 1990 *Kluwer Academic Publishers, Dordrecht. Printed in the Netherlands.*

2. LES CHANGEMENTS STRUCTURAUX DURANT LA PERIODE 1970–1988

Vers la fin de la décennie des années 70 et au début de la présente, les banques espagnoles connurent une période de crise qui toucha un certain nombre d'entités, généralement de petites dimensions. Les difficultés commencèrent à la suite de la hausse des prix des produits énergétiques. L'appareil productif espagnol, très dépendant du pétrole, en subit gravement les conséquences. La crise gagna rapidement les banques industrielles, nuisant sérieusement à la qualité de leur actif. Mais là ne fut pas la seule raison de ces problèmes. Un certain nombre de banques, crées quelques années auparavant à l'abri des premières normes libératrices du système, se trouvèrent en difficulté à cause du manque d'expérience bancaire de leurs responsables, qui furent incapables de résister au changement de signe du cycle économique.

La crise énergétique constitue la toile de fond d'une série de transformations auxquelles, cependant, ont activement contribué d'autres facteurs, parmi lesquels il faut citer les changement dans le financement du déficit public, la réorganisation des marchés, la déréglementation de l'économie et l'internationalisation progressive de cette dernière.

a. Le financement du déficit public

Malgré la crise économique, le déficit public s'est maintenu à des niveaux relativement bas jusqu'à 1981, année où il a commencé à augmenter rapidement. D'après la définition large du "déficit", c'est-à-dire celle qui fait référence au besoin de financement du secteur public et qui est, d'autre part, la plus significative du point de vue financier, le déficit atteignit, en 1985, un chiffre équivalent à 7% du PIB, pour ensuite diminuer doucement. La dette publique, qui en 1980 représentait 20% du PIB, a atteint, en 1988, le chiffre de 46% du PIB, bien que son augmentation se soit ralentie ces dernières années. C'est ainsi que les intérêts de la dette publique, qui, pendant la décennie des années 70, constituaient à peine un fardeau pour l'économie, en sont venus à répresenter vers la fin de la décennie actuelle plus de 3% du PIB.

Le financement des importants déficits de la décennie des années quatre-vingt ne put être réalisé au moyen d'un appel direct au public, car ni les marchés de capitaux internes, ni la capacité d'épargne des familles et des entreprises ne pouvaient s'accommoder sans tensions aux quantités requises par l'Etat. Le résultat de cette évolution fut qu'on imposa aux banques et aux caisses d'épargne des coefficients obligatoires de souscription de dette publique, à des prix inférieurs à ceux du marché. De 1979 à 1989, la quota de "l'actif d'émission publique" sur l'actif total du système bancaire, est passé de 8,5% à 21%.

b. La réorganisation des marchés

La configuration du bilan des banques a été aussi marquée par les changements qui ont eu lieu au sein des marchés financiers, parmi lesquels on remarque l'augmentation de la demande de crédit à la consommation, qui, tout au long de ces dernières années, a tendu à se généraliser et qui a provoqué un intérêt croissant de la part des banques envers ce secteur du crédit, traditionnellement occupé par les caisses d'épargne. Il faudrait citer, dans ce domaine, le développement du crédit hypothécaire ainsi que d'autres formes de crédit directement liées à la consommation des familles. Un autre élément important a été le développement du marché boursier, sévèrement touché par la crise industrielle de la décennie des années soixante-dix. On y voit l'influence considérable de l'entrée de capital étranger, à la suite de l'adhésion de l'Espagne à la CEE. Tout autour du marché de valeurs, qui subit actuellement une profonde réorganisation, on a créé de nombreux services et activités. On a également commencé à développer les fonds de pension et, d'une façon générale, toute une série d'opération financières qui se trouvent à mi-chemin entre celles qui sont traditionnelles dans le secteur bancaire et celles réalisées par les compagnies d'assurances.

c. La déréglementation

Depuis 1974 environ, le secteur bancaire espagnol a été l'objet d'une dé-réglementation progressive qui touche presque tous les aspects de son activité. En premier lieu, la liberté d'ouverture de succursales est pratiqement totale depuis 1974, ce qui a mené à une forte saturation des reseaux bancaires, qui rend très difficile la pénétration de banques étrangères dans le secteur bancaire de détail. De leur côté, les taux d'intérêt ont été totalement libéralisés. La suppression de limitations se fit de manière progressive, et elle a permis d'ajuster le prix de l'argent aux conditions déterminées par la politique monétaire. En contrepartie, les fluctuations des taux d'intérêt ont augmenté, ce qui fait que ce risque spécifique est plus grand, aussi bien pour les entités financières que pour leurs clients, et que la gestion des marchés monétaires est devenue beaucoup plus technique.

D'une façon générale, il s'est produit un rapprochement des activites des banques et des caisses d'épargne, parallèle à la libération, depuis 1978, des conditions d'accès au marché espagnol pour les banques étrangères, ce qui a mené, en très peu d'années, à une participation significative de celles-ci dans le crédit aux entreprises. Le secteur bancaire a assimilé ce processus sans trop de problèmes, en dépit du fait que cette déréglementation s'est accompagnée, depuis 1978, d'un durcissement des normes de surveillance et de contrôle bancaire de la part du Banco de España, qui, dans ses directives, s'est inspiré systématiquement des normes et orientations communautaires.

d. L'internationalisation

Ces dernières années ont ete témoins d'une intégration de plus en plus large de l'économie espagnole dans les échanges mondiaux, et européens en particulier, de biens et services. A son tour, l'ouverture de l'économie a provoqué d'importants mouvements de capital qui, en grande partie, ont transité par le système bancaire. Les entreprises espagnoles se financent de plus en plus en devises, tandis que d'importants investissements, aussi bien réels que financiers, sont canalisés vers l'Espagne. Pour se faire une idée de l'importance de ces mouvements, rappelons les entrées de capital brut à long terme qui, en 1988, dépassèrent 30 milliards de dollars.

Ces mouvements se sont produits bien que la libération des mouvements n'ait été amorcée qu'en ce qui concerne les sorties de capital (libéralisation d'investissments directs et, avec un caractère limité, d'investissments de portefeuille et en immeubles). A moyen terme, l'adhésion de la peseta au SME et l'entrée en vigueur des directives communautaires sur les mouvements de capitaux, pleinement applicables à l'Espagne à la fin de 1992, conditionneront aussi bien la structure des opérations du secteur bancaire avec l'extérieur, que la trajectoire des taux d'intérêt.

3. LES RESULTATS DU SECTEUR BANCAIRE

L'évolution décrite plus haut se reflète, logiquement, dans le bilan et le compte de résultats des banques espagnoles durant la période décrite. Jusqu'à 1984, le bilan des banques a crû plus vite que le PIB nominal, mais, à partir de cette année-là, la croissance se fit plus lente à la suite, en partie, de l'apparation de nouveaux instruments financiers qui ont remplacé quelques-unes des formes traditionnelles d'endettement.

Si l'on compare les chiffres du début de la décennie des années soixante-dix (Tableau 1) avec ceux des dernières années, on constate une modification sensible du compte de résultats de l'ensemble des banques espagnoles; la marge financière (rendement moyen de l'actif moins le coût moyen du passif) a montré une claire tendance à l'augmentation liée à l'élévation des taux d'intérêt nominaux qui a eu lieu depuis 1975. Dans un climat de taux élevés, le secteur bancaire sut "rentabiliser" la situation et ajuster sa politique aux fluctuations des marchés. Le changement de tendance, qui se produisit lors des premières années de la décennie actuelle, provoqua une diminution de la marge, à l'exception notable de l'année 1988. Etant donné, d'autre part, que les banques espagnoles ont augmenté le recouvrement de services et

Tableau 1. Bilan des banques espagnoles. (En pourcentage de l'actif moyen.)

	Marge financière	Autres produits	Dépense exploitation	Provisions	Résultat
1970–72	3,41	0,31	2,54	0,11	1,20
1978–80	4,37	0,62	3,50	0,73	0,82
1986–88	4,01	0,74	2,70	0,81	1,07

Source: Banco de España.

diversifié leur offre, la marge ordinaire d'exploitation, qui est la somme des deux concepts, a subi une augmentation sensible. Dans le chapitre des dépenses, et après une phase d'augmentation qui atteignit son point culminant en 1979, la tendance s'inversa pour situer l'ensemble des dépenses des banques espagnoles à des chiffres semblables (en pourcentage de l'actif moyen) à ceux enregistrés au début de la décennie des années soixante. Malgré cette évolution si favorable, le chiffre des bénéfices nets a montré une légère tendance à la diminution, due, essentiellement, à l'importance des sommes que le secteur bancaire s'est vu obligé de consacrer à l'assainissement de son actif, conséquence, à son tour, de la crise économique.

Le tableau 2 permet d'établir des comparaisons avec d'autres pays. Les indices de l'Allemagne, des Etats-Unis, du Royaume-Uni et de la France, sont obtenus à partir des rapports de quelques banques importantes, tandis que ceux de l'Espagne procédent du compte de résultats consolidé du secteur bancaire. En 1987, on réalisa aux Etats-Unis et au Royaume-Uni d'importantes provisions pour risque-pays. Les comparaisons sont significatives jusqu'au niveau des résultats d'exploitation. On remarquera l'Espagne par sa large marge financière, ainsi que par les coûts d'exploitation, également plus importants.

Tableau 2. Comptes de resultats de pays de la CEE. (Pourcentage sur l'actif moyen total, 1986.)

	Allemagne	Royaume-Uni	France	Belgique	Espagne
Revenus financiers nets	2,35	3,10	2,72	1,62	4,16
Revenus non financiers	0,60	1,61	0,46	0,56	0,66
Revenus totaux nets	2,95	4,71	3,18	2,18	4,82
Coûts d'exploitation	1,85	3,12	2,12	1,71	3,09
Bénéfices d'exploitation	1,10	1,59	1,06	0,47	1,73
Provisions	0,41	0,74	0,68	0,02	0,95
Bénéfice A.I.	0,69	0,85	0,38	0,45	0,78

Source: OCDE.
– Sont inclus dans les revenus financiers les résultats du trading de valeurs.
– Sont incluses dans les coûts d'exploitation les dotations pour pensions de retraite.

4. LES FUSIONS BANCAIRES

Un des arguments couramment invoqués afin de justifier les fusions bancaires a trait aux économies d'échelle et à la réduction de coûts relatifs qui s'ensuit et qu'impliquent, du moins en théorie, les dites fusions. Le besoin d'affronter une stratégie résolue de réduction de prix découle des tendances profondes du marché, qui, sans aucun doute, toucheront les principales composantes du compte de résultats du secteur bancaire.

– le contrôle de l'offre monétaire réduira l'augmentation nominale du bilan bancaire et écartera la possibilité d'obtenir des bénéfices liés, d'une façon ou d'une autre, aux processus inflationnistes;

– les taux d'intérêt élevés finiront par céder dans un contexte de liberté de mouvements de capitaux, cette tendance étant renforcée par l'entrée de la peseta dans le SME.

De cette façon, la diminution des taux d'intérêt, le développement des transactions en monnaie étrangère, ainsi que l'augmentation de la concurrence entre les institutions financières, rendront très difficile le maintien du différentiel d'intérêt à son niveau récent, ce qui fait qu'on peut s'attendre à un arrêt de la progression de la marge financière, qu'il faudra compenser par d'autres voies, parmi lesquelles on remarquera, de façon prioritaire, celle d'une moindre élévation des coûts. L'impossibilité pratique d'obtenir ces transformations par la voie unique d'une meilleure gestion des coûts amène à penser au besoin de promouvoir des changements structuraux. Vue de cette perspective, la dynamique créée par une fusion bancaire est suffisamment forte pour provoquer ces changements qui, en fin de compte, doivent se refléter dans une rationalisation des réseaux de guichets, dans une gestion optimale des ressources informatiques et dans l'offre d'une gamme complète de services. La capacité d'obtenir des économies d'échelle demeure latente dans tout processus de fusion, et l'art consiste à exploiter ces économies et à éviter, dans la mesure du possible, les "déséconomies".

Ce ne sont pas là les seules raisons qui justifient une fusion bancaire. L'augmentation de la dimension permet de mieux garantir l'indépendance de la nouvelle entité face à des possibles actions hostiles; elle ouvre la possibilité d'entreprendre des opérations qui, autrement, n'auraient pas pu être réalisées; elle consolide, du moins dans le cas espagnol, la possibilité d'opérer en tant qu'interlocuteur privilegié de l'autorité monétaire. De ce point de vue, la situation espagnole était relativement exceptionelle au sein du contexte européen, où l'Histoire a crée, dans la plupart des pays, un noyau central de deux ou trois grandes banques autour desquelles se structure, en fait, le système bancaire, et qui opèrent comme les agents principaux dans la transmission de la politique monétaire au reste des agents économiques.

En tout cas, l'opportunité des fusions n'est pas une vérité absolue, puisqu'elle dépend de la capacité des entités impliquées de faire apparaître les économies d'échelle latentes et d'esquiver les "déséconomies", ce qui, à son tour, est étroitement lié à la situation relative des banques fusionnées et à leur dynamisme. L'option des Bancos de Bilbao et Vizcaya de constituer le BBV se base, en dernier ressort, sur la capacité de gestion, largement reconnue, des deux entités, sur leurs ressources humaines et sur la solidité de leurs bilans respectifs. Les deux banques étaient des 'leaders' sur le marché espagnol, avec d'excellents résultats commerciaux. La fusion permettra d'aborder les nouvelles conditions créées par l'ouverture des frontières et le marché unique de 1993. Durant les quelques mois écoulés, outre la rationalisation du réseau extérieur de la nouvelle entité, une banque a été achetée en Belgique et un accord de collaboration a été conclu avec une importante banque française, impliquant, entre autres choses, un échange de réseaux dans les deux pays.

Quant aux aspects formels de la fusion, les faits se sont jusqu'à présent déroulés d'une façon accélérée: le 24 Janvier 1988, les Conseils d'Administration des deux banques signèrent le protocole de fusion, qui fut approuvé par les Assemblées extraordinaires d'actionaires le 1er Juin. Les banques préexistantes disparurent le 1er Octobre, date de naissance du BBV. Du point de vue de l'actif, la nouvelle banque est la vingt-septième de l'Europe, tandis que du point de vue de ses ressources en capital, elle occupe la seizième place. Elle est en Espagne, et avec une grande différence, la première entité financière, quel que soit le point de vue considéré.

Seul le temps permettra de juger la validité du pari réalisé par les deux entités espagnoles. Jusqu'à présent, les résultats obtenus confirment la pertinence des analyses qui menèrent à la fusion. Les banques espagnoles ont conscience des défis du marché unique de 1993 et elles ont déjà commencé à y faire face.

Part C
Is There An Efficiency/Stability Trade-off?
Issues in Banking Supervision and Regulation

X. Competition, Diversification and Structural Change in the British Financial System

DAVID T. LLEWELLYN

Analysing the structure of the British financial system when the industry is in the midst of an uncompleted phase of major structural change and financial innovation as great as any experienced this century, immediately presents major methodological problems. The business of banking is changing in two fundamental ways: (1) banks and other financial institutions have increasingly become multi-product firms encompassing a range of services far wider than the traditional role of asset-liability transformation; in particular fee income and off-balance-sheet business have increased in importance for banks; and (2) the traditional "structured" or specialist basis of the British financial system has given way to a more conglomerate structure which has eroded the traditional distinctions between the major areas of finance.

The theme of this paper is that the British financial system is in the midst of a period of major structural change as all types of financial institutions are diversifying their range of business under the impact of greatly intensified competitive pressures, international pressures, major changes in the structure and style of regulation, technology and changes in the market environment. In the process traditional distinctions between specialist financial institutions are being eroded, non-bank financial institutions are conducting traditional "banking business", banks are conducting "non-banking" financial business, and non-financial companies (e.g. retail stores) are also entering into the business of financial services. The major factor creating structural change is competition: the competitive environment has intensified considerably over the 1980s in particular. The UK represents a case-study of the power of competitive pressures to induce structural change in a financial system. As the goal of completion of the internal market in the EC by the end of 1992 is unambiguously about competition, the case study of the role and power of competition in the UK may have implications for how 1992 could affect financial systems in other EC countries. It is for this reason that Section II of the paper offers an analysis of how competitive pressures might be expected to influence the evolution of a financial system.

The structure of the paper is as follows. Section I reviews the nature and form of structural change and financial innovation in the British financial

D. E. Fair and C. de Boissieu (eds), Financial Institutions in Europe Under New Competitive Conditions, 117–145.
© 1990 Kluwer Academic Publishers, Dordrecht. Printed in the Netherlands.

system. Section II considers the role and impact of the most powerful pressure – competition – producing structural change and what might be predicted for a financial system subject to more intensive internal and international competitive pressures. Section III considers two potential "problem areas" related to recent trends (profitability and the viability of financial conglomerates), and some developments in retail banking.

I. STRUCTURAL CHANGE

Central structural issue

At the risk of oversimplification, financial services can be broadly divided into six categories: commercial banking, investment/merchant banking, insurance, fund management, housing finance, and securities trading. The central strategic issue of any financial system is that of *separation* versus *integration* though in practice it is almost invariably a question of the balance between the two polar cases. In the former, different categories of finance are conducted by specialist institutions with clear demarcation lines between different types of activity and institution. With an integrated or conglomerate system all (or a wide variety of) functions are performed by single institutions with little to delineate the different functions of different institutions.

Regulatory arrangements in this area are different in different countries which creates potential competitive distortions for those institutions which conduct business in several countries. Under host-country regulatory regimes institutions may be able to conduct business in foreign countries which they are prevented from conducting in their own. Conversely, under home-country regulatory regimes foreign institutions may be able to conduct business in a country which is prohibited to domestic institutions. The globalization of banking and financial markets, and the increasing integration of markets both domestically and internationally, create pressures on regulation when it is not competitively neutral as between institutions within a national system and between countries. Thus, regulation (legal or informal) which enforces limits on the range of business (e.g. between investment and commercial banking) is likely to be undermined via global competitive pressures. Eisenbeis (1989) suggests that regulation which constrains one set of institutions creates opportunities for non-domestic institutions to secure competitive advantages, induces domestic residents to use foreign institutions and markets, and drives domestic institutions overseas.

In those countries where regulation, or restrictive practices, has traditionally enforced separation, these impositions have tended to be liberalised over the 1980s. This has been the result of several interacting and simultaneous pressures: global competitive pressures; the evolving diversification strategies of financial institutions seeking competitive advantages through the offer (sometimes on a global basis) of a full range of financial services and the alleged synergies associated with economies of scope; the intensification of competitive pressures in institutions' traditional markets and business areas; and the requirements of competitive neutrality in regulation which has become an increasingly significant issue as, through financial innovation, distinctions are eroded between different types of financial intermediation mechanisms (e.g. banks and capital markets) and instruments. In the UK the prevailing political orthodoxy of the 1980s has been that diversification should not be impeded because it implies financial services being supplied under more competitive conditions with a presumed benefit (in terms of efficiency, choice and price) to the consumer.

Many countries are moving further along the "structural spectrum" towards the conglomerate end. It is a process that, once begun, is difficult to halt as the process itself creates competitive distortions to the extent that allowable diversification between potentially competing sets of institutions is not symmetrical and equal in both directions. A major factor in the early 1980s behind the demand by UK building societies for an extension of their powers was the move by the banks into the mortgage market. Similarly, banks in many countries (including those where regulation impedes it) have sought to diversify into the securities industry both to regain business lost through securization but also because, as a result of financial innovation, the distinction between banking and capital market facilities has become less powerful.

The main arguments in favour of allowing banks and other institutions to diversify relate to the potential risk-reducing qualities of a diversified business; the ability to increase and widen the source of profits with potential systemic advantages; in order to enhance the competitive environment in which financial services are provided, and to generate alleged benefits of economies of scale but most especially of scope.

On the other hand there are several reasons why separation might be desired. It is one way of dealing with potential conflicts of interest that can arise when institutions conduct a wide range of business. It also makes regulation easier in that if the objective is to regulate *functions* there is a clearly defined set of *institutions* performing each function. It also means that to a large extent regulation can be "sub-contracted" to the functional sectors themselves: such self-regulation through "clubs" has been a distinctive feature of regulation in the UK and it has many advantages (Llewellyn, 1986). The regulatory authorities might also take the view that risks are reduced through limiting the range of business activities, and that systemic risk is lowered by, for instance, reducing the danger of contamination of one part of the business (e.g. banking) by risks in other parts (e.g. insurance). Diversification also

120

widens the range of activities against which the lender-of-last-resort function and deposit insurance are provided.

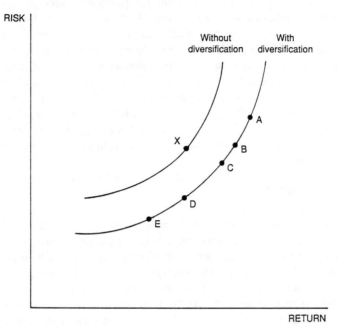

Fig. 1. Risk-return trade off.

Dependent upon the type and correlation of risks involved, diversification can have the effect of improving the risk-return trade-off (Boyd and Graham, 1986) but in the process induce institutions to incur more rather than less risk. Diversification may improve upon the set of risk-return opportunities available to a financial institution as indicated in Figure 1. If, prior to diversification, the institution chose point X, the new opportunities available to it involve a choice of several possibilities compared with the previous set of options: (i) more risk with a higher return than before, (A); (ii) a higher return for the same risk (B); (iii) a higher return and lower risk (C); (iv) lower risk and the same return (D); and (v) a lower return with a lower risk (E). There is no necessary presumption that institutions will choose a less risky portfolio and some analysis argues that institutions will do so only if shareholders of the institution are risk averse and unable to diversify their asset portfolios directly in the securities market. It is theoretically possible that allowing diversification will have the effect of increasing risk, and the evidence from US studies is ambiguous. Gilbart (1988) finds there is no *a priori* reason for supposing that diversification reduces overall risk as it depends upon a complex of factors including the expected profitability of the new area, its inherent riskiness, the correlation with existing parts of the business, the relative size of the different business areas, and the extent of any synergies implied with alleged economies of scope. Clark (1988) in a survey of economies of scale and scope suggests that in general large diversified deposit institutions have not enjoyed a cost advantage over smaller, more specialised institutions. Boyd and Graham (1986) find no evidence either way with respect to risk enhancement or reduction. Overall, US studies point to no unambiguous conclusions about the effect of diversification on risk, efficiency, and profitability. There seems to be little evidence of significant economies of scale.

Separation may also be favoured as a means of minimising any alleged possibility of a concentration of power in the financial system which in turn has two dimensions: issues related to competitiveness, and the increased systematic cost if conglomerates fail. Diversification may have the effect of reducing risk in the sense of reducing the *probability* of failure. On the other hand, it may raise the systemic *cost* of failure because a wider range of financial activities is involved. If diversification reduces risk (probability of failure) there is a trade-off in allowing diversification between lower risk and higher systemic cost which may mean a regulator would choose not to allow diversification even though risk would be reduced, or to allow diversification but providing the components were separately capitalized.

Diversification: strategic options

This central issue relating to the structure of the financial system has five dimensions:
1. The extent of allowable diversification by financial institutions.
2. The distinction between whether a bank or other financial institution provides an *own-service* from its own resources (implying that the risk is on the balance sheet and for which capital has been allocated) or whether it acts solely as a *marketing agent* for another company such as, for instance, when a bank or building society acts as an agent for an insurance company.
3. The separation between financial and non-financial companies.
4. The distinction between diversification and ownership, and
5. The extent to which diversification requires separate management and capitalization.

The first issue relates to the extent to which financial institutions are able to offer a wide range of financial services. When *separation* is the norm, as historically it has been in the UK, the separation relates to differences between types of financial institution, between banking and the capital market, and between finance and industrial and commercial companies. Such separation may be imposed by regulation or be chosen for business reasons though in some cases it may reflect restrictive practices and self-imposed anti-competitive arrangements.

Diversification is an ambiguous concept most especially when considering risk characteristics. A financial institution (say, with an existing specialised and a narrow range of business) wishing to diversify by offering a wider range of services has three basic strategic options: (1) it can develop what can be termed *own diversification* where new business (e.g. potential insurance liabilities for a bank) is developed internally and placed on the balance sheet as the institution provides the service itself with its own resources; (2) it can purchase an existing supplier of the service (e.g. a bank buys an insurance company), or (3) it can enter into an agency arrangement whereby it sells the product of an existing independent supplier of the service: *agency diversification*.

There is a major difference between the first two and the third. In the former case the risk of the new business is borne by the diversifying institution, the balance sheet is constrained, and equity capital must be allocated to the new business to cover the new balance sheet exposure risk. Comparing options (1) and (2) in principle the firm is indifferent when the cost of purchasing an existing company equals the start-up cost of providing the new service from within the firm. On the other hand, there is a risk premium to be taken into account through developing the diversified business internally (it could prove not to be successful or more difficult to develop) whereas the purchase route immediately absorbs an on-going and presumably successful business. It also means that the acquiring institution buys the reputation and skills of the other firm and immediately gains the scale of the firm rather than building up scale through organic growth. Thus option (2) is an attractive option for a diversifying institution and in general is the method used when banks diversified into securities trading.

In terms of risk analysis the crucial distinction is between *own* and *agency* diversification. In the former case the relevant criteria relate to how the new business affects the risk characteristics of the new combined balance sheet and exposure (e.g. covariance of risks etc). In practice a major form of diversification is where an institution provides a wide range of services but by acting as a sales agent for other institutions which absorb the balance sheet and capital risks. Obvious recent examples are where building societies have arrangements with life assurance companies and sell the latters' products. The fees earned raise the rate of return on assets and equity and such returns may not be highly correlated with existing returns. Whereas *own* diversification raises issues with respect to risk, *agency* diversification focuses more upon the efficiency of delivery systems.

The *agency* form of diversification has become a significant feature of the

British financial system and may become a feature of EEC trans-national business arrangements in the financial sector. A parallel could be drawn with other industries. The majority of goods are not bought directly from the manufacturer but from a store selling a wide range of goods produced by different manufacturers. The rationale is simple: the optimum scale and structure of production is different from the optimum scale and structure of distribution with the result that the producer (for a fee) sub-contracts the sales process.

Traditionally, services are different as, by their nature, they are delivered directly by the producer. There is no inherent reason why this must be the case. There are many advantages to such *agency* diversification: institutions may link complementary expertise; the different institutions may offer mutually advantageous economy of access by utilising each other's delivery systems; they share each other's reputation advantages; they avoid many of the management problems of a diversified business; learning costs are avoided as are the substantial "start-up" costs involved with *own diversification*, and it generates fee income without encumbering the balance sheet. At the systemic level the *agency* route enables firms to diversify without raising the number of suppliers.

An intermediate route, between *own* and *agency* diversification, is where joint-venture companies are formed between different types of financial institution with each contributing its own expertise. A recent example in the UK is with the National Provincial Building Society which is to establish a life assurance company as a joint venture with a major insurance company (General Accident).

The third dimension of diversification relates to the extent to which a formal separation is made between financial and non-financial companies, and the extent to which the latter are able to offer financial services. This amounts to the issue of whether, for business or regulatory reasons, finance should be regarded as an exclusively specialist activity. In most countries there is a traditional distinction between finance and non-finance companies though this is breaking down. In the US, for instance, Sears Roebuck is one of the largest suppliers of financial services, and in the UK Marks and Spencer has a banking licence and supplies a range of financial services including credit. Allowing non-finance companies to own banks could offer the advantages of diversification and widen the sources of capital for banks though, as noted by Corrigan (1987), this is questionable unless the underlying profitability of banking is sound. The difficulties are, however, substantial: (i) the potential conflicts of interest are serious, (ii) the commercial company might be motivated by a desire to gain access to a cheap source of finance such as insured deposits (Roberts, 1987), (iii) it potentially widens the area of the lender-of-last-resort function, (iv) the question arises as to whether it is appropriate for unregulated and unsupervised commercial companies to own banks, and (v) the bank within the holding company could be used to supply cheap loans to other parts of the group as any diminution of profits and/or rise in risk is unlikely, except in the extreme case, to raise the cost of funds to the bank. Again the issue arises as to whether the risk to the shareholder of the holding company is more efficiently diversified directly in the capital market by holding equity in a diverse range of companies or via a holding of equity in a conglomerate. Only if there are clear and identifiable synergies is the latter a more efficient diversification strategy.

The issue of *separation* versus *integration* relates both to the range of allowable business, and the extent of interlocking ownership structures both within the finance sector (e.g. whether a bank can own an insurance company) and between financial institutions and non-finance companies. These are distinct and separate issues in that, for instance, while Marks and Spencer has a banking licence and sells financial services, it is open to considerable doubt at this stage whether the Bank of England would allow it to purchase an existing clearing bank or an insurance company, (Leigh-Pemberton, 1987).

A fifth issue, in the event that diversification into major new and different areas is allowed, relates to the extent to which the different functional areas can be managed and capitalized in an integrated manner, or whether integration by ownership is allowed while the management and/or capitalization must be kept separate. The latter is one way of handling the potential conflicts of interest involved in conglomeration and avoiding the risks of contamination though, by the same token, it denies the economies of scale in the use of capital (Barge 1985) and may impede marketing and delivery strategies.

The major remaining form of separation in the UK is that between insurance underwriting and banking. Loehnis (1987) notes that, while there has been no legal inhibition, the regulatory authorities have discouraged banks from entering into insurance (most especially general insurance) business due largely to fear of conflicts of interest between depositors and policyholders, and the risk of contamination. The Governor of the Bank of England (*Banking World*, August 1987) has said:

> We would not find it so difficult if the size between them were disproportionate in the sense that an insurance company which knows its business could probably safely carry a much smaller bank with its different sorts of risks, and vice versa. If you had two very large institutions I think the problem of two totally different operations which are basically highly geared could lead to the difficulty of measuring capital and liquidity. This could set a problem not only for the group management and the group board, but also for the supervisors. We would perhaps be more reluctant about the acquisition if the two parts were of more equal size. There may

well be a difference too, in assessing risks, capital liquidity, gearing and so on, between life insurance and general insurance. I cite that as a simple illustration of the problem of the expertise required to make the right judgements.

The issue is discussed further in Bank of England (1984). Opinion seems to be shifting in favour of a more accommodating stance with respect to links between banking and insurance. There are now a number of UK insurance companies with interests in small deposit-taking companies and some large commercial banks own small insurance subsidiaries. The Trustee Savings Bank has recently purchased an insurance company and a major mutual building society (Britannia) plans to purchase a mutual life assurance institution. Loehnis (1987) has stated that: "what we want to avoid is insurance companies and banks of similar size forming links, but that would not necessarily preclude the building up of one within the other by organic growth, and in a few specific cases permission has been given for a significant minority stake in one to be held by the other." However, it is open to question whether in the UK this would extend to an ownership link or merger between a major insurance company and a major bank.

Nevertheless, banks and building societies in the UK see strategic advantages in offering insurance services. This is partly because insurance is often linked with existing business (e.g. home insurance when houses are purchased) and because many insurance products have savings components. Banks and building societies have entered the insurance market through several routes: purchase of insurance companies, joint-ventures, internal development of insurance business, and via agency arrangements. Steinherr (this volume) views the recent tendency to merge banking and insurance activities as motivated by the general quest for "global finance". As he notes, banking and insurance products can be either close substitutes (they both deal with risk and may have savings components) or complements as in the example cited earlier. Either way it is a reasonable business strategy to offer both products.

Structural change and financial innovation

A central feature of the British financial system over the 1980s has been an unprecedented combination (both historically and internationally) of structural change and financial innovation (Bank of England, 1983). Structural change is about how the basic functions of a financial system are performed by markets and institutions, the business structure of component institutions and markets, and changes in the market and institutional mechanisms through which financial intermediation and other services are provided.

Financial innovation has two central features: the creation of new financial instruments, techniques and markets, and the unbundling of the separate characteristics and risks of individual instruments and their reassembling in different combinations (Llewellyn 1988a). In the process four central features of financial innovation emerge: it increases the range, number and variety of financial instruments; it combines characteristics of instruments in a more varied way and widens the combination of characteristics thereby reducing the number and size of discontinuities in the spectrum of financial instruments (a process of "spectrum filling"); it has the effect of eroding some of the differences between different forms of intermediation as, for example, where Floating Rate Notes and Note Issuance Facilities link banks and capital markets; and it has the effect of integrating financial markets as many instruments straddle several simultaneously. Eisenbeis (1987) also suggests that some financial innovations create instruments which perform functions similar to those traditionally provided by financial intermediaries which may have the effect of lowering the demand for the services of intermediaries.

There has been a close parallel in the UK between structural change in the financial system and the process of financial innovation in two respects: they both imply an erosion of traditional distinctions and boundaries, (a distinction between *institutional* and *instrument* integration), and both have been induced by the same pressures of competition, technology, changes in regulation, international competitive pressures, and changes in the market environment. Structural change in the financial system has involved the erosion of traditional demarcations between different sub-sectors of the system: *institutional integration*. Similarly, financial innovation has the effect of eroding distinctions between financial instruments and intermediation mechanisms: *instrument integration*. Over the 1980s, structural change and financial innovation have been twin components of the same process: the development of a more integrated, less specialist financial system. In the process there has been a steady erosion of traditional distinctions in several dimensions: between the business of different types of institutions, between instruments, between wholesale and retail sectors (for instance, money market interest rates are now available on retail deposits, and corporate banking products such as CAPS and COLLARS have become available in the retail mortgage market), between capital market and banking facilities and also between functions as, for instance, where NIFs offered by banks represent a form of insurance. In the process the British financial system has shifted perceptibly from its historical differentiated form to a more conglomerate structure.

Historic characteristics and structure

For most of this century the structure of the British financial system was remarkably stable; historically it has been a highly structured system based on specialist and differentiated financial institutions and markets with clear functional demarcations between them (Revell 1973). The City of London historically has organised itself on a highly specialist basis. In particular, and in common with many other financial systems (most notably the US, Canada, Japan and Australia) but in contrast to many in Europe, there has been a clear functional distinction between the major business areas of commercial banking, investment banking, housing finance, insurance, fund management and securities trading. However, this structured system, and in contrast to the experience in other structured systems, has not been predominantly a product of official and legal regulatory limits on the range of business activities (except in the case of building societies) but more a function of restrictive practices, anti-competitive mechanisms, and self-imposed constraints. On the other hand (and for reasons already outlined), the regulatory authorities have been sympathetic to this structured approach.

Current trends

The major structural changes that have dominated the more recent evolution of the British financial system (most especially since 1980) relate to competition, the process of diversification, the undermining of the historic structured system, the form and extent of regulation, the increasing internationalization of finance, and the acceleration in the pace of financial innovation. The reasons behind these developments are discussed in Llewellyn, 1989. At the same time the business of "banking" has changed: a shift from wholesale to retail banking, the provision of a wide range of financial services, and the development of off-balance-sheet business (Lewis, 1988). The traditional monopoly of banks in the money transmission service has also been challenged most notably by building societies.

Overwhelming all other forces has been the role of competition as the competitive environment has intensified within and between sub-sectors of the system. In the process the specialist basis of financial institutions has been powerfully eroded as diversification has produced a trend towards financial conglomerates. This has been a comparatively easy process in the UK as historic demarcations have been largely self-imposed rather than forced by legislation. At the same time regulation has become more formalized and explicit, and competitive pressures have undermined most of the traditional features of self-imposed regulation based upon restrictive practices.

The dominant change, and one that has been both created by competitive pressures and in itself reinforcing them, is the process of diversification and the erosion of the historic structured basis of the financial system. The process of diversification has involved existing institutions widening the range of products and services, and institutions purchasing firms in other sectors. The 1980s has witnessed mergers and purchases between banks, securities traders and brokers of various kinds, insurance companies, investment managers and advisers and estate agents. Banks, building societies and insurance companies now offer a full range of financial services both via branch network and agency arrangements. This has been occurring across the full range of financial institutions and markets. The clearing banks have bought securities trading firms and merchant banks, and they also own unit trusts (thus merging four areas of finance that have traditionally been kept separate). One bank has also bought an insurance company. At the same time the process of diversification into a limited range of financial services includes non-finance companies such as the BAT company, and Marks and Spencer (which holds a banking licence). Marks and Spencer, a nation-wide retail store, launched its own unit trust in October 1988 which it sells through a directly-owned subsidiary. Several national retail stores (with access to a large number of personal customers) offer credit card services and personal loans. Thus conglomeration has come to straddle financial and non-financial companies.

Building societies are similarly diversifying. From being a set of highly specialised institutions, whose business was exclusively to collect retail savings deposits to finance mortgage loans, they are emerging as diversified retail banks encompassing consumer lending, insurance underwriting, stock exchange brokerage services, portfolio management and money transmission services which have hitherto been the monopoly of a small number of clearing banks.

Securities industry

The most far-reaching structural change centres on the securities industry following "Big Bang" in 1986, (Goodhart, 1987; Hall, 1987). This represents an instructive case study of the pressures inducing structural change. Historically, this sector has been highly regulated through practices enforced by the London Stock Exchange (LSE). Since 1908 stock exchange practice was based upon a strict "single capacity" rule which meant that member firms were either brokers or jobbers (marketmakers) in securities (equities and government and corporate bonds but not eurobonds) but could not be both. Prior to "Big Bang" the stock exchange consisted of 4,852 individual members in 209 member firms (predominantly partnerships). Most of these firms (192) were brokers acting as agents for investors (arranging deals on their behalf with the jobbers for a minimum commission). Traditionally, member firms had to be partnerships. But changes to this rule in 1969 allowed member firms to become limited companies and to take outside shareholders though a limit of 10 per cent was placed on shareholdings in a member firm by any single non-member. This was raised to 29.9 per cent in 1982 but the fact that member firms could not be wholly owned by a single non-member meant that firms could not be part of wider groupings.

Thus, the historic distinction and separation between banking and securities trading (enforced by law in some countries) was in the UK financial system the product of self-imposed arrangements. No change in the law was required to end this major feature of the British financial system.

The rule book of the LSE was never applied to the very much larger eurobond market in London where trading arrangements have always been different in four major respects: banks were not excluded as traders and market-makers; there was no single capacity operation; no fixed minimum commission charges were enforced, and trading has always been screenbased rather than on the floor of an exchange. In fact it was the set of rules and restrictive practices enforced by the LSE that induced the eurobond market to develop outside the ambit of the stock exchange. In 1986 the LSE and International Securities Regulatory Organisation (the selfregulatory organisation set up by the eurobond market) were merged to form a unified securities market known as the London International Stock Exchange and regulated in common by The Securities Association.

As a result of "Big Bang" and de-regulation in the stock exchange and the securities industry, British and foreign banks have become major elements in the securities industry as part of integrated financial groups comprising commercial banking, merchant banking, securities broking and market-making, together with fund management components. In October 1986 fixed commissions for securities trading in the London market were ended following the agreement between the government and the Stock Exchange. In March of the same year Stock Exchange rules were changed to allow one hundred per cent outside ownership of stock broking and jobbing firms. The resulting massive capital injection by a wide range of British and foreign banks has changed the UK market in two major respects: the hitherto separate and specialist role of market-maker and broker (enforced by internal regulation since 1908) has been abandoned, and all the major securities firms have become parts of integrated financial institutions. In terms of US experience, this is tantamount to May Day in 1975 and the abolition of Glass-Stegal occurring simultaneously (Jacomb, 1985).

This represents a substantial package which has been a major, if not central, ingredient of structural change in the British financial system evident during the 1980s. The catalyst was the decision of the government to refer the rule book of the LSE to the Restrictive Trades Practices Court. But the old system would have changed without this due to global competitive pressures. The restrictive practices were causing the LSE to lose market share even of domestic trading of domestic securities. Stock exchange firms were undercapitalised which made it difficult to compete with the more highly capitalised firms in the US. After the abolition of exchange controls the international portfolio diversification of major institutions was handled predominantly by foreign securities firms and this clearly exposed the weaknesses of the British market (Leohnis, 1987). The abolition of exchange control in 1979, coupled with development in information and trading technology and the growing power of large institutional traders who could take advantage of these factors to by-pass the LSE, meant that uncompetitive practices could not be sustained. Perhaps the most indicative symptom of an unsustainable system was the development of the eurobond market outside the traditional market and set of restrictive practices. This represents a major example of the power of global competitive pressures, and the impact of technology, having a decisive influence on the structure of a financial system. In effect, restrictive practices could be sustained in a cohesive and cartelised industry while there was no significant external competition. It was the development of information and trading technology that eventually undermined the self-imposed restrictive practices and induced a major structural change in the financial system.

II. ANALYSIS OF COMPETITION

A central theme has been that the dominant pressure inducing structural change in the financial system has been competition and the greatly intensified competitive environment that has prevailed in the 1980s. The financial system of the 1980s has been an industry subject to increased competitive pressures both within and between sub-sectors. There are several reasons why competitive pressures have intensified. The powerful international dimension has already been noted in the securities industry though it applies also more generally. Increasingly competition in finance has developed in a global dimension (Llewellyn, 1988c). Secondly, technology has had a major impact in lowering the entry costs into some services. Thirdly, the general regulatory climate has favoured the development of competitive pressures and, as noted by Broker (1989), in many countries regulatory authorities have become more focused upon the question of efficiency in the financial system and how this can be enhanced by competition. Above all, competition has been a product of new strategic objectives of financial institutions which across the board have developed diversification strategies by offering a wider range of services.

In order to focus the discussion it is instructive to consider what would normally be predicted in an industry that is subject to more competition. This is summarised in Table 1 and the experience of the recent evolution of the financial system indicates that the model applies as much to the finance industry as to any other. The analysis of competition in finance has a particular bearing with respect to 1992 and the EEC because the completion of the "internal market" is unambiguously about competition. The framework

Table 1. Impact of competition.

(1)	The most efficient firms would become yet more efficient and the average efficiency of the industry would rise.
(2)	The pricing of the product would tend to eliminate any excess demand that might previously have existed.
(3)	Internal cross-subsidies, and pricing structures not based on cost or risk considerations, would tend to disappear.
(4)	The industry would likely experience more mergers as the less efficient firms find the competitive environment too demanding.
(5)	There would be considerable pressure towards the elimination of any cartel that might exist over the fixing of the industry's prices.
(6)	Restrictive practices would be competed away through circumvention.
(7)	Overall profitability is likely to decline.
(8)	The overall risk characteristics of the industry are likely to increase.
(9)	Firms seek to diversify.
(10)	Exits.

outlined in this section is one that is directly relevant to a consideration of the likely impact in some EC countries of the 1992 arrangements.

Efficiency

The first proposition, though perhaps the most important, is in practice difficult to test in practice. Nevertheless, all sectors are under pressure to improve efficiency and control costs. Certain indications, however, suggest that the basic efficiency of the system has increased. In wholesale banking domestic and international competition has eroded lending margins, and the abolition in 1983 of the building society cartel (where the margin used to be set at a level sufficient to maintain the less efficient societies in business) has increased pressure on less efficient building societies. Across the board clearing banks are also under increased pressure to control operating costs.

One particular aspect of efficiency associated with competitive pressures has developed in the mortgage market with the emergence of securitised mortgages and partnership arrangements. In both cases overall efficiency is raised because some institutions concentrate on that part of the lending process in which they have a comparative advantage. Both mechanisms are based upon there being three functions in a loan: an *initiating procedure, administration* of the loan, and the *holding of the asset.* Traditionally all three functions have been performed by the same lending institution which seeks a borrower and makes the loan, administers the loan contract, and holds the loan as an asset on the balance sheet. There is no reason, however, why the functions should not be split if different institutions have different comparative advantages and efficiency in different functions. A building society or a retail bank may have a comparative advantage in the first two functions and hence would be efficient at initiating and administering mortgages. On the other hand, because of funding or capital constraints, it may be less efficient than some other institution (such as a wholesale bank with no retail branches) at holding the asset. In this case, overall efficiency is increased if each institution exploits its comparative advantage: the first institution initiates and administers the loan, while the second holds the mortgage as an asset. This particular innovation raises efficiency through a process of decomposing the lending process and exploiting the different comparative advantages.

A similar analysis applies to some new financial instruments (such as swaps) where each borrower funds in his most efficient way (even though that is not his preferred way) and subsequently makes a swap with another borrower who has the opposite comparative advantage and preferences.

Elimination of excess demand

The second proposition in Table 1 is that competition has the effect of eliminating any excess demand (queues) that might exist which implies that the price is set below the market clearing level. The building society cartel was operated in this way with queues for mortgages being the norm prior to 1983. An excess demand implies that some consumers would be prepared to pay a higher rate of interest than that being charged. This was sustainable for two reasons both associated with an uncompetitive mortgage market: (i) the building societies were part of a cohesive, co-operative industry and until 1983 operated a collective cartel, (ii) they were not subject to external competition as banks entered the mortgage market in a significant way only in 1981. If competition develops (either internally or from outside) competitors bid away the excess demand by raising the rate of interest to the market-clearing level. Thus the effect of competition in this case is to raise the mortgage rate, eliminate excess demand, and increase the supply of loans. In practice, excess demand has been eliminated in the mortgage market since the entry of banks in the early 1980s.

Cross-subsidies

All multi-product firms have the problem of identifying and allocating costs to each business area (including capital costs). Proposition (3) in Table 1 relates to pricing policies. When competitive conditions vary between different business areas of an institution there is scope for "cross-subsidising". This implies a pricing policy which does not fully reflect differences in cost and risk, and frequently means that prices are set high in one market (where competition is less) and low in another such that the former effectively "cross-subsidises" the latter. This need not imply offering one service at a loss but may mean that fixed costs are not allocated to it. As competition intensifies such cross-subsidies are normally competed away. In effect, new entrants target on the "subsidising" component of competitors business which undermines the latter's ability to price the "subsidised" component at a low level.

Two examples of how competition has eroded "cross-subsidies" are in the mortgage market and securities trading. Traditionally, and when not subject to external competition, building societies charged higher rates of interest on large mortgages compared with smaller mortgages even though they were in practice less risky and cheaper to administer. This implied a perverse pricing strategy with low risk and large mortgages cross-subsidising higher risk and more costly mortgages. This would not be sustained in a highly competitive market as new entrants would secure a high risk-adjusted rate of return by competing away the large mortgages (by slightly undercutting building societies) and leaving building societies with the less profitable business. This is how the banks behaved when they entered the mortgage market in the early 1980s. This had the effect of forcing building societies to reverse their pricing policies and it is now more common for large mortgages to be offered at a lower rate of interest.

A second example is in the pricing of securities trading. As a result of the stock exchange fixing minimum dealing charges large institutional traders were not able to bargain over commission charges which implied that they did not secure the benefits of their large volumes. This had the effect of a cross-subsidy to personal customers whose charges were lower than would otherwise have been the case had charges for institutional traders been lower than the minimum allowed. One of the predictable features of "Big Bang", as was also the case following similar changes on the New York Stock Exchange in 1975, is that charges for large traders have been reduced and some evidence that those for small traders have risen.

The position becomes more complex when a particular "product" performs several services simultaneously, and when it is difficult to unbundle the components. In this case it is difficult to identify and price separately the subsidising and subsidised components. An example is with "free banking" on current accounts which are both deposits and a part of the money transmission service offered by banks. Generally, banks do not charge for the use of current accounts (while they remain in credit) but similarly do not pay interest on credit balances. This implies a cross-subsidy from those who hold large average balances (effectively an interest-free loan to the bank) to those who make many transactions and hence impose costs on the bank which are not recouped from the customer. This implicit cross-subsidy would be eliminated if the market rate of interest were paid on all outstanding balances while the economic cost was charged for all services. This would induce customers to maintain higher average balances and at the same time seek to reduce their costs by, for instance, greater use of credit cards so as to minimise the number of transactions.

Leaving aside the question of tax-efficiency (i.e. interest received is taxed while the subsidy received by no charges is not) the problem arises because consumers are using both "services" of a current account and everyone is a subsidiser and a recipient of a subsidy. The position is therefore not as clear cut as when the subsidising and receipt of the subsidy involve different customers who can be targeted by competitors. However, although it is more difficult in practice to identify the subsidising and subsidised customers, the pricing arrangement makes it potentially attractive for competitors to bid for transactions balances. With the change in regulation in the 1986 Building Societies Act several building societies have done this. Banks have also begun to pay interest on current accounts with large average or minimum balances and, in some cases, without simultaneously levying charges.

Mergers

Proposition (4) has been a feature of the building society sector with the number of societies declining from 273 in 1980 to 138 by the end of 1987. There will likely be substantial pressures for a further concentration in the industry. To the extent that scale is a factor in market success (eg in computer facilities and the ability to offer a wider range of services) this will be reinforced in the medium term. Regulation will also be a pressure on smaller societies in that they do not have the same range of powers (either on asset or liability diversification) as the larger societies.

It is likely, therefore, that the number of societies will continue to decline and the industry will become yet further concentrated. In practice future concentration will more likely involve a merging of medium-sized societies. In effect, the 20 per cent of business undertaken outside the ten largest societies will be undertaken by considerably fewer societies. The number of institutions will be reduced in three ways. The traditional route has been through mergers and this will continue. But since the 1986 Building Societies Act all societies now have the option of converting from mutual to PLC status and this can be done either as an independent institution or with a view to being absorbed by an existing institution such as a bank or insurance company. Some medium-sized institutions will appear attractive to other institutions as a route to selling retail financial services to the personal sector. This conversion and absorption route could imply more competitive pressures for the larger societies in that it gives greater access to the personal sector to a wider range of competitor institutions.

Cartels and restrictive practices

Competitive pressures make it difficult to sustain a non-market-clearing pricing structure. Similarly, if a cartel fixes prices at a level that creates excessive profits competition may develop from outside the cartel. It was competitive pressure from the New York stock exchange (where large UK investors could transact at lower dealing charges) that was the major factor undermining the minimum commission charges enforced by the London Stock Exchange. For a cartel to be effective the industry must be cohesive and not subject to external competition. This was true of the building society and the stock exchange price-fixing arrangements until the early 1980s. In the case of the former the cartel was abandoned in 1983 after the entry of banks into the mortgage market. Competition from New York, after technology developments made it feasible for UK investors to trade in New York, was the dominant factor undermining the price-fixing arrangements on the London stock exchange. This argument is a particular example of the more general proposition that competition undermines all forms of restrictive practices through circumvention. If it is technically possible to do so, customers seek to avoid the restrictions by dealing outside the cohesive group maintaining them.

Erosion of profitability

A normal expectation is that competition has the effect of eroding profitability most especially as new firms enter the industry. This has clearly been the case in international banking, wholesale banking generally, and in securities trading in the UK since "Big Bang". It is not, however, invariably the case and the outcome depends upon how the industry operated before the entry of competition and specifically upon whether it was previously seeking to maximise profits. An instructive case study is provided by building societies where profitability (absolutely and in terms of the rate of return on assets and capital) has risen in the 1980s notwithstanding the more competitive climate. This is associated in part with the operation of the cartel prior to 1983 which had the effect of maintaining the mortgage rate below the market-clearing level. With the abolition of the cartel, profits rose as the same margin was earned on an increased volume of mortgages. Thus profits can be increased due to the stock-adjustment effect of moving to a market-clearing, profit-maximising position.

Risk

A major issue in finance is the extent to which (if at all) de-regulation (externally imposed or internally generated) induces "excessive" competition and excess capacity with the potential for increased instability in the financial system. Competition may have the effect of increasing risk in two ways: (i) by increasing the variability of profits, and (ii) by inducing lending criteria to be relaxed. This latter seems to have been the case in international lending during the 1970s, and the evidence indicates that the risks on building society mortgage lending increased in the early stages following the entry of banks. This was associated, in part, with lending bigger multiples of borrowers' income and a high proportion (sometimes one hundred per cent) of the value of the property. It is likely that risks rose to the extent that, by previously maintaining excess demand, building societies rationed-out less credit-worthy borrowers. An alternative is via the effect on interest rates in that a more competitive environment might be expected to raise both the volatility of interest rates (competing institutions engage in active liability-management) and their absolute level to the extent that in the non-competitive (cartelised) regime interest rates were set below the market clearing level.

Diversification

Competition developing in a firm's existing market is likely to induce diversification. This has been true across the board in the financial system as has been described. For instance, a major competitive influence on building societies has been a strategic decision adopted by their banking competitors over the 1980s to target the personal sector for retail deposits, lending to this sector, and the provision of financial services generally. Diversification may be seen as a means of restoring profits eroded by competition developing in a firm's traditional business.

Exits

In the final analysis, and failing other strategies, the ultimate effect of competition is to induce exits from the industry as the industry becomes "overcrowded" and the more efficient force the exit of the less efficient. In practice this has not been a common reaction in the financial system. However, one example has been in the securities industry. One of the features of "Big Bang" was a substantial rise in the number of market-makers both in the gilts and equity markets. New entrants were anticipating a sharp rise in turnover following the abolition of minimum commissions. In practice the required increase in turnover to enable the much larger number of market-makers to remain profitable was not a realistic proposition. In the event, and especially after the stockmarket collapse in October 1987, the volume of transactions actually declined sharply. This subsequently induced several equity and government bond market-makers to withdraw within the first two years of the new market structure. At the same time several firms have announced that they will no longer service personal accounts below a certain figure.

Excess capacity and profitability

Partly as a result of banks' strategic shift towards retail banking and financial services during the 1980s, competitive pressures have intensified in retail banking and this is likely to be intensified further as a result of the 1992 EEC arrangements to be discussed in the next Section. The possibility arises that the provision of retail financial services is becoming an overcrowded industry. A wide range of institutions (clearing banks, insurance companies, foreign banks, building societies and even non-financial firms) have targeted the personal sector simultaneously. There are many reasons why financial institutions or firms generally seek to diversify: to maintain profitability in the context of more competition in traditional markets, to reduce risk by less concentration, to reap economies of scope, to reduce excess capacity, because of a presumed high profitability of existing suppliers or because competitors have higher costs, to compete away cross-subsidies etc. The profitability of diversification, however, depends in part upon what is happening to the demand for the product. If demand is rising strongly it can make profitable an area that, for a particular institution, might not have been profitable before. The demand can be met by new institutions without taking business from others. If, on the other hand, demand is static the net result is that all have a smaller volume of business, and it is almost certain that profitability is lowered.

Given the extent and magnitude of the shift towards selling financial services to the personal sector, it is difficult to avoid the conclusion that strategies are being built on optimistic assumptions about the size and profitability of the market. Competition (domestic and international) eroded the profitability of parts of wholesale banking in the 1970s as more firms (often foreign banks) entered the market. The same is likely to happen in the retail sector in the 1990s.

It is normally (though by no means invariably) to be expected that increased competition leads to a decline in profitability. It is, therefore, something of a paradox that in the case of both the clearing banks and building societies basic profitability increased over the 1980s at a time when the competitive environment intensified considerably. Profitability is measured not in terms of absolute profits but by the rates of return on assets (ROA) and equity (reserves for building societies, i.e. ROE). In the case of banks the low figure for 1987 reflects a distortion due to the exceptional provisions for bad debt made in that year. The sample includes the four largest banks and four large building societies. Table 2 shows that for building societies there has been a sharp trend rise in the ROA since 1982 from 0.80 per cent to 1.25 per cent. For banks the ROA rose sharply after 1984. The ROE measures show a trend rise for building societies after 1982 (from 24 per cent to 31 per cent) and for banks there has been a very sharp rise from 17 per cent in 1983 to 26 per cent in 1986.

When considering the reasons for the apparent paradox, and drawing implications for the future, a distinction is made between *cyclical, stock adjustment*, and *trend*, factors. To the extent that the explanation for the rise in profitability relates to either of the first two, the rise is likely to be temporary. *Stock adjustment* factors occur when there is a once-for-all single and finite shift to a new position which is neither subsequently reversed nor continuous at the same rate. The change may be substantial while the stock adjustment is being made but is nevertheless finite in nature.

In general, bank profitability (as measured by ROE and ROA) can rise for five reasons:

1. Through an endowment effect which raises overall profitability.
2. Because the nature of the business is changing in a way that generates profits without increasing assets. Off-balance-sheet earnings raise the measured ROA and ROE even though the underlying profitability of the asset base might be declining.
3. Margins are raised on all business perhaps because of strong demand.
4. The asset mix changes with a switch from low to high margin assets. In this case (as happened in 1986 and 1987 for both domestic and inter-

Table 2. Banks and building society rates of return.

		1980	1981	1982	1983	1984	1985	1986	1987
[1]	Rate of Return on Assets								
	– Banks	1.37	1.24	0.85	0.83	0.81	1.09	1.21	0.10
	– Building Societies	0.70	0.89	0.80	1.00	0.85	1.14	1.20	1.25
[2]	Rate of Return on Equity								
	– Banks	23.3	23.0	17.2	16.9	19.1	25.5	26.1	2.2
	– Building Societies	22.4	27.7	24.0	28.4	25.8	30.5	30.8	31.0
[3]	Rate of Return on Capital								
	– Banks	x	x	11.8	11.3	11.3	12.5	13.1	1.3
[4]	Equity/Assets Ratio								
	– Banks	5.9	5.4	5.0	4.9	4.2	4.3	4.6	5.0
[5]	Capital/Assets Ratio								
	– Banks	x	x	7.2	7.3	7.2	8.7	9.2	8.6

national business) margins in both can decline while overall the ROA is increased.

5. Because there is a fall in the cost of bank liabilities relative to other market interest rates.

The endowment-effect (given that banks do not pay interest on all deposits) is cyclical in nature and associated with the movement in interest rates. There has been something of this effect operating at times during the 1980s though the impact has been steadily declining, and will decline further as competition has the effect of eroding the proportion of accounts upon which no interest is paid.

A major factor in profitability trends has been a change in the nature of the banking business. Banks are not exclusively asset-liability transformers (absorbing deposits with one set of characteristics and creating assets with a different set). Increasingly they earn income off the balance sheet through the provision of various services. This necessarily increases the measured rate of return on assets. Over the 1980s the proportion of the banks' total income generated through off-balance-sheet activity rose from 11 per cent in 1980 to 17 per cent in 1987. Thus the measured ROA and ROE can be maintained because the nature of the business is changing. Banks have also benefited from the cyclical effect of an exceptionally strong and sustained demand for mortgages and consumer credit.

Perhaps the most important contribution came from a strategic shift (stock-adjustment) that banks made from wholesale to retail banking activity during the 1980s. Competitive pressures during the 1970s substantially eroded the profitability of wholesale banking (domestic and international) which, combined with the strong growth in the demand for retail loans, induced a major strategic shift by banks towards the retail sector. Such business is considerably more profitable and hence such a shift will necessarily raise measured profitability. This represents a competitive response of diversification in order to maintain overall profitability.

Analysing profitability trends is a complex process. Nevertheless, abstracting from the detail, the rise in bank profitability (in terms of the rate of return on assets and equity) over the past few years has been dominated by four factors:

1. a change in the nature of banking business with the growth of fee income and other off-balance-sheet business;
2. the cyclical effect associated with the unprecedented rise in the demand for credit and most especially from the personal sector;
3. a stock-adjustment effect of a shift, at the margin, from wholesale to retail banking.
4. The rise in the ROE was associated in part with a substantial rise in loan capital issued by banks following a change in capital regulations in the

early 1980s by the Bank of England. This had the effect of allowing a multiple rise in bank assets on the basis of a fixed volume of equity and hence the ROE would rise. As there is a regulatory limit on the extent tot which loan stock can be counted as capital, the shift towards loan capital was a stock adjustment rather than a continuing flow and hence is not a means of continuing to raise the ROE.

Thus to a significant extent the predicted long-run effect of increased competition on profits has been concealed by two stock adjustments and a strong cyclical effect.

To some extent two potential problems for banks during the 1980s (a capital constraint and the impact of competition on profitability) have been concealed. The former was because of the facility to raise capital via subordinated debt. Over the period 1980-87 the six major clearing banks raised a total of £ 7.3 billion in such capital due to an accommodating change in the Bank of England's regulation with respect to capital (Llewellyn, 1988b). The stock adjustment to the regulatory limit having been made, capital must now be raised predominantly through equity: retained earnings (which implies profits) and new issues. The problem with this is that, given current price-earnings ratios which for the bank sector overall currently stand at 5.6 against 12.9 for all shares in the FT 500 Index, the average cost of new capital will rise sharply.

The decade of the 1980s may therefore come to be viewed as a transitional phase. During the 1970s, competitive pressures in wholesale banking eroded profitability. The 1980s could prove to be transitional in the sense of the various stock adjustments and the cyclical effect. In which case the 1990s could be a period when competitive pressures begin to seriously erode overall bank profitability. It is difficult to avoid the conclusion that the 1990s will be a more difficult period for bank profitability most especially if the retail financial services sector is becoming over-crowded. There are several grounds for a less optimistic view of future profitability than might be suggested by recent trends:

- the underlying effect of competition;
- the ending of the beneficial stock adjustments;
- the lesser ability to engage in cross-subsidising most especially with respect to current accounts;
- the further erosion of the banks' traditional "endowment effect" as the average cost of retail funds rises;
- the ending of the boom in consumer lending;
- a reduction in the underlying profitability of credit cards;
- a rise in the average cost of capital in the context of banks having reached the regulatory limit (as a proportion of the capital base) with respect to loan-stock capital.

The banks will respond and this is likely to include a further attempt to expand off-balance-sheet income which will change yet further the nature of banking business.

Financial conglomerates

The second problem area identified relates to the trend towards diversification and the emergence of financial conglomerates the wisdom of which might be questioned on grounds of efficiency. There is no certainty that financial institutions have the necessary management skills to handle a very diversified business where the technicalities can be complex. There may also be doubt in some cases about whether, for instance, the different ethos and cultures of clearing banks, merchant banking and broking can be mixed; the "deal-orientated" culture of securities trading does not easily fit within the ethos of a clearing bank (Gardener, 1988). Evidence indicates that alleged "synergy" is difficult to identify and achieve when totally different cultures and practices are brought together. This appears to be most evident in the case of the American banks who bought or created UK securities trading firms.

Those who are sceptical of the financial conglomerate strategy believe that conflicts of interest cannot be avoided and that the costs of policing all the complex boundaries (Chinese Walls and compliance officers) in an attempt to avoid them are high, and the risk remains of losing clients when breaches are published. These costs may outweigh the alleged benefits of synergy and economies of scope even when they can be identified. In some cases size has proven to be a problem with unwieldly structures, internal tensions together with information and control problems.

This in turn raises the question of the extent to which the different facets of a conglomerate are managed independently, and of the type of control systems within the administrative structure. The dilemma is that, if the different areas are integrated so as to secure the advantage of the consumer of a "department store", then questions arise about whether such a diverse but integrated business can be effectively managed. On the other hand, if (perhaps because of a regulatory requirement) different elements of the conglomerate are established as semi-autonomous companies, the question arises as to whether there is any advantage to the user of financial services and whether the firm secures the alleged synergies. Loehnis (1987) considers the distinct possibility that in the UK regulatory context costs of supervisory compliance might come to outweigh the potential gains in synergy within a financial conglomerate.

Within the financial sector where conglomerates are emerging a warning that diversification may not always be successful is provided by the "lifeboat" organised by the Bank of England in 1974. Here the biggest institutions that had to be rescued were former successful specialist HP finance houses, such as UDT, Bowmaker and Mercantile Credit, which had recently diversified into lending to property developers. The wideranging diversification of business by the big UK banks has not always been conspicuously successful. Another example of such diversification by commercial banks is to be found in their move into medium-term sovereign lending. Some of the problems encountered may be attributable to many of the banks being new to this type of business. In general, the traditional wisdom and expertise of bankers engaged in international lending is located in the merchant banks, not the clearing banks.

There are also implications for the role of the central bank as a lender-of-last-resort in that, while a functional approach to regulation may be adopted, it is companies and not functions that become insolvent. With a diversified company the central bank cannot readily discriminate between those activities which need to be supported in the national interest and those which can be allowed to fail most especially, for instance, if depositors interpret the failure of a subsidiary with dedicated capital as a sign of weakness of the banking group. It is not clear that, requiring dedicated capital to bank subsidiaries effectively protects the bank either from contagion or a responsibility to support its subsidiaries.

None of the factors that have induced the globalization of finance (competitive pressures, financial innovation, technology, de-regulation, abolition of exchange control etc) have a specifically European dimension, (Llewellyn, 1988c). At the same time, there has been little globalization of retail banking. Whilst this has been true to date, the position could change in the 1990s. Potentially the arrangements envisaged for the post 1992 EC represent a major change in the market environment for all financial institutions and suppliers of financial services.

There are considerable differences in the price, range, and quality of financial services available in different EC countries. There are three main factors accounting for this: (i) differences in basic efficiency in different financial systems, (ii) different types of constraining regulation imposed in different countries, and (iii) differences in the basic internal competitive environment which sustains a higher level of cost and/or profits in some systems compared with others. In principle, a high price in one national system would be competed away either through the entry of foreign firms or by the users of financial services using foreign mechanisms, (Llewellyn, 1988c). The same effect could be achieved via a "contestable markets" mechanism (Baumol, 1982). In practice, though it varies considerably between countries and for different users (especially wholesale versus retail customers), this process can be impeded by exchange control, together with information, access and transactions costs. The Second Banking Directive will add a specifically European dimension to competition in financial services. It is a major change for it establishes the principle of freedom of establishment and the provision of cross-border services within the Community. The over-riding principle is that if an institution is authorised in one member country it is deemed to be similarly authorised in *all* other Member states; an institution wishing to provide services in another Member state does not need separate authorization whether the provision of services is via location in other countries or via cross-frontier trade.

Clearly, the greatest impact will be felt in those countries where internal regulation is most constraining, where internal competitive pressures are weakest (perhaps because of cartels or restrictive practices), and where entry barriers have been most formidable. For instance, the impact within the British financial system may not be substantial: competitive conditions are already demanding, there is no exchange control, all major EC banks already have a presence in London, there are few restrictions on the range of business, and foreign branches in London are not required to have dedicated capital. In other words, there have been no regulatory limits preventing EC institutions developing business within the UK; in general entry into the UK will be no easier after 1992 than it is now. On the other hand, British institutions will gain through greater access to other EC markets.

Retail banking

The central issue for competing banks and other financial institutions is access to potential customers and the creation of effective delivery systems for financial services. Whatever the type of business being considered, for provision to be effective an institution needs access to potential custiomers and this is likely to be secured differently for retail as opposed to wholesale banking services, and different banks will develop different approaches. Access can be secured in five basic ways: (i) by building a location, i.e. establishing a European network of branches, (ii) by mergers, where two institutions of different nationality merge so that a single institution has universal access in both countries, (iii) through the purchase of a company in another country which has ready access to customers, (iv) through developing business links with institutions in other countries so that the partner gives access to its customer base and acts in some cases as an agent (see the concept of "agency diversification" discussed above), or (v) via trade though there has to be effective communication between the customer in one country and the suplier of a financial service in another.

Some banks and other financial institutions will seek a pan-EC strategy via transnational mergers. There are several examples to date including that of UAP (the largest French insurance group) and Sun Life Assurance (UK) planning to exchange shareholdings and co-operate on future international development. Prior to that UAP had acquired a major stake in the largest Belgian insurance group. In some countries (perhaps Spain and Italy) there will be powerful competitive pressures on small banks to merge or join larger groups. In 1987 Deutschebank acquired Bank of America's 100-branch network in Italy, and Credit Lyonnais of France acquired Nederlander Crediet Bank (a Dutch subsidiary of Chase Manhattan Bank) which absorbed 127 branches and a 7 per cent market share. Other examples include the acquisition by Banco Santander of Spain of a substantial equity stake in Instituto Bancario Italiano and its exchange of equity with the Royal Bank of Scotland, and the participation of Midland Bank in Euromobiliare.

An alternative strategy is the development of joint-ventures and various forms of co-operative arrangements. The "link" method is potentially powerful and is likely to emerge as a major business route because it enables different institutions to exploit their different comparative advantages. This has recently been used in the UK mortgage market and has enabled foreign institutions without an internal branch network to access retail customers. In practice, and given the expense of developing a new branch network, this is likely to be a major implication of the Second Directive and its effect upon the future evolution of European financial institutions. Such links, and joint ventures designed to exploit different comparative advantages, will become increasingly common between institutions in different countries. Foreign institutions will be holding assets which have been originated and administered by domestic institutions. This will prove to be a major way of foreign institutions gaining access to personal customers without the necessity of a branch network.

Overall, the major implications of the 1992 ambitions will be to further intensify the competitive environment in which (most especially retail) financial services are provided. This cannot fail to have major strategic implications for the suppliers of financial services perhaps most especially with respect to business linkages between different nationalities of financial institutions. This could represent a further significant element in structural change of financial systems.

REFERENCES

Bank of England, (1983) "Competition, Innovation and Regulation in British Banking", *Quarterly Bulletin*, September.
Bank of England, (1984) "Insurance in a changing Financial Services Industry", *Quarterly Bulletin*, June.
Barge, J. (1985) "Goodhart's Law Strikes Again", *The Banker*, July.
Baumol, W. K. (1982) "Contestable Markets: An Uprising in the Theory of Industry Structure", *American Economic Review*, 72: 1–15.

Boyd, J. H. & Graham, S. L. (1986) "Risk, Regulation & Bank Holding Company Expansion into Non-banking", Federal Reserve Bank of Minneapolis, *Quarterly Review*, Spring.

Broker, G. (1989) *Competition in Banking*, OECD.

Clark J. A. (1988) "Economies of Scale & Scope at Depository Financial Institutions: Review of the Literature", Federal Reserve Bank of Kansas City, *Economic Review*, Sept.

Corrigan, E. G. (1987) Commentary in *Restructuring the Financial System*, Federal Reserve Bank of Kansas City.

Eisenbeis, R. A. (1987) "Can Regulatory Reform Prevent the Impending Disaster in Financial Markets?", in *Restructuring the Financial System*, Federal Reserve Bank of Kansas City.

Eisenbeis, R. A. (1989) "The Impact of Securitisation & Internationalisation on Market Imperfections", in Gardener, E. P. M., *The Future of Financial Systems & Services*, London, Macmillan.

Garderner, E. P. M. (1988) "A strategic perspective on banking financial conglomerates in London after the crash", Bangor University, *mimeo*.

Gilbart, R. A. (1988) "A Comparison of Proposals to Restructure the US Financial System", Federal Reserve Bank of St Louis, *Review*, July.

Goodhart, C. A. E. (1987) "Structural Changes in the British Capital Markets" in Currie, D. *et.al.* eds. *The Operation & Regulation of Financial Markets*, London, Macmillan.

Hall, M. J. B. (1987) *The City Revolution: Causes & Consequences*, London, Macmillan.

XI. Frankfurt Financial Centre Challenged by 1992

NORBERT WALTER

Within the last few years competition among the leading financial centres in the world has intensified markedly. This reflects the ongoing process of globalization, which itself is the result of various developments. The tendency towards globalization goes back to the late 1960s when a rapidly growing world trade induced a parallel expansion of international capital flows. In the 1970s the oil price explosion and the recycling of petro-dollars boosted those flows to new heights. In the 1980s globalization was more and more the result of genuinely-based developments in the financial markets rather than on events in the real economy. Deregulation, securitization and an immense progress in communication technologies became the main driving forces.

Deregulation was a precondition as well as a consequence of the increase in global business. On the one hand globalization would not have reached its current dimension without the repeal of restrictions on cross-border capital flows. On the other hand in many countries the impetus to deregulate was to attract business and to secure or to enlarge the countries' share in international markets.

Securitization, i.e. the trend to put claims and participation rights into security form also enormously enlarged the volume of international capital flows. Both deregulation and securitization allowed the creation of sophisticated new financial instruments like Floating Rate Notes, Euro-Notes or Euro-Commercial Papers and thus contributed to the wave of financial innovations in the 1980s.

No matter how important these influences have been, banking around the clock and around the globe would not have developed to the extent we experience today without modern communication technology. New generations of computers have made the processing and transmission of even immense proportions of data faster and cheaper. Due to global communication networks information generated at one place is immediately available at any other place throughout the world. With the support of computers it is also possible to analyse the development on the financial markets in real-time.

In Europe competition between financial centres moved forward to a new

D. E. Fair and C. de Boissieu (eds), Financial Institutions in Europe Under New Competitive Conditions, 147–155.

stage by the EC Commission's 1992 initiatives for a single European market. The 1992 initiatives generate numerous opportunities and challenges for Europe's financial centres as they lead to a marked increase in business on the one hand but also inevitably intensified competition on the other hand. The single market programme is an enormous stimulus for economic growth. Throughout Europe companies are already preparing ground for 1992 as high rates of investment in machinery and equipment in many countries show. In the 1990s, economic growth will be stronger than in the previous decade by quite a margin. The single market in addition encourages price stability since its main impact is achieved through cost reductions and boosts to productivity. European bond and share markets are profiting from these developments not least because they go hand in hand with increased capital requirements of firms. Companies do not need capital only to enlarge their production capacity or for diversification and restructuring – including merger and acquisition activities – but also to be able to intensify market research and product development. Also, the privatization of nationalized industries is likely to get further impulses from the single market initiatives. Even public enterprises will to a greater extent depend on private financing means.

Additional benefits result from the integration of the European financial markets themselves. An integrated financial area means free movement of capital within Europe, the unhindered provision of cross-border financial services throughout the Community and full freedom for suppliers of such services to establish themselves in any member country.

Obviously such far-reaching liberalization will stimulate business, for example by intensifying arbitrage or by allowing broader use of financial innovations. This in turn will lead to increased financial market liquidity that may encourage substantial participation by institutional investors, including those from other countries, for example Japan.

Although financial markets will strongly expand as a consequence of the realization of the single market, there will be much more competition among European financial centres at the same time. When capital is free to move within Europe and national frontiers are no longer barriers for banking then activities like investment banking which do not need a special location will tend to concentrate at places which offer the best opportunities, i.e. abundant skills, a broad spectrum of products, high market volumes and low transaction costs.

Europe 1992, however, does not emerge as a "big bang" at the turn of the year 1992/93, but stands for a long-term process, which is already under way. As far as the integration of financial markets is concerned, a number of concrete measures has already been implemented, e.g. the lifting of restrictions on trade credits, on trading in unlisted securities and on the admission of securities to the capital market. Most of the remaining restrictions on capital movements are to be abolished by mid-1990. From 1993 on, banks are to be allowed to offer their services throughout the entire EC.

Facing these challenges European financial centres have already started a competitive race for market shares. At present, London – despite its undeniable problems – seems to be positioned best. None of its European competitors has a similar tradition and reputation. With the "big bang" in 1986, which was not only a deregulation programme but also a splendid marketing idea, the City gained new glory although the euphoria of the first year faded as a result of the crash in October 1987. The British public is well aware of this tradition and the City's importance for the country's economy. Therefore not only Conservative governments have backed Britain's financial centre.

Although London has lost its top position as the most important financial centre on the globe and is now ranked behind Tokyo and New York, it still has an outstanding position. The city offers a wide range of market segments. It is the centre of the euroDM credit and money market. More than 2,500 companies are listed at the London Stock Exchange. And there is no other stock exchange where so many foreign shares are traded. All important banks and investment companies have established branches in London and made it a basis not only for their European activities but also for their globally oriented strategies. All these factors, the truly international character and the breadth and depth of the market give London an edge over its European competitors. The City, however, does not rest on its laurels: on the contrary, there are ongoing efforts to enlarge the market shares by aggressive strategies. Some months ago, for example, Mr. Andrew Hugh Smith, Chairman of the London Stock Exchange, announced ambitious plans. He wants to centralize trading in all European blue chips and bonds in London. Experts expect that a league of about 200 European blue chips and government bonds will crystallize as a consequence of the single market initiatives.

It is for the stock exchanges on the European continent to stop London's expansion plans otherwise they won't be more than regional exchanges with no international weight one day. The more they are willing to improve their own competitiveness, i.e. by abolishing superfluous regulations and by adapting to trends in the international markets (the growing importance of new instruments and new trading techniques), the better the chance that they will be successful.

Nevertheless, it will be difficult for the centres in continental Europe to catch up with the leading financial centres of the globe. At present, therefore, the race is primarily for predominance on the European continent. In France, obviously, there is a high degree of consensus between the government and all financial institutions involved that Paris should win and a lot has been done within the last few years to reach this target. Four measures were decisive in this context:

1. The establishment of the Second Marché for shares of small- and medium-sized companies in 1983.
2. The creation of new instruments, e.g. new money market papers.
3. The opening of the Marché à Terme des Instruments Financiers (MATIF) in 1986. The development of MATIF is a real success story as it very soon became one of the most important financial futures exchanges on the globe (at present No. 3 behind Chicago and Tokyo). MATIF is still very active and innovative as we have seen in April 1989, when it started to offer a euroDM interest future. MATIF also intends to be Europe's first financial futures exchange to join the globex system – an automatized international trading system which offers financial futures contracts outside official trading hours.
4. Far-reaching deregulation measures, e.g. the abolition of the broker's monopoly, a measure similar to the "big bang" in London which will provide open access to the stock exchange for French as well as for foreign banks and will markedly reduce transaction costs.

Switzerland is another important financial market on the continent which is strengthening its position. Switzerland does not participate in the European single market. Consequently 1992 means great challenges for the country. Contrary to its European competitors Switzerland does not profit from trade creation and other positive effects of the 1992 initiatives. Furthermore, the country has to face stronger competition from EC financial centres which gain new room for manoeuvre by the far-reaching deregulation measures. Switzerland, however, seems to have recognized the signs of the times as various measures and plans to cope with the future testify. With the opening of SOFFEX – a fully computerized market for options in 1986 – an important step forward has been taken. By the end of 1989 SOFFEX will also start trading in financial futures. Another goal is the establishment of modern computerized information and payment transactions systems. No matter how important these measures are, Switzerland should not concentrate on technical improvements alone, given institution disadvantages like high taxes (withholding tax of 35 per cent, stamp duty ranging from 0.15 to 0.30 per cent and some highly cartelized market segments.

Other countries and financial centres too all preparing for 1992. For Amsterdam, Madrid, Milan and other places the main problem is whether they will be able to maintain their current position or whether they will lose most of the trading in Dutch, Spanish or Italian blue chips to places like London, Paris or Frankfurt.

Frankfurt has started the race for market shares with some delay. Although Germany did not completely miss the trend towards deregulation and innovation, for many years things did not change much here compared with the dynamic developments in other countries. Despite the "Restliberalisie-rung", regulation of the markets is still high owing to – in part – obsolete ideas of consumer protection or of monetary policy supervision. In fact, it acts as a brake on innovation. Securitization is also still strongly underde-veloped. This continues to rob the German capital market of that breadth and depth which international issuers and investors are used to at competing financial centres. Furthermore German tax policy was not conducive to making the German financial centre more attractive for international financial market transactions. Old obstacles such as the securities transfer tax have remained in place; new ones, for example the withholding tax, have been introduced, though abolished again after an outcry from the public.

No surprise, there was growing concern among the German banking community which frequently pointed to the measures in other countries and asked for similar efforts in Germany. At present it seems as if the warnings were not without effect. 1989 so far has seen a busy German legislature, active monetary authorities and an alert banking community in order to strengthen the country's financial markets.

A spectacular step was without doubt the repeal of the 10 per cent withholding tax on July 1st, only half a year after its introduction. The highly unpopular withholding tax was an evident example of the lack of sensitivity and myopia of German politicans with regard to financial matters. The tax was introduced despite all warnings that its fiscal benefits would be very limited in comparison to the damaging effects it would have on German financial markets. Enormous capital outflows in the second half of 1988 and the first months of 1989 and a depressed value of the DM showed that the critics were right. Although the hasty abolition of the tax does not foster confidence in the wisdom of German politicians the country's financial markets surely will profit.

Furthermore, the Federal Government has announced an amendment to the Act relating to capital investment companies and the Act relating to the supervision of insurance companies. The purpose of these measures is to enable or make it easier for institutional investors to participate in financial futures business. Moreover, it is intended to abolish the need to obtain state approval for the issuing of bonds (under §§ 795, 808a Civil Code). This measure is highly overdue, because the approval procedure often protracts issuance, an implication impacting extremely negatively in times of market volatility.

Monetary authorities too widened the room for manoeuvre of investment bankers in setting new conditions for the issue of external DM-bonds. The abolition of the two day notification period for new DM-eurobonds allows issuers to respond faster and more flexibly to often rapidly changing market situations. The reduction of the minimum maturity for public issues and private placements – now down to two years – considerably enlarges the range of maturities available, thus new instruments like medium – term notes, already common in other countries, can be established in Germany, too.

Furthermore, since the beginning of the year, so-called "stop loss" and "stop buy" orders have been possible on the German exchanges, too. In all this, Frankfurt, which now accounts for roughly 70 per cent of German market turnover (equities and bonds) naturally plays a central role.

With the approval of the Länder governments to reforms of the German stock exchange law in June the last legislative barriers to the Deutsche Terminbörse (DTB), the planned new financial futures and options exchange, are pulled down. Contrary to fears of pessimists no agonizing debate about the status of the regional stock exchanges blocked the reforms so that DTB should start on time in January 1990. Investors in the Federal Republic will then also be able to hedge their portfolios using financial futures and options. It is planned to begin trading with 14 share options and with futures contracts based on a synthetic Federal bond and on the German share index (DAX). The lack of such hedging instruments has so far contributed to the fact that foreign capital investors have only gone into the German capital market on a short-term basis. The development of an efficient market for suitable contracts may then eliminate one reason for the high volatility of German capital markets. It is a great step forward, too, that DTB will be completely computerized. The electronic trading and settlement system will ensure transparency and promptness – a quality German financial markets are well-known for.

Closely connected to the establishment of DTB is the completion of the computerized "Inter-Banken-Informations-System" (Ibis) in January 1990. For the time being the main task of Ibis will be to improve the information base for trading outside the official trading hours of the German stock exchanges (11.30 a.m. to 1.30 p.m.). As Ibis will provide real-time information about market developments for those taking part in the telephone trade, i.e. institutional investors, transparency will increase enormously. Because of the close link between the cash and the futures market there is an urgent need for such an improvement, given the fact that DTB opening hours (10 a.m. to 4 p.m.) go far beyond those of the stock exchange. Ibis also marks the first step towards a fully computerized stock exchange, which will come when Ibis is no longer used only for generating information but enlarged as a trading system. Thus a dual system is likely to develop in Germany with computer trading attracting the orders of the highly professional institutional investors on the one hand, and the traditional trading on the floor left for business with private investors on the other hand. Whether both systems will survive in the long run is not yet clear. Of course, it would be best if it were for the market to decide. Although these are dreams of the future, it is obvious that the establishment of DTB and Ibis will entail fundamental structural changes in German financial markets. It is to be expected, for example, that the seven regional stock exchanges will lose business and that, especially, trading in German blue chips will concentrate in Frankfurt.

All this will undoubtedly make German financial markets more attractive. Nevertheless deregulation and innovation cannot stop here given the ongoing efforts in other countries. Further steps are necessary. Above all the securities transfer tax should be abolished as soon as possible. The deadline which the German legislature has set itself – January 1st, 1992 – is far too late. Under present conditions there is little incentive, even to innovative market participants, to make use of new financing instruments. Securities transfer tax, for example, has meant that certificates of deposit, although permitted in the Federal Republic since May 1986, have achieved practically no importance here. This tax – together with intermediaries' fees for brokerage – contributes much to our high transaction costs. According to figures published by the Working Association of German Stock Exchanges, they represent 0.58 per cent of market value for a big order in Frankfurt, compared with 0.41 per cent in Paris, 0.25 per cent in London and only 0.14 per cent in New York. Given such figures, it is understandably difficult to attract business back to Frankfurt.

What the German financial centre also needs, of course, is lower company taxation. This is particularly urgent against the background of the European internal market. When they are free to offer services, as planned, financial institutions will be more influenced by differences in tax burden when they decide where to set up their bases. The Federal Government has at least indicated that it is planning relief measures for the next legislative period. Substantial improvements should be agreed in good time and on a binding basis. It is particularly important to improve the position of the international investor, especially the shareholder. Without a change in stance vis-à-vis the investor, all efforts to improve the attractiveness of a financial centre will ultimately fail.

In the field of monetary policy, relief measures are also required, for example in connection with the minimum reserve requirement. The effect of this is that euromarket business is bypassing the Federal Republic. Even if the minimum reserve is to be retained – which is not absolutely necessary for a functioning monetary policy – there are various possibilities for eliminating the resulting competitive disadvantages, for example by paying market interest rates for the reserves.

Due to the somewhat belated start and the continued efforts of its international competitors Frankfurt has to make double efforts if it is to catch up with the leading financial centres in the world and to keep the top position on the European continent. Frankfurt, however, should be in a position to manage this considering not only the fundamental structural reforms that are under way but all those principal advantages which are in favour of the place.

For several years now, West Germany has been world champion in exports. Its economy plays a prominent role within the EC. More than a quarter of the Community's GNP is produced in Germany. Economic growth has improved now for two years and will remain at a relatively high level in the coming years, not least as a result of dynamic capital investment. Continued economic growth and a substantial reduction in German income tax will entail expanding disposable incomes of private households. This means high savings well into the 1990s even if the savings ratio is going to decline slightly.

Furthermore, West Germany has a well-founded and solid banking system, with globally operating universal banks.

Another, probably the best trump card is the fact that Deutsche Bundesbank, the German central bank, has its domicil in Frankfurt. The importance of the Bundesbank goes far beyond its task as a lender of the last resort for German banks. In fact, it plays a dominant role among European central banks. Since the start of the European Monetary System the Deutsche Bundesbank has been setting the tone in European monetary policy. As a result of the stability–oriented Bundesbank policy the Deutsche Mark has proved to be the "anchor" of economic and monetary policy for our European neighbours. Even more the Deutsche Mark has become by far the most important international reserve currency after the US dollar. At the end of 1988 all Deutsche Mark assets held by foreigners totalled about DM 720 bn.

As European monetary integration proceeds, it will be important to stake, assert and underpin the claim very early on that Frankfurt should be the domicile of the EC central bank. We should make no mistake about it: the basis for this question will be established early. Monetary union is not a component of the European Commission's internal market programme, and no one can say at this point when it will be achieved. But it will come.

Frankfurt has charisma as a centre for European monetary policy. With its autonomous and federally structured central bank, the Federal Republic offers a suitable model for the EC central bank. The Bundesbank is our best export item for Europe. If the United Kingdom were to stay out of the exchange rate and intervention mechanism of the EMS, Frankfurt's dominance in the European Monetary System would presumably be absolutely certain.

Frankfurt's chances of becoming the domicile for the EC central bank are good because the city is in the centre of Europe. As one of the nodal points of world air transport it has optimum global links. On the other hand, it would have desirable geographical distance from any city, domicile of other important EC institutions, be it Brussels or Strasbourg. To choose Frankfurt would testify to the political independence of the European central bank. Moreover, not one of the important institutions of the EC is yet in the Federal Republic. That, too, may be a reason for shaping European monetary policy from here in future.

As much as the Frankfurt financial centre would benefit from being selected as the location for the European central bank, it can ultimately only prosper in this role in an intellectual climate which attaches central importance to research and training in the financial sector. We in the Federal Republic generally have well-trained employees with an already relatively strong international orientation. Countries such as France and the United Kingdom, where there is sometimes a striking lack of interest in speaking or learning a foreign language, are in a somewhat more difficult position. But to be really competitive as a financial centre, a facility must be set up to provide specialized training and training for excellence in this sector at an international level. One solution would be to establish a European financial university. This would strengthen Frankfurt's case for becoming the leading financial centre in Europe.

XII. The European Insurance Industry and the Impact Competition from Banks Will Exert on It

OLE AERTHØJ

I have chosen to focus on the following two main topics:

a) the differences in insurance distribution within Europe, and the way the industry is affected by competition from banks, and

b) a description of the transition from a conventional insurance company to a financial supermarket, which my employer, Baltica, has undergone during recent years.

I. INTRODUCTORY COMMENTS ABOUT THE EUROPEAN INSURANCE INDUSTRY

Based on the assumption that most of the participants in this Colloquium have a background in banking or other bank-related activities, I thought it could be worthwhile to make a few comments about the European insurance industry in terms of volume, competitors, legislation etc.

As can be seen from Figure 1, *Europe represents a total premium income of 32 per cent of world premiums*. Within Europe there are vast differences in the *annual premium paid per capita*, as can be seen from Figure 2. These differences are very fundamental when you try to understand the expansion strategies which have been adopted by the insurance companies at present. It is a well known fact that the high growth markets are to be found in the Mediterranean region (in particular in life insurance), whereas many of the mid- and north-European markets seem rather saturated.

When looking at the list of major European insurance companies we find that they are quite large operations. Allianz of West Germany, for example, booked 1987 *premiums* of US $ 16 billion. Except for Japanese competitors, this figure is only exceeded slightly by three US companies, namely State Farm, Prudential and Aetna. If you compare this with the large Japanese companies, however, they are in an entirely different class! Nippon books 1987 premiums just above US $ 40 billion, which is 2.5 times bigger than Allianz, or 50 times bigger than Baltica, which is the largest insurance company in Denmark.

So in the insurance industry as well, the Japanese have achieved leadership.

D. E. Fair and C. de Boissieu (eds), Financial Institutions in Europe Under New Competitive Conditions, 157–174.
© 1990 Kluwer Academic Publishers, Dordrecht. Printed in the Netherlands.

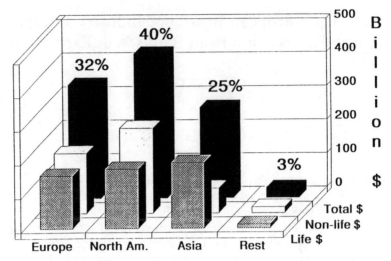

Figure 1. World-wide insurance premiums, 1987.

Figure 3a shows a list of the 15 largest insurance groups in the world. Figure 3b gives a ranking of the 15 largest insurance companies in Europe, and finally Figure 4 gives the size of the largest company in each of the 12 EEC member states.

If you compare size by looking at market values, it may be surprising

Figure 2. Premiums per capita in Europe.
Source: Swiss Re/Sigma 3/1989.

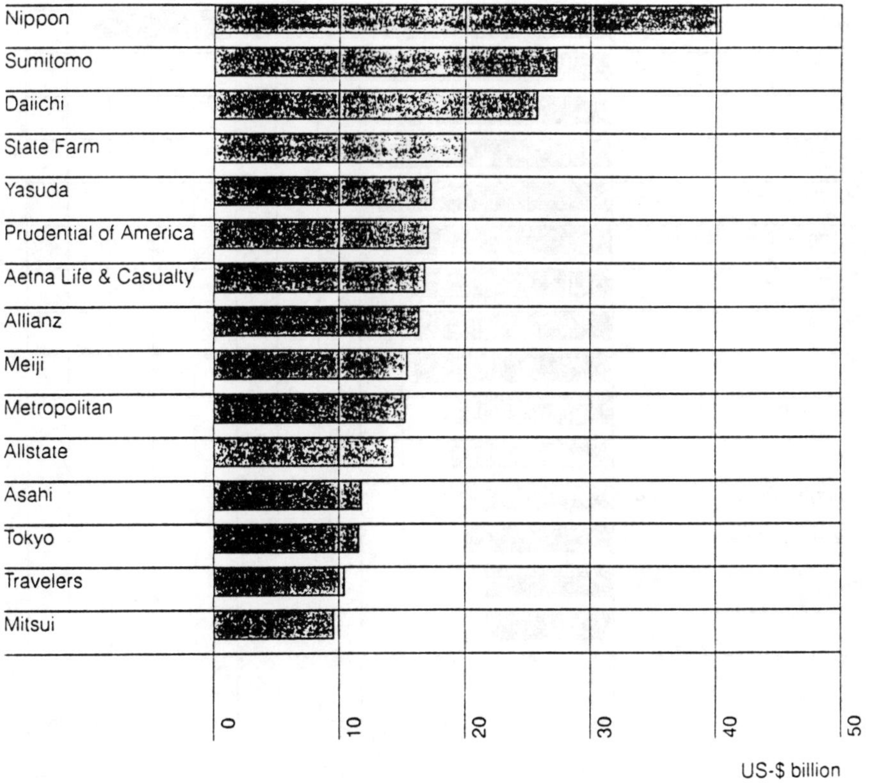

Company					
Nippon					
Sumitomo					
Daiichi					
State Farm					
Yasuda					
Prudential of America					
Aetna Life & Casualty					
Allianz					
Meiji					
Metropolitan					
Allstate					
Asahi					
Tokyo					
Travelers					
Mitsui					

US-$ billion

Figure 3a. The largest insurers in the world in 1987 (overall business).

to many observers, that Italy's Generali represents the highest *market value* of any financial institution (including banks) outside Japan. In Business Week's "the Global 1000", Generali ranks no. 82 on the list, with a market value of almost US $ 15 billion, whereas the next non-Japanese financial institution is American Express with a market value of US $ 13.5 billion. The highest ranking European bank is Deutsche Bank at no. 143, with a market value of $ 10 billion.

II. EEC HARMONIZATION OF INSURANCE REGULATION

Second Non-life Directive

One of the hottest issues within the European insurance industry in recent years has been the EEC's attempt to harmonize the industry by issuing a

160

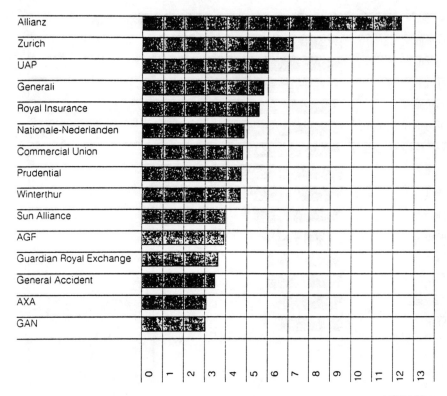

US-$ billion

Fig. 3b. The largest insurers in Europe in 1986 (overall business).

Group	Country	Total income
Allianz	West Germany	9,263
Generali	Italy	5,391
Nationale Nederlanden	Netherlands	5,065
Royal	UK	4,785
UAP	France	4,183
La Union y el Fenix	Spain	981
AG	Belgium	894
Irish Life	Rep. of Ireland	589
Baltica	Denmark	550
Imperio	Portugal	106
Ethniki	Greece	83
Le Foyer	Luxembourg	60

Fig. 4. Top group per EC Market (m ECU) 1986.

constant stream of Directives. The most momentous Directive is the Second Non-life Directive which was finally approved by the Council at the end of 1986, after 13 years of negotiations of the draft!

Whereas it has long been possible for all companies within the Community to establish themselves in other member states, the Second Non-life Directive makes it possible to sell insurance products to clients in other community states, without being formally established there. Thus from mid–1990 when this Directive should be incorporated into the national legislations of the member countries, it will be possible – but perhaps not practical or economical – for insurance companies to market and sell their products throughout the entire EEC.

Industry internationalization

However, the industry has not sat around waiting for the EEC to liberalize the rules regulating the insurance business. If you consider the 15 largest companies listed in Figure 3b, many of these companies are already receiving the larger part of their premium income from abroad, mostly through ownership of foreign subsidiaries. Many of the companies have built up their foreign activities partly by *organic growth* and partly by *acquisitions.* A good example of this is the Generali, which in 1987 earned only 34 per cent of the premium from their home market, Italy: 66 per cent of the premium came from foreign activities which are nicely spread over many markets.

Allianz in 1987 received 36.4 per cent of their premium from abroad, but the Germans have created their international portfolio predominantly through a few major acquisitions (Cornhill in the UK and RAS in Italy). Thus one could claim that Allianz internationalized the easy way compared to companies like Generali or Zürich.

Reciprocity

As in banking, the insurance industry has spent a lot of time discussing reciprocity in an EEC context. The Second Non-life Directive did not contain a provision about reciprocity. Consequently, for example, an American insurer can avoid the hassle of applying for twelve different permits for a pan-European operation. Instead, it could establish a subsidiary in Paris, and run all other European operations as branch offices of the Paris company.

As you will appreciate, this is quite the contrary of the legal situation under the Second Bank Directive, where there is a reciprocity clause.

I personally find it difficult to understand why there should be such a difference between EEC policy towards third party countries regarding banking and insurance. Apparently, the Commission is also having second thoughts, as a more recent proposal for a Second Life Directive contains a provision regarding reciprocity.

What will ultimately be the Commission's policy with respect to reciprocity is difficult to assess at this point in time, but clearly they cannot continue with two different approaches.

Before I close this topic, I would like to add a few comments about the commercial strategy chosen by American and Japanese insurance companies in Europe. When asked about their European strategy, it seems the *Americans* are opting for organic growth. Many of them have been in Europe for decades, so they have a base on which they can build. With a weak dollar, acquisitions might not be attractive to the Americans.

When looking at the *Japanese*, and their financial strength, one would expect them to grow via acquisitions. Nonetheless this has not been the case so far. Several joint venture agreements between major European insurers and Japanese companies have been signed in the last couple of years. To me it seems reasonable to anticipate that these less binding cooperation agreements are their first step in an approach that will ultimately lead to significant acquisitions in the EEC.

III. THE DIFFERENT DISTRIBUTION METHODS IN EUROPEAN INSURANCE

Now having made some introductory comments about the European insurance industry and the regulatory environment it functions in, I shall turn to a brief description of the *distribution channels* used to sell insurance products. To understand what changes the future will bring to distribution of insurance products, it is worth dwelling on the current situation for a moment. Furthermore this description will reveal some national characteristics, as far as distribution is concerned.

Generally speaking, insurance products are sold through the following channels:
– employed sales force
– tied agents
– agents working for several companies
– brokers
– banks
– direct marketing.

The chart presented as Figure 5 demonstrates some of the differences to be found in Europe. As can be seen, there are *vast national differences* between e.g. Germany and the United Kingdom. In Germany most products are sold through tied or exclusive agents, whereas brokers are almost unknown distributors. In the UK on the other hand, insurance distribution

Germany

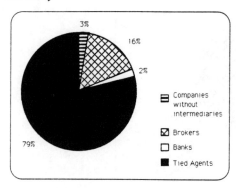

United Kingdom

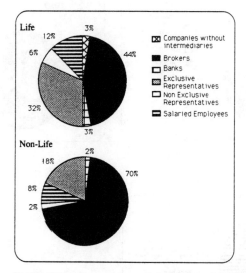

Fox-Pitt, Kelton: *European Insurance Perspective — June 1989*

Fig. 5. Percentage of premiums for each distribution channel.

is dominated by insurance brokers.

If you turn to countries like Holland and France, Figure 6, you will find a much more polarized picture, where there is a good spread amongst brokers, agents, banks, and an employed sales force. In Denmark on the other hand, the insurance companies sell almost exclusively through their *own sales organisation*. Even industrial and marine business are predominantly written on a direct basis.

164

Netherlands

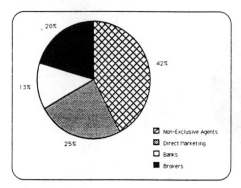

France (Life business)

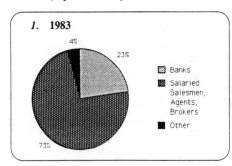

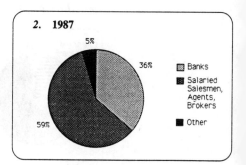

French Non-Life Business (1987)
Source: L'Argus

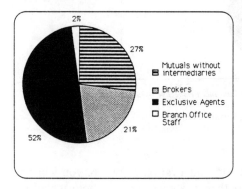

Fig. 6. Percentage of premiums for each distribution channel.

Fox-Pitt, Kelton: *European Insurance Perspective — June 1989*

In Spain, *direct selling*, i.e. selling through your own sales force, is used extensively by the mutuals. The leading mutual in Spain, MAPFRE, for example, has got 1,360 branches across the country, all staffed by MAPFRE. The privately-owned insurance companies use *agents* for their distribution:

As has been mentioned earlier, there are two types of agents: the agent representing several principals, and the exclusive or tied agents. In a country like Switzerland, almost *all agents are tied to one principal.* In countries where agents have traditionally produced business for several insurance companies, there is a fine line between agents and brokers. Normally,however, the latter will canvas the market, and will not have been left with any authority to represent a given company.

In the UK, the *Financial Services Act* has made life very complicated indeed for the non-tied agents. Thus, within life insurance there has been a sharp increase in the number of tied agents, including a number of building societies which are serving as agents in the British context. An estimate by Swiss Bank Corporation/Savory Milln states, that one third of Britain's 45,000 independent agents have changed over from independent to tied agents from mid 1987 to mid 1988. The equivalent proportion of Britain's 14,500 estate agents have gone through the same transition process.

Brokers vary enormously in size. It is difficult to see any similarities between a "High Street" broker in Weybridge, and Sedgwick with its world wide operations and its 12,000 employees. Brokers can be divided into different types, representing different characteristics:
– "High street" broker (non-specialized)
– niche brokers
– mass-market broker (belonging e.g. to a bank or an association)
– mega brokers (5 to 10 in total).

It is interesting to note that out of the first 20 UK brokers, seven of them are mass market brokers, i.e. brokers owned by a bank or an association like the A&A.

If you look at insurance broking in Europe it is a well known fact that the home base for insurance broking is London. This is where you find the trend-setters, and this is where the large European brokers are domiciled. If you go to the Continent, insurance broking it still in its infancy. Many of the so-called mega-brokers are now setting up pan-European operations, and I have no doubt that insurance broking – certainly within the commercial segment – will increase considerably on the Continent in the years to come.

This perhaps would be the right place for me to comment on the *geographic centre for financial activities* (London or Frankfurt). In the world of insurance, in my opinion, there is no place above or even close to London as the centre.

Germany, as far as insurance is concerned, has been a very closed market for many years, which has prevented it from playing any significant role at all. If one should look for a competitor to London it would have to be Paris.

Direct marketing is currently being tried in most markets, but shows quite different results. As the pie-chart regarding Holland in Figure 6 shows, direct marketing seems to be reaching a significant level there. Also in the UK, direct marketing is becoming a more common way of distributing the unsophisticated products, e.g. motor or house content insurance. The breakthrough of direct marketing in insurance, I believe, is hampered by the fact that most composite companies are reluctant to promote this way of distribution, owing to consideration towards their existing sales force.

Banks too, are beginning to play a role in distribution of insurance products throughout Europe. Of course distribution through banks has a bias towards life-insurance, which by its very nature often competes with the bank's own long term saving products.

As can be seen from the pie-charts related to the French life insurance in Figure 6, the banks have gone from representing 23 per cent of the sales of life insurance products in France in 1983 to representing a 36 per cent share in 1987. That is an impressive increase indeed, especially when one considers that generally consumers are conservative people.

IV. COMPETITION BETWEEN BANKS AND INSURANCE COMPANIES

Having looked at the size (and strength) of the trend-setting insurance companies in Europe (Section I), and learnt some of the characteristics of insurance distribution (Section III), now let us turn to the competition between banks and insurance companies.

However, before we start this analysis, let me introduce a distinction of paramount importance: when you discuss operational competition between banks and insurance companies, i.e. competition on the level of selling products to the end-consumer, you have to distinguish between competition for *corporate clients* and for *private customers*. Unfortunately there is not one definition of these terms, but the corporate client will typically represent a need for sophisticated advice, whereas the private client needs standardized products (motor, home fire and contents).

I do not believe that we will see much competition between the two types of financial suppliers in respect of corporate clients – that is certainly not before the mid-1990s. The battle, I think, will be fought on the *mass market* where the products are commodities. I would include life insurance in the mass market, despite the fact that some life insurance products require a well trained sales force. The skills required, however, are related to personal income issues and tax rules, and that of course comes very close to the skills required to sell bank products.

As mentioned before, when I introduced the term "operational competition", you can compete in many ways. Competition, in my view, can be circumvented by e.g. acquiring your competitor, or entering into an alliance with him. Consequently, in this paper I shall be dealing with three types of *interaction* between banks and insurance companies:
– "competing" by way of merging with or acquiring each other;
– strategic alliances regarding joint sales;
– operational competition.

Mergers and acquisitions

Mixed ownership between banks and insurance companies is not a new phenomenon, however most national legislations have been strict about not allowing insurance companies to be major share holders in banks and vice versa.

Nonetheless, looking at Europe you will find countries such as Spain and Turkey, where traditionally there have been very *close ties between the two sectors*. In both instances, it seems that it has been the banks who have been in the controlling seat.

If there are *major cross-holdings*, competition turns to collaboration, and you very quickly promote cross-selling if that seems feasible. Thus, in Spain today, the banks are playing an increasing role in the distribution of life products. In Turkey, banks are extremely powerful in the distribution of insurance products. Of the 25 largest banks in Turkey, there are hardly any which do not have equity interest in an insurance company or vice versa. A common covenant on a loan in Turkey is for the applicant to take out insurance in the lending bank, which provides the bank with a 30 per cent commission as well as security for the assets on which the loan is granted. Not bad business at all!

In France the 1989 merger between CIC and GAN is a good example of combining insurance and bank operations. Both companies are controlled by the government. As for further comments about government ownership, please refer to the next heading.

Over the last year or so, there have been several examples of north European insurance companies buying (or making cooperation agreements with) Italian or Spanish banks. These deals, having been signed by Swiss, German, and British companies, have mostly been centred around distribution of life products in these Mediterranean markets.

Recently, there has also been an example of a *foreign insurance company and a local bank joining forces* in the field of insurance: thus two joint shareholders in Hambros Bank, namely British Guardian Royal Exchange and Istituto Bancario San Paolo di Torino, bought three Rome-based insurance companies early this year.

In Scandinavia we have not seen much in terms of significant cross-holdings between banks and insurance companies. What we have seen, however, is the insurance companies setting up niche banks within their own sphere, but I shall revert to that in Section V. below.

Strategic alliances

This, I believe, is the most obvious way for companies to handle the competitive challenges of the 1990s. Therefore, I am somewhat surprised that we have not seen more strategic alliances formed over the last few years than is the case.

Germany and France represent the markets where we have recently seen significant alliances formed. In Germany, Allianz' alliance with Dresdner Bank received enormous press coverage, not least because many people saw it as a revenge for Deutsche Bank's decision to set up a life insurance company of its own.

In France the alliance between BNP and UAP is a perfect example to demonstrate that alliances between banks and insurance companies are not just fancy ideas being discussed in the offices of the McKinseys or the Boston Consulting Groups of this world, but that even the French Government – who owns these colossal financial institutions – believe in the demolition of traditional financial borderlines. The deal included a minor swap of shares, which is insignificant for the integration of activities.

Operational competition

If you take a broad view of Europe today, I would claim that *the competition between insurance companies and banks is still minimal.* Yet, there are countries where the competition is building up, and where banks are really making inroads into life insurance, but even in such countries the banks are mainly competing for the commission which follows the sale of the product, i.e. acting solely as intermediaries.

Competition, in my opinion, will not continue in this way. I see ahead of us competition where *banks will produce insurance products* within their own sphere, i.e. becoming underwriters rather than intermediaries. What is happening at the moment, is just the beginning of the true competition between insurance companies and banks. If a bank is able to train its staff to sell insurance products – which is not as simple a task as you may think – then it should be no problem for the bank to add on a production unit responsible for the actual underwriting.

There are of course counter arguments to this. One is the restrictions posed by national legislation, but future liberalization should remove this obstacle.

Another – and much more important argument against full competition between banks and insurance companies – is the conservatism of the consumer. If you do not offer something new and innovative to the customer, it will take many years before a majority of private clients change their habits of buying financial products. Let me add to this, that creating innovative products is not an easy task, especially not when the innovation should add value. If you are just combining existing products the only way to make them attractive is by introducing cost savings in the handling of such products.

Future developments

In 1986, Arthur Andersen & Co. carried out a study where 600 bankers, business-men and academics throughout Europe responded to a questionnaire about the future of the European banking industry.

In the study, it became clear – not surprisingly – that small to medium-sized institutions would be *most vulnerable as targets for acquisitions* (Figure 7a). Thus 72 per cent of the respondents saw companies with total assets of less than $ 150 million as likely take-over candidates, whereas only 7 per cent saw the likelihood of institutions with assets above $ 40 billion as candidates for take-over.

Interestingly enough, the European bankers saw themselves more as *hunters than hunted* (Figure 7b)! Eighty-four per cent found it unlikely that European banks would be acquired, whereas 51 per cent found it likely that banks would be acquiring non-bank financial institutions.

I personally believe that we will see at least as many insurance companies buy banks as vice versa, but I admit it is difficult to substantiate. Looking at the list of market values, however, insurance companies are moving rapidly up the ranking list, and furthermore many insurance companies today seem overcapitalized which I do not believe is a general problem within the banking sector.

In this paper, I have concentrated on the competition between banks and insurance companies. This of course does not mean that *other entrants* are not to be expected on the international financial scene. However, when the bankers were asked by Arthur Andersen who would be the most likely entrants to the banking area, they saw insurance companies as the most likely entrant (69 per cent). (Figure 8a).

Targets for Acquisition (by Asset Value)

Small to medium-sized institutions most vulnerable

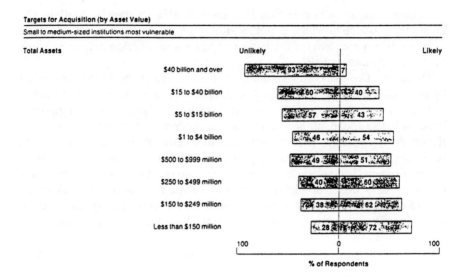

Likelihood of Acquisition Activity by European Banks

European banks as hunters rather than hunted

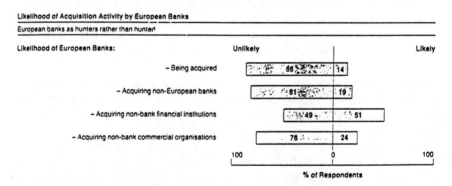

Fig. 7. (Upper panel) Targets for Acquisition (by asset value). (Lower panel) Likelihood of acquisition activity by European banks.

Conversely, when looking at the most feasible areas for banks to enter, insurance broking is exceeded by several other types of services such as stockbroking, information services etc. (Figure 8a). Nonetheless, insurance broking on the whole is considered one of the likely areas for bank expansion, as can be seen from the chart.

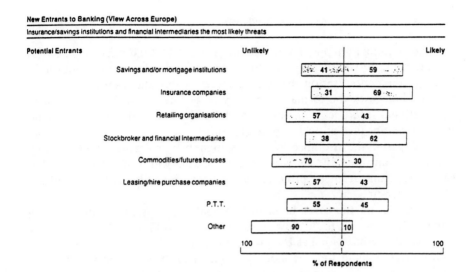

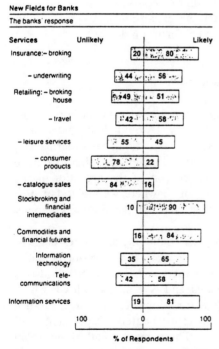

Fig. 8. (Upper panel) New entrants to banking (view across Europe). (Lower panel) New fields for banks.

Conclusion

So what is going to happen? Well, as one of our dear humourists here, Storm P., once said: "It is difficult to tell fortunes – in particular about the future!" I believe the concentration that we have seen within the insurance industry will continue with the formation of very large international entities. These multinational insurance companies will have the financial power to expand their operations further by way of acquisitions.

The largest of the insurance companies might be moving into retail banking, but other than these, the activities within banking will be confined to niches such as fund management, project financing, investment banking and perhaps mortgage lending, etc.

The banks, on the other hand, will probably let insurance underwriting follow their first strategic move into insurance broking, but not until the anticipated liberalization has been implemented.

Moreover, I could well see more strategic alliances being formed between banks and insurance companies, and some of them are likely to be international deals.

Let me end this section by mentioning, that of course the different profit potentials in different markets will affect the expansion strategies. I have found it outside the sphere of this paper to comment on this here.

V. THE BALTICA STORY

SUERF asked me to provide "leading examples of competition across traditional financial borderlines". In all modesty, I would claim that Baltica represents one of the best examples today of a true financial supermarket, which is able to supply a vast number of financial products. I shall therefore conclude my paper by offering a brief description of the activities of the Baltica Group, and explain how we have got to where we are today. For reference purposes, I enclose as Figure 9, a chart of the Baltica company structure.

Baltica is the largest *insurance company* in Denmark, and dates back to 1915. Like most other Danish insurance companies, it is a result of many mergers and acquisitions accomplished over the years. The most recent one was the merger between Baltica-Scandinavia and Nye danske Lloyd, which took place in 1982. Until 1985 we were a traditional composite insurance company with an overall market share of approximately 20 per cent, and listed on the Copenhagen Stock Exchange. The company had about *3,300 employees*, of whom about 1,000 were directly involved with field sales.

In June 1985 a *Holding company* was established over and above the insu-

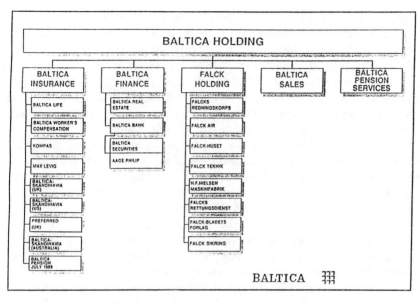

BALTICA ⌗

Fig. 9. Baltica holding, June 1989.

rance company, which at the same time enabled us to create a *finance company* as an affiliate to Baltica Insurance. Baltica Finance's first tasks of course, were to carry out the banking activities related to the insurance company, but soon Baltica Finance developed their own activities. Thus they moved into *stockbroking* in October 1985, and today, after another acquisition of a stockbroking company we are one of the largest stockbrokers in Denmark. In 1986 a *Property Investment Company* was created and listed on the Stock Exchange, and in 1987, *Baltica Bank* was founded. The bank remains a niche bank, predominantly working within corporate finance. However, the bank is also responsible for the *Baltica Car Loan* for private individuals, which is offered as a package offering: financing of the automobile, insurance, replacement car in the event of breakdown, financing of repairs, accident/ life insurance etc. The Car Loan is a good example of a true *combination product*.

The latest development within Baltica Finance has been the 1988 opening of a chain of *Real Estate Agents*, run on a franchise basis. The creation of Baltica Real Estate introduced several innovations to the housing market in Denmark, and the creation received quite a bit of resistance from the competitors. Some people saw it as a threat that big financial companies could use their strength to produce a comprehensive and cohesive package of the financial services you need when you are buying or selling a house. However, the Baltica move quickly led to a total shake-up in the real estate market, and today the market has been totally reorganized. Of course the local mortgage lending institutions are taking part in the reorganization as well.

With effect from the beginning of 1988, Baltica acquired 100 per cent of *Falck*, a company of some 7,500 employees, operating 3,500 *ambulances, fire-fighting trucks* and other vehicles. Founded in 1906, the company today holds a very dominating position when it comes to ambulance services, auto assistance and, although to a lesser degree, also fire fighting.

Contrary to the insurance industry, Falck benefits from a top image standing in Denmark. Consequently, we gained some of the goodwill when we acquired this family owned company. However, the company retains its own logo, image and history, and continues to offer emergency services to all Danes, regardless of the insurance company they use.

As a natural consequence of having these different activities in our organization, it was decided to move the insurance sales force of around 1,000 people into a separate company known as *Baltica Sales*, thus making it possible for them to sell services from other parts of the Group as well.

Thus, today we are a company with 11,000 employees and an annual turnover of 10 billion Danish Kroner ($ 1.4 billion). We rank amongst the 10 largest companies in Denmark, and have within our sphere insurance, banking, stockbroking and Falckservices.

In 1984 we defined what we called the *Security-concept*. By this we mean being able to provide a variety of products solicited by the consumer, when he wants to buy, maintain or protect himself or his assets. With our current organization we have come a long way in positioning ourselves as a true composite supplier of "security products" in Denmark.

The next phase for us, is to expand internationally. The main geographic focus for this strategy is Europe. Today we have four subsidiaries abroad, two in the UK, one in the US and one in Australia. In addition, we recently bought a 10 per cent share of Hambros Bank in the UK, thus placing ourselves as one of the four major shareholders in this bank.

In 1988 the Baltica Holding stock was listed on the London Stock Exchange, and investor presentations are now held on a frequent basis in major financial centres throughout Europe.

Let me end this paper by reverting to the main topic of this colloqium, namely the *breakdown across the traditional financial borderlines*.

In my crystal ball, I see a process towards the demolition of traditional industry divisions within the financial community. The respective *markets will be moving at quite a different pace* owing to differences in legislation, market saturation and former traditions. The over-all development however, will inevitably be influenced negatively by *conservative consumers, whose buying habits are extremely difficult to change.*

XIII. Competition in the British Housing Finance Market

IAN M. LUMSDEN

I. INTRODUCTION

This paper considers the development of competition within and between the national markets for housing finance. It is based primarily on recent experiences in the British markets, with particular emphasis on the response of the British building societies to the rapid increase in competition from national, European and international sources.

The paper considers the influence of deregulation in the British markets and considers the likely impact which the European legislative programma will have both in the UK and in other European Community countries to achieve the completion of the internal markets. A number of options for diversification open to specialist housing finance institutions are considered. Some recent examples of diversification activities are discussed.

II. COMPETITION

The British housing finance markets over the last ten years have undergone a dramatic change. This is best illustrated by looking at the market share positions of the main institutional suppliers of mortgage finance for the purchase of residential property.

As Table 1 shows, building societies have been the dominant suppliers of loans for house purchase in the UK. Ten years ago they had 80 per cent of net advances but this market share fell to 50 per cent in 1987 as a result of a significant increase in competition for the supply of house purchase finance. Building societies' loss of market share came at a time when the total market was growing rapidly. From Table 1 it would appear that over the last ten years the demand for house purchase finance has increased almost sevenfold. This is not really the case. A more accurate interpretation would be that the supply of mortage finance has increased sevenfold.

One of the prime features of the British housing finance markets up to the early 1980s was rationing. Building societies, the dominant suppliers, operated within a cartel agreement which acted in a way which held mortgage rates significantly below market clearing levels. In practice this meant that

D. E. Fair and C. de Boissieu (eds), Financial Institutions in Europe Under New Competitive Conditions, 175–190.
© 1990 Kluwer Academic Publishers, Dordrecht. Printed in the Netherlands.

Table 1. Loans for house purchase.

Period	Building societies £m	Local authorities £m	Insurance companies and pension funds £m	Monetary sector £m	Misc, financial institutions £m	Other public sector £m	Total £m
1979	5,271	294	227	597		72	6,461
1980	5,722	454	264	593		300	7,333
1981	6,331	269	88	2,448		353	9,489
1982	8,147	555	6	5,078		355	14,141
1983	10,928	−306	126	3,531	225	21	14,525
1984	14,572	−195	250	2,043	445	− 43	17,072
1985	14,711	−502	200	4,223	425	59	19,116
1986	19,541	−506	435	4,671	2,379	61	26,581
1987	14,580	−431	769	10,055	3,952	51	29,772
1988	23,677	−313	796	10,877	5,008	143	40,188

Source: Financial Statistics, Table 9.4, HMSO

Notes

1. The figures for insurance companies and pension funds are less reliable than those for other institutions.
2. The monetary sector includes the banks and trustee savings banks.

Table 2. Average mortgage and 3 month LIBOR.

Year	Average mortgage rate %	Average 3 month LIBOR %	Interest rate differential %
1979	11.94	13.74	−1.80
1980	14.92	16.71	−1.79
1981	14.01	14.04	−0.03
1982	13.30	12.37	0.93
1983	11.03	10.20	0.83
1984	11.84	10.03	1.81
1985	13.47	12.32	1.15
1986	12.07	11.02	1.05
1987	11.61	9.77	1.84
1988	10.96	10.41	0.55

mortgage rates were generally lower than capital market rates, e.g. 3 month London Interbank Offered rate (LIBOR). As a result, the refinancing of mortgage loans in the capital markets, a common feature of the United States and continental European housing finance markets, was uneconomic in the UK. The British housing finance system was, therefore, dependent on the retail savings market for its funding.

This was still the case when the British clearing banks were released from credit restrictions which had had the effect of keeping them out of the housing finance markets. The banks' change of emphasis towards the retail savings which they needed to attract to refinance their mortgage lending put severe pressure on the building societies' interest rate cartel which finally broke in October 1983. As a result the cost of retail funds increased to the point where the mortgage rate rose above three month LIBOR and, therefore, it became cost effective to refinance mortgages in the capital markets. (See Table 2 for details).

To help contend with this significant change in the competitive environment building societies pressed for and were given new powers to raise funds in the capital markets. Most of the largest societies made considerable use of these powers, a trend which has continued strongly over the last six years, as Table 3 clearly demonstrates. The net wholesale funding position of building societies peaked in 1986 as pressure on retail savings increased as a result of competition from the British government's continuing privatization pro-gramme and a strong bull equities market. This position changed quite dramatically following the stock market collapse in October 1987 as retail savers returned to the safety and security of building society investments.

It was within this market framework that the 'new lenders' emerged as a major competitive force in the British housing finance markets. These new lending institutions did not come within either the banking or the building society sector as they were not deposit-takers. They raised all their funds on the capital markets and distributed their loans to retail customers through existing intermediary channels such as mortgage brokers and real estate agents.

Table 3. Building societies wholesale funding.

Calendar year end	Retail inflow (net increase in shares and deposits outstanding) £m	Net wholesale funding £m
1980	7.159	
1981	7,196	102
1982	10,515	252
1983	10,564	1,635
1984	13,217	2,228
1985	13,428	3,093
1986	12,684	6,141
1987	14,417	3,150
1988	20,904	5,471

Source: Table 20 – Housing Finance No. 3 July 1989.
Building Societies Association.

As Table 1 shows they achieved a remarkably high degree of market penetration in a very short space of time. They were helped by a rapidly growing mortgage market which allowed the entry of new suppliers more easily than during a static or declining market.

The new lenders had a particular interest in encouraging the development in the UK of a United States style secondary mortgage market. Some of the new lenders had capacity constraints based on the levels of their initial capital. Some had the indirect motive of creating a market in mortgage-backed securities in which they had considerable trading experience in the United States. A secondary mortgage market had not developed in the UK because the basic reasons for its existence in the United States – fixed rate mortgages and geographic restrictions between the various States – did not exist in the UK. This is still mainly the case today.

In addition to competition from these new lenders, building societies have also had to contend with the entry of specialist mortgage lenders from other Member States of the European Community as they began to position themselves in anticipation of the completion of the internal market in financial services. For example, some of the Danish specialist mortgage banks have established an operational presence in London to provide a mortgage service to Danish housebuilders developing residential property in the south of England. Of the French housing finance specialists, UCB, the mortgage subsidiary of Compagnie Bancaire acquired a small lending institution in London. Société Generale have linked with Skipton Building Society to distribute "French" mortgage funds in the UK. In addition many of the foreign banks already established in the UK turned their attention to the housing finance sector.

III. REGULATION

With buoyant demand for house purchase loans, the break-up of the cartel, increased competition from the banks and a general trend towards deregulation, it was not surprising that there was increasing pressure from building societies for greater freedom. The 1962 Building Societies Act under which building societies were operating was based broadly on legislation drafted in the last century. The 1986 Act was broadly welcomed by building societies in that it gave powers to engage in a number of new activities related to the British housing and retail financial services markets. There were, however, a number of key restrictions imposed by the Act which caused societies problems in a market place which was changing at a much greater pace than had been foreseen. This brought about a revision in powers and limits in 1988 which has resulted in an Act which now poses few serious limitations

on what building societies can do. In summary the main areas in which building societies can operate are as follows:
- *Wholesale funding:* building societies can raise up to 40 per cent of their liabilities from capital markets from a wide variety of instruments
- *Lending:* loans secured by first mortgage to owner-occupiers of residential property: currently at least 90 per cent of a building society's commercial assets have to be in this category but the proportion will be reduced in stages to 75 per cent by the beginning of 1993. The remaining 10 per cent (rising to 25 per cent) of commercial assets can be in the form of other loans secured on land, investment in subsidiaries, the direct ownership of land and property for residential development and unsecured loans
- *Services:* building societies can offer a broad range of services under six main groupings. These are banking services, investment services, insurance services, trusteeship, executorship and land services. The definitions of these are very wide-ranging but a few of the main activities now permitted to building societies are: money transmission, unsecured personal loans, foreign exchange and currency services, managing unit trusts and pension schemes, owning up to 15 per cent of a general insurance company and up to 100 per cent of a life assurance company, estate agency and property survey and valuation services.

In addition the Building Societies Act created a regulatory framework which differed from that for the UK banks. It established a risk-asset weighting system which requires in certain circumstances, building societies to have higher levels of capital backing than the banks for identical assets, e.g. unsecured personal loans. The BIS regulations and the proposed EC harmonisation of solvency ratios will encourage the removal of this disparity.

IV. STRATEGIC RESPONSE

For the first time in their history building societies faced major strategic choices in their response to deregulation and increased competition. Not surprisingly there have been some significant differences in the way different building societies have responded. Table 4 shows the range of services now being offered by the largest societies. Within this, however, there are major differences in emphasis and priority. For example, Halifax Building Society, the largest in the UK, has built up a network of almost 700 estate agency offices whereas the Woolwich, now the third largest Building Society, has only 40 outlets. As with the banking sector greater emphasis is being placed on generating off-balance-sheet income. Building societies are mutual institutions and, therefore, retained earnings are the primary source of capital to support growth and diversification strategies. This is likely to remain the

Table 4. New activities of the top 15 building societies as at beginning of July 1989.

New activity	Halifax	Abbey National	Nationwide Anglia	Woolwich Equitable	Alliance & Leicester	Leeds Permanent	National & Provincial
Investment advice, polarisation	Tied to Standard Life, but offers independent advice through subsidiary	Tied to Friends Provident, but offers independent advice through subsidiary	Independent but under review	Tied to Sun Alliance, but offers independent advice through sub sidiary	Independent, but will tie to Scottish Amicable from 1st August	Tied to Norwich Union	Independent, but will tie to own life subsidiary. Indep. subsidiary planned
General insurance	Yes	Yes	Yes	Yes	Yes	Yes	Yes
Estate agencies, and no of branches	Yes 696	Yes 426	Yes 471	Yes 548	Yes 112	Yes 140	No 0
Unsecured loans	Yes - own money	Yes - own money	Yes - own money	Yes - own money	Yes - own money	Yes - 50% joint venture with North West Sec.	Yes - with Forward Trust
Secured loans	Yes - own money	Yes - own money	Yes - own money	Yes - own money	Yes - own money	Yes - own money	Yes - own money
Cheque book account and cheque card	Planned this year - own clearing	Yes - own clearing	Yes - cleared through Co-op	Planned this year - cleared through B of E	No	No	No
Credit card	Visa (own brand, joint venture with Bank of Scotland)	Under consideration	Access (Midland Bank's)	Under consideration	Visa (Bank of Scotland's)	Visa (own card)	Visa (own card)
ATM Network and no of own machines	Own network 1200 machines	Link 678 machines	Link & Matrix 323 machines	Link & Matrix 198 machines	Matrix 107 machines	Matrix 101 machines	Matrix 52 machines
PEP's	No	Own share pep launched in July	No	Independent advice through subsidiary	No	No	Yes - execution only
Unit trusts	No	Under consideration	No	Under consideration	No	No	Yes - execution only
Pension plans	Independent advice through subsidiary	Own brands through branches, independent advice through subsidiary	No	With Sun Alliance through branches, independent advice through subsidiary	No	No	Independent advice
Stock-broking	No	Under consideration	No	Under consideration	No	No	Yes - with Allied Provincial (execution only)
Off-shore foreign services	Jersey - expatriate savings	Jersey and Gibraltar - mort services and expatriate savings Spain and Italy - mortgage lending	Isle of Man - expatriate savings	Under consideration	No	Isle of Man - expatriate savings	Isle of Man - expatriate savings
Property development	Financing of third party projects only	Yes	Yes	Yes	Financing of third party projects only	Yes	Yes
Conversion to plc?	Not envisaged in present plans Advisers: NM Rothschild	Yes Advisers: Kleinwort Benson Warburgs	Not envisaged in present plans Advisers: Warburgs	Not envisaged in present plans	Under consideration Advisers: Schroders Hoare Govett	Not envisaged in present plans Advisers: Hambros	Under consideration Advisers: JP Morgan Cazenove

Note: The link and Matrix ATM network collectively have approximately 2,220 machines of which about 500 are shared. Halifax's own network has joined LINK. Matrix will merge into LINK early next year.

Bradford & Bingley	Cheltenham & Gloucester	Brittannia	Bristol & West	Birmingham Midshires	Yorkshire	Northern Rock	Town & Country
Independent	Tied to Legal & General	Independent, but will tie to own subsidiary if acquisition of FS Assurance is completed	Independent but under review	Independent	Independent	Tied to Legal & General	Tied to Legal & General
Yes	Yes	Yes	Yes	Yes	Yes	Yes	Yes
No	Yes	Yes	Yes	Yes	Yes	Yes	Yes
0	19	50	60	28	18	61	13
Yes - own money	Yes - with Lloyds Bowmaker	Yes - with Lloyds Bomaker	Yes - with Lloyds Bomaker	Yes - own money	Yes - with Forward Trust	Yes - with Chartered Trust	Yes - with Co-op
Yes - own money	Yes - own money	Yes - own money	Yes - own money	Yes - own money	Yes - own money	Yes - own money	Yes - own money
No	No	No	Under consideration	Yes - cleared through TSB	No	Yes - cleared through Co-Op	Yes - own money
No	No	No	No	Visa (TSB's)	No	Planned this year	Visa (own card)
Matrix	No	Link	Matrix	Link – Some own mach. planned this year	Link	Link	Link
56 machines		27 machines	54 machines		27 machines	15 machines	20 machines
Yes - with James Capel	No	No	No	Yes - with MIM Britannia	Independent advice through 'advice centers'	No	No
No	Yes - execution only	No	No	No	Independent advice through 'advice centers'	No	No
Own deposit based brands, and independent advice	Yes - with Legal & General	Independent advice	Own deposit based brand, and independent advice	Via independent broker	Independent advice	AVC's to companies when unit linked	Yes - with Legal & General
No	Yes - with BZW (execution only)	Yes - with Henry Cooke Lumsden	No	No	Yes - with BWD (in which has equity stake)	No	No
Isle of Man - expatriate savings	No	Isle of Man - expatriate savings	Guernsey - expatriate savings and estate agent Jersey - estate agent	No	No	No	No
No	Yes	No	Financing of third party projects only	Yes	No	Yes	Under development
Not envisaged in present plans	Under consideration	Not envisaged in present plans	Not envisaged in present plans	Not envisaged in present plans Advisors: Morgan Grenfell	Not envisaged in present plans	Not envisaged in present plans	Not envisaged in present plans

case despite new powers to raise other forms of capital. As an alternative, building societies have the power to convert from a mutual institution into a public limited company (plc) and operate as a bank under the Banking Act. Abbey National, the second largest building society, has recently completed its conversion into a bank using these new powers. It is now the fifth largest bank (in terms of market capitalization) in the UK.

Returning to the question of the strategic response of building societies to their new environment, one or two particular themes emerge. Perhaps the main distinction is based on size – the largest societies have more options than the smallest. Within this context management resources become a critical factor. Rationalization within the building society industry is a process which has been going on since the turn of the century as Table 5 shows. There will be continuing pressure for further mergers as competition intensifies. This could bring in a European dimension which is considered in more detail below.

Building societies have perhaps three possible ways of diversifying:
– *horizontally within the UK;*
– *vertically within the UK;*
– *horizontally into other EC markets.*

As can be seen from Table 4 most societies have adopted the first option by introducing personal consumer lending products, including credit cards, insurance services and a range of off-balance-sheet activities which exploit their core strengths of distribution networks and stable customer base. Although this gives the impression that building societies are becoming more like banks, the Building Societies Act still requires societies to concentrate on personal sector operations.

A smaller number of societies have concentrated their efforts on vertical

Table 5. UK building societies: progress.

Year	No. of Societies	No. of share investors 000's	No. of borrowers 000's	Amount advanced £m	Total assets £m
1900	2,286	585	–	–	60
1930	1,026	1,449	720	89	371
1950	819	2,256	1,508	270	1,256
1960	726	3,910	2,349	560	3,166
1970	481	10,265	3,655	1,954	10,819
1980	273	30,636	5,383	9,506	53,793
1988	130	43,813	7,369	46,929	188,844

Source: Table 21 – Housing Finance No. 3 July 1989.
Building Societies Association.

diversification around their core housing finance products. This involves the development of an integrated house-buying service which includes estate agency, property valuation, property development and housebuilding and possibly the ownership of rented property. These services may in future be supplemented with the provision of legal services, if the necessary legislation is introduced to permit this. Vertical integration has given societies tighter control of their sources of business as mentioned later with the acquisition of estate agencies.

At present the signs are that only a few of the largest societies will contemplate extending their services to other parts of the European Community. Prior to its conversion to a bank Abbey National was the only British building society to have established an operational presence elsewhere in continental Europe. The largest society, the Halifax, has set up a new business unit to implement its European strategies. A few other societies are taking similar steps.

V. THE SINGLE EUROPEAN MARKET

As discussed above a few building societies will exploit opportunities which arise in other parts of the Community following the opening up of the European financial services markets after 1992. The majority, however, are likely to regard the 1992 programme as a source of increased competition in the UK housing finance markets. The UK financial services markets are already widely accepted as the most open and competitive in the European Community. This has been clearly demonstrated in Section I. Competition is not confined to financial institutions from other parts of Europe – it includes competitors from Japan, USA and Australia. There are still a number of European specialist housing institutions which have not yet been given the freedom to operate outside their domestic markets. Some will be developing plans to enter the UK mortgage market although these may be deferred until the next upturn in demand.

Broadly speaking there are four main entry routes into the financial services markets of other Member States – cold start, acquisition, joint venture or direct cross-border operation. As far as British building societies are concerned this final option is not yet available although the implementation of the Second Banking Co-ordination Directive may require changes to the Building Societies Act 1986 to permit direct operation across European borders. Cold starts, i.e. the creation of a new subsidiary with its own management, administration and distribution in a costly and high risk option. Cold starts or direct operations may be preferred in some of the smaller markets where there is little or no availability of suitable acquisitions or joint venture partners.

Table 6. Recent mergers, alliances and acquisitions within the EC Financial Services Sector.

Bank	Major recent moves in Europe	Recent domestic acquisitions
Belgium		
ASLK-CGER Bank	Banque U.C.L. Luxembourg, 51% 1987	–
Banque Bruxelles Lambert	Banque Louis Dreyfus, Paris merchant bank, 100% since 4/89; Crédit European, Luxembourg, banking, 100%, 1987; BBL Finance Ireland, Dublin, 100% 1987; Euroventures Benelux, Holland, venture capital joint venture, 1988	Infotrade; Trasec; Eurodata Services Belgium; Oridata Base
Crédit Communal de Belgique	CREGEM Finance Netherlands; CREGEM Investment (Ireland); CREGEM International Luxembourg, 1990	–
Generale Bank	Amsterdam-Rotterdam Bank, Netherlands, 10%, 1988; Cogeba-Gonet, Switzerland, private banking, 100%	T.C.D., insurance broker, 77.34%; Credit Europ; Belgofactors, 50%
Denmark		
Copenhagen Handelsbank	–	Morville Group, stockbrokers, 1987
Privatbanken	–	A. Vollmond & Co Securities, 100%, 1989
France		
Banque Nationale de Paris	BNP Mortgages, UK, former subsidiaries of Chemical Bank, 1988; United Overseas Bank, Geneva, 50%, 1988; BNP Norge, 75% 1988; BNP AK Dresdner Bankasi, 30%, 1988; BNP Securities London, stockbrokers, 75%	Du Bouzet, Paris, 1987; Union des Assurances de Paris, agreement to cross-sell financial products; Crédit Universal, 87%
West Germany		
Commerzbank	ADIG Investment Luxembourg, investment fund, 37.5%, 1988; Jean de Cholet-Gilles Dupont, Paris, broker, 3%, 1988	Leonberger Bausparkasse, home loan association, 40%; Commerz Unternehmens-beteiligungs, interests in small companies; Commerz International Capital Management, asset manager 100%
Bayerische Hypotheken-und Wechsel-Bank (Hypobank)	Richard Ellis Financial Services, UK, joint venture, property finance, 1989; joint venture, property finance, Spain, with Banco Popular Espanol, 1989; Bayernhypo Finance, Netherlands, founded 1986; Hypo Property Finance, Ireland, founded 1988; Hypo Capital Management Luxembourg, founded 1989	Heimstat Bauspar, Munich, building society, 75%, 1988; Hypo Immobilien Service, Germany, founded 1988; Hypo Capital Management, Germany, founded 1988

Table 6. Continued.

Bank	Major recent moves in Europe	Recent domestic acquisitions
West Germany (cont.)		
Bayerische Vereinsbank	Közep Europai Hitelbank, Budapest, joint venture; Banque International de Credit et de Gestion, Monaco, joint venture; ADIG Investment Luxembourg, investment bank, 37.5%	–
Ireland		
Bank of Ireland	Bank America Finance, London, home mortgages, 1987	Irish Civil Service Building Society
Italy		
Banca Commerciale Italiana	Comit Sociedade de Investimentos, Lisbon, financial intermediation services, founded 1989; Banca Internazionale Lombarda, joint venture with Banque Paribas, UBS, Mediobanca and Assicurazioni Generali, 1988; S G Warburg Group, London 2.2%, 1986	–
Banca Nazionale dell'Agricoltura	–	Nagrafin Fiduciaria, 20%, 1988; Nagrafin Investmenti, 62%, 1988; Interbanca Banca per Financiamenti a medio e Lungo Termine, 49.4%; Bolefin Factor, 62%, 1987; Assiaudit, 45%, 1986
Banca Nazionale del Lavoro	Hesse Newman, Hamburg, universal bank, 100%, 1988; Sogegred, Zurich, trading company, 64%, 1987	Lavoro Broker Assicurazioni, insurance brokerage, 1987; Lavoro Vita, life insurance, 1987; Lavoro Commissionaria, stock exchange brokerage, 1987
Cassa di Risparmio delle Provincie Lombarde (Cariplo)	Cie, International de Banque, France, 1988; Istituto Bancario Italiano (100% controlled by Cariplo) is exchanging shareholdings with Banco Jover, of the Banco Santander Group	Cia, Finanziaria Italiana, merchant banking, 1988; PAROS, insurance broker; Cassa di Risparmio di Calabria, bank, 16.67%, 1987; Cassa di Risparmio di Spoleto, bank, 33.3%, 1987
Istituto Bancario San Paolo di Torino	Hambros, London raised stake to 12%, 1989; Banque Vernes et Commerciale de Paris, merchant banking, raised stake to 100%, 1988; Credit Commercial de France, Paris, 1%, 1988; Cie. Financières de Suez, Paris, 1.1%, 1987	Acquired three insurance companies from Acqua Marcia Group in joint venture with Guardian Royal Exchange, 1989; Crediop, medium and long term credit to the public sector, 40%, 1989

186

Table 6. Continued.

Bank	Major recent moves in Europe	Recent domestic acquisitions
Netherlands		
Algemene Bank Nederland	Acquired Vienna branch of Bank of America, 1988; Algemene Bank Nederland (Luxembourg), founded 1988; ABN Financial Services (International), Ireland, offshore financing, 1988; Alicon Borsmaeglerskab, Denmark, bond trading, 50%, 1988	Interests in many leasing companies
Spain		
Banco Hispano Americano	Acquired 75% of subsidiary of Continental Illinois Bank, Belgium, 1988; Euroventures, venture capital, joint venture; Hispano Americano Sociedade de Investimentos, Lisbon, 1987	–
Banco Popular Espanol	Europensions, joint venture with Allianz (Germany) and RAS (Italy), pension plans, 60%, 1988; joint venture with Allianz and RAS for life insurance products, 30%, 1989	–
Banco Santander	Banco de Comercio e Industria, Portugal, corporate and investment banking, 10%, 1988; Royal Bank of Scotland, strategic alliance in which Santander acquired 10% of RBS and RBS 2.5% of Santander, 1988; CC Bank, Germany, 50% joint venture with RBS, 1988; Credit du Nord Belge, 50% joint venture with RBS, 1988; Istituto Bancario Italiano, 30%, 1989	Grupo Banco Comercial Espanol, 74% 1987; Bansalibar, Ceivasa, Carmosa, Fibansa, Norvasa, majority control, 1988
United Kingdom		
Barclays Bank	Puget-Mahe, Paris, stockbroker, 44%, 1988	Barclays de Zoete Wedd, stockbroker, 100%, 1987
Lloyds Bank	Finance Plus, French government bond market maker, 30%, 1987	Abbey Life Insurance, 57.6%
Midland Group	Midland Montagu, Stockholm, formerly Carnegie-Montagu, interest increased to 100%, 1989; Midland Montagu Bank, Stockholm, founded 1989; Euromobiliare, Italy, investment bank 46%, 1988; Sundal	–

Table 6. Continued.

Bank	Major recent moves in Europe	Recent domestic acquisitions
United Kingdom (cont.)		
National Westminster Bank	Collier, Oslo, stockbrokers, 100%, 1987; Midland Montagu AS, Oslo, founded 1986 Banco Natwest March, Spain, shareholding increased to 83.6%, 1989; bought five branches of Banque de l'Union Européenne, France, and added to NWB France, 1988; Sellier, France, stockbrokers, 100%, 1988; Banco NatWest March bought 88% of Banco de Asturias, 1988	Wood Mackenzie, 1988
Royal Bank of Scotland Group	Banca Santander, Spain, commercial cooperation agreement, in which RBS owns 2.5% of Santander and Santander owns 10% of RBS, 1988; CC Bank, Germany, 50% joint venture with Santander, 1988; Crédit du Nord Belge, 50%, joint venture with Santander, 1988	–
TBS Group	Hill Samuel Espana, marketing of fund management, 49%; Bansander Noble Lowndes, Spain 25%, Andre de Lorrard Noble Lowndes, France, 5%, Neuberger Nobel Lowndes, Germany, 50%, employee benefits consultancies; Haliden, Ireland, personal financial products, 50%; TSB Private Bank International, Luxembourg, founded 1988	Graham Motors, 1988; Hill Samuel Group, 1987; Target Group, 1987; Boston Financial, 1987

Source: "Banks' Winning Gambits for 1992", Institutional Investor – June 1989

The major issues concerning entry into another European market are access to suitable channels of distribution, availability of good quality local management with local market knowledge, access to cost-effective sources of refinancing, and possibly some local production capacity.

Retail financial services products throughout Europe are mainly delivered through branch networks unique to the owning institution. There is now a growing tendency for branches to sell a wider range of financial services, some of which are provided by other suppliers. This is increasingly the case with insurance products. This development can go beyond the sale of products. Table 6 shows insurance companies have featured quite prominently in the spate of recent mergers, alliances and acquisitions within the financial services sector throughout the European Community. In some European countries insurance is already an integral part of the banking sector with almost all insurance companies owned by banks, e.g. Spain. In contrast the insurance sector in West Germany and the UK is more independent but still relies heavily on banks and specialist lending institutions for the intermediation of core insurance products. The West German situation is changing as the trend towards 'Allfinanz', the financial services supermarket, grows. This is most clearly demonstrated by the recent decisions of Deutsche Bank to form its own Bausparkasse and Insurance Company.

On a cross-border basis the Spanish distribution channels of Winterthur, the large Swiss insurance company, have been made available to Abbey National through a recently created joint venture company, Abbeycor Nacional, which also includes Cor Group, a local capital market specialist in Spain. Looking at this situation in reverse it is clear that British building societies could provide a suitable entry route into the UK markets for European and other foreign institutions. This could take the form of an agency agreement or at the other extreme a takeover following demutualization.

In some markets new channels of distribution are beginning to open up. The issue of credit cards and loan products by multiple retailers has followed the American example in most European markets but as yet there is no sign of this taking on a cross-border dimension. This may, however, follow any European diversification of the major retailing groups.

In the field of housing finance the pivotal role of the real estate agent in intermediating credit and insurance products is being increasingly exploited in continental Europe. In the UK markets where the majority of housing finance is used to turn over the existing stock, the importance of the estate agent as the point of sale for financial services increased dramatically with the removal of mortgage rationing. The major financial services suppliers reacted in the UK by acquiring a large proportion of the independent estate agency groups to form national branded chains. The long-term effects of this defensive strategy have still to be seen but it could be argued that a similar acquisition/concentration process could take place in the housing finance markets of continental Europe as the emphasis changes from financing the purchase of new houses to financing the purchase of existing properties.

Availability of good quality management resources will be a constraining factor to financial institutions broadening their European operations. To a certain extent the acquisition route may help to limit this problem. Institutions contemplating a pan-European operation will have to have in place a management development programme geared to providing certain core skills for application in other European markets. This is in addition to language-learning programmes which will have to become a standard feature of broader-based European institutions. Local skills may have to be acquired in the country of operation. Where these are in short supply their price will go up. This could have a major impact on the start-up costs for cold start or joint venture operations, where local market knowledge will be a critical factor.

On the funding side the housing finance markets throughout Europe are supplied from both retail savings and wholesale funds. In the UK variable rate instruments dominate the mortgage markets whereas in other European markets, notably West Germany, fixed rate finance is the norm. Access to the domestic capital markets will be much easier than access to local retail savings where savings banks tend to be mutual or municipally owned. At a European level the capital markets already function efficiently as the development of new instruments, particularly currency and interest rate swaps, enable the transfer of capital from one market to another. The development of the ECU as a common European currency will take a long time to reach the stage where it can play a major role in cross-border retail financial services activities. One of the major funding problems facing long-term credit institutions is the availability of long-term debt instruments in the emerging housing finance markets in southern Europe. This could lead to a growing acceptance of variable rate financing as well as to the development of longer-term fixed rate or indexed debt instruments.

The need for maturity, rate and currency risk management in addition to credit risk management will put greater responsibility on directors, management and supervisors as financial institutions develop their European operations. Risk management techniques are available as are staff with experience in their use. The need for stronger and evenhanded regulation and supervision is recognised in many of the European Directives which relate to the financial services sector. Minimum harmonisation of standards for capital adequacy, large debt exposure, etc, goes some way to creating the European level playing field.

VI. SUMMARY

Increased competition has been a major feature of the housing finance markets in the UK and is becoming so elsewhere in Europe. Deregulation is breaking down the traditional boundaries between the institutional suppliers of retail financial services. The strategies adopted by British building societies in coping with their changing environment may well be mirrored in other parts of the European Community.

The housing finance markets in the European Community will become more open, producing opportunities for some of the larger building societies to expand their operations into other Member States. Joint ventures and acquisitions will be more favoured than cold starts or direct cross-border operation as these are likely to provide more immediate access to distribution, local management and market knowledge. Funding will be a key competitive factor with capital market operations being easier to establish than the development of a retail savings base. Although the major emphasis will be a realignment of the supply of financial services, wider choice of products at more competitive prices will benefit European consumers of financial services.

XIV. Competition in Retail Banking: Threat or Promise?

LESLIE T. JOHNSON

I. INTRODUCTION

It was Voltaire, the eighteenth century French philosopher, who said that, "if you see a banker jump out of the window, jump after him – there's sure to be a profit in it." And the group who appear to have taken these words to heart are the banks themselves. In the name of competition, they have followed each other in introducing new technology, new products and new management structures.

But competition, in any meaningful sense of that word, has existed amongst the large UK retail banks only since 1971. Prior to this date the banks operated as cartels, and only competed amongst themselves by means of their branch networks. Fees and interest rates, charged and paid, were subject to various agreements in both England and Scotland which dated from the nineteenth century, and these were condoned by the authorities on the basis that the agreements helped hold interest rates down.

In 1971 the authorities introduced a new policy 'Competition and credit control'. Under this new policy, the clearing banks agreed to abolish the various cartel agreements and to actively compete with one another. However, real competition emerged only gradually and it was not until the 1980s that the clearing banks began to compete with each other, and with other financial institutions.

This paper seeks to examine how the clearing banks have changed their strategies during the 1980s in order that some pointers of likely behaviour in the future can be ascertained; it also seeks to ask whether the authorities should be concerned with the changes discussed. The plan of the paper is as follows: in Section II we examine the amount of competition that has occurred and the new domestic markets that the banks have entered. In Section III the implications of the change in behaviour are considered. Cost reduction and the use of new technology are examined in Section IV. In Section V the effects that 1992 are likely to have upon the clearing banks are considered, and some tentative conclusions are offered in Section VI.

Before continuing, a word of caution must be given regarding the statistics

D. E. Fair and C. de Boissieu (eds), Financial Institutions in Europe Under New Competitive Conditions, 191–202.
© 1990 *Kluwer Academic Publishers, Dordrecht. Printed in the Netherlands.*

used in this paper. Reliable statistics for the UK clearing banks are notoriously difficult to obtain. Individual banks have claimed, for example, that whilst they know how many branches they have, they do not know how many were opened/closed in any particular year. In a similar way, records are not kept for how many staff are employed on UK banking business as opposed to a global staff figure. Fortunately, three of the largest clearing banks (Barclays, Midland and National Westminster) are quoted on the New York Stock Exchange and, as such, have to file a separate report each year (Form 20-F) to satisfy the requirements of the Securities and Exchange Commission. These reports provide far more information than the Annual reports issued in the UK and the data used in Sections II and III of this paper have been obtained from the Form 20-F reports. However, there is still a suspicion that the three banks do not use the definitions in identical ways. Therefore, cross-bank comparisons are not strictly reliable and the data should be seen as indicating trends.

II. COMPETITION AND NEW PRODUCTS

Competition for the UK clearing banks has increased rapidly during the 1980s in both the international/corporate sector and the domestic personal sector. In this paper we will concentrate our attention on the competition faced in the domestic personal sector, because that is the sector that has become increasingly important to the banks, in particular since 1984. As competitive pressures increased in the international/corporate sectors with the development of new markets and new players along with the increasing problems of the international debtor countries, the banks turned to the domestic personal sector to increase their lending business and profitability.

Table 1 shows that lending to the domestic personal sector by the three clearing banks (Barclays, Midland and National Westminster) has more than doubled since 1984 to stand at over £ 41 billion and now accounts for some 42 per cent of all domestic lending. It can be expected that this trend will continue during the 1990s.

This increase in business has come about, primarily, from the increase in lending for house purchase, as well as aggressive marketing campaigning by the banks. Traditionally, the clearing banks did not grant house mortgages, except for their staff and a few individual customers, leaving that product to be provided by the building societies (savings and loan associations). However, the banks decided to enter the mortgage market in 1981, primarily for political reasons,[1] and the monetary sector has increased its share of total net house purchase lending from some six per cent in 1980 to 32 per cent in 1988.[2]

As can be seen from Table 2, both Barclays and Midland have more than doubled their lending for house purchase, and mortgages now account for

Table 1. Barclays, Midland and National Westminster Bank Domestic Lending 1984–88 (£ billions).

	1984	1985	1986	1987	1988	Percentage increase 1984–88
Corporate[1]	32.77	34.83	38.39	44.24	58.25	78%
Personal	19.39	22.29	26.75	33.12	41.87	116%
Total	52.16	57.12	65.14	77.36	100.12	92%
Personal as % of total	37%	39%	41%	43%	42%	

Source: See text.
Note : [1] These figures exclude lending to government agencies and overseas residents.

Table 2. Personal lending 1984–88 (£ billions).

	1984	1985	1986	1987	1988	Percentage increase 1984/88
Barclays						
Mortgage	–	3.09	3.52	5.28	7.96	157%[1]
Non-mortgage	–	6.01	6.79	7.93	9.36	56%[1]
Total	7.99	9.10	10.31	13.21	17.32	117%[1]
Midland						
Mortgage	1.30	1.60	3.00	3.60	4.50	246%
Non-mortgage	3.02	3.38	3.72	3.87	4.66	54%
Total	4.32	4.98	6.72	7.47	9.16	112%
National Westminster						
Mortgage	–	–	5.71	7.71	9.63	69%[2]
Non-mortgage	–	–	4.01	4.73	5.76	44%[2]
Total	7.08	8.21	9.72	12.44	15.39	117%

Source: Respective Bank's Annual Report on Form 20-F various years and are partially estimated.
Notes : – Not available.
 [1] 1985/88.
 [2] 1986/88.

some 46 per cent and 49 per cent respectively of personal sector lending.

The competition for the personal sector business is also increasing because of changes in legislation. For example, under the Building Societies Act 1986, societies are now able to offer unsecured loans and cheque accounts. The Nationwide Anglia and the Abbey National building societies introduced interest-bearing cheque accounts, and both claim to have opened in excess of one million accounts each since the end of 1987. In addition, the Halifax has announced that it will be offering a cheque account in late 1989, whilst the Alliance and Leicester is currently taking over Girobank plc, which was previously owned by the Post Office.

These new competitive pressures forced the major clearing banks to offer interest-bearing cheque accounts from early 1989. It is too soon to say how much this additional cost will amount to because the conditions attached to the new accounts mean that not all customers will change their accounts. In addition, Barclays Bank announced in January 1989 that it was abolishing all transaction charges for its personal customers, which would have cost Barclays £ 88 million in 1988, and £ 84 million in 1987.

Other new personal business areas that the clearing banks have entered have been travel, car hire, insurance underwriting and estate agencies. There have also been the well publicised entries into and withdrawals from, gilt and equity market-making, and the provision of clearing services for the futures markets.

There are, of course, risks attached to entering any new market and an indication of these risks can be seen by considering the recent experiences of estate agencies. From 1985 to September 1988 the number of estate agencies in the UK increased from some 14,000 to some 17,000. Most of these new offices were opened by banks, notably Lloyds Bank, building societies and insurance companies as they sought to establish national chains. With a buoyant property market it seemed to be a good strategy which would provide increased opportunities for selling mortgage and insurance products.

However, the property market turned down in late 1988 and over 1,000 offices have been closed since then. Lloyds Bank has closed 40, whilst the Prudential insurance group has closed 60 and made a loss of some £ 25 million for the first half of 1989.[3]

III. IMPLICATIONS OF NEW PRODUCTS

The most important implication of the increase in lending to the personal sector is bad debts. Table 3 shows that personal sector bad debts written off have increased rapidly since 1984. Whilst the amounts involved may appear relatively small, given the amounts of lending, a comparison with Table 2 shows that bad debts have increased faster than lending. It is also interesting to note that, unlike the personal sector, domestic business sector bad debts have been contained, and indeed reduced in relative terms. This has probably been due to the strength of the UK economy over the past few years.

Unfortunately the figures shown for the Midland Bank in Table 3 include

Table 3. Domestic bad debts written off by domestic offices 1984–1988[1] (£ billions).

	1984	1985	1986	1987	1988	% Change 1984/88
Barclays						
Business	123 (74%)	105 (63%)	117 (61%)	90 (36%)	93 (41%)	−24%
Personal	44 (26%)	61 (37%)	76 (39%)	160 (64%)	103 (53%)	+134%
Total	167	166	193	250	196	+17%
Midland						
Business	402 (91%)	97 (55%)	121 (64%)	94 (70%)	50 (53%)	48%[2]
Personal	40 (9%)	79 (45%)	68 (36%)	41 (30%)	44 (47%)	44%[2]
Total	442	76	189	135	94	−47%
National Westminster						
Business	113 (81%)	120 (72%)	141 (69%)	178 (67%)	140 (55%)	+24%
Personal	26 (19%)	47 (28%)	63 (31%)	88 (33%)	114 (45%)	+338%
Total	139	167	204	266	254	+83%

Source: See Table 2.

Notes : [1] Midland Bank figures are for the UK, USA and Continental Europe, but exclude 'overseas residents'.

[2] 1985/88 See text.

the United States and Continental Europe and so are not comparable with the other two banks. It is also likely that the Midland's figures for 1984, in particular the business sector write-off, include the problems of Crocker.

In the UK the amount lent for nearly all house purchase is below the valuation or purchase price. Therefore, in the event of a bad debt situation the lender should receive all moneys back, unless there is a drastic fall in the housing market. It therefore follows that personal sector bad debts written off are due to non-mortgage lending and Table 4 shows this distinction. In 1988 bad debts written off varied between one and two per cent of non-mortgage lending by the three banks. However, the banks are expecting bad debts to increase and announced in July 1989 that they are to increase their provisions against bad debts in the personal sector.

The increase of bad debts has probably arisen because of the greater marketing efforts by the three banks. For example, Barclays has set sales targets for each member of its branch staff and has appointed Regional Sales Managers to ensure that targets are achieved. The suspicion is that prudent lending considerations are being ignored in the pursuit of increased lending and market share. There is also some evidence that practices that would not have been allowed in the past, unauthorised overdrafts for example, are now accepted quite happily by the banks.

Table 4. Personal bad debts written off 1984–88 (£ millions).

	1984	1985	1986	1987	1988	Percentage increase 1984–88
Barclays						
Written off	44	61	76	160	103	134
As % non-mortgage lending	–	1.0	1.1	2.0	1.1	
Midland[1]						
Written off	40	79	68	41	44	10
As % non-mortgage lending	1.3	2.3	1.8	1.0	0.9	
National Westminster						
Written off	26	47	63	88	114	338
As % non-mortgage lending	–	–	1.6	1.9	1.9	

Source: See Table 2.
Notes : – Not available.
[1] See note 1, Table 3.

The bullet that will have to be bitten by the banks is the repossession of houses. Until now no figures have been published for this activity, but it is known that the number of re-possessions by the building societies has more than doubled from 10,870 in 1984 to 22,930 in 1987. In addition, there were a further 61,220 loans more than six months in arrears at the end of 1987.[4] Whilst these figures are small in relative terms, less than one per cent of all loans, the trend indicates a future problem for the banks.

IV. COST REDUCTION

One way for the banks to attack the competition is to become more efficient by reducing costs. Both Barclays and National Westminster Banks have announced that they are seeking cost reductions over the next few years; Barclays wanting to save some £ 200 million per year. From the UK retail bank viewpoint this can be achieved by reducing the size of the branch network and/or increasing the amount of technology used to reduce staff numbers.

Of course, as Tables 5 and 6 show, whilst the UK has the largest number of branches per institution, it is not the only country which has reduced the size of its branch network, although some countries have increased the number of branches during the 1980s, Spain and the Netherlands in particular. Because of the different relative sizes of the various institutions, Table 6 shows the number of branches per institution.

In contrast to the reduction in the number of branches, most OECD countries have increased the number of staff employed by banks during the

Table 5. Selected OECD countries – number of bank branches 1980–86.

Country	1980	1983	1986	Change 1980/86	% Change
Austria	596	661	705	109	18.3
Belgium	3,658	3,680	3,646	– 12	–0.3
Denmark	3,644	3,502	3,424	– 220	–6.0
Finland	2,721	2,839	2,925	204	7.5
France	20,245	21,395	21,100	855	4.2
W. Germany	33,871	35,611	39,812	5,941	17.5
Greece	697	748	795	98	14.1
Italy	8,416	9,025	9,705	1,289	15.3
Japan	8,034	8,550	9,251	1,217	15.1
Luxembourg	244	241	250	6	2.5
Netherlands	5,577	5,406	7,388	1,811	32.5
Norway	565	640	702	137	24.2
Portugal	N/A	1,426	1,510	N/A	N/A
Spain	25,682	31,052	32,615	6,933	27.0
Sweden	1,479	1,450	1,424	– 55	–3.7
Switzerland	4,817	5,005	3,948	– 869	–18.0
UK	14,488	14,197	13,666	– 822	–5.7

Sources: UK = CLSB.
All other countries = OECD.

Table 6. Selected OECD countries – average number of branches per institution.

Country	1980	1983	1986	% Change
Austria	74.50	82.63	88.13	18.3
Belgium	44.07	43.81	42.40	–3.8
Denmark	15.25	15.63	15.85	4.0
Finland	4.15	4.35	4.71	13.4
France	49.62	49.87	57.49	15.9
W. Germany	10.97	11.72	8.92	–18.7
Greece	174.25	187.00	198.75	14.1
Italy	39.33	44.02	48.53	23.4
Japan	105.71	112.50	120.14	13.7
Luxembourg	2.20	2.11	2.05	–6.8
Netherlands	64.85	58.76	91.21	40.7
Norway	23.54	29.09	24.21	2.8
Portugal	N/A	83.88	55.93	N/A
Spain	72.75	84.15	93.45	28.5
Sweden	105.64	103.57	101.71	–3.7
Switzerland	11.15	11.61	8.81	–21.0
UK	1,811.00	1,774.62	1,708.25	–5.7

Sources: As per Table 5.

Table 7. Selected OECD countries – number of staff (000s) employed by banks.

Country	1980	1983	1986	% Change 1980/86
Austria	21.1	21.6	22.1	4.7
Belgium	47.8	47.4	49.2	2.9
Denmark	48.0	49.0	55.0	14.6
Finland	38.2	40.4	44.2	15.7
France	–	368.00	366.2	–
W. Germany	–	–	–	–
Greece	21.4	24.0	28.4	32.7
Italy	210.4	226.3	235.3	11.8
Japan	334.0	337.0	320.0	– 4.2
Luxembourg	7.6	9.0	11.4	50.0
Netherlands	91.5	90.7	104.1	13.8
Norway	14.1	15.8	17.9	26.9
Portugal	–	58.4	59.2	–
Spain	244.9	241.7	240.7	– 1.7
Sweden	20.1	21.4	23.5	16.9
Switzerland	82.4	91.8	105.4	27.9
UK	278.4	280.7	313.0	12.4

Sources: As per Table 5.

period 1980-86, with the notable exceptions of Japan and Spain as can be seen from Table 7, the largest increases having occurred in Luxembourg, Greece, Switzerland and Norway.

In the UK, staff costs now account for some 60 per cent of non-interest expenses for the clearing banks and for 1988 totalled some £ 4.98 billion for the three clearing banks, clearly an area for cost-saving exercises.

One way of reducing staff requirements is by using technology to replace personnel, and the most common is by the use of Automated Teller Machines (ATMs). The UK clearing banks have invested heavily in this technology as can be seen from Table 8.

However, the provision of technology will not necessarily mean that customers will use it. For example, one UK retail bank has provided ATMs since the 1960s; but it was not until 1987 that the number of ATM cash withdrawals exceeded the number of cheques cashed across branch counters.

There is also some evidence from the United Kingdom that the siting and reliability of ATMs is important from a usage point of view. For example, as the number of machines installed increases, we would expect the usage rate to also increase. However, as is illustrated by Figure 1, since 1985 as Barclays Bank has increased the number of its ATMs, so this use has decreased. In comparison, Clydesdale Bank, at the other extreme, has increased both the number of ATMs and their usage rate.

Table 8. Number of branches and ATMs in the United Kingdom.

(end December)	1980	1981	1982	1983	1984	1985	1986	1987
Branches								
Retail banks	14,756	14,738	14,669	14,487	14,359	14,271	13,987	13,803
Building societies	5,684	6,162	6,480	6,643	6,816	6,926	6,954	6,962
ATMs								
Retail banks	1,735	2,846	4,055	5,628	6,524	8,074	8,884	10,113
Building societies	–	–	6	112	291	652	1,286	2,072
Average no. ATMs per branch								
Retail banks	0.12	0.19	0.28	0.39	0.45	0.57	0.64	0.73
Building societies	–	–	–[1]	0.02	0.04	0.09	0.18	0.30

Source: Author's calculations based on CLSB, *Abstract of Banking Statistics*, vol. 6, May 1989, Tables 6,21 and and 6.24.
Note: [1] Insignificant.

Given the high fixed costs of ATM installation, the usage rate is important in order that average total costs can be minimised. Unfortunately, there is no evidence currently available to explain why the customers of Barclays and Clysesdale banks should appear to behave so differently.

However, it can be expected that the trend towards using ATMs will continue, providing that the technical problems that are becoming apparent, mainly customer claims that they had not used the machine, can be resolved.[5] In this connection a recent report[6] has recommended that the Australian practice be adopted whereby the banks have to prove that the machine was used, rather than the reverse.

v. 1992

According to most commentators, 1992 will mean a greater increase in competition amongst banks and other financial institutions in the EC countries. This may be, but it will depend upon the delivery system strategy adopted by the bank and the willingness of customers to use a 'foreign' institution. There are 13 main delivery strategies that can be adopted by a bank as shown in Table 9. There are advantages and disadvantages with using any of them, but the biggest problem facing a bank will be staff. If home staff are deployed overseas, then there is the disadvantage that they will not know the local

200

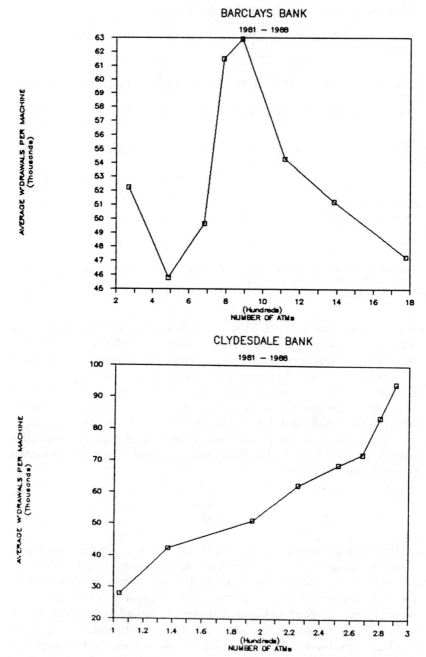

Fig. 1. ATM installation and usage rate.

Table 9. Bank delivery system strategy.

1. Full service branch
2. Limited service branch
3. Speciality branch
4. Fully automated branch
5. Thin branches
6. ATMs
7. Financial supermarket
8. Department store financial supermarket
9. Eftpos
10. Intelligent terminals
11. Home banking
12. Card-based systems
13. Telemarketing and distance delivery systems

market conditions and will be seen as being 'foreign'. If overseas staff are used, then there is the problem of promoting those staff within the domestic organisation.

With non-branch strategies, the staffing problems can be overcome but you are then reliant on the local postal/telephone systems for the efficient delivery of the product. Given the recent international experiences of the British banks where they have lost money on their international branches, it seems that 1992 may only bring further problems.

There are also the implications for monetary policy to be considered. Let us take a simple example. The Bank of England, say, sets relatively high nominal interest rates as part of its conduct of monetary policy. A non-UK, say West German bank, realises that, because of lower domestic interest rates, it can offer loans in the United Kingdom at a much lower rate than UK banks can and so advertise such a service. Will the authorities permit their monetary policy to be so evaded, or will the German bank simply increase its lending margins? And either way, given the current state of customer protection legislation, who will accept the responsibility of explaining exchange rate risk?

VI. CONCLUSIONS

In this paper we have tried to highlight the most important changes that are occurring in the UK personal financial sector. All of these changes have been due to an increase in competition that an individual bank now faces, and can expect to continue to face. Whilst the personal customer has benefited from the fact that it is now easier to borrow than ever before, we have pointed out that this strategy by the banks has inherent dangers, most notably the risk of increasing bad debts. A down-turn in the economy or a change in government taxation policy could cause losses from bad debts to increase rapidly.

Of course, by its very nature, banking is a risk business, and we are not suggesting that this risk element should, or could, be removed. Rather, it is the change in the strategy of the UK banks to one of increasing lending at all costs and, simultaneously, moving into non-traditional markets that we question.

Technology is beginning to be accepted by the average customer but it has been a long process and one which is still continuing. But as costs become under greater pressure, so it can be expected that the amount of technology used will increase whilst staff numbers will be reduced.

For the authorities, the problem that they face is in deciding whether the banks should be permitted to enter new, non-traditional, markets. In this connection it is perhaps worth membering the old adage that 'the cobbler should stick to his last'.

NOTES

1. They wanted the government to withdraw the special tax concessions enjoyed by the building societies. The strategy failed.
2. Source: *CLSB abstract of banking statistics*, vol. 6, May 1989.
3. *Financial Times*, 1 July 1989, p. 5.
4. Source: *Housing Finance*, Building Societies Association, January 1989, Table 11.
5. In 1988 the most common complaint to the Banking Ombudsman was that customers who had not used an ATM were having their accounts debited with a cash withdrawal.
6. *Banking services: law and practice*. Report by the Review Committee, Chairman: Prof R. B. Jack, CM 622, February 1989.

XV. La Concurrence dans le Domaine des Valeurs Mobilières

GEORGES MARTIN et MARC VAN TURENHOUDT*

1. CADRE GÉNÉRAL

Les conditions de concurrence sur les marchés financiers ont connu ces dernières années des évolutions particulièrement importantes. Dans certains pays, elles sont déjà radicalement modifiées. Dans d'autres, elles sont en train de l'être. Le vocabulaire imagé utilisé pour désigner ces changements (on se souvient du "Big Bang" de Londres...) est illustratif de la profondeur des bouleversements en question.

Les marchés boursiers, qui font plus particulièrement l'object du présent article, sont fréquemment soumis à des réglementations détaillées et à des contrôles relativement lourds. En cela, ils offrent des similitudes avec l'activité des banques et des compagnies d'assurances notamment. Ces différents domaines ont en commun qu'ils touchent à la protection de l'épargne, au financement de l'économie dans son ensemble, et à des notions comme l'intérêt général, qui justifient souvent certaines limitations de la concurrence.

Dans bien des pays, les activités bancaires par exemple ont pourtant été soumises beaucoup plus tôt et plus intensément à la concurrence internationale que les activités boursières. Ce qui est vrai pour le marché des obligations – le développement de l'énorme marché des euro-obligations qui, contrairement aux marchés domestiques cloisonnés, échappe quasi complètement aux contrôles nationaux – ne s'est pas vérifié pour le marché des actions, sinon tout récemment et sur une échelle encore relativement modeste, avec la naissance du marché des "euro-equities".

Parallèlement, les marchés des nouveaux instruments financiers – options, futures, etc. – ont connu en quelques années un développement explosif dans un nombre croissant de pays. Les marchés traditionnnels des valeurs mobilières se sont ainsi largement diversifiés, avec l'éclosion de cette gamme variée de nouveaux instruments.

---

* Les vues exprimées dans cette étude n'engagent que ses auteurs et ne représentent pas nécessairement la position de l'institution qui les emploie.

D. E. Fair and C. de Boissieu (eds), Financial Institutions in Europe Under New Competitive Conditions, 203–219.
© 1990 Kluwer Academic Publishers, Dordrecht. Printed in the Netherlands.

La présente étude se concentre sur deux aspects de ces évolutions aux facettes multiples:
- les réformes récemment mises en oeuvre, en cours ou envisagées au plan national, sur diverses bourses européennes, avec une attention particulière au cas de la Bourse belge qui, pour être relativement tardif, n'en est pas moins représentatif de la tendance générale;
- les projects d'harmonisation européenne en la matière, avec une évaluation de leurs conséquences pour les conditions de concurrence sur les marchés nationaux.

Nous nous efforcerons, dans une dernière partie, de tirer quelques conclusions et quelques orientations probables des tendances constatées.

2. LES RÉFORMES BOURSIÈRES NATIONALES – LE CAS BELGE

Le mouvement de dérégulation des marchés financiers s'est amorcé dans les années 70 aux Etats-Unis. C'est sans doute la Bourse de New York qui a connu, en 1975–1976, le premier "Big Bang" avant la lettre, avec une dérégulation des courtages qui conduisit à une profonde transformation des conditions de concurrence, prenant notamment la forme d'une véritable guerre des prix qui dura plusieurs années et fit un certain nombre de victimes parmi les firmes concernées.

Ce n'est que 10 ans plus tard, en 1986, que la première grande réforme du même type vit le jour en Europe. Elle eut pour cadre la City de Londres. On y trouvait un important ingrédient supplémentaire que les bourses américaines n'avaient pas connu, mais que plusieurs autres bourses européennes ont expérimenté par la suite (celles de Paris, Copenhagen, Madrid et Bruxelles notamment): alors que la *dérégulation des commissions* avait été la caractéristique principale de la réforme américaine, la *déspécialisation des intermédiaires* ou, si l'on préfère, la fin du monopole ou du quasi-monopole d'une catégorie précise d'intermédiaires, a joué sur un certain nombre de places européennes un rôle au moins aussi important dans la transformation des conditions de concurrence. Plusieurs bourses ont combiné à des degrés divers les deux aspects: dérégulation des courtages et déspécialisation des intermédiaires.

Le but de ces différentes réformes était partout le même: accroître l'efficacité des marchés nationaux, à la fois dans l'intérêt des épargnants et des investisseurs d'une part, et dans celui des émetteurs publics et privés d'autre part, et accessoirement, dans bien des cas, accroître l'attractivité et la compétitivité internationales de la place boursière concernée. Ce dernier aspect a pris une importance croissante dans un passé récent, au fur et à mesure que se précisait et se rapprochait la perspective du grand marché européen des services financiers.

A. La déspécialisation des intermédiaires

1. L'accès actuel aux marchés

En matière d'accès aux marchés boursiers, l'Europe connaît deux traditions différentes. Une série de pays, en particulier les pays germaniques – Allemagne, Autriche, Suisse, Grand-Duché de Luxembourg,... – connaissent de longue date le régime de la banque universelle. Dans ces pays, les établissements de crédit ont le droit d'opérer directement en bourse. Malgré la spécificité de leur système, les Pays-Bas se rapprochent également de ce modèle.

Dans la plupart des autres pays européens, et notamment dans les pays de culture latine et de tradition juridique napoléonienne, comme la France, l'Italie, l'Espagne et la Belgique, l'accès au marché boursier est réservé à des intermédiaires spécialisés, les agent de change, qui bénéficient du monopole de l'exécution des ordres.

Tel était du moins le cas jusqu'il y a peu, car cette situation est en train d'évoluer rapidement. Encore convient-il de noter que, sur la plupart des places où les banques n'avaient pas accès à la Bourse, les réformes récentes ne leur ont offert ou ne leur offriront dans les prochaines années qu'un accès *indirect*, non pas en tant que banques, mais à travers des prises de participation dans des "sociétés de bourse" existantes ou à travers la création de filiales spécialisées dans ce type d'activité. Tel fut notamment le cas à Londres, à Paris et à Madrid, et tel sera prochainement le cas à Bruxelles.

La Bourse belge fournit à cet égard un exemple typique. Depuis le milieu des années 30 et la suppression du régime de la banque mixte en Belgique, les banques se sont vu interdire le droit d'intervenir directement en Bourse. Si elles peuvent recevoir les ordres de la clientèle, l'exécution de ceux-ci est réservée aux seuls agent de change inscrits au tableau établi par la Commission de la Bourse. Les agents de change exercent leur profession en nom personnel. S'ils l'exercent en société, il ne peut s'agir que d'une société en nom collectif ou en commandite simple, dans laquelle l'agent de change conserve sa responsabilité personnelle illimitée. La société anonyme est donc exclue, et par conséquent aussi un appel relativement aisé à des capitaux extérieurs.

De plus, l'agent de change est un simple exécutant des ordres reçus, rétribué par des commissions fixes. Il n'agit ni comme contrepartiste ni comme "market maker". Il est supposé de la sorte agir dans le seul intérêt du client et ne pas devoir prendre de risques inconsidérés pour assurer sa rentabilité.

Le statut des intermédiaires en Bourse a conservé un caractère corporatiste se caractérisant notamment par un monopole (c'est-à-dire le droit d'exercer la profession réservé exclusivement aux personnes agréées par la profession elle-même), des dirigeants élus par les membres, une participation prépondérante de ceux-ci à la législation, le contrôle des conditions d'accès et d'exercice de la profession, une tarification commune et uniforme.

Les conditions d'accès à la profession d'agent de change sont typiques de cette situation: pour être agréé par la Commission de la Bourse, organe composé d'agents de change élus par leurs pairs, il faut avoir accompli un stage de six années consécutives chez un ou plusieurs agents de change belges et être parrainé par deux agents de change au moins. Ces conditions ont eu notamment pour conséquence qu'aucun agent de change étranger, même ressortissant d'un autre Etat de la CEE, n'a essayé jusqu'à présent de les satisfaire.

Les banques partagent avec les agents de change le droit de collecter des ordres de la clientèle; grâce à leur vaste réseau d'agences, elles récoltent d'ailleurs la majorité de ces ordres. Elles doivent toutefois ristourner aux agents de change qui exécutent les ordres en Bourse une proportion élevée du courtage perçu: actuellement 60%, jusqu'il y a quelques années les deux tiers.

Le monopole des agents de change est toutefois relatif dans la mesure où il ne concerne, dans la pratique, que les ordres inférieurs à BEF 10 millions. L'interdiction d'exécuter en dehors du marché du pays ne s'applique en effet pas aux cessions de titres portant sur des montants supérieurs à BEF 10 millions. Ceci explique le développement en Belgique d'un important marché "hors bourse" sur lequel les banques sont très actives et les courtages sont libres.

2. Les principales caractéristiques de la réforme projetée

A la demande du Ministre des Finances de l'époque, de difficiles négociations ont été amorcées dès le milieu de 1986 entre les représentants du secteur bancaire et du secteur boursier afin de préparer une réforme du marché belge. Les divergences de points de vue entre les deux professions étaient toutefois si fondamentales que ces négociations n'ont abouti à aucun résultat significatif. Il a fallu plusieurs interventions des pouvoirs politiques pour débloquer la situation et aboutir enfin, dans les derniers mois de 1988, à un accord global sur les grandes lignes d'une réforme qui, entre-temps, a été coulée en un projet de loi qui devrait normalement être adopté avant la fin de 1989.

Les principales caratéristiques de cette réforme sont les suivantes:

a) Les agents de change pourront se transformer en sociétés commerciales, et en particulier en *sociétés anonymes*. Cette disposition facilitera la constitution de sociétés de bourse et le regroupement des très nombreuses firmes existantes (plus de 200 à l'heure actuelle, de très petite taille pour la plupart) en entités plus importantes.

b) *Le capital des sociétés de bourse s'ouvrira* progressivement à des actionnaires belges et étrangers autres que les agents de change. Les établissements de crédit et les compagnies d'assurances pourront, dès l'entrée en vigueur de la loi, acquérir 25% du capital des sociétés de bourse. Dès le 1er janvier

1991, cette limite sera supprimée, et à partir du 1er janvier 1992, de nouvelle sociétés de bourse pourront être créées, sans avoir à passer par le rachat de sociétés existantes. De plus, n'importe quelle autre société ou personne physique pourra devenir actionnaire de sociétés de bourse moyennant l'accord préalable de la Commission bancaire et financière chargée, dans le cadre de la nouvelle législation, du contrôle prudentiel de ces sociétés.

c) La création des sociétés de bourse n'entraînera pas la disparition des *agents de change personnes physiques*. A l'intérieur de ces sociétés, les transactions sur valeurs mobilières cotées en Bourse ne pourront être effectuées que par ou sous la direction d'agents de change, soumis à une déontologie et à un contrôle particuliers. Ces agents de change devront également être majoritaires au sein du Comité de Direction des sociétés de bourse.

d) Les exigences auxquelles seront soumises les sociétés de bourse en matière de *fonds propres* seront sensiblement renforcées. Des exigences de *solvabilité* particulières seront imposées aux sociétés de bourse qui voudront se livrer à des activités plus risquées comme la prise ferme ou la contrepartie.

e) Une des questions sur lesquelles les points de vue ont divergé le plus longtemps est celle de la *centralisation du marché*.

Le seuil sous lequel les transactions doivent passer par le mécanisme d'enchères de la Bourse sera porté de BEF 10 millions actuellement à BEF 20 millions pour les actions cotées sur le marché au comptant, BEF 25 millions pour les obligations et BEF 30 millions pour les actions cotées sur le marché à terme.

Toutefois, quel que soit le mécanisme d'exécution des ordres (donc également pour les blocs de montant élevé), toutes les transactions sur actions devront être confiées aux sociétés de bourse à partir du 1er janvier 1992.

En ce qui concerne le marché des obligations, au-delà du seuil de 25 millions, continuera à subsister un marché de blocs sur lequel pourront opérer aussi bien les sociétés de bourse que les établissements de crédit.

De manière à assurer que les prix pratiqués sur les différents marchés soient convergents, un écart maximum devra être respecté entre les prix fixés pour une même valeur selon le mécanisme des enchères en Bourse pour les opérations de taille petite ou moyenne, et selon d'autres mécanismes de négociation pour les ordres dépassant les seuils fixés. En outre, toutes les opérations effectuées sur les marchés des blocs feront l'objet d'une obligation de "reporting" auprès des autorités du marché, en ce qui concerne tant les prix que les quantités.

f) Par ailleurs, l'introduction d'un *marché continu et informatisé* est déjà relativement avancée en ce qui concerne les actions; de même, des études concernant l'organisation de plusieurs *nouveaux marchés* sont en cours et devraient aboutir prochainement.

g) Enfin, le *contrôle du marché* proprement dit sera confié à l'ancienne Commission de la Bourse, alors que le *contrôle prudentiel* des intermédiaires opérant sur le marché relèvera d'une *Commission bancaire et financière* aux pouvoirs élargis. C'est à cette Commission bancaire et financière qu'appartiendra l'agrément des sociétés de bourse. Si ces dernières devront acquérir un certain nombre de parts de la Société de la Bourse de Valeurs mobilières, coopérative chargée d'administrer la Bourse, le marché boursier belge ne connaître donc pas, comme certaines autres places, la notion de "sièges" attribués en nombre limité et à un prix parfois très élevé aux candidats désireux d'avoir accès à la Bourse.

Les banques se sont fermement opposées pendant les négociations à toute notion de numerus clausus, en ce qui concerne en particulier les nouvelles sociétés de bourse qui pourront être créées à partir de 1992, lorsqu'il ne sera plus obligatoire de racheter une société existante pour avoir accès au marché.

B. La dérégulation des commissions

Cet ingrédient essentiel de la dérégulation des marchés boursiers a caractérisé notamment la réforme des Bourses de New York et de Londres. Plus récemment, Paris, après avoir ouvert le capital des sociétés de bourse aux actionnaires extérieurs, et notamment aux banques, a également décidé de supprimer la fixation de courtage uniformes.

Une des conséquences de la libération des courtages sur les opérations de bourse est fréquemment un renchérissement sensible pour les petites opérations et, à l'inverse, une compression des marges pour les opérations importantes. Il est vrai que, lorsque les courtages sont fixés uniformément par ou avec le consentement des autorités, les petites opérations sont fréquemment déficitaires et sont en fait, au moins dans une certaine mesure, subventionnées par les opérations de plus grande taille. Cette situation est encore aggravée lorsque le courtage doit être partagé entre les institutions qui recueillent les ordres et les intermédiaires autorisés à les exécuter. Théoriquement, une telle situation devrait encourager la petite épargne à s'orienter vers le capital à risque. Dans la pratique, toutefois, l'effet peut être exactement contraire: les intermédiaires financiers seront en effet tentés de promouvoir des produits plus rentables et de décourager les placements en actions.

Une autre conséquence typique du coût administratif élevé des petites opérations et de la difficulté de les rentabiliser est la tendance de plus en plus généralisée, dans de nombreux pays, à pousser le petit investisseur à se tourner de préférence vers des formes de placement collectives en valeurs mobilières: fonds communs de placement, SICAV, etc. Cette tendance comporte de nombreux avantages à la fois pour les intermédiaires financiers et pour les épargnants, et contribue à renforcer l'institutionnalisation des marchés boursiers, sur laquelle nous reviendrons plus loin.

Dans un certain nombre de pays, dont font partie notamment la Suisse, les Pays-Bas et la Belgique, les tarifs des courtages ne sont libres qu'à partir d'un certain seuil, les opérations inférieures à celui-ci continuant à se voir appliquer des tarifs uniformes.

La réforme de la Bourse de Bruxelles n'a pas modifié fondamentalement cette situation. Une double préoccupation l'a inspirée: renforcer la compétitivité internationale de la Bourse belge sans pour autant décourager l'accès à la Bourse de l'épargne populaire.

Dans cette optique, un nouveau barème des courtages, plus fortement dégressif (légèrement plus élevé pour les petites opérations, nettement plus bas pour les opérations moyennes, complètement libre pour les grosses opérations) a été approuvé par le Ministre des Finances et entrera en vigueur au moment de l'adoption de la loi de réforme. Le partage des courtages entre les sociétés de bourse et les établissements financiers autorisés à recevoir des ordres de bourse sera également réaménagé dans un sens plus conforme à la part apportée par chacun à la valeur ajoutée de la transaction. Pour les grosses opérations, le montant de la rétrocession sera lui aussi entièrement négociable.

Enfin, toujours dans le but de favoriser la compétitivité de la Bourse belge, il a été décidé de plafonner le montant de la taxe sur les opérations de bourse de manière à pénaliser beaucoup moins les opérations importantes.

En vertu de l'accord passé à la fin de 1988 entre les différentes parties à la table de négociations, le mode de fixation des courtages et des rétrocessions devrait toutefois être réexaminé dès 1991, vraisemblablement dans le sens d'une plus grande liberté. On peut en effet se demander dans quelle mesure la fixation de courtages uniformes par l'autorité publique se justifie encore, et surtout, si une telle situation ne sera pas remise en cause, à plus ou moins brève échéance, par les autorités européennes à la lumière de l'application des règles de concurrence du Traité de Rome aux services financiers.

Déjà, la Commission européenne a clairement confirmé que les services bancaires étaient soumis aux règles de concurrence contenues dans le Traité de Rome. Jusqu'à présent, elle a réservé sa décision en ce qui concerne les taux d'intérêt, dans la mesure où ils sont considérés comme relevant de la politique monéraire, prérogative des Etats souverains. Tel n'est toutefois pas le cas, de toute évidence, de la tarification des opérations de bourse, dont la fixation uniforme devrait donc tôt ou tard être remise en cause dans les pays de la Communauté européenne où elle est encore pratiquée.

Le fait que les sociétés de bourse d'un pays donné conviendraient entre elles du niveau des courtages serait totalement contraire à l'article 85 du

Traité de Rome. L'autorité publique a toutefois, en principe, le droit d'imposer des courtages uniformes pour des raisons de politique économique. Une telle intervention ne peut cependant avoir pour objet de prolonger ou conforter des pratiques concertées qui violent les règles communautaires sur la concurrence, ni faire obstacle aux objectifs du Traité qui sont notamment la libre circulation des services et des capitaux et l'établissement d'un régime assurant que la libre concurrence n'est pas faussée à l'intérieur du Marché Commun.

3. EVOLUTION DES CONDITIONS DE CONCURRENCE SUR LE PLAN EUROPÉEN

A. Dispositions en matière financière

Ces dernières considérations nous amènent, après avoir prêté attention aux principales caractéristiques des réformes boursières nationales, à nous pencher sur les effets considérables que la réalisation progressive du grand marché européen des services financiers devrait avoir sur les conditions de concurrence dans et entre les marchés nationaux de valeurs mobilières.

On vient de le voir, indépendamment même du grand marché européen de 1992, la simple application des règles communautaires en matière de concurrence au domaine boursier devrait conduire dans les prochaines années à décartelliser les marchés nationaux qui sont encore soumis aujourd'hui, à des degrés divers, à des formes de fixation concertée des prix patronnées par les autorités nationales.

Mais les intentions de la Commission européenne vont beaucoup plus loin dans ce domaine.

La dernière phase de la libération des mouvements de capitaux au sein de l'espace financier européen est en voie d'achèvement puisque nous ne sommes plus qu'à quelques mois du 1er juillet 1990. En ce qui concerne les actions, obligations et les parts d'OPCVM, cette libre circulation était d'ailleurs déjà réalisée en vertu de la directive du 17 novembre 1986 amendent et complétant celle du 11 mai 1960. Cette directive est entrée en vigueur le 28 février 1987. La libre circulation des capitaux constitue évidemment une condition nécessaire, mais non suffisante, de la levée de tous les obstacles à la concurrence entre les marchés financiers nationaux.

On rappellera brièvement les grands principes sur lesquels s'est appuyée ces dernières années la Commission européenne pour s'efforcer d'éliminer le plus rapidement possible les obstacles subsistants. La stratégie de la Commission se résume à prendre un certain nombre de mesures en vue de réaliser le degré d'harmonisation minimale des réglementations nationales qui permet la *reconnasissance mutuelle* de l'équivalence de ces réglementations par les autorités de contrôle des différents pays, de cette première règle de la reconnaissance mutuelle découlent en toute logique les principes de la licence unique et du contrôle exercé exclusivement par les autorités du pays d'origine.

En d'autres termes, une fois que les différentes réglementations nationales ont atteint un degré suffisant d'harmonisation, l'institution financière agréée par les autorités de contrôle de son pays d'origine ne doit plus demander son agrément dans les autres pays de la Communauté; elle peut y exercer son activité, via une succursale ou même sans établissement (liberté d'établissement et libre prestation de services par-delà les frontières) en se conformant uniquement aux règles auxquelles elle est soumise dans son pays d'origine.

Une longue liste de directives, de recommandations et même de codes de conduite européens touchant les intermédiaires et les opérations sur valeurs mobilières ont déjà été approuvés ces dernières années ou devraient l'être encore d'ici à la réalisation du grand marché intérieur au 1er janvier 1993. Nombre de ces dispositions sont déjà transposées dans les législations et réglementations nationales. D'autres le seront dans les moins ou les années qui viennent. Certaines n'existent encore qu'à l'état de projet, voire d'ébauche.

Pour mémoire, les principales dispositions européennes en matière financière (dont certaines encore à l'état de propositions) concernent le code général de conduite en matière de transactions relatives aux valeurs mobilières, les prospectus d'offre publique de valeurs mobilières et d'admission de valeurs mobilières à la cote officielle, les conditions d'admission à cette cote, les informations périodiques à publier par les sociétés cotées en Bourse, les opérations d'initiés ("insider trading"), les offres publiques d'achat et d'échange, les informations à publier lors de l'acquisition ou de la cession de participations importantes dans une société cotée (directive dite "anti-raider"), la taxe sur les opérations de bourse et plusieurs directives sur les organismes de placement collectifs en valeurs mobilières ("OPCVM"), organismes pour lesquels la réalisation du grand marché intérieur est devenue une réalité le 1er octobre 1989.

B. Deuxième directive de coordination bancaire

Un texte important, qui a presque atteint le terme de son processus d'adoption et qui aura un impact considérable sur la concurrence dans le domaine des valeurs mobilières, est la *deuxième directive de coordination bancaire*. Bien que concernant uniquement les établissements de crédit, pour lesquels elle vise à réaliser le degré d'harmonisation qui permettra la mise en oeuvre des principes de reconnaissance mutuelle et de contrôle par le pays d'origine, cette directive comporte, entre autres caractéristiques, celle de s'inspirer fortement du modèle germanique de banque universelle et de reconnaître, dans cet esprit, l'ensemble des activités sur valeurs mobilières comme faisant partie intégrante de l'activité bancaire. Il en résulte notamment qu'à ces activités s'appliquera le principe du "passeport unique", et donc la faculté pour une banque agréée dans un pays de la Communauté d'exercer, à travers des succursales ou par prestation directe de services, toutes les activités en matière de valeurs mobilières sur tout le territoire de la Communauté.

Cette directive mettra donc fin aux restrictions qui pourraient exister encore dans certains pays d'Europe entre les activités de banque commerciale et celles de banque d'investissement. La banque européenne de demain pourra non seulement détenir des actions à titre de placement et se livrer à des opérations de trading, mais effectuer pour compte propre ou pour compte de la clientèle toutes opérations sur valeurs mobilières, détenir des participations, même dans des entreprises non financières (moyennant toutefois certaines limites par rapport à ses fonds propres), et avoir accès, au moins indirectement (c'est-à-dire par l'intermédiaire d'une filiale spécialisée), à toutes les bourses de la Communauté.

Une importante réserve toutefois: dans cette directive comme dans beaucoup d'autres, est admis le principe de la 'discrimination à rebours" qui permet éventuellement aux autorités de contrôle d'un pays de la Communauté de se montrer, si elles le souhaitent, plus restrictives à l'égard de leurs propres établissements financiers, en limitant ou interdisant de leur chef certaines de ces activités. Par contre, ces autorités nationales ne pourront interdire à un établissement bancaire étranger de s'y livrer sur leur territoire s'il y est autorisé par les autorités de contrôle de son pays d'origine. Il y a donc là une situation quelque peu ambiguë qui pourrait se retourner contre les banques de certains pays de la Communauté. Toutefois, selon toute vraisemblance, la pression de la concurrence amènera les autorités de contrôle nationales à s'aligner progressivement sur les normes prévues par la directive européenne et à ouvrir aux établissements qu'elles contrôlent l'exercice de l'ensemble des activités visées par cette directive.

Il est donc inévitable que, dans les prochaines années, la concurrence s'intensifie fortement sur les marchés financiers, et en particulier sur les marchés boursiers, dans les pays de la Communauté où subsistent certaines barrières entre des groupes déterminés d'intermédiaires spécialisés et les banques, en ce qui concerne les activités d'émission, de négociation et de gestion en matière de valeurs mobilières.

C. Directive sur les services d'investissement

L'application aux banques des principes de la licence unique, de la reconnaissance mutuelle et du "home country control" dans le cadre de la deuxième directive de coordination bancaire conférerait même à ces dernières un avantage concurrentiel anormal par rapport aux institutions non bancaires spécialisées dans les activités sur valeurs mobilières. C'est une des raisons pour lesquelles la Commission européenne a présenté une autre proposition de directive concernant, celle-ci, *les services d'investissement dans le domaine des valeurs mobilières*. Cette proposition de directive est en quelque sorte le complément logique de la proposition de deuxième directive de coordination bancaire.

Il convenait en effet que toutes les entreprises qui fournissent des services dans le domaine des valeurs mobilières soient mises sur pied d'égalité. L'objectif de la directive sur les services d'investissement est précisément de créer pour l'ensemble des "entreprises d'investissement" (il faut entendre par là toute personne physique ou morale offrant à titre professionnel certains services dans le domaine des valeurs mobilières), les conditions de la "reconnaissance mutuelle". A cette fin, la directive se propose d'harmoniser un certain nombre de règles prudentielles concernant ces entreprises d'investissement. Elle comporte, en annexe, une liste des activités et des instruments visés qui couvre tout le champ des services en matière de valeurs mobilières et de nouveaux instruments assimilés à celles-ci.

Il faut toutefois constater que, pas plus que la deuxième directive de coordination bancaire, la proposition de directive sur les services d'investissement ne sera en mesure, à elle seule, de coordonner efficacement l'ensemble des règles dont l'harmonisation paraît indispensable pour permettre la reconnaissance mutuelle et donc la prestation vraiment libre de services, dans toute la Communauté sur base d'un agrément unique. La Commission en est consciente puisqu'elle a déjà mis en chantier un project de directive complémentaire sur les exigences spécifiques en matière de fonds propres découlant des risques inhérents aux activités sur valeurs mobilières.

A cet aspect devraient encore s'en ajouter plusieurs autres, notamment une coordination minimale de systèmes nationaux de protection de la clientèle, et sans doute aussi un sérieux effort d'harmonisation en ce qui concerne les réglementations nationales ayant pour object l'organisation et le fonctionnement des marchés boursiers ainsi que les règles de bonne conduite ("conduct of business rules") qui visent à éviter les conflits d'intérêts, tant au sein des entreprises d'investissement qu'entre celles-ci et leur clientèle d'une part, leurs actionnaires d'autre part. Le fait, notamment que, ces réglementations concernant l'organisation des marchés, la déontologie professionnelle et les systèmes de protection des clients soient laissées provisoirement à la compétence des autorités nationales risque en effet d'entraver la réalisation d'un véritable marché unique des services financiers non seulement en raison de la disparité des règles dans ce domaine, mais parce que le risque n'est pas imaginaire que certaines autorités de marché aient tendance, au nom de l'intérêt général et de la protection des consommateurs, à édicter ou à maintenir des exigences réglementaires qui pourraient constituer des entraves à la libre prestation des services.

D. Etablissements de crédit et services d'investissement

Un passage du projet de directive illustre ce genre de risque. Dans l'attente d'une coordination ultérieure, dont le timing n'est pas autrement précisé, les Etats membres garderaient la possibilité d'interdire aux succursales d'établissements de crédit étrangers de devenir directement membres d'une bourse ou d'un marché de titres organisé sur leur territoire lorsque les règles locales en la matière refusent également cette faculté à leurs propres institutions de crédit. La possibilité existe toutefois de tourner cette difficulté en acquérant une entreprise existante ou en créant une filiale qui respecte les règles fixées par les autorités de la bourse d'accueil. Ce passage de la directive confirme donc que les Etats membres qui n'accordent aux banques que l'accès indirect à leur marché boursier pourront, au moins temporairement, maintenir cette exigence, même à l'égard des banques des Etats membres qui accordent l'accès direct. Au travers de leur Fédération européenne, les banques de la Communauté ont fait savoir à la Commission qu'elles estimaient rétrograde et discriminatoire le maintien d'une telle situation. Elles n'ont pas perdu tout espoir que, dans une version ultérieure du projet, cette restriction concurrentielle soit abolie, mais il n'en est rien jusqu'à présent.

Encore ne faut-il pas exagérer la portée de cette restriction puisque le droit d'accès des banques à la bourse et aux autres marchés organisés de titres est bien reconnu, même si dans certains cas il ne pourra être qu'indirect. D'autre part, la possibilité d'offrir tous les services visés par-delà les frontières (et donc, par exemple, d'exécuter pour le compte d'un ressortissant du pays A des transactions sur un marché organisé du pays B) devrait à terme priver de leurs effets les restrictions nationales existantes.

Un débat est en cours à l'heure actuelle en ce qui concerne l'application de la directive sur les services d'investissement aux établissements de crédit visés par la deuxième directive de coordination bancaire. La liste des opérations autorisées par cette dernière comportant les opérations relatives aux valeurs mobilières, il en découle logiquement qu'à la différence des autres entreprises d'investissement, les établissements de crédit déjà autorisés, en vertu de leur agrément bancaire, à exercer les activités couvertes par la directive sur les services d'investissement, ne devront pas solliciter un nouvel agrément en application de cette dernière.

Plus fondamentalement toutefois, les banques constatent qu'elles doivent déjà satisfaire à la plupart des obligations prévues par la directive sur les services d'investissement (par example en matière de capital minimum, d'honorabilité des dirigeants, de contrôle des participations importantes, etc.) en vertu d'autres textes, et en particulier, de la deuxième directive de coordination bancaire. Il paraît donc au secteur bancaire qu'il serait plus logique, afin d'éviter toute confusion ou double emploi, que les banques de la CEE ne soient soumises qu'à la deuxième directive bancaire et qu'elles tombent entièrement en dehors du champ d'application de la directive sur les services d'investissement. Bien entendu, les quelques dispositions de cette dernière concernant des aspects de l'activité d'investissement non couverts par la deuxième directive bancaire seraient transposés dans celle-ci de manière à créer des conditions de concurrence équivalentes entre les établissements de crédit et les autres sociétés d'investissement. Ces aspects se réduisent d'ailleurs essentiellement à deux: la création dans chaque pays d'un système de garantie destiné à protéger spécifiquement les investisseurs, et l'élaboration de règles destinées à réduire au minimum les conflits d'intérêt, notamment avec la clientèle, inhérents aux activités dans le domaine des valeurs mobilières. Le débat à ce sujet n'est pas clos.

4. QUELQUES TENDANCES RÉCENTES ET ORIENTATIONS POUR L'AVENIR

Il ne fait aucun doute que les réformes nationales inspirées par des préoccupations de dérégulation qui ont d'abord retenu notre attention, et plus encore l'intense effort en vue de créer un véritable marché libre et intégré des services financiers au niveau de la Communauté européenne, vont accroître considérablement la concurrence au sein des marchés nationaux et entre ceux-ci.

– Le premier bouleversement qui paraît inévitable est la fin progressive des marchés cloisonnés et des monopoles locaux qui subsistent encore. Ceux-ci seront bientôt non seulement dépourvus de sens, mais illégaux au regard de la législation européenne.
– Cette disparition des monopoles nationaux plus ou moins protégés devrait déboucher à son tour sur une délocalisation croissante du marché pour toutes les valeurs importantes, qu'il s'agisse d'actions ou d'obligations.
– Directement liée aux deux points précédents, mais résultant également du rôle croissant joué par les investisseurs professionnels et institutionnels sur les marchés de valeurs mobilières, une troisième tendance qui se dessine a trait au rôle probablement plus restreint des marchés de détail nationaux, auxquels accède directement le particulier, par rapport aux marchés de gros traduisant l'importance croissante d'une nouvelle forme d'intermédiation financière.

A. *Disparition progressive des monopoles nationaux*

Nous l'avons déjà souligné, il ne fait pas de doute que les règles européennes en matière de concurrence s'appliquent également aux tarifs et courtages des opérations sur titres. Les interventions des autorités nationales dans ce domaine ne peuvent contrevenir aux objectifs du Traité.

Tout aussi important est le fait qu'aucune règle ne pourra être maintenue ou instaurée, qui aurait pour effet de créer une distorsion de concurrence à l'égard d'un intermédiaire ou d'un marché étranger. Particulièrement intéressant à ce propos est le récent débat, dans le cadre des réformes boursières française et belge notamment, autour du principe de la centralisation des opérations. L'objectif de celle-ci est d'accroître la transparence et la liquidité du marché. Si, par exemple, trop d'opérations sont exécutées en dehors d'un marché boursier déterminé, non seulement cette situation risque d'être préjudiciable à la profondeur de ce marché et de rendre sur celui-ci le mécanisme de fixation des prix plus volatil, mais le réalisme des prix fixés sur le marché boursier (en général le marché réservé aux petites et moyennes opérations) peut se ressentir du manque d'information des opérateurs sur le volume et le prix des grosses opérations traitées en dehors de ce marché.

On ne peut nier qu'il y ait là un problème réel. Il convient toutefois de tenir compte également d'autres considérations. La première est que les mécanismes d'exécution des petites opérations sont généralement mal adaptés aux exigences de ce qu'il est convenu d'appeler le "marché des blocs", où s'exécutent les opérations de gros montant pour le compte d'une clientèle professionnelle bien informée et ayant ses exigences propres (par exemple, une exécution rapide, un prix certain, pas de fractionnement de l'ordre en plusieurs parties traitées à des prix différents, etc.). Une deuxième considération importante est que l'objectif légitime de la transparence peut être atteint par des exigences précises en matière d'information des différents marchés organisés permettant un rapprochement rapide et efficace des prix par le jeu des arbitrages, sans que l'on doive recourir nécessairement à la contrainte de l'exécution de tous les ordres sur un même marché et/ou au travers d'un même mécanisme d'exécution. Un troisième aspect à prendre en considération est que, lorsqu'une même valeur est traitée sur plusieurs marchés différents d'un même pays ou de plusieurs pays, l'intérêt du client peut aller à l'encontre du principe de la centralisation et exiger que l'intermédiaire s'adresse au marché où l'ordre sera exécuté aux conditions les plus favorables.

Il y aurait d'ailleurs violation des principes fondamentaux du Traité de Rome en matière de concurrence et de libre prestation des services, ainsi que des règles relatives à la libre circulation des capitaux, si l'on voulait contraindre un intermédiaire financier qui reçoit un ordre de bourse relatif à une valeur cotée sur plusieurs places différentes de la CEE de l'exécuter sur une de ces places à l'exclusion des autres. Cette règle s'applique indifféremment aux titres nationaux et aux titres étrangers. En d'autres termes, les autorités nationales n'auraient pas plus le droit d'imposer par exemple l'exécution à Bruxelles d'une opération portant sur des actions d'une société belge que d'une opération portant sur des actions d'une société française cotée à la Bourse de Bruxelles, si ces actions sont également cotées sur d'autres bourses de la CEE.

Les autorités belges ont cru pouvoir tourner cette difficulté en imposant la centralisation de l'exécution des ordres portant sur les actions non pas sur le marché boursier, mais auprès des sociétés de bourse agréées qui restent libres d'exécuter l'ordre éventuellement sur le marché des blocs, ou même sur une bourse étrangère. Il est toutefois à craindre que même cette approche prudente se retourne finalement contre le marché belge. En effet, les grands établissements, étrangers notamment, qui sont habitués à traiter des actions internationales pour le compte de leur clientèle, et qui peuvent exécuter ces ordres soit directement, soit au travers d'une filiale qu'ils possèdent déjà sur d'autres marchés européens où ces actions sont également cotées, hésiteront probablement à les exécuter sur le marché belge s'ils sont obligés à cette fin soit de créer ou d'acquérir une société de bourse en Belgique, soit de faire exécuter l'ordre par une société de bourse existante en lui abandonnant un courtage.

B. Délocalisation croissante des marchés de gros

La probabilité est d'ailleurs grande de voir se développer petit à petit, parallèlement aux différents marchés nationaux, un marché de plus en plus délocalisé pour toutes les valeurs importantes. La combinaison des principes de l'agrément unique et de la libre prestation transfrontalière des services conduit à une situation dans laquelle un marché se créera directement entre certains des intermédiaires agrées des différents pays sans que ce marché soit localisé physiquement ou géographiquement dans un pays particulier. Avec les moyens disponibles aujourd'hui en matière d'informatique et de télécommunications, ce marché sera plus que probablement un marché entièrement sur écrans. Il n'y a d'ailleurs aucune raison qu'il se limite aux frontières de la Communauté européenne: vraisemblablement, ce marché boursier délocalisé réservé aux professionnels développera plus encore qu'aujourd'hui des interconnections étroites avec les intermédiaires américains et asiatiques, dans le cadre d'un marché ouvert en continu, 24 heures sur 24.

Il résulte de cette tendance que des exigences comme la centralisation, l'accès uniquement indirect des banques, ou à fortiori le respect d'une échelle de courtages fixes, perdront toute signification sauf en ce qui concerne les marchés locaux où ne se traiteront plus guère que les valeurs sans rayonnement international. Ce qui, bien sûr, ne leur enlèvera pas leur utilité, au contraire.

Ces marchés continueront en effet à servir de pépinière aux valeurs qui, progressivement, y apprendront à s'attaquer à des marchés plus importants et plus ouverts, au niveau européen d'abord, et pour certaines d'entre elles, au niveau mondial ensuite.

C. Rôle plus restreint des marchés de détail

On peut prévoir aussi, avec un risque d'erreur limité, un rôle progressivement plus restreint du "marché de détail" auquel les particuliers ont individuellement accès. Il est probable que certaines sociétés d'investissement, bancaires ou non bancaires, se spécialiseront dans ce créneau de la petite clientèle. Sans être nécessairement voué à se rétrécir en chiffres absolus, ce segment de marché devrait probablement connaître une régression relative par rapport aux marchés dominés par les différentes catégories d'investisseurs professionnels et institutionnels. Plusieurs raisons expliquent cette tendance. Les différentes formes de placements collectifs du type fonds communs de placement, SICAV, etc., connaissent structurellement une croissance plus rapide que les placements individuels en actions et en obligations. Les risques accrus résultant d'une plus grande volatilité des taux d'intérêt et des taux de change ne sont évidemment pas étrangers à cette tendance qui se fonde sur les avantages d'une gestion professionnelle et d'une meilleure répartition des risques que celle qui est normalement accessible à un particulier. Dans le domaine des placements en actions, en outre, après la période d'euphorie qui a marqué la première moitié des années 80, le krach boursier d'octobre 1987 a brutalement rappelé les risques inhérents à ce type de placements et l'intérêt de rechercher les formules qui les minimisent. En outre, la gestion de fortune et la gestion fiduciaire connaissent un succès croissant auprès des particuliers, parallèlement à d'autres phénomènes comme l'élévation continue du niveau de vie et le vieillissement de la population européenne.

Par ailleurs, de nouvelles formes d'épargne prennent une place grandissante dans le patrimoine financier des ménages: les préoccupations concernant la capacité des systèmes légaux de protection sociale à faire face aux exigences de plus en plus lourdes concernant les pensions amènent, dans la plupart des pays industrialisés, le développement rapide de diverses formes institutionnalisées d'épargne contractuelle en vue de la retraite, que ce soit au niveau des entreprises de manière collective (fonds de pension, assurances-groupe complémentaires, plans d'épargne) ou sous une forme libre et individuelle (assurance-vie, épargne-pension, etc.), mais le plus souvent, avec un certain encouragement fiscal de la part des Etats. Il se crée de la sorte, à une échelle et à un rythme différents selon les pays, mais d'une manière de plus en plus généralisée, un énorme réservoir d'épargne collective confiée à la gestion d'intermédiaires professionnels comme les compagnies d'assurance et les banques, et s'orientant massivement vers les marchés financiers.

Le développement rapide de ces formes institutionnelles et collectives d'épargne financière à long terme s'orientant vers les investissements mobiliers contribue, avec les autres tendances décrites plus haut, à créer une nouvelle forme d'intermédiation financière où des entreprises spécialisées placent et gèrent, pour le compte des particuliers et d'autres entreprises, des masses gigantesques de capitaux.

Ainsi voit-on, dans une mesure croissante, les marchés de gros prendre le pas sur les marchés de détail, où les particuliers interviennent individuellement. Il en résulte une mutation des structures de marché exigeant notamment des sociétés plus grandes et plus capitalisées, disposant d'un personnel plus qualifié et plus spécialisé, et se livrant une concurrence très vive, au niveau des commissions comme de la qualité des services. La structure de marché traditionnelle, dans laquelle les intermédiaires jouent un simple rôle de commissionnaire, c'est-à-dire d'exécutant passif et rémunéré par une commission fixe, et où le "juste prix" est celui résultant de la confrontation d'un très grand nombre d'ordres de petite taille, reste sans doute valable pour certains segments des marchés boursiers, mais cesse d'être le modèle dominant.

Il en résulte un défi pour les autorités qui, elles aussi, devront dépasser les schémas traditionnels où, bien souvent, la protection du "petit épargnant" était préoccupation prioritaire, sinon exclusive. Aujourd'hui déjà, l'institutionnalisation et l'internationalisation des marchés, la taille des intermédiaires et les moyens technologiques mis en oeuvre posent les problèmes de supervision en termes tout à fait différents.

Au sein de la CEE, l'intégration des marchés nationaux va encore accélérer ce processus, contribuant à renforcer la concurrence, mais en même temps, à démanteler les barrières qui assuraient parfois une rentabilité relativement facile, et donc à accroître les risques. La collaboration supranationale entre les autorités de contrôle deviendra une dimension inéluctable des marchés financiers. Des efforts d'harmonisation des conditions de concurrence entre les différentes places financières, amorcés plus tôt dans le domaine bancaire, s'imposeront comme une nécessité dans le domaine des valeurs mobilières également. La CEE est en train de poser les premiers jalons dans ce sens, mais le problème se pose dès aujourd'hui à une échelle internationale bien plus large.

Part D
The Role of the Banks in the
Restructuring of European Industry

XVI. Why Do We Have This M & A Wave?

IVO G. CAYTAS and JULIAN I. MAHARI

Different people are wont to provide different answers to a perplexing issue: why has the 'urge to merge' affected industries worldwide all of a sudden with the amazing intensity we observe in virtually every industrialized country?
   Reasons obvious from the outset include:
1. Deregulation turned into a global movement due to the almost simultaneous ascendance to power of conservative parties in all major industrial nations.
2. Technology requires R&D investments that involve risks unmanageable for smaller units. If the torch is to be passed on, it has to be to someone able to shoulder the necessary investments.
3. Respect for bureaucracies has reached rock bottom. And there it will remain, for a while at least. Profit Centers and entrepreneurial 'small is beautiful' drives have cast doubt on the efficiency of large organizations. Virtually none of the stunning major market breakthroughs of the last two decades can be traced back to a bureaucratic corporate giant.

There are also some less-than-obvious reasons of undiminished intellectual power:
1. There is an unrivalled profit level to be achieved in record time by just changing things. Everything in business is, to some extent, a matter of justification. You don't have to be right as long as you have a compelling argument. Whoever okays the proposal does not spend his own funds. But with growth rates sharply restricted in most industries, anything that looks like dramatic change is valued as such.
2. When you start changing things, you can change more than you actually need to if the pretext is strong enough. Thus, you can cut costs after an M&A transaction to an extent that would face violent opposition if proposed under normal circumstances.
3. Extraordinarily large sums change hands. Hence, even the crumbs falling to providers of ancillary services are larger. They go to consultants, lawyers, accountants, bankers – people who get paid to see a deal get done and not to see it drown in the ifs and whens of paralyzing analysis. The incentive is overpowering to "help people manage change", as a major Drexel ad campaign claims. Analysis there must be, but with incentives like this,

D. E. Fair and C. de Boissieu (eds), Financial Institutions in Europe Under New Competitive Conditions, 223–233.
© 1990 *Kluwer Academic Publishers, Dordrecht. Printed in the Netherlands.*

analysis turns into a race for the best supporting argument.

Perhaps most disillusioning: there is no credible lobby opposing M&A. Who should that be? A crowd of senior executives clinging to their seats, a group of gentlemen well near retirement age with six- and seven-digit salaries pushing slogans like 'never change a winning team' or 'don't change horses in the midst of a river'? Unions picketing unprofitable shops that would long have been closed by their previous owners had they just found a socially acceptable occasion? Young Unemployed Previously Prosperous now Insolvent Executives (also known as Yuppies) laid off and now back on the trail "in search of excellence"? Politicians whose campaigns are funded and whose treasuries are filled by contributions and taxes splashed around generously before, during, and after such transactions? None of these so far have mustered the stamina to oppose the single most powerful driving force in capitalist society: the profit incentive.

It is important to understand how this mechanism came into being: in the beginning, tender offers targeted asset-rich, undervalued companies. They were restructured, stripped of some expendable assets, and financial "value" was created by mobilizing hidden reserves and untapped potential. In the meantime, markets have seen so many acquisitions go through that a ritual of price adjustment takes place almost automatically. A bid for a major corporation ups the stock price of all those similarly situated and invites other bidders. The more it all becomes a familiar process, the more the outcome is anticipated, expected, and thus facilitated. Long-standing socio-cultural objections to "unfriendly" bids are reduced to a mere squabble over price as nobody any longer expects shareholder loyalty to hold the incumbent management in place. Once this is achieved, an efficient market is within reach: transactions are examined and opposed with regard to their terms and not in principle.

M&A is, in fact, a veritable revolution against the security of mediocrity. It exposes to the cold winds of change everything that has gone unquestioned for a while in corporate structures. Every era has its iconoclastic period in business, and the M&A wave will continue well into the 1990s. For those faint of heart, it is a powerful incentive for "new thinking", for those overzealous there is a warning sign posted not to become the undertakers of the trade that they feed on. Political intervention and a carelessly triggered recession both lurk around the corners.

M&A is pure challenge. It may not be for the ultimate good of industry, as we do not have a deadline of reference set to test its beneficial or detrimental effects. The next really *big* recession may very well turn into a temporary disaster, but what about the splashy times until then? To this day and age, economic theory has not excelled in predicting reasonably *who* will be most affected by a recession, how, when, and why. It is safe to predict that the weakest will be hit worst, as they always are, but the weakest will be a shrinking segment of society this time: unskilled labor, people unwilling to move, people unwilling to change, people in dying industries. With growth rates like these, not much is added to the cake. But it can be split *very* differently between the same old participants in the game. That's what competition is about: while markets expand, rising sales do not hurt anyone since relative shares stay the same or may even shrink. But when opportunities are scarce, competition quickly becomes a burden to civilization: it can't stay civilized in the long run. Thus, creating opportunities, at the expense of whoever does not complain, is the common objective of all those who see their green pastures slowly turn yellow. That is precisely what is happening presently.

While the financial industry faces shrinking margins and listless business in substantial segments of its business, it is under extreme pressure to create new, untested, glamorous and promising playing grounds. Only persistent innovation keeps imitators at bay for a while, and imitation is nowhere easier. With all the talk about 'competence', it seems more like another 'c' word makes or breaks deals: contacts.

Although in today's highly professionalized environment, any proposal stands a fair chance to be examined on its merits, the crucial time factor is closely correlated with the issue of access. M&A can only be dealt with effectively on a top decision maker's level. The person you talk to has to have authority to decide, or at least to profoundly influence and shape the decision, or else invaluable days and weeks will be lost, personal interests entirely unrelated to the transaction will enter into play, and there is no telling which force will have what effect over what period of time. On the other hand, business research indicates an exaggerated tidal wave of items that are declared "top management responsibility", and the resulting over-crowding of desks has not quite produced the desired results. While ultimate responsibility rests at the top, substantive preparatory work obviously has to be carried out by lower echelons, and this is precisely the reason why polite compromises, careful hedges, and amazing restraint are typical of firms where the one who decides is compelled by organizational necessities to share responsibility and workload with others who are less interested but still play a game of their own. M&A is entrepreneurial, not organizational: always a matter of substantial risk in committing sizeable funds to a specific gamble on the future, it is easy to handle for a strong personality with a small handful of assistants, such as most raiders structure their operations; it is still possible to handle in enormous, anonymous organizations with thinly spread respon-sibilities like GM, Nestlé, or Mobil; but it does not work well at all in a bureaucratic and still internally competitive environment typical of commercial banks, less-than-giant major industrial corporations, and any group that is averse to quick, expensive, and visionary decisions with a considerable downside risk. The latter could be viewed as a subtle description of virtually all of mainstream central European industry.

Leveraged buyouts (LBOs) have become an integral part of the international restructuring arsenal. Defaults have been few while rates of return have exceeded most other investment opportunities offered worldwide.

Prior to the October 1987 stock market crash, money flowed into LBO funds as if investors had at last found the golden goose laying the golden egg. Then the crash hit. Stock prices plummeted, and investors recoiled with horror. Their visions of taking firms private and then going public again at lofty multiples evaporated. In a span of several hours, as the market took its worst drubbing since the great depression, the LBO perspective quickly receded into oblivion.

But in the two years since the crash, the dream has returned. Indeed, the macro-economics surrounding the deals may well be better than ever. Stock prices have adjusted since their inflated pre-crash levels but have remained relatively stable.

Many investment groups eyeing deals prior to the crash are finding post-crash prices irresistible. While they were worried about a continued free fall in stock prices immediately after Black Monday, the period of stability since has convinced many to re-enter the market. Deals that looked marginal in pre-crash conditions now look positively alluring. Plus, investors walk away with a veritable bonanza – interest rates have fallen. Since most LBOs are financed with at least 80 to 90 per cent debt, lower rates make any deal more attractive. Both edges of the investment sword have been sharpened with lower stock prices and lower interest rates. The only major cloud on the horizon is the growing chance of a recession that could cripple a firm's cash flow, which in turn would reduce its ability to repay lenders and provide investors with their expected rate of return.

THE SHAREHOLDER REVOLUTION

Executive power has been wisely used and sometimes blatantly abused in the past. Corporate raiders sowed the seeds of shareholder discontent a few years back, when they started to argue that many companies are poorly managed. Then, last year, institutional investors set out to challenge a growing number of companies to put to a vote the poison pills they had installed to thwart raiders. More and more institutions since have hoisted the activist banner. Their resolutions are aimed at more issues at more companies, such as confidential voting and shareholder access to the proxy statement, that would upset the existing balance of power between management and shareholders. Even though proxy victories have proved largely elusive, results were so encouraging that institutional investors seem determined to try again and keep coming back until they succeed.

Most managements, though, are readying for a fight. There is a more coordinated and more serious effort to hold down the vote. Proxy solicitors have been working hard, and banks are made more and more aware of a direct link between their voting record in support of management and the share of business they are awarded. Part of the effort is a stepped-up utilization of scientific "findings" that support management interest. For example, a group closely related to management interests discovered in 1988 that companies protected by poison pills command substantially higher premiums when they are taken over than companies without such provisions on their books. The implication and its message to shareholders is clear: poison pills add shareholder value, so don't vote against them. Less than a week later, the opposition counter-attacked: it surveyed prominent economists, each of whom concluded that the study and its methodology were se flawed that the conclusions were virtually meaningless.

Still, it is clear that shareholder activism is growing, extending far beyond the social issues, such as disinvesting in South Africa, that were focused on in the past. Management is going to have to learn to live with a whole class of investors who want to exercise their power on the central issues facing corporate governance.

THE EURO-BUYOUT

The restructuring wave which began in the United States at the turn of the decade is starting to reach Europe in earnest. The idea is basically the same, for a management group to buy a company by borrowing against its assets, and a lot of the money is coming from the same American coffers. But far from being a me-too affair, the European LBO has its own causes and its own perils. It is a safe bet that after 1992, a large number of large European companies will reorganize and rationalize by shedding inessential units or acquiring synergy. Britain already is a hotbed while on the Continent, most deals are still comparatively small. Although financiers have augmented their available funds to buy substantial equity stakes in Europe, much more than the availability of money is at issue. Across Europe, an entire generation that founded companies after World War II is approaching retirement age and facing often difficult succession problems. Luckily for them, a new breed of entrepreneurs has grown up, attempting to run bigger companies, and in their vanguard, the marriage brokers appear. As in the United States, European LBO candidates tend to be in staid, cash-rich businesses, and some deals occur as a direct result of restructuring by US parents. Parallels to the US notwithstanding, there are vast cultural, legal, and tax divides that make Europe a dangerous turf for uninitiated buyout artists. In West Germany, reluctance to accept new ideas has a lot to do with having lost two wars and many investors having lost all their property twice. Swiss companies are still able to disenfranchise hostile shareholders, while in France, Italy, and Spain the laws make it hard to borrow money secured by assets that are yet to be bought. Throughout Europe, labor laws are stacked against the sweeping layoffs that mark a number of American LBOs. Many euro-deals involve a founding family selling a private company, and it is never easy to figure out what one is worth. Even when the target is a subsidiary of a publicly traded company, it is more troublesome to deal in Europe than in the United States: plants may have to be acquired in a dozen countries and borrowings to be arranged in half a dozen currencies. There is also palpable resistance to American-style financial engineering that burdens companies with 90 per cent debt and leaves only 10 per cent equity. Financial gearing is slow to approach the Continent.

SECURING FUTURE EARNINGS

Fears of undesired tender offers cause managements to invest heavily into quick-payoff projects and starve commitments that would yield income years from now. They are doing it for a number of reasons, most commonly the desperate wish to raise the company's stock price in order to fend off prospective acquirers. Ironically, the strategy these days is often backfiring: investors see the prodigal policies for what they are and disinvest anyway. Overall, corporate commitment to growth remains high. But we can cite a disturbing number of businesses that are falling prey to myopic management. The tendency seems to be spreading: most companies are making at least some decisions today that are not in the long-term interest of shareholders. Figuring out which projects make economic sense is theoretically simple. A manager maps out the expected costs and revenues over the years and then, using a percentage figure as the cost of money over time, calculates the project's present value. If it is positive, the project should be done. In practice, of course, the exercise is not nearly so simple, since no one can be sure what the expenditures or revenues or cost of money will be. One could assume the worst – or assume that investors will assume the worst – and scorn projects that could take years to pay off. Or one may abandon textbook analysis and follow a different rule: Any project that pays off after the manager in charge changes places is not worthwile. Paradoxically, the high price/earnings ratio of many stocks probably discourages executives from investing in the long term. Investors are less willing to buy promises of growth when P/E multiples are this high. Even if the growth materializes, the P/E could drop sharply if the stock market dives, making the investment unattractive. Though in theory they should not, high P/Es shorten investors' time horizons and at the same time executive outlooks.

The same effect can result from excess frugality. A company managed by accountants is bound to let erstwhile successes fade away under the misconception of payoff deadlines and product development expectations. If executives believe prospects for the business are not worth funding, they tend to pocket the remaining profits and let the business slowly waste away. Outsiders can tell when an operation is not properly financed. Excess borrowing is one tip-off, as nothing collapses future prospects more quickly. A great swell of debt transforms managers from long-term planners into frantics scurrying about trying to keep it from drowning the company. In their haste to free up cash for debt service, these managers often cut funding for new projects, trim the research budget, slim down the payroll, even skimp on capital spending and maintenance. Investors are affected once their company cannot refurbish equipment, its competitive position erodes, and profits drop. The only opportunity for making money in the stock of such poorly managed companies is for shortsellers.

A CHANGED INVESTMENT ATTITUDE: MERCHANT BANKING

Traditional investment banking used to be a strictly intermediary affair. The firm would represent a client for a fee, providing advice and financing without committing its own equity. There was a potential for losses if fees could not be generated in sufficient amounts to cover costs, or if underwritten issues could not be placed in the market for the calculated price. However, profits were limited to the fee, and risk-taking was an unmentionable part of a banker's vocabulary. Times change.

In 1989, the merchant banking variety of investment banking has the banker step in not as an intermediary only, but as a (sometimes managing) partner by his client's side. Although commissions and fees still account for a sizeable portion of revenues, the emphasis continues to shift to an active investment of a bank's own funds. In other words, investment bankers are out to own industrial and service corporations, just as the clients they advise. The role of well-paid hirelings is shifting to supporting status only, while the ability to mobilize large amounts of money taps the most important strategic advantage in the business. The roots of this type of merchant banking go back to the era of J.P. Morgan, when a fusion of finance and commerce helped lay the foundation of industrial America. The resurgence of this phenomenon tilts the United States closer to the systems of Japan, Germany, Italy , or France, where banks are customary majority shareholders in trade and industry. The difference is that in those countries, it's a small world for major players, and it is virtually impossible for anyone belonging to the financial establishment to promote a course of action that is flagrantly opposed to the prevailing perspective. That makes the implementation of changes via financial routes much harder to accomplish. The American advantage is the free-for-all spirit without a clear power center and without a dominating consensus. Nobody is strong enough there to enforce a code of do's and don'ts that are not dictated by the parties' self-defined interest. No universal retortive action looms for antagonizing one or the other Fortune 500 firm, loyalties are rationalized and therefore substitutional, no close-knit elite guards access to the feasibility of certain transactions.

However, freedom has not brought only benefits to those power investors. Firms like Kohlberg Kravis Roberts focus solely on equity investment. Most other investment banks in the race, however, provide a multitude of other fee-based services, such as underwriting high-yield debt. That could blur their judgment as investors, with negative consequences for the companies they acquire. The other significant difference is that companies acquired by LBO specialists are very often broken up and sold off for quick profits. The new type of bank/investor claim that they are interested in a long-term position, willing to keep their acquisitions largely intact for up to 10 years. On the eventual resale or recapitalization of a company or a division, they can realize substantial capital gains.

Investment bankers insist they can expand their customary short-term horizons by putting their firm's own capital on the line, this assuring that their interests are completely synchronized with those of their co-investors and the companies they acquire. To facilitate the shift from dealbroker to owner, they strive hard to promote a different breed of banker: more value is being placed on longer-term viewpoints and experience in basic detailwork such as inventory control and cash management. It will also be necessary to rotate bankers to industrial holdings to expose them profoundly to the industrial world they are expected to relate to. A pool of operating talent is assembled that might be capable of dealing with the questions that confront the industrial holding companies banks are more and more resembling nowadays. Ironically, the more adept investment banks become at owning companies, the more they risk damaging their franchise as advisors to major corporations. The merchant banking tendency is deeply troubling some corporate clients as there is an inherent conflict of interest when an agent becomes a principal at the same time. For instance, it is not quite sure clients will get the first shot at what the bank itself might be willing to buy. A situation might be created where corporations never find out there was an opportunity to buy a particular target company. This problem is particularly acute for traditional LBO firms that have long relied on banks to bring them deals. A bank might also be excluded from lenders' meetings where sensitive strategic and financial information is shared by an industrial corporation once it acquires a competing operation. Investment bankers downplay such issues. There are always conflicts in their business, they argue, they just have to be managed right. Competition with a client cannot be ruled out any longer, but in one or the other form, this has happened all the time in the past as well. If banks have relied in the past on relationships to get business, they might change that in the course of the 1990s to a situation where they get the business in part because they have a major stake in their clients.

In the near future, the pressure to embark on merchant banking might become overpowering. Banks that try to resist will find it increasingly difficult to compete with those that are generating vast capital gains from their principal deals. Likewise, the more profitable firms will be able to compensate their professionals better, which is a major strategic advantage. However, with so many inexperienced new players rushing to get into the business, and so much money at large to support them, the chance for disaster is growing. Corporations could be tempted to take on too much debt in their eagerness to derive the benefits of private ownership. Ultimately, of course, market discipline will set in: investment banks that fail will not be able to attract investors the next time.

Another hazard to be watched closely is the impact highly leveraged transactions have on bondholders. While equity owners benefit from the gearing, bond ratings usually fall into a bottomless precipice at the sheer announcement of a buyout. This reflects the fact that extra debt means extra risk for unsecured creditors. It is likely that some legislative action will be taken in due course, perhaps limiting the debt/equity ratio or requiring some form of collateral to be posted. It is almost inevitable: equity investors tend to be entrepreneurial in mind, while bond creditors represent the vast majority of fixed-income security holders that mirror the general investing public's perspective. With numbers so clearly stacked against equity interests, political reaction to rebalance the situation cannot be too far ahead.

UNLIKELY PLAYERS

However, much of the potential for M&A has not even been tapped yet. There is an unlimited supply of actors who have yet to enter the field and are very likely to do so sooner or later as the bidding for corporate control becomes more and more of a standard event.

In thousands of companies large and small, employees are starting to act as if they own the place. In more and more, they are entitled, because they do. The employee stockholder is a phenomenon very familiar in the United States, breaking ground in Japan, but not much of a force to reckon with in Europe yet. Employee Stock Ownership Plans, or ESOPs, are rapidly gaining adherents among corporate managements everywhere. By giving workers a stake in the operation, a company can boost morale and productivity. As an M&A tool ESOPs are useful for both financing corporate control transactions and staving them off. In some countries, investors who launch a bid can reduce their borrowing costs if they set aside part of their stock for employees. At the same time, a corporation seeking to repel an offer can use employee shares as a way to put a sizeable share of the company into relatively friendly hands. In Japan, ESOPs have been initiated as a means of fending off foreign buyers. Today, more than 90 per cent of all companies listed on Japan's eight stock exchanges have some kind of employee participation scheme. In West Germany, ESOPs are subsidized by the Government but have not reached significance since allotment is strictly limited to a modest sum per employee. Nevertheless, interesting developments can be expected if a certain number of firms follow existing precedent and fall prey to a most unexpected hostile bidder: their own employees. Much the same interest lies ahead in the case of unions beginning to mobilize their remarkable funds for changing sides and accepting entrepreneurial responsibility through owning firms outright.

Not at all unlikely, just a little bit less familiar, is the sight of large corporations going after each other. This sort of transaction is facilitated by their borrowing capacity just as much as by their liquid reserves, also known as war chests. The Time/Warner/Paramount situation reminded us once again that white gloves do not necessarily mean tender manners.

As funding is the key to M&A success, the role of resourceful commercial banks is likely to increase as they realize that regardless of remaining reservations, they do not stand a chance to keep out of the restructuring business as it develops into a major occupation of the financial markets. For a commercial bank, it is very important to go into transactions not only as an adviser on the M&A side, but also to finance it. Under liberalized lending policies, many of those loans take the form of mezzanine or subordinated debt that is a sophisticated form of underwriting. Banks hold these papers for a long time and have to project on business risks over 10-15-year periods. Private placement and bank syndication will develop to complement each other as a valuable blend of services offered in support of mostly friendly transactions.

AN OVERALL PERSPECTIVE ON M&A

Like everyone, the M&A industry worries about the economy in general and interest rates in particular. After a decade of booming business, the need to adjust to impending change is viewed with trepidation. Virtually all agree that the future will be tougher on antitrust, but just how much nobody can predict. There is also consensus that the present favorable environment will not last forever, but experience shows that a stock market drop does not affect M&A considerably. Not even a recession might: the present level of leveraging has produced a mountain of debt that will call for restructuring once severe conditions threaten layers of high-yield bonds. There is a lot of business generated by pressing worries, and prime objects will be cheap for those who can afford to pay in acceptable currency.

Our long-term prognosis on M&A is extremely favorable, regardless of the fact that a recession might certainly reduce the number and volume of deals. The ones most likely to be cut are transactions riding on the coat-tails of a market trend, and little pity should be wasted for those. Intelligent, creative visions will continue to benefit from the enhanced awareness of the specific requirements and utilities of an efficient market for corporate control, and market liquidity for such projects is unlikely to dry up as international opportunities outside the industrialized world remain scarce. Banks badly hurt in sovereign lending are very likely to continue support for a controllable mega-risk even of the size of KKR's buyout of RJR Nabisco and Jimmy Goldsmith's bid for B.A.T. Size, to an extent, is a guarantee for success, as failure would be impossible to afford. Nobody wants to speculate about what might happen if this assumption should ever fail. In more than just one way, we might find ourselves in a home-grown dilemma of the size of the international debt crisis. But it is more than likely that such and comparable doomsday scenarios will not, for all their predictable political impact, be allowed to occur without a government-sponsored "soft-landing" of sorts.

Or so we care to delude ourselves.

XVII. The Merger Game: Playing Against the Odds

DAVID J. RAVENSCRAFT

A new round of the merger and acquisition game has begun in Europe. This round may attract a record number of players. There were 1,900 recorded acquisitions in the European Economic Community from January to September of 1988, a 16 per cent increase over the same periode in 1987. Over the next five years, "something over 20,000 European companies will be involved in mergers and acquisitions," according to Lawrence Banks of Robert Fleming & Co. Ltd.[1] If realized, this would exceed the number of acquisitions in any of the US merger waves.

The game's attraction, of course, is its high stakes. For companies, the prize is a slice of forthcoming integrated European market. For shareholders, it is the large premiums paid to shareholders of the target firms which in the US has totaled to $ 296 billion over the last ten years.[2] For investment bankers and merger lawyers, it is the high fees paid for each transaction. For society, it is the increased efficiencies that should accompany merger and acquisitions.

However, the value of a game also depends on the probability of winning. The merger game has been played numerous times in many different countries. This paper reviews the evidence on prior mergers in order to measure the chances of merger success. As the title suggests, the paper concludes that, from the perspective of the bidding companies, the odds are against mergers and acquisitions achieving the desired efficiency gains. The paper draws from past experience a list of the major causes of merger failure which must be overcome if the odds are going to be improved. Since every game is somewhat different, this paper also discusses the relationship between previous merger activity and the current situation in Europe.

I. LESSONS FROM PREVIOUS MERGERS AND ACQUISITIONS

Ravenscraft-Scherer research

Have mergers and acquisitions resulted in improvements in economic efficiency? To answer this question, F. M. Scherer and I compiled and analyzed

D. E. Fair and C. de Boissieu (eds), Financial Institutions in Europe Under New Competitive Conditions, 235–249.
© 1990 *Kluwer Academic Publishers, Dordrecht. Printed in the Netherlands.*

a large statistical data base of approximately 6,ooo US acquisitions occurring between 1950 and 1977. Each acquisition was linked to the Federal Trade Commission Line of Business (FTC LB) data. For the years 1974–1977, the FTC required 471 of the largest US companies to report detailed data on each of their business units. The typical company had almost 8 manufacturing lines of business (LB) yielding a total of over 3,000 manufacturing LBs per year. With this sample, it was possible to analyze the incidence of acquired line sell-offs, and for the surviving product lines, how 1974–77 profitability varied with diverse kinds of merger experience.

Rather than finding evidence of improved efficiency, we found the opposite – on average profitability deteriorated after the acquisition. The typical target company's profitability prior to the acquisition was 8 percentage points above its industry average suggesting that acquiring companies sought "stars" or well-managed companies with established brands. After the acquisition, profitability declined to normal if we ignore the premium paid and subsequent asset re-evaluations (i.e., pooling-of-interest accounting). If the premium paid and asset re-evaluations are included (i.e., purchase accounting), then post-acquisition profitability was three percentage points below the industry average of the acquired business units. The rate in decline of profitability for acquired companies was significantly faster than comparable highly profitable firms which remained independent, indicating the decline was more than just regression to the mean.

This profitability decline represents the good news about acquisitions. The bad news is that almost one-third of all acquisitions are subsequently undone through divestiture. Many unprofitable acquisitions had been sold off prior to 1974, so they were not included in the above declines. Our analysis of 285 business units fully divested between 1975 and 1981, confirmed that sell-offs during the 1970s were indications of managerial failure. For these sell-offs, we had data on pre-divestiture profitability. Three or five years before the sell-off commenced, profitability of the affected unit went into a sharp decline. In the year before the full sell-off, the average ratio of operating income to assets of the divested business unit was *minus* 1.09 per cent or almost 14 percentage points below the industry average.

Furthermore, we found a clear link between acquisition and divestiture. Our multivariate analysis of divisional sell-offs reveals that a divestiture was twice as likely for lines with a merger history than for those without, all else equal. Finally, we did not find any *statistical* evidence that the conditions that led to a sell-off had pre-merger antecedents.[3] For a sample of 215 acquisitions that were subsequently sold off, pre-merger profitability differed trivially from that of acquired but retained companies, holding firm size and the method of accounting constant.

Not all acquisitions are created equal and we did find important differences between acquisition types. Not surprising, conglomerate acquisitions displayed the worst performance both in terms of lower profitability and higher sell-offs. However, horizontal acquisitions also experienced profit declines. Only for tender offers did we find any evidence supporting the hypothesis that mergers are an attempt to replace inefficiently managed companies. In the year before the acquisition, targets of tender offers displayed profit rates slightly below their industry average. The new management, however, did not do any better. Profitability failed to improve in the years following a successful tender offer. The only acquisition category for which we found efficiency improvements was mergers-of-equals. When two firms of roughly equal size combined, profitability increased from normal to slightly above normal, although this increase was insignificant in many specifications and did not include any premium paid or asset revaluations.

Our research also contains an important corollary. A minority of firms expanded into new business units through internal growth rather than acquisitions. Controlling for industry effects and accounting methods, internally grown business units had significantly higher profit rates than acquired lines. Internal growth also lead to a lower rate of divestiture. Thus, it appears that firms have been too quick in choosing the acquisition route as a means of expanding.

Additional evidence on post-acquisition performance

Other studies confirm our acquisition-related performance decline results. Dennis Mueller studied changes in market share for the top 1,000 US companies over a 22 year period, 1950–1972.[4] Acquisitive companies experience dramatic reductions in market shares relative to companies with little or no merger activity during this period. Although horizontal acquisitions fared better than conglomerate, they too experienced a decrease in their combined market share. Work by Michael Porter suggests that the Ravenscraft and Scherer estimate of 33 per cent divestiture rate was too low.[5] By studying an even longer time period, 1950–1986, he found a 60 per cent divestiture rate for the 33 companies in his sample. He concludes the "track record of corporate strategies has been dismal" (p. 43). Porter also confirmed the finding that internally developed business units had a much higher survival rate than acquired lines. The evidence from two earlier US merger waves and preliminary estimates from the current 1980s US merger wave also fails to find average gains from acquisition activity.[6]

Poor acquisitions performance does not appear to be the domain of US companies. Mueller organized an international comparison of merger activity across seven countries, Belgium, Federal Republic of Germany, France, The Netherlands, Sweden, the United Kingdom and the United States.[7] From this project he concluded, "the rather consistent lack of evidence that mergers led to or were expected to lead to significant increase in profits is inconsistent with all the neoclassical theories of mergers" (p. 314–115). The similarity in results between the US and European countries was particularly surprising given "the much heavier incidence of horizontal merger activity in the European countries" (p. 315). McDougall, Round, Crouch and Wirth attempted to extend this international comparison to Australia for the 1970–1981 period.[8] They found that: "while neither study has provided much systematic support for the efficacy of a strategy of corporate acquisitions, it is noticeable that acquiring firms in Australia suffered more from the takeover experience than their overseas counterparts, despite the fact that the Australian acquirers generally exhibited superior pre-takeover performances" (p. 174). Not even the Japanese seem to be able to generate synergies from acquisitions. In a sample of 46 Japanese acquisitions occurring between 1980–1987, Odagiri and Hase found insignificant declines in the acquiring firms profitability and growth.

The history of post-merger performance is sobering. For many time periods and across many countries, profitability and market share performance fail to improve after the acquisition and many mergers are subsequently undone.

The stock market evaluation

Against this backdrop of poor merger performance, the stock market has consistently remained optimistic about mergers. Bradley, Desai & Kim demonstrate that the net gain to bidders and targets from tender offers over the period 1963–1984 has remained fairly constant at about seven per cent of the combined stock value.[9] Net gains to bidders and targets from mergers and acquisitions also tend to be significantly positive although somewhat smaller than in tender offers.[10] Similar net gains to shareholders have been found in Australia (Bishop, Dodd and Officer), Canada (Eckbo) and the UK (Franks, Harris and Mayer).[11]

While the stock market and post-merger performance results are difficult to reconcile fully, there are some potential explanations for these differences or overlapping conclusions that can be drawn. First, a net gain to shareholders does not necessarily translate into increased post-merger performance. The shareholders' gain may stem from undervalued assets or they may be the result of transfers from workers, bondholders, suppliers, local communities or governments to shareholders. Shleifer and Summers argue that the transfers from workers and communities may be large in some cases.[12] Declines in bond prices resulting from recent leverage buyouts and takeovers (e.g., RJR Nabisco Inc. and B.A.T. Industries PLC) shows the potential for transfers from bondholders.

Second, the message the stock market is sending to the bidders is not exactly positive. Most stock market studies of recent US mergers and acquisitions reveal a negative and often statistically significant return to the bidder at the time of the merger announcement.[13] On average, the bidder stock price drops between 1 to 3 per cent on the announcement of an acquisition. The stock price decline may not stop at the acquisition announcement. Some researchers have found continued bidder stock price declines for several years after the acquisition. According to Magenheim and Mueller, these price decreases maybe as large as 15 to 40 per cent.[14] Post-acquisition bidder losses could swamp the combined bidder and target gains observed around the merger announcement. This would bring the stock market evidence in line with other post-merger performance findings.

Third, according to *Mergers and Acquisitions*, divestitures and LBOs accounted for over 50 per cent of all US mergers and acquisitions over the last several years. Thus, a significant part of the current US merger wave involves restructuring and the shedding of previous acquisitions that no longer make sense. This restructuring and the stock gains that are associated with them can hardly be viewed as supporting the efficacy of mergers and acquisitions. In a recent issue, *Mergers and Acquisitions* warns that a similar fate may face some European firms. "In an intriguing parallel with the American stock market of the 1960s, the biggest and most active European acquirers were darlings of the overseas equity markets in the early 1980s. But recently, they have been treated more rudely by investors who are demanding stellar follow-up performances" (March/April 1989, p. 60).

Thus, even stock market data suggests that many mergers and acquisitions have not worked and that on average this activity probably destroys rather than creates value for the acquiring company. Stock market studies, however, do show a positive combined return to bidders and targets. Therefore, mergers and acquisitions result in a net gain to shareholders. The problem is, the source of the shareholder gains is not well understood. The accounting and divestiture results indicate that the gain does not stem from increases in post-merger performance.

II. MAJOR CAUSES OF MERGER FAILURE

History suggests that the odds are against at least the bidder in the merger game. Therefore, it appears that the "rules of the game" are stacked against successful acquisitions. This section discusses some of the main problems that can lead to failed acquisitions.

Managerial control loss

For many (if not most) mergers the skills and expertise of the acquired company's personnel are critical to the continued success of the acquired businesses. Yet, research shows that the turnover rate for acquired company's management is almost twice as large as non-acquired companies. Over 60 per cent of the acquired company's top managers turn over in five years.[15] A major cause of this turnover is the reduction in the incentives of target managers who change from top executives to line managers. For example, in the fourth largest US merger in 1988, Eastman Kodak acquired Sterling Drug. Kodak was counting on Sterling's management experience to become a major player in the pharmaceutical industry. Within six months five senior managers resigned including Sterling's CEO John Pietruski. According to a *Wall Street Journal* interview, he called the transition from being the head of a publicly traded company to a division "a culture shock". "You're no longer the top guy. Someone else is. I had less ability to dictate the organizational structure, or devise tactics to run the company and make basic decisions."[16] The less experience the acquiring company's managers have in the target company's industries, the more serious is this loss of expertise.

Conflict in corporate culture

In a recent survey by Business International of 150 executives mostly based in Europe, "cultural differences between the two companies" was cited as the greatest acquisition difficulty.[17] A clash in corporate cultures can create havoc even for acquisitions with large potential synergies. Take GE's 1988 acquisition of the US investment banking firm Kidder Peabody & Co. "GE believed the synergies could be great," according to the *Wall Street Journal*. "Kidder could take some of GE Capital's loans, make securities out of them and sell them to customers. GE Capital could invest in LBO candidates identified by Kidder... But differences in culture and business philosophy sharply handicapped those efforts. Employees of the two units didn't like each other."[18] As a result, the two divisions often competed rather than cooperated. The conflict resulted in the loss of a number of key Kidder personnel. Similar corporate clashes have hurt General Motors acquisition of Electronic Data System (EDS) and IBM's acquisition of Rohm.

The potential conflict in culture escalates in cross-border takeovers. In a 1988 UK conference for Acquisition Professionals, Patrick Grafton of BHF-Bank stated "buyers must pay strict attention to potential clashes in corporate culture resulting from national differences... Corporate culture has been a deal killer."[19]

Asymmetric information or latent problems

Acquirers are at an information disadvantage. Targets know much more about the condition of their firm (and for diversifying acquisitions their industry) than the buyer. This is a classic "lemons" problem which is most often associated with used cars.[20] Target firms can take advantage of this asymmetric information by voluntarily selling the firm when trouble is on the horizon. In friendly mergers, bidders do have access to the target's books, but even the most careful inspection may not disclose all the pitfalls. When the US conglomerate Textron bought Talon company in 1968, Talon had 42 per cent of all US zipper sales. Interviews with Talon insiders suggested that Textron bought Talon at its peak and paid far too much.[21] In the year of the acquisition the Japanese firm YKK stepped up its imports into the US. Due in part to YKK technological lead and lower production costs, Textron's Talon division steadily declined in the 1970's. By 1979, Talon had outright losses. It was sold in 1981 for one-third of the price paid. In at least ten of the 15 case studies of acquisitions that were subsequently sold off, analyzed by Scherer and myself, detectable latent problems unnoticed or unheeded by the buyer grew eventually to be a source of considerable post-acquisition distress.

Hostile takeovers face a slightly different problem. Management's opposition may be a sign that the firm is not a lemon. However, management may fight even if there are latent problems if they feel they are more likely to solve the problems or their main concern is protecting their job. Since hostile bidders often have access to only public documents, they cannot make the same detailed check of the companies' books that occurs in friendly acquisitions. Relying on mainly public financials was costly to Merv Griffin's troubled 1988 takeover of Resorts International. "We found a surprising number of things about the company that were different from what we anticipated," said David Hanlon, Resorts new CEO.[22]

Winner's curse

When the Canadian and US retail giants Campeau Corp. and R. H. Macy & Co. battled it out for the US retail firm Federated Department Stores Inc. in early 1988, the bidding got intense. Campeau's initial bid started at $ 47 a share. To win Campeau had to bid $ 73.50. The *Wall Street Journal*'s front page headlines the day after the bidding war ended was: "Campeau at Last Gets Federated – Now Can He Make a Go of It? To Win, Canadian Took on Huge Debt at a Time When Chains Are Hurting. *From Macy's, a Sigh of Relief*."[23] (emphasis added). Macy's chairman, Edward Finkelstein, went on to say, "We're both lucky to get out of this alive... I'm very pleased

I don't have to deal with it and he does." Such bidding wars are becoming increasingly common. Who wins a bidding war? One answer is the firm that can bring the most synergies or the better management to the deal. An alternative possibility stems for the winner's curse hypothesis – the winner in a bidding contest is the individual or firm with the most optimistic expectations about the future of the company and the economy. Evidence supporting the winner's curse hypothesis has been found in bids for off-shore oil, timber tracts and takeover targets.[24] When the 'winner's curse' is combined with the hubris possessed by many executives, overly optimistic projections can prevail.

Bad luck

In any gamble, luck plays a role. Some merger failures can be traced to unforeseen events. For example, in early 1973 Bendix Corporation acquired a mobile home and recreational division from Boise Cascade Corporation. The timing could not have been worse. The oil crises of late 1973 and early 1974 caused the sales of recreational vehicles to plummet. Bad luck, however, only explains individual merger failure. It cannot account for the consistently poor performance of mergers overall, since good luck presumably balances out the losses.

Agency problems

According to finance theory, the shareholders are the owners of the company and the managers are agents hired to maximize shareholder value. Agency problems arise when the agents do not have the same incentives as the individuals who employ them. Evidence suggests that the incentives of the managers and shareholders often do diverge. Cross-sectional studies of senior executive compensation have discovered a startling fact. Rather than being based on performance, compensation levels are determined by firm size and indirectly growth. On average, a 10 per cent increase in firm size will lead to a 3 per cent increase in a CEO's salary and bonus. After reviewing the executive compensation evidence, Baker, Jensen and Murphy reach the obvious conclusion. The evidence "suggests that CEOs can increase their pay by increasing firm size, even when the increase in size reduces the firm's market value. This could explain some of the vast amount of inefficient expenditures of corporate resources on diversification programs that have created large conglomerate organizations over the last 20 years" (p. 609).[25]

A more subtle form of the agency problem arises in diversification programs aimed at decreasing the company's risk. Many mergers are undertaken to smooth the earnings of the bidder's cyclical business or to move from a declining to a growth industry. However, since shareholders can diversify risks on their own, this form of risk reduction does not increase shareholder value.

Vague goals and poor planning

The Business International survey discussed above also found that "clarity of purpose and objectives" was the most critical success factor in managing an acquisition."[26] However, the attainment of efficiencies in acquisitions are often only vaguely outlined in merger planning. For example, Michael Porter notes, "If you believe the text of countless corporate annual reports, just about anything is related to just about anything else! But imagined synergy is much more common than real synergy. GM's purchase of Hughes Aircraft simply because cars were going electronic and Hughes was an electronic concern demonstrates the folly of paper synergy."[27] Even in horizontal mergers, expected efficiency gains can be more assumed than actual. Sutherland's analysis of the UK 's Monopolies Commission reports concludes that "the net savings, when they are quantified at all are rather strikingly small."[28] A similar observation has been made in discussions I have had with US antitrust officials.

An obvious solution to many of the above problems is more careful acquisition planning. Indeed, almost half of the Business International survey respondents said that if they had the acquisition to do over again, they would "be much more thorough in the analysis beforehand."[29] However, in today's competitive merger market, planning time is not a luxury that is often afforded. The second bidder in a tender offer battle may have only a couple of days to come up with a competing offer. And, in the heat of the battle careful analysis can be overtaken by the desire to win. An illustration of this timing problem is provided by Jemison and Sitkin. They describe an acquisition in which a team of 150 specialists (most of whom had never worked together) were assembled within a 30 hour period for a deal that took only 6 days.[30] It is easy to see how major problems can be overlooked in this type of process.

III. EUROPE 1992 AND THE US DEREGULATION MOVEMENT

Thus far, I have emphasized the downside risks of mergers and acquisitions. There are many positive motives for merging that can produce significant efficiency gains.[31] One of the most important merger motives underlying the current US merger wave has been deregulation in key industries. Substantial changes in the organization of markets necessitates changes in firms' organizational structure. Mergers are one way of achieving these changes.

The US deregulation movement pales in comparison to the organizational changes that are occurring in the push for an integrated Europe. Regulatory constraints have limited many firms' ability to obtain economies of scale or to spread the large fixed costs of such items as R&D. As a consequence, in many European industries, like heavy equipment and telecommunications, the number of firms greatly exceeds the comparable number in integrated markets such as the United States. Rationalization of plants to eliminate this overcapacity is needed. Thus, the potential for successful mergers and acquisitions in Europe may be more promising than many in the past.

Three factors will help determine whether these economies can be achieved through mergers and acquisitions. First, fragmentation of Europe results from not only regulation but also from custom, language, culture and the historical infrastructure inherited by each country. The question becomes, absent regulatory constraints, can standardization be achieved, or will product differentiation prevail? The answer will vary from industry to industry. Standardization and the accompanying economies of scales were achieved even under the old rules in the elevator industry, but product differentiation and profitable regional firms are likely to continue in the major domestic appliance industry.[32]

Second, acquisitions are not the only means of adapting to a changing environment. The historical evidence suggest that internal growth has outperformed acquisitions. The Japanese, for example, appear to be very successful in global expansion through building new plants instead of acquiring them. The building of new plants has a number of distinct advantages over the combining of existing plants. New plants allow the introduction of the latest technology. For example, US steel firms who have developed minimills have outperformed steel firms involved in horizontal acquisitions.[33] Economies of scale are also easier to capture through a new large-scale plant than the combination of two older smaller plants. Furthermore, countries or states seek out new plant locations often through financial incentives, whereas they may restrict the rationalization of old plants particularly when they are accompanied by a loss of jobs.

Third, positive motives do not negate the problems faced by acquisitions. Most causes of merger failure apply to cross-border acquisitions. Integrating corporate cultures is particularly difficult in these acquisitions. The inexperience of acquirers in the target's country makes retaining key personnel important, a difficult task in acquisitions. Latent problems in the target firm may also be harder to identify given this inexperience.

Competition for good European acquisition cadidates, which is already evident, is likely to intensify leading to the potential for overpayment due to the 'winner's curse'. Even the goals of globalization and integration are poor reasons to merge unless these concepts are specifically operationalized in context of each acquisition.

Deregulation of banking and airlines in the US

Only time will tell whether the merger incentives created by a changing regime in Europe will dramatically increase the odds of merger success. However, some additional insight can be obtained from a closer look at US mergers in industries that underwent deregulation. Two industries stand out in this regard – banking and airlines. Partial deregulation of the banking industry began with the Depository Institutions Deregulation and Monetary Control Act of 1980 and was extended with the Garn-St. Germain Act of 1982. These acts increased competition in banking by phasing out interest-rate ceilings and removing restrictions on new services, in particular, money market funds. Airline deregulation began in 1978 with the Airline Deregulation Act, which initiated the elimination of non-safety-related airline regulations and the Civil Aeronautics Board over a period of several years. A substantial amount of merger activity followed in both of these industries. In fact, the banking and transportation industries account for approximately 15 to 25 per cent of the 1980's merger wave in the US.

The results of mergers and acquisitions from the banking sector are easily summarized because they closely parallel the general evidence. Studies of post-merger data fail to find a gain in performance. Stock market data, on the other hand, find positive gains to the target bank and positive net gains to both bidder and target. However, like the overall economy findings, the bidder firm incurs declines in shareholder value.[34] Thus, deregulation does not seem to have improved merger performance in banking relative to the rest of the economy.

The failure to find efficiency gains in banking is not entirely surprising for two reasons. First, banking studies have not found evidence of economies of scale (declining long run average cost as a bank increases its size at a given location) or economies of scope (lower costs due to having banks in numerous different locations).[35] Second, over the last couple of years US regional banks have consistently outperformed national money centers.

The change in the airline industry due to deregulation is both complex and dramatic. Thus, a brief summary of the changes is difficult. However, a number of general trends can be identified. First, while problems have developed, deregulation has clearly increased social welfare. Second, after an initial period of expansion, a few airlines, all of whom have roots in the regulated period, have come to dominate the industry. The five largest airlines own more of the passenger traffic today than they did prior to deregulation. Third, partly because of the development of the "hub and spoke" system and computerized reservation systems, entry into the industry is very difficult. The only major early entrant, People Express, failed. Fourth, mergers played a key role in both the increased efficiency gain and the increased concentration. Finally, many of these changes were not anticipated by either the proponents or opponents of deregulation.

As a consequence of this dynamic environment, airline merger performance differs significantly from the typical performance discussed thus far – with one important exception – diversification through merger does not appear to work in airlines either. The only attempt to diversify into general travel from airlines (United Airlines) was dismantled under the threat of a hostile takeover. Although no hard data exists, the majority of *horizontal* airline mergers appear to have increased the performance of the combined firm and many acquisitions helped financially distressed target companies. The stock market anticipated this improved performance with average stock price increases for *both* the bidder and target airline companies around the merger announcement.[36] Nevertheless, airline mergers have been controversial for several reasons. First, integration problems and loss of managerial expertise have not been inconsequential. Second, many experts question whether the gains have been shared with consumers. In fact, for some mergers the gains may have come at the expense of consumers. Due to lack of antitrust enforcement, prices have increased after several of the mergers. Morrison and Winston conclude that one-half or more of the six most recent airline mergers have decreased travelers' welfare.[37] Finally, despite the focus on horizontal acquisitions, one of the top seven airline companies was taken over and three others are currently takeover targets or rumored takeover targets. Firms must wonder what it takes to keep from being a target of a takeover.

IV. CONCLUSION

Like any investment, mergers and acquisitions are a gamble. In the merger game, the target shareholders are like the house, they always take their cut and therefore strongly support the game. The bidding firms and capital providers are the gamblers, they must assess the odds and the amount they wish to risk. History suggests that the odds are against bidder's success. Hopefully, by documenting these odds and the problems that cause mergers to fail, this paper will deter some gamblers and help sharpen the skills of those who choose to play.

Unlike pure gambling, however, mergers and acquisitions need not be a zero sum game. Thus, improving the skills of the participants, so that it is a positive sum game, is the responsibility of all players – shareholders, management, investment bankers, and government. The integration of Europe increases the potential for a positive sum outcome. But, evidence from the US deregulation movement suggests that substantial changes in the organization of markets does not guarantee merger success. This experience further indicates that governments must be on guard so that the merger gains do not come at the cost of consumer welfare. The US experience should serve as a warning: the firms that get blinded by the limelight of Europe 1992 and ignore history are likely to be the hostile candidates and leveraged buyouts of 1993.

NOTES

1. "Jockeying for Position in a Unified Common Market: An Emphasis on Fundamentals in the Pre-1992 Buying Rush," *Mergers and Acquisitions* March/April 1989 p. 57.
2. Jensen, Michael, "Takeovers: Their Causes and Consequences," *Journal of Economic Perspectives* 2, (Winter 1988) p. 21.
3. The next section will discuss some qualitative evidence that latent problems did exist in some cases.
4. Mueller, Dennis C., "Mergers and Market Share," *Review of Economics and Statistics* 67, (May 1985) pp. 259–267.
5. Michael E. Porter, "From Competitive Advantage to Corporate Strategy," *Harvard Business Review* (May–June 1987) pp. 43–59.
6. With respect to earlier US merger waves, see Hogarty, T. F., "Profits from Mergers: The Evidence of Fifty Years," *St. John's Law Review*, vol. 44, 1970, pp. 378–91 and Livermore, Shaw, "The Success of Industrial Mergers," *Quarterly Journal of Economics* 49 (November 1935) pp. 68–96. For an analysis of the most current US wave, see Patience, John and Chris Sortwell, "Creating Economic Value Through Diversification," manuscript, McKinsey and Company, New York and Herman, Edward and Louis Lowenstein, "The Efficiency Effects of Hostile Takeovers." in *Knights, Raiders and Targets: The Impact of Hostile Takeovers*, John Coffee, Louis Lowenstein and Susan Rose-Ackerman, eds. (New York: Oxford University Press, 1987). The recent trend towards leveraged buyouts may represent an exception. Kaplan finds increases in operating performance in the first two years after a LBO. Kaplan, Steven "A Summary of Sources of Value in Management Buyouts," in *Leveraged Management Buyouts*, edited by Yakov Amihud (Homewood, IL, Dow Jones-Irwin, 1989).
7. Mueller, Dennis C. ed., *The Determinants and Effects of Mergers: An International Comparison*, Cambridge, MA, Oelgeschlager, Gunn & Hain, Publishers, Inc., (1980).
8. McDougall, F. M., D. K. Round, A. G. D. Crouch and A. Wirth, *The Effects of Mergers and Takeovers in Australia*, (Melbourne, Victoria, Australian Institute of Management, (1986).
9. Bradley, Michael, Anand Desai and E. Han Kim "Synergistic Gains from Corporate Acquisitions and their Division Between the Stockholders of Target and Acquiring Firms," *Journal of Financial Economics* 21 (1988).
10. For example, see McConnell, John J. and Debra K. Dennis "Corporate Mergers and Security Returns" *Journal of Financial Economics* 16, (1986) pp. 143–187.
11. Bishop, S., P. Dodd and R. R. Officer, *Australian Takeovers: The Evidence*, (Sydney, Centre for Independent Studies) 1987. Eckbo, E. "Mergers and the Market for Corporate Control:

The Canadian Evidence," *Canadian Journal of Economics* 19 (1986), pp. 236–260. Franks, Julian R., Robert S. Harris and Colin Mayer. "Means of Payment in Takeovers: Results for the United Kingdom and the United States," in *Corporate Takeovers: Causes and Consequences*, Alan J. Auerbach ed. (Chicago, University of Chicago Press, 1988).

12. Shleifer, Andrei and Lawrence H. Summers, "Breach of Trust in Hostile Takeovers," in *Corporate Takeovers: Causes and Consequences.*

13. For a review of these studies see, Black, Bernard S., "Bidder Overpayment in Takeovers," *Stanford Law Review* 41, (February 1989) pp. 597–660.

14. For example, see Magenheim, Ellen B. and Dennis C. Mueller, "On Measuring the Effect of Acquisitions on Acquiring Firm Shareholders," in *Knights, Raiders, and Targets: The Impact of the Hostile Takeover.*

15. Walsh, James P. "Top Management Turnover Following Mergers and Acquisitions," *Strategic Management Journal* 9 (March-April 1988) pp. 173–183.

16. *Wall Street Journal*, Thursday August 11, 1988.

17. Business International, *Making Acquisitions Work: Lessons from Companies' Successes and Mistakes*, (Business International, Geneva, 1988).

18. *Wall Street Journal*, Friday, January 27, 1989.

19. *Mergers and Acquisitions*, March/April 1989, p. 58.

20. See Akerlof, George A. "The Market for "Lemons": Quality Uncertainty and the Market Mechanism," *Quarterly Journal of Economics*, 84 (August 1970) pp. 488–500.

21. See, Ravenscraft and Scherer *Mergers, Sell-offs, and Economic Efficiency.*

22. *Wall Street Journal*, Wednesday, July 5, 1989.

23. *Wall Street Journal*, Monday April 4, 1988.

24. For example, see Varaiya, Nikhil P. "The 'Winner's Curse' Hypothesis and Corporate Takeovers" *Managerial and Decision Economics*, 9 (1988) pp. 209–219.

25. Baker, George P., Michael C. Jensen, and Kevin J. Murphy. "Compensation and Incentives: Practice vs. Theory" *Journal of Finance* 43 (July 1988) pp. 593–616.

26. Business International, *Making Acquisitions Work* p. 18.

27. Porter, "From Competitive Advantage to Corporate Strategy," p. 54.

28. Sutherland, A. *The Monopolies Commission in Action* (London, Cambridge University Press, 1969). Also see Utton, M. A. "British Merger Policy," in *Competition Policy in the UK and EEC* George, K. D. and D. Joll eds. (London, Cambridge University Press, 1975) and Meeks, G. *Disappointing Marriage: A Study of the Gains from Merger* (London, Cambridge University Press, 1977).

29. Business International, *Making Acquisitions Work*, p. 17.

30. Jemison, David B. and Sim B. Sitkin, "Acquisitions: the Process Can Be a Problem," *Harvard Business Review* (March-April 1986) pp. 107–116.

31. For a listing of 15 different motives for merging, see Ravenscraft, David J. "The 1980s Merger Wave: An Industrial Organization Perspective," in *The Merger Boom, Conference Series No. 31* eds. Lynn Browne and Eric Rosengren, Federal Reserve Bank of Boston, 1988, pp. 17–37.

32. On the elevator industry, see Svensk, Robert E, and France J. Aguilar "DAAG Europe (A)" Harvard Business School case no. 374–037. On the major domestic appliances industry, see Fuller, Baden C., P. Nicholaides, and J. Stopford, "National or Global? The Study of Company Strategies and the European Market for Major Domestic Appliances," Working paper Series no. 28, Centre for Business Strategy, London Business School, June 1987.

33. Due, in part, to its emphasis on mini-mills and new plant development, Nucor Corp. has consistently been one of the most profitable firms in the steel industry. In contrast, LTV's acquisition of Republic Steel in 1984 led to bankruptcy.

34. For the most recent evidence on mergers in the US banking industry, see *Bank Mergers:*

Current Issues and Perspectives, Benton, E. Gup, ed. (Boston, Kluwer Academic Publishers, 1989).

35. See Berger, Allen N. , Gerald A. Hanweck, and David B. Humphrey, "Competitive Viability in Banking: Scale, Scope, and Product Mix Economies," *Journal of Monetary Economics* 19 (November 1987).

36. Ironically, one of the largest stock price increases occurred in the Texas Air Corp. acquisition of Eastern Airlines which at this point appears to be one of the least successful. The share price of both Texas Air and Eastern increased by almost 40 per cent in the two weeks surrounding the merger announcement. Three years latter, Texas Air's Eastern Airline subsidiary declared bankruptcy causing the parent Texas Air Corp to incur substantial losses.

37. See, Morrison, Steven A. and Clifford Winston, "Enhancing the Performance of the Deregulated Air Transportation System," *Brooking Papers: Microeconomics* 1989, pp. 61–123. They state: "The effect of the six mergers on travellers' welfare has been mixed: half the mergers have reduced it, and, assuming that frequent flier mileage continues to be provided and continues not to be subject to tax, half have improved it. ... Furthermore, the mergers have largely foreclosed any opportunity to integrate the air transportation system more effectively, thus undermining deregulation's long-run performance," (p. 69).

Part E
Competition in Traditional Non-bank Areas; Securities Trading, Housing Finance and Insurance; Financial Conglomerates

XVIII. Les Effets de la Réglementation et le Comportement des Banques

PATRICK ARTUS et JEAN-PAUL POLLIN

La régulation centralisée de certaines activités économiques se justifie théoriquement dans trois situations d'imperfection de marchés: lorsque la concurrence est impossible (cas du monopole naturel) ou destructrice, lorsque existent des externalités entre les décisions individuelles, ou encore en présence d'asymétries d'information entre les cocontractants. Chacun de ces arguments peut être invoqué pour expliquer la nécessaire régulation du système bancaire.

D'abord parce que le pouvoir de création monétaire confère aux institutions qui le possèdent un poids dans l'échange qui peut contrarier le jeu des mécanismes de marché. Dans la mesure où elles ont la possibilité de faire reconnaître leurs titres de dettes comme instruments de règlement, les banques ont une capacité d'action pratiquement illimitée sur l'allocation des ressources. Si elle n'est pas maîtrisée, l'expansion du système bancaire risque donc d'aboutir à une concentration du pouvoir économique. D'autant que l'on admet souvent, à tort ou à raison, que les banques bénéficient de fortes économies d'échelle et d'envergure.

Par ailleurs l'activité financière est par nature exposée à des problèmes d'externalités et d'asymétries d'information. Dans les économies monétaires modernes, les transactions réelles ont pour contrepartie des transferts d'actifs, dont une bonne partie est illiquide. Pour l'essentiel, en effet, les titres émis par les agents économiques ne peuvent être échangés et cotés sur un marché, parce que leur qualité est trop incertaine. L'asymétrie d'information entre prêteurs et emprunteurs engendre des effets de sélection adverse et d'aléa de moralité qui limitent les opérations de finance directe. Or le rôle des institutions financières, spécialement des banques, est de remédier à cette défaillance du marché et d'assurer la liquidité d'actifs a priori non négociables. En évaluant la solvabilité de l'emprunteur, en contrôlant l'affection des fonds empruntés (donc en résolvant le problème d'asymétrie d'information), elles permettent la réalisation de transactions financières impossibles dans une organisation de marché. En garantissant la valeur des crédits accordés, en transformant les caractéristiques de ces dettes, elles les rendent indirectement acceptables comme moyens de règlement. C'est en ces termes qu'il faut comprendre le principe de l'intermédiation, et c'est aussi dans cette approche

D. E. Fair and C. de Boissieu (eds), Financial Institutions in Europe Under New Competitive Conditions, 253–274.

des fonctions du système bancaire que se trouve le fondement le plus convaincant de sa régulation.[1]

Car la transformation que réalisent les banques les soumet à une instabilité potentielle: le processus n'est viable que si les agents ne retirent pas en même temps leurs dépôts dont la contrepartie est largement illiquide. Face à l'éventualité de retraits massifs, chaque déposant a intérêt à récupérer son placement le plus rapidement possible et l'équilibre est donc instable. Ce résultat s'interprète comme la conséquence d'un phénomène d'externalité puisque c'est la décision de retrait de certains agents qui détériore l'organisation des paiements et conduit à une situation inefficiente. De surcroît les défaillances bancaires vont provoquer la rupture de relations de crédit qui reposent sur la connaissance des emprunteurs, acquise dans la durée et faiblement transmissible. Il s'ensuit un accroissement du coût de l'intermédiation, et donc une hausse du coût du crédit et/ou un rationnement des financements disponibles, c'est-à-dire un resserrement des possibilités de choix intertemporels. Des contributions récentes ont d'ailleurs montré que c'est en ces termes qu'il faut analyser l'incidence des crises financières sur l'activité économique.[2]

On sait que le problème peut être résolu par la mise en place d'un système d'assurance capable, quelle qu'en soit la forme, de garantir la liquidité d'une banque connaissant des difficultés temporaires. La crédibilité des interventions envisageables dans ce cadre doit suffire à dissuader tout movement de course aux dépôts. Malheureusement l'instauration d'un tel dispositif nécessite un contrôle prudentiel de l'intermédiation, car l'assurance fait naître un autre phénomène d'aléa de moralité: en garantissant la valeur de leurs dépôts, on incite les banques à prendre des risques accrus. En fait on retrouve ici les problèmes d'asymétrie d'information déjà évoqués, sous une forme différente mais avec des conclusions semblables. Parce que les marchés sont incapables d'évaluer et d'orienter correctement les décisions des institutions financières, il faut par une régulation centralisée gérer l'information utile et fixer des limites à ces décisions.

La coexistence nécessaire des marchés et de l'instance de contrôle nous ramène à des questions relativement classiques. Il s'agit de savoir comment il est possible de combiner le jeu de la concurrence avec celui d'une organisation hiérarchique qui encadre l'action des intermédiaires financiers. Ou, ce qui revient au même, il s'agit de définir les formes optimales du dispositif de régulation afin de préserver à la fois la stabilité et l'efficacité du système d'intermédiation.

Cet article se propose de répondre en partie à ces questions en cherchant à analyser l'efficacité des différents types de réglementation bancaire. Dans une première partie nous passerons en revue les grandes lignes de la littérature portant sur cette question, tandis que dans une seconde partie on l'illustrera par quelques analyses simples.

1. L'ANALYSE ÉCONOMIQUE DES RÉGLEMENTATIONS BANCAIRES: UN ÉTAT DE LA
LITTÉRATURE

De façon générale, l'intervention publique peut revêtir deux formes principales selon qu'elle entend modeler les structures de marchés, ou selon qu'elle cherche à infléchir directement le comportement des agents. Dans le premier cas, il s'agit de réglementer le contexte dans lequel s'exerce une activité économique donnée, dans le second on contraint certaines décisions individuelles.

Une telle distinction est sans doute aisément critiquable, car il n'y a pas de réelle indépendance entre ces deux types de réglementation. Il est bien évident que les contraintes imposées aux institutions financières affectent la structure des marchés sur lesquels elles interviennent, et l'on montrera que les règles définissant l'activité bancaire conditionnent les formes et l'efficacité de l'assurance-dépôts.

Cette classification reste cependant utile d'une point de vue analytique et nous allons nous en servir pour dresser une typologie de la réglementation bancaire.

A. La régulation des structures bancaires

Le problème est ici de déterminer les structures de marchés qui assurent une production efficiente de services financiers, tout en préservant la sécurité du système. De ce point de vue, on peut encore distinguer deux grandes catégories d'actions:
– celles qui concernent la concurrence dans le secteur et qui visent soit à régler l'entrée, soit à contrôler la taille des institutions,
– celles qui concernent la segmentation fonctionnelle des activités financières, c'est-à-dire qui définissent le champ d'activité ouvert aux diverses institutions.

1. La question de la taille optimale
Ce qui est en jeu dans le premier cas, c'est le principe d'une taille optimale des banques et le risque que peut faire courir une concentration excessive du pouvoir financier. Mais, à la réflexion, ce genre de question s'avère moins intéressant qu'il n'y semble à première vue.
– D'abord parce que les études portant sur les économies d'échelle dans les banques permettent difficilement de conclure à l'existence d'une taille optimale. Il semble que la décroissance des coûts ne concerne que les institutions de petite taille. Passé un certain volume de dépôts ou d'actifs, la taille ne paraît pas conférer d'avantages de compétitivité. Aux Etats-Unis la plupart des études montrent que la taille optimale se situerait entre 25 et 75 millions de dollars de dépôts, ce qui est très faible et conduit

à s'interroger sur la viabilité des méga-banques. En France, les travaux récemment menés sur ce point ne permettent pas réellement de conclure, mais il en ressort que que les économies d'échelle, si elles existent, sont très limitées.[3]

Au demeurant ce genre d'étude est très discutable aussi bien sur le plan de la méthode que dans son principe.[4] La mise en évidence d'économies d'échelle dans l'industrie n'a jamais été chose facile, mais sa transposition à l'activité financière caricature les faiblesses de la démarche. En l'occurrence on traite globalement de l'ensemble des coûts liées aux diverses activités d'une banque; c'est-à-dire que l'on mélange des services qui n'ont que peu de rapports entre eux, qui relèvent de fonctions de production très différentes et dont l'addition n'a pas grand sens. Sans doute l'activité de trading prise isolément suppose pour être rentable un certain volume de transactions, ce qui est en revanche moins évident pour les opérations d'ingénierie financière. Mais dans l'un et l'autre cas la mesure de l'effet de taille n'a rien à voir avec le montant des dépôts ou du total du bilan.

De surcroît, lorsque l'on parle de coûts bancaires, il faut aussi s'intéresser au coût des ressources dont l'évolution n'a rien à voir avec celle des coûts opératoires. Des observations tendent même à montrer qu'il existe une relation inverse entre ces deux types de coûts, ce qui n'a rien de surprenant: les banques à réseaux qui ont à supporter des frais importants pour la collecte et la gestion des dépôts bénéficient en contrepartie de ressources moins onéreuses.[5] On comprend que dans ces conditions la mise en évidence d'une taille optimale est pour le moins hasardeuse.

– D'autre part l'internationalisation des activités financières ôte beaucoup de son intérêt à cette question. Dans ce contexte il est en effet illusoire de penser réglementer la concentration financière: l'hétérogénéité des structures bancaires dans les différents pays exclut certainement toute négociation sur se point. D'autant que si le marché des services financiers devient mondial, il y a toute chance pour que les conditions de concurrence soient respectées, puisque même des unités de grande taille seront dans cette hypothèse relativement petites par rapport au marché.

– Enfin on rappellera que l'efficience d'un marché ne dépend pas princi- palement du nombre d'agents qui y interviennent. Ce qui importe c'est plutôt la forme du jeu entre les firmes sur ce marché, ou encore le niveau de concurrence potentielle; une structure oligopolistique ou monopolistique n'est donc pas nécessairement sous-optimale. La théorie des marchés contestables, même si elle est moins révolutionnaire qu'elle ne veut le paraître, a permis de renouveler l'approche du problème et mis l'accent sur le rôle des conditions d'entrée et de sortie d'une activité donnée.[6] Or de ce point de vue, certaines innovations technologiques récentes ont sans doute contribué à faciliter l'entrée sur les marchés de services financiers.

Par exemple le développement de la banque à domicile devrait permettre à des institutions financières d'entrer dans la distribution de produits bancaires sans avoir à se doter d'un réseau d'agences. On peut en attendre un accroissement de la concurrence potentielle sur ces marchés.

Au total on voit bien qu'il n'existe pas de réel danger que se constituent, dans le secteur bancaire, des positions de monopole venant affecter l'optimalité de l'équilibre économique. La question d'une limitation réglementaire de la taille des banques est donc pratiquement sans objet.

2. La régulation fonctionnelle

En revanche la question de la séparation fonctionnelle des activités financières semble plus pertinente mais aussi plus complexe à analyser. Le problème est ici de savoir si l'on doit permettre à une même institution de produire et d'offrir tous les services financiers (et l'autoriser ainsi à bénéficier d'é-conomies d'envergure) ou s'il faut au contraire réserver la production de ces services à des institutions spécifiques, réellement autonomes.

De nombreux arguments ont été invoqués pour expliquer la présence d'économies d'envergure dans le secteur financier, et donc pour justifier de la plus grande efficacité des institutions multiproductrices.[7] On peut observer tout d'abord qu'il existe de fortes substitutions entre les divers actifs financiers, de sorte qu'au stade de la distribution il est préférable de proposer toute une gamme de produits (de placement, de financement, de paiement...) plutôt que de les vendre séparément. La gestion de trésorerie n'est optimale que si l'on a la possibilité de combiner au mieux les services de paiement et de placement; une partie des innovations financières ont d'ailleurs eu pour principe de créer une étroite relation entre ces services. De même que l'optimisation des financements se trouve largement facilitée si l'on peut trouver auprès d'un même organisme l'ensemble des instruments disponibles: les MOF reposent précisément sur l'exploitation de cette idée.

Au demeurant certains auteurs ont soutenu que la production simultanée d'un ensemble de services était une des caractéristiques de l'intermédiation.[8] Plus précisément E. Fama a émis l'idée que les banques obtiennent un avantage comparatif dans la distribution du crédit, du fait des informations sur les mouvements des comptes que leur assure leur fonction complémentaire de gestion de moyens de paiement.[9]

Il faut ajouter que la possibilité de participer au financement des entreprises sous diverses formes peut permettre de résoudre en partie les problèmes d'aléa de moralité et donc de résoudre les coûts d'agence. Cette idée a notamment été développée par J. Stiglitz qui s'est efforcé de montrer que la détention conjointe de titres de dettes et d'actions d'une même entreprise permettait d'exercer un meilleur contrôle.[10] De même l'instauration de relations de long terme entre apporteurs et utilisateurs de capitaux contribue à résoudre les problèmes de contrôle, en situation d'asymétrie d'information. Or il est naturellement plus facile de conserver des relations durables entre une entreprise et sa banque si celle-ci a la capacité d'offrir une gamme complète de moyens de financement. C'est peut-être pour toutes ces raisons que ce sont les pays dans lesquels les relations entre institutions financières et entreprises sont les plus riches et dans lesquels les banques ont des compétences larges, qui ont réalisé sur longue période les meilleures performances macro-économiques.[11]

Enfin le fait de combiner dans une même institution des activités différentes doit permettre une diversification des risques et donc d'obtenir une plus grande stabilité des résultats. R. Litan a ainsi calculé, sur la période 1965-81, que les banques américaines auraient pu réduire sensiblement (de 45%) la volatilité de leurs bénéfices si elles avaient été autorisées à s'implanter dans les activités qui leur étaient interdites par la réglementation en vigueur.[12]

Ceci dit le modèle de la banque universelle n'a pas que des avantages. D'abord parce qu'il présente des inconvénients du point de vue de la facturation des services: on observe en effet que la tarification des institutions multi-activités comporte en général de fortes péréquations (des subventions croisées) qui sont contestables aussi bien du point de vue de l'équilibre économique que de la compétitivité des banques. C'est le cas particulièrement en France où la facturation insuffisante de la gestion des moyens de paiement a pour contrepartie un coût excessif du crédit. Il en résulte une mauvaise utilisation des moyens de paiement et une fragilisation des banques à réseaux qui risquent d'avoir du mal à supporter la concurrence d'institutions spécialisées dans la seule distribution du crédit.

Peut-être ne s'agit-il là que de la conséquence de contraintes institutionnelles ou de l'incapacité à sortir d'un système dépassé. En pratique il est d'ailleurs toujours délicat de mettre au point une comptabilité analytique satisfaisante dans les activités de service. Mais peut-être aussi s'agit-il d'une difficulté plus fondamentale liée aux caractéristiques du problème posé: on a pu démontrer en effet que dans le cas d'un monopole naturel multi-produits il n'existe pas nécessairement de système de tarification ne comportant pas de subventions croisées.[13] Or, dans ces conditions, une concurrence destructrice peut se développer amenant certaines entreprises à se positionner sur les activités qui font ressortir des opportunités de profit. Alors même que la firme en situation de monopole naturel est économiquement plus efficace, elle peut se trouver déstabilisée par son incapacité à trouver un système de prix viable. C'est là bien sûr un cas particulier mais qui illustre la possible fragilité de l'entreprise multi-productrice.

Cependant la critique essentielle que l'on peut adresser au modèle de la banque universelle concerne la sécurité des dépôts. Car même si, comme on vient de le dire, la diversification des activités permet de réduire le risque global de l'institution, il n'empêche qu'elle accroît le problème des asymétries d'information, parce qu'elle complique l'évaluation des risques et qu'elle rend de ce fait plus incertaine la valeur des dépôts. Qui plus est, l'existence d'institutions financières couvrant plusieurs activités peut être incompatible avec un dispositif d'assurance des dépôts, dans la mesure où il devient possible de transférer à cette assurance des risques étrangers à la gestion des moyens de paiement ou à la distribution du crédit. C'est-à-dire que le dispositif serait amené à couvrir des risques sans rapport avec son intention initiale. On peut même imaginer que des institutions soient incitées à prendre des risques excessifs sur certains types d'activité (par example le trading en valeurs mobilières), sachant qu'à partir d'un niveau de pertes donné celles-ci seraient prises en charge par le système d'assurance-dépôts. On retrouve ici l'argument de l'aléa de moralité, mais de façon totalement injustifiée puisqu'il n'y a aucune raison de garantir toutes les activités financières.

Dans de telles conditions il n'y a d'autre solution que de rendre plus exigeant le contrôle des activités bancaires. Car plus on ouvre le domaine d'activité des intermédiaires financiers et plus il faut élargir le champ de la régulation, contrepartie de l'assurance-dépôts. Dans la mesure où il n'est pas possible de dissocier, notamment dans les résultats, les différentes opérations initiées par une même banque, il faut que le dispositif de surveillance couvre l'ensemble de l'institution.[14] A la limite, si on accepte l'existence de conglomérats à vocation financière, industrielle et/ou commerciale, il faudrait logiquement que le contrôle prudentiel porte aussi sur les activités non financières du groupe. On comprend que l'ambition est alors démesurée et risque d'engendrer une bureaucratie déraisonnable. C'est pourquoi il faut sans doute admettre l'idée de séparations institutionnelles entre certaines activités financières (et bien sûr entre les activités financières et les activités industrielles ou commerciales), même si l'on peut discuter sur la forme et sur les frontières de cette segmentation.[15]

Récemment plusieurs auteurs se sont efforcés de montrer que la meilleure solution serait celle qui associerait une structure de groupe à un cloisonnement des activités: chacune d'entre elles relèverait d'une institution distincte qui serait coiffée par une holding.[15] Cette organisation permettrait de sauvegarder les économies d'envergure au niveau de la distribution et peut-être de l'échange d'informations, tout en préservant la séparation des risques. Elle concilierait donc le respect de l'efficience et les exigences du contrôle prudentiel. Mais pour qu'elle soit viable il faudrait que la gestion des dépôts (et de leurs contreparties) puisse être parfaitement isolée des autres activités; ce qui signifie notamment que les transactions entre les diverses institutions constituant le groupe devraient s'opérer à des conditions aussi favorables que celles qui prévalent, à un moment donné, sur le marché. Or même si l'on peut prendre quelques garanties et édicter des réglementations en ce sens, on conviendra qu'il est extrêmement difficile de vérifier la réalisation d'une telle condition. De sorte qu'une des filiales du groupe aura toujours l'opportunité de transférer ses risques (c'est-à-dire ses pertes effectives ou potentielles) à la filiale bancaire, afin de bénéficier de l'assurance-dépôts.

Dès lors il n'y a guère d'autre possibilité que de cloisonner strictement l'exercice des activités financières, comme le fait le Glass-Steagall Act, ou alors de réglementer assez précisément l'activité de gestion des dépôts pour éviter tout transfert de risque. C'est à cette dernière solution que se réfère la proposition visant à imposer aux institutions collectrices de dépôts un ratio de liquidité de 100%. Il s'agirait en effet de contraindre les banques à garder, en contrepartie des dépôts reçus, des actifs parfaitement liquides (c'est-à-dire négociables à tout moment sur un marché) et portant un risque minimal (des titres publics à échéances courtes). Dans un tel schéma les transferts entre institutions seraient impossibles et la sécurité des dépôts serait quasi complète. Mais nous montrerons un peu plus loin que cette proposition comporte un certain nombre de faiblesses. On rejoint en effet à ce stade l'étude de la régulation des comportements.

B. La régulation des comportements bancaires

En fait la régulation des structures trouve rapidement ses limites lorsqu'il s'agit de résoudre les problèmes d'asymétrie d'information qui ont été précédemment évoqués. Car ce qui est en cause, c'est l'incapacité des marchés, quelle que soit leur forme, à évaluer correctement des choix de portefeuille des banques, et donc la qualité des placements qu'elles proposent. L'impossibilité de conclure des "contrats complets" oblige alors à contraindre les décisions bancaires de façon à exclure (ou limiter) des comportements qui léseraient les déposants ou le système d'assurance-dépôts. En d'autres termes il faut que la discipline d'une réglementation se substitue à la discipline défaillante des marchés.

Dans cette perspective, différentes mesures peuvent être envisagées qui tournent toutes autour du même principe et qui sont du reste largement substituables. Nous nous intéresserons ici essentiellement à l'efficacité des types de réglementations envisageables en négligeant pour l'essentiel le coût de leur application. L'appréciation de ce coût ne pose d'ailleurs pas de difficulté particulière sur le plan analytique: de façon générale il se mesure par l'écart qu'introduit la réglementation à la solution optimale, dans l'hypothèse de contrats complets.

1. Les formes de l'assurance-dépôts

Les formes d'organisation de l'assurance-dépôts constituent un premier type de réponse à nos préoccupations. En particulier il peut être intéressant de se demander s'il est préférable que le dispositif soit géré de façon privée (par des associations professionnelles ou des groupements d'institutions) ou s'il doit plutôt être placé sous le contrôle de l'État. La question est importante puisqu'elle conditionne notamment le principe de monnaies émises de façon concurrentielle, s'opposant au pouvoir traditionnellement reconnu à la puissance publique en ce domaine.[17] Ceci a donné lieu à de nombreux débats auxquels les innovations financières récentes ont redonné une actualité mais dont les détails ne concernent pas vraiment notre propos.

On retiendra cependant que l'action d'une Banque Centrale, en tant que prêteur en dernier ressort, est fatalement plus efficace que toute organisation privée dans la prévention des paniques bancaires. Dans la mesure où la puissance publique a la capacité de taxer les agents (donc de répartir les coûts d'une course aux dépôts) et de garantir sans limite la liquidité des institutions financières, son intervention (ou seulement l'éventualité de son intervention) possède une crédibilité absolue. Ce point a notamment été développé par Diamond et Dybvig qui écrivent par exemple: "Parce que les organismes d'assurance n'ont pas le pouvoir de taxer, ils doivent détenir des réserves pour rendre crédible leur garantie. Ceci met en évidence une des raisons pour lesquelles l'État possède un avantage naturel dans la prise en charge de l'assurance-dépôts".[28]

Toutefois ces caractéristiques de l'intervention publique ne suffisent pas à garantir son optimalité. Car un système qui reposerait uniquement sur la toute puissance du "prêteur en dernier ressort" subirait à plein le phénomène d'aléa de moralité: le jeu entre les banques de second rang et la Banque Centrale se traduirait par un biais inflationniste. De plus un tel système induirait une discrimination entre les différentes banques. En effet, si une Banque Centrale peut se permettre le luxe de laisser de petites banques tomber en faillite, il lui est en revanche impossible de refuser son aide à une grande institution en difficulté. De ce fait l'existe d'une assurance-dépôts gérée de façon privée est une condition essentielle au maintien d'une diversité et d'une certaine concurrence dans le secteur bancaire. Il est donc souhaitable que la Banque Centrale réserve ses interventions aux situations de déséquilibres macro-économiques graves ou laissant à une organisation indépendante le soin de régler les problèmes micro-économiques.

Ceci étant, de nombreuses propositions ont été faites pour tenter de résoudre, ou du moins de réduire, le phénomène d'aléa de moralité. On peut songer de ce point de vue à deux types d'actions complémentaires et visant:
- d'une part à inciter les déposants à surveiller les choix de portefeuille de leur banque et à s'intéresser aux risques pris. Par exemple on a suggéré de limiter le montant de la garantie (soit en niveau, soit en pourcentage) comme c'est déjà le cas dans un certain nombre de pays. Mais ceci laisse subsister des risques de paniques, au moins sur les gros dépôts. Dans un

ordre d'idée un peu différent, on a aussi imaginé de moduler la garantie en fonction de la rémunération servie sur les dépôts, ce qui éviterait au moins des surenchères entre banques puisque cela obligerait les déposants à supporter un risque accru en contrepartie de taux d'intérêt plus élevés. Nous reviendrons sur ce point à propos de la régulation des taux.

– d'autre part à dissuader les banques d'utiliser l'assurance-dépôts pour accroître leurs risques. En ce sens la proposition la plus souvent évoquée consiste à ajuster la prime en fonction du niveau des risques de chaque institution. Théoriquement c'est une réponse satisfaisante au problème de l'aléa de moralité, mais pratiquement la mesure des risques est extrêmement délicate.[19] Car ce qui doit être pris en compte ce ne sont pas simplement les risques de crédit, mais aussi les risques de taux d'intérêt ou de taux de change. Comme de surcroît ils ne sont pas indépendants les uns des autres, leur compréhension doit être globale. Or on touche ici à des questions qui sont à la fois complexes sur le plan analytique et inextricables du point de vue des informations nécessaires pour les traiter. De sorte que la mesure du ou des risques d'une institution financière est pratiquement trop imprécise et trop évolutive pour servir à la définition d'une prime d'assurance. Il n'existe donc pas de forme optimale du dispositif d'assurance qui puisse totalement écarter les difficultés soulevées par les asymétries d'information.

2. La réglementation des fonds propres

Une autre façon de résoudre l'aléa de moralité consiste à rendre la faillite plus coûteuse pour les actionnaires de la banque en obligeant celle-ci à respecter un ratio minimal de capitalisation. Cela revient à demander aux actionnaires d'assurer pour partie, et sur leur propre capital, les dépôts collectés. Ils prendront ainsi en charge une part plus grande du coût de la panique si la banque était amenée à liquider en catastrophe ses actifs. On peut attendre d'une telle mesure à la fois qu'elle limite l'intervention du fonds d'assurance et qu'elle incite les banques à une gestion plus prudente de leurs risques.

On sait que ce type de régulation a été retenu et même privilégié dans bon nombre de pays. Et c'est du reste cette formule qui a servi de base à l'ébauche d'un contrôle prudentiel à l'échelle internationale.

Cependant il n'est pas certain que l'imposition d'un ratio de capital implique une réduction des risques bancaires. Si l'on retient la logique d'un modèle de portefeuille, on peut facilement montrer qu'un coefficient de capitalisation va conduire les banques à sélectionner des actifs plus risqués, quelle que soit leur attitude à l'égard du risque.[20] Elles vont en effet chercher à compenser la réduction qui leur est imposée de l'effet de levier par un accroissement du risque de leurs actifs. Dans certains cas (dans le cas d'institutions ayant un comportement plus risqué), cela peut conduire à une augmentation de leur probabilité de faillite. On tombe alors sur la même zone de difficulté que celle que nous venons de rencontrer à propos de la fixation de la prime d'assurance.

Car pour éviter cet effet pervers il faut moduler les exigences de fonds propres en fonction de la structure du portefeuille. Plus précisément il faut imposer des ratios de capital spécifiques à chaque actif. Toujours en se situant dans le cadre de l'analyse de portefeuille, on peut montrer que ces ratios dépendent des rendements attendus sur les actifs et sur les dettes, de leur structure de variance-covariance, et de la probabilité maximale de faillite tolérée.[21]

Dans une certaine mesure, c'est une solution de ce type qui est retenue par le ratio COOKE puisque chaque catégorie d'actifs y fait l'objet d'une pondération différente dans la comptabilisation du risque global, auquel on rapporte les fonds propres. Mais d'une part le mode de calcul ne fait qu'additionner les risques présumés de crédit et de contrepartie, sans chercher à apprécier leur diversification. D'autre part les risques de taux d'intérêt et de taux de change sont pour l'instant négligés, alors qu'ils constituent ajourd'hui un facteur important d'instabilité potentielle. Enfin les risques relatifs à la structure des ressources ne sont également pas traités.

Mais on conviendra que pour s'approcher de la formule théoriquement satisfaisante les informations nécessaires, et partant le coût de la réglementation, seraient exorbitants.

3. La réglementation de la liquidité

Nous avons déjà expliqué que l'instabilité potentielle du système bancaire tenait à l'illiquidité de ses actifs, ou plus précisément à la fonction de transformation qu'il assume. Par conséquent toute mesure visant à accroître la part des actifs aisément négociables dans le portefeuille des banques tend à prévenir les risques de panique. En ce sens l'imposition d'un ratio de liquidité joue un peu le même rôle que la réglementation des fonds propres. Dans leur application les deux types de mesure se recouvrent d'ailleurs en partie. Mais ici il ne s'agit pas de savoir comment répartir le coût de la panique, le problème est plutôt de s'assurer que les banques sont capables de faire face à leurs engagements.

Naturellement la sécurité n'est complète que si les banques sont capables d'assurer à tout moment la liquidité de la totalité des dépôts. C'est pourquoi différents auteurs ont évoqué l'idée d'une couverture à 100% des dépôts par des actifs liquides.[22] Une telle disposition permettrait pratiquement de faire l'économie du système d'assurance et des problèmes qui l'accompagnent. Concrètement les banques auraient l'obligation d'investir toutes leurs ressources à vue dans des actifs négociables, sans risque de défaut et à échéance courte. Les dépôts auraient ainsi pour contrepartie des actifs de valeur certaine, et qui surtout pourraient être liquidés instantanément.

Répétons que c'est cette dernière propriété qui importe, la certitude de la valeur des dépôts n'est pas ici essentielle. Il est du reste intéressant de remarquer qu'il serait possible, et souhaitable à certains égards, de confier la gestion des moyens de paiement à des fonds de placement investis en valeurs mobilières.[23] Les règlements s'effectueraient par des mouvements sur des comptes-titres, des parts de SIVAC ou de FCP; ils aboutiraient donc à des transferts directs ou indirects de titres liquides entre les agents. Les comptes seraient rémunérés mais pour que le système soit stable, leur valeur se modifierait au jour le jour en fonction des prix de marché des actifs détenus par les fonds. De sorte que la valeur des dépôts serait indépendante des retraits effectués, ce qui exclut toute incitation à une panique bancaire. Il est vrai qu'un système fondé sur l'incertitude de la valeur des dépôts est assez éloigné de la conception que nous avons, pour des raisons historiques, des propriétés de la monnaie. Mais il n'est ni irréaliste ni révolutionnaire. Après tout l'inflation soumet également les dépôts à vue à une incertitude sur leur valeur réelle, qui peut être tout aussi lourde de conséquences. De plus certaines innovations financières récentes ont façonné des moyens de règlement qui fonctionnent selon des principes très proches du modèle que nous évoquons.

Mais quelle que soit la formule retenue, on ne résoudra pas l'instabilité du système de financement et de paiement en exigeant une liquidité parfaite des actifs bancaires. Cette solution en effet revient à nier la spécificité de l'intermédiation et elle ne sert qu'à déplacer le problème posé. Car dès lors qu'il existe dans l'économie des actifs qui ne peuvent faire l'objet d'une évaluation et d'une cotation sur un marché, il faut que des intermédiaires opèrent une certaine transformation de ces actifs. Si les institutions qui ont en charge la gestion des moyens de paiement sont contraintes à ne détenir que des titres négociables, il faudra que d'autres intermédiaires financiers prennent en charge les actifs illiquides. On retrouvera alors d'une façon ou d'une autre le déséquilibre entre les caractéristiques des ressources et celles des emplois, et la question des crises d'illiquidité se reposera dans les mêmes termes.[24]

De surcroît, il est bien possible que le volume de titres négociables soit insuffisant pour assurer la liquidité nécessaire de l'économie, c'est-à-dire pour servir de support aux transactions désirées. Il est vrai que le développement des procédures de titrisation devrait contribuer à résoudre cetre difficulté. Mais il est vrai aussi qu'à court terme la titrisation ne touchera qu'une part modeste des crédits distribués dans l'économie.

Au total il est clair que l'imposition d'un ratio de liquidité ne constitue qu'une réponse partielle au problème de l'instabilité bancaire. Elle a par ailleurs un coût qui s'exprime dans la déformation de la frontière efficiente des portefeuilles bancaires. Mais il n'est pas dans notre propos de rentrer dans la comparaison de ses coûts et avantages.

4. La réglementation des taux d'intérêt

On justifie traditionnellement la réglementation des taux d'intérêt créditeurs en disant que la concurrence pour les dépôts est susceptible de conduire à des surenchères entre les banques et peut les conduire à des prises de risque dangereuses. De sorte que la rémunération servie aura pour contrepartie des risques excessifs par rapport à l'optimum collectif.

L'argumentation est cependant moins claire et moins convaincante qu'il n'y paraît. Car si l'on fait l'hypothèse d'un fonctionnement concurrentiel des marchés financiers, on ne voit pas pourquoi les institutions financières chercheraient à surpayer des dépôts alors qu'elles ont la possibilité de se refinancer, à taux donné, sur le marché monétaire; il existe donc sûrement un plafond aux taux créditeurs.[25] De même qu'en l'absence d'assurance-dépôts il n'y a guère de raison pour que les banques prêtent à des taux inadaptés par rapport aux risques pris.

Ici encore la difficulté ne peut provenir que de la distorsion introduite par l'assurance-dépôts dans l'arbitrage rendement-risque. D'un côté le prix des ressources bancaires est insensible aux risques pris (dans le cas d'une prime d'assurance fixe) puisque les déposants n'ont aucun intérêt à surveiller l'emploi qui est fait de leurs placements. D'autre part, dans la mesure où les pertes potentielles des actionnaires de la banque sont plafonnées, celle-ci peut être incitée à investir dans des actifs plus risqués, notamment lorsque la marge d'intérêt est faible. En d'autres termes c'est parce que l'assurance-dépôts déforme la prise du risque que l'on est conduit à des décisions sous-optimales. Dans ces conditions, la réglementation des taux créditeurs, parce qu'elle permet d'élargir la marge d'intérêt, de diminuer la probabilité de faillite et donc de rendre plus coûteuse la prise de risque, contribue à réduire l'incidence de l'aléa de moralité.

Cette conclusion favorable à la réglementation des taux peut être également obtenue en partant d'une argumentation différente. Elle repose sur l'incertitude dans laquelle se trouvent les banques, quant aux caractéristiques des dépôts qu'elles collectent.[26] Il s'agit encore d'un problème d'asymétrie d'information mais qui joue cette fois aux dépens des institutions financières. Dans la mesure où elles ne peuvent connaître la stabilité des dépôts qui leur sont consentis, elles n'ont en effet d'autre solution que de proposer des contrats spécifiant un taux de rémunération et une pénalité en cas de retrait prématuré. Ce procédé doit normalement inciter les déposants à révéler la durée probable de leurs placements afin de permettre aux banques d'adapter leurs actifs en conséquence. Mais on montre qu'il existe pas nécessairement de contrats d'équilibre, c'est-à-dire qu'il peut exister des cas où des surenchères vont s'effectuer entre les institutions financières. La seule façon de bloquer ce processus déstabilisant est alors de fixer un plafond de rémunération sur les dépôts.

On voit donc qu'il existe de solides justifications à une réglementation des taux créditeurs. Mais il est vrai qu'une telle mesure comporte également un coût important par l'affaiblissement de la concurrence qu'elle est susceptible d'induire entre les différentes institutions financières.

2. L'INCIDENCE DES RÉGLEMENTATIONS BANCAIRES: QUELQUES ILLUSTRATIONS

Après avoir cas par cas résumé les arguments essentiels de l'analyse économique de la régulation bancaire, nous allons maintenant illustrer et éclaircir quelques uns des points évoqués. Ceci permettra également de comparer les effets des différentes formes de réglementations dans la mesure où elles sont pour partie substituables.

On gardera cependant présent à l'esprit que les résultats obtenus dépendent largement des hypothèses que l'on a retenues concernant la nature et la technologie de l'intermédiation, les objectifs de la banque ou encore les conditions d'équilibre des marchés. Or les choix en ce domaine sont très ouverts. Nous présentons ici les principales conclusions d'une analyse plus approfondie.

A. Réglementation de la rémunération des dépôts et assurance des dépôts

Il est facile de montrer la similitude entre les effets de l'assurance des dépôts et ceux de la réglementation de la rémunération de ceux-ci. On considère une banque
qui a comme ressources des dépôts et du capital, et qui peut investir soit dans un actif risqué, soit dans un actif non risqué. La nature du risque est la suivante: le placement risqué peut soit réussir (avec une certaine probabilité), soit échouer, auquel cas les sommes investies sont perdues. L'espérance de son rendement est le taux d'intérêt sans risque. Si, après réalisation des rendements, la valeur de marché des actifs de la banque est inférieure à celle de ses dépôts, la banque est en faillite, les actionnaires perdent tout et les déposants récupèrent la valeur nette de la banque. Les actionnaires et les déposants sont neutres vis-à-vis du risque; les premiers maximisent donc l'espérance de la valeur nette du capital qu'ils ont investi; lorsque la rémunération des dépôts est libre, les seconds exigent de recevoir un rendement anticipé égal au taux sans risque à condition bien sûr qu'ils puissent mesurer le risque pris par la banque dans ses investissements.
On montre alors les résultats suivants:
– *Il est équivalent qu'il y ait une assurance des dépôts avec une prime exogène (indépendante du risque pris), une réglementation de la rémunération des dépôts ou une inobservabilité du risque pris par la banque qui conduit les déposants*

à accepter une rémunération forfaitaire. Dans les trois cas, la banque est amenée à mettre toutes ses ressources sous la forme de l'actif risqué. Ceci est dû au fait que les actionnaires peuvent au plus perdre leur capital; l'espérance de la valeur de la banque est donc une fonction convexe du rendement de l'actif risqué, ce qui conduit à prendre le plus de risque possible.

- *Il est parallèlement équivalent que les déposants puissent assurer le risque pris et obtenir un rendement espéré des dépôts égal au taux sans risque ou que l'agence d'assurance des dépôts demande une juste prime égale à l'espérance de contribution de cette agence.* Dans les deux cas, plus de risque pris se traduit de façon transparente par un coût accru des dépôts, ce qui implique que *les actionnaires deviennent indifférents vis-à-vis du risque pris.* Si de plus les déposants ont de l'aversion pour le risque, ils exigent une prime qui varie avec la probabilité de faillite, ce qui amène les actionnaires à annuler celle-ci.

- Si les déposants ne peuvent pas observer le risque pris par la banque et que celle-ci déclare la quantité des actifs risqués qu'elle détient, elle est *incitée à tricher* et à déclarer qu'elle détient suffisamment peu d'actifs risqués pour que dans la situation d'échec de ces placements elle ne soit pas en faillite. Les déposants ne demandent alors, s'ils sont naïfs, que le taux sans risque, et la banque prend le risque maximum. Si les déposants sont rationnels, ils anticipent ce comportement et demandent la rémunération correspondant à la situation totalement risquée.

- Deux éléments peuvent venir réduire le risque pris par la banque lorsque la rémunération des dépôts est contrôlée ou que la prime d'assurance est forfaitaire:

  i) si la banque subit un *coût connexe de collecte de l'information sur le risque inhérent aux actifs qu'elle achète* (ce qui introduit un élément fort semblable à de l'aversion pour le risque dans son objectif), il n'est pas du tout certain qu'elle prenne une position risquée, si ce coût est suffisamment fort pour compenser l'avantage lié au plafonnement de la perte.

  ii) si, lorsque la banque est en faillite, les actionnaires non seulement perdent leur capital mais subissent un *coût forfaitaire de faillite*, ils peuvent être amenés à annuler la probabilité de cette dernière si le coût de faillite est suffisamment grand pour compenser l'avantage procuré par la prime de risque.

B. *Réglementation de la rémunération des dépôts et compétition pour les dépôts*

Les développements ci-dessus illustrent les inconvénients de la réglementation de la rémunération des dépôts. Cependant, elle peut empêcher les banques de se livrer à une surenchère stérile pour gagner des parts de marché, amenant des faillites en chaîne.

Considérons le modèle traditionnel de *compétition pour les dépôts*. Il y a un grand nombre de banques qui se concurrencent, ce qui implique que le profit réalisé par chacune d'entre elles tend vers zéro. Les banques ont accès à un refinancement à taux d'intérêt donné, et proposent des contrats de dépôt. Les déposants sont de deux natures: les uns ont une probabilité faible de retirer leur argent au bout d'une période, les autres ont une probabilité forte de le faire (parce qu'ils ont un besoin de liquidité, une "durée de vie" plus faible); seuls les déposants et pas les banquiers savent de quel type ils sont.

Les banquiers ont le choix entre:

- proposer deux contrats de dépôts qui leur permettent de discriminer entre les types de déposants. Les contrats spécifient la rémunération des dépôts selon qu'ils sont conservés une ou deux périodes. Les déposants maximisent l'espérance de l'utilité de la valeur de leur placement; les deux contrats proposés sont discriminants (et permettent d'aboutir à un équilibre avec séparation) si chaque type de déposant a intérêt à révéler son type en choisissant le contrat qui lui est destiné et pas celui destiné à l'autre type de déposant.
- proposer un seul type de contrat de dépôt non discriminant qui soit optimal pour les déposants.

On peut alors montrer les résultats suivants:

- Le cas favorable (stable) est celui où le contrat non discriminant est moins favorable pour le type de déposant qui a une faible probabilité de retirer son argent (*type 1*) après une période que le contrat discriminant qui lui est proposé. Ce contrat est par contre toujours plus favorable pour les déposants à forte probabilité de vie courte (*type 2*) puisque, jouant sur les deux populations, il permet à la banque de ne pas perdre d'argent en jouant sur les profits qu'elle fait à la seconde période. Si on est dans ce cas, seul l'équilibre avec discrimination est possible puisque les déposants de type 1 refuseront le contrat sans discrimination.
- Le cas défavorable (instable) est celui où le contrat non discriminant est préféré par les deux populations de déposants. En effet, si une banque est localisée sur ce type de contrat, une autre banque peut venir et proposer une rémunération des dépôts légèrement plus faible en première période et plus forte en seconde période. Elle attirera alors les déposants de type 1 qui ont une forte probabilité de conserver leurs dépôts en seconde période, gagnera de l'argent sur ces déposants alors que la première banque ne gardant que les déposants de type 2, perdra de l'argent et fera faillite. Dans ce type de situation, *aucune banque ne peut empêcher une autre banque de lui prendre ses meilleurs déposants et de lui faire faire faillite*.

Mais on voit que pour éviter cette compétition stérile, il suffit d'édicter une *règle de réglementation de la rémunération des dépôts*: si celle-ci ne peut être supérieure à celle versée à l'équilibre non-discriminant, la surenchère devient impossible. Cette règle est donc justifiable si on craint que les banques se placent effectivement dans un contexte de forte compétition, sans aucun "accord amiable" pour la définition des parts de marché.

C. Règle de capitalisation ou de fonds propres

Comme nous allons le voir, les résultats vont sensiblement *dépendre du type de modélisation adopté pour le comportement bancaire*, la maximisation de l'espérance de la valeur nette avec possibilité de faillite, ou la réalisation d'un choix de portefeuille général avec aversion pour le risque.

1. Maximisation de l'espérance de la valeur nette

Si on suppose que la banque a le choix entre plusieurs actifs risqués, de rendements non indépendants, on peut montrer les résultats suivants:

– Dans le cas général, *si la rémunération des dépôts n'est pas aléatoire, c'est l'actif le plus risqué* (celui dont le rendement a la plus forte variance) *qui est détenu dans le portefeuille*. Les covariances entre les rendements n'interviennent pas puisqu'on a toujours une solution en coin (la part d'un actif dans le total de bilan étant nulle ou égale à 1). Ceci résulte comme précédemment de ce que l'espérance de la valeur de l'entreprise croît avec l'incertitude. Par contre, *si l'actif le plus risqué a son rendement très corrélé avec la rémunération des dépôts et si celle-ci est aléatoire* (et pas les autres actifs), *ce sont les autres qui sont détenus* puisque avoir plus d'actif risqué réduit le risque de la banque en couvrant le risque de taux d'intérêt sur les dépôts.

– Une *baisse du rapport* exigé capital/dépôts (ou de façon équivalente capital/total de bilan) est supposée ici amener les actionnaires à *accroître les fonds propres* de la banque. Lorsque ce rapport augmente:

   i) il est plus probable que les actionnaires décident de ne détenir que de l'actif le plus risqué même si la rémunération des dépôts est aléatoire; l'accroissement de la quantité de capital implique en effet une probabilité accrue d'augmenter le risque en détenant cet actif.

   ii) Cependant *la probabilité de faillite est réduite* (puisque la banque a plus de fonds propres), *sauf si la rémunération des dépôts est très corrélée avec le rendement* de l'actif le plus risqué. Dans ce cas en effet, plus de capital relativement aux dépôts investi dans cet actif peut accroître la probabilité de faillite puisque la baisse du rendement de cet actif n'est plus suffisamment compensée par la baisse de la rémunération des dépôts.

   iii) Introduire un *ratio de fonds propres spécifique à chaque actif* ne permet pas, si la rémunération des dépôts n'est pas aléatoire, d'éviter que seul l'actif le plus risqué soit détenu, car cette introduction ne remet pas en cause la convexité de l'espérance de la valeur de la banque par rapport à la quantité détenue de cet actif.

2. La banque faisant des choix de portefeuille

Nous changeons là complètement notre représentation du comportement de la banque et supposons qu'elle réalise un choix de portefeuille avec aversion pour le risque, en maximisant l'espérance d'utilité du rendement de son capital vue sous forme espérance-variance.

Elle est toujours confrontée à N placements, un sans risque, les autres risqués, et collecte des dépôts dont la rémunération peut aussi être aléatoire. Le choix de la structure de son actif entre les différents placements est traditionnel dans les modèles de choix de portefeuille: le vecteur des parts optimales dépend de la matrice de variance-covariance des rendements, du vecteur des covariances des rendements avec la rémunération des dépôts et du vecteur des excès de rendement anticipé des actifs risqués par rapport à l'actif sans risque.

– Considérons d'abord le cas d'une *règle de capitalisation indifférenciée selon les actifs*. La hausse du ratio capital/dépôts impose aux actionnaires d'accroître les fonds propres (ils ne peuvent pas restructurer leur bilan pour respecter le ratio, ce qui sera le cas avec une règle différenciée). *Si la rémunération des dépôts n'est pas aléatoire, une hausse du ratio capital/ dépôts accroît la quantité détenue des actifs dont il est au départ détenu une quantité positive* (si elle est négative, c'est-à-dire s'il y a vente à découvert, elle devient encore plus négative). En effet, la hausse du coefficient de capital réduit le levier, donc la rentabilité des fonds propres, ce qui est compensé par une hausse de la détention de tous les actifs risqués. *Si la rémunération des dépôts est aléatoire, les effets deviennent ambigus.* Imaginons qu'elle soit très corrélée avec le rendement d'un des actifs risqués; la hausse de la part du capital dans les ressources qui réduit la part des dépôts peut impliquer une réduction de la part de cet actif dans les emplois afin de diversifier le risque.

– Lorsque la règle de *capitalisation est différenciée* (il y a un rapport capital/ actif par actif), il faut distinguer soigneusement deux cas.

Cas 1: La règle est respectée par des apports en capital des actionnaires: le niveau de fonds propres varie donc. Dans ce cas, *si l'aversion pour le risque de la banque est faible*, le comportement des actionnaires est de maximiser le rendement, donc de choisir les parts des actifs risqués de manière à obtenir un capital très faible. Si le coefficient de capital appliqué aux actifs risqués est plus élevé que celui appliqué aux actifs non risqués, la banque vend donc à découvert des actifs risqués, ou du moins n'en détient pas, *un coefficient élevé sur ces actifs est donc dissuasif. Si l'aversion pour le risque est forte,* au contraire une hausse du coefficient de capital réduit la variance du rendement, ce qui permet à la banque *d'accroître la part des actifs risqués.*

Cas 2: *La règle est respectée avec un capital restant fixe mais en changeant la structure de l'actif pour jouer sur les écarts entre ratios de capital:* on voit alors que la hausse du coefficient de capital appliqué à un actif réduit la part de cet actif au profit des autres, ce qui est naturel puisque cette réaction permet de respecter la règle de capitalisation.

On a aussi vu que l'analyse des effets de la mise en place de ratios de fonds propres fait intervenir des éléments qui ne sont pas toujours clairement explicités dans la littérature:
– représentation du comportement de la banque avec ou sans aversion pour le risque;
– degré d'aversion pour le risque, qui centre l'analyse sur le rendement ou la variance;
– caractère aléatoire ou non de la rémunération des dépôts et corrélation de cette rémunération avec les rendements des placements;
– respect des règles de capitalisation par modification de la quantité de capital ou de la structure de l'actif des banques.

Selon le cas, une hausse du ratio de capital minimal sera efficace non pour réduire le risque pris par la banque – quel que soit l'effet de cette hausse sur le risque, il apparaît toutefois qu'elle réduit le risque de panique bancaire de course pour retirer les dépôts. Cette course (les "bank runs") se produisant lorsque les déposants réalisent que, compte tenu des retraits qui ont déjà été opérés, ils ne pourront pas récupérer leurs dépôts s'ils ne précèdent pas les autres déposants qui ne se sont pas encore présentés. Ceci intervient par exemple lorsque la préférence pour la liquidité se réduit brutalement dans la population. Evidemment, un surcroît de capital permet aux banques de faire face (en anticipations) aux retraits et évite la course aux dépôts.

Ces résultats tendent à montrer qu'il n'existe pas de système de régulation totalement efficace, car la multiplication des cas de figure possibles laisse subsister une forte marge d'incertitude sur l'effet des mesures envisageables. Mais on retiendra surtout de ce qui précède le principe d'une interdépendance entre les diverses composantes de la réglementation. La forme de l'assurance-dépôts conditionne l'influence du ratio de capitalisation sur les choix de portefeuilles bancaires, de même que la manipulation de ce ratio joue un rôle analogue à celui du plafonnement de taux créditeurs... L'efficacité d'un système de réglementation doit donc être appréciée de façon globale, et il n'est pas possible de considérer une à une chacune de ses composantes.

Cette remarque complique sans doute le problème d'harmonisation des réglementations nationales, dans le contexte d'internationalisation des activités financières. Car l'application d'une même disposition n'aura généralement pas la même incidence dans les différents pays. Par exemple l'effet du ratio COOKE sur la stabilité et l'efficience des systèmes bancaires dépendra de l'ensemble des divers dispositifs de régulation dans lesquels il va s'insérer. Sa signification et ses difficultés de mise en oeuvre seront donc différentes aux Etats-Unis, au Japon et en Europe. On comprend qu'il ne sera pas simple de pousser plus loin la coopération.

La question se pose évidemment de savoir si une telle harmonisation est souhaitable. La réponse que l'on y apporte généralement consiste à dire que si l'objectif de la régulation bancaire est simplement de protéger les déposants (de pallier l'existence d'asymétries d'information), alors il est préférable de laisser jouer la concurrence entre les réglementations nationales. Les investisseurs arbitreront entre la stabilité et l'efficience des divers systèmes. En revanche s'il s'agit de résoudre un problème d'externalité (s'il s'agit de se garantir contre les effets d'interdépendance qui jouent entre les différentes institutions financières), alors il faut certainement organiser une coopération entre les autorités monétaires nationales. On ne peut tolérer que la sécurité des systèmes de paiement et de financement de certaines économies soit affectée par les défaillances de banques opérant dans un pays où la réglementation est excessivement laxiste.

La tâche est évidemment difficile. Les dispositions mises au point dans le cadre du comité COOKE n'offrent pour l'instant que des garanties minimales. Elles sont sans doute bien insuffisantes pour assurer complètement la stabilité des systèmes bancaires. En l'occurrence il convient peut-être aussi de s'interroger sur l'arbitrage entre le gain en efficience que procure l'internationalisation des activités financières et les risques d'instabilité qu'elle comporte.

NOTES

1. La théorie de l'intermédiation a été récemment renouvelée par le littérature sur les asymétries d'information. Les deux articles essentiels sur ce point sont ceux de: D. Diamond, "Financial Intermediation and Delegated Monitoring", *Review of Economic Studies*, juillet 1984, et D. Diamond et P. Dybvig, "Bank Runs, Deposit Insurance and Liquidity", *Journal of Political Economy*, juin 1983.
2. Cf. tout particulièrement B. Bernanke, "Nonmonetary Effects of the Financial Crisis in the Propagation of the Great Depression", *American Economic Review*, mars 1983.
3. Cf. par exemple M. Dietsch, *Economies d'échelle, économies d'envergure et structure des coûts dans les banques de dépôts françaises.* Note ronéotée, version provisoire, novembre 1988.
4. On trouvera dans un travail récent de U. Muldur et P. Teston, une revue et une critique

de ce type de travail. Cf. "Bilan critique sur la littérature économique en matière d'indicateurs de coût et rendements d'échelle dans la banque", Document de travail, *CDC*, mars 1989.

5. On trouvera l'illustration de ce point dans U. Muldur et M. Sassenou, "Structure des coûts et efficacité des banques françaises", Document de travail, *CDC*, mai 1989.

6. Cf. W. Baumol, J. Panzar et R. Willig, *Contestable Markets and the Theory of Industry Structure*, Harcourt Bruce Jovanovich, 1982.

7. La notion d'économie d'envergure s'exprime dans la propriété de sous-additivité de la fonction de coût. On dit qu'il y a sous-additivité lorsque pour un ensemble de biens: $N = \{1, ...n\}$, pour les vecteurs de production $Q = \{q_1, ...q_n\}$, $Q^i = \{q_1, ...q_i\}$ et $Q^{n-i} = \{q_{i+1}, ... q_n\}$, on a:

$$C(Q) < C(Q^i) + C(Q^{n-i})$$

$C(Q)$ représentant le coût de production associe au vecteur Q, $C(Q^i)$ le coût de production associé au vecteur $Q^{i.}$.

8. Cette idée est exprimée par T. Campbell et W. Kracaw dans "Information Production, Market Signalling and the Theory of Financial Intermediation", *Journal of Finance*, septembre 1980.

9. Cf. E. Fama, "What's different about Banks?", *Journal of Monetary Economics*, 1985.

10. Cf. en particulier J. Stiglitz, "Credit Markets and the Control of Capital", *Journal of Money, Credit and Banking*, mai 1985.

11. Cf. C. Mayer, "New Issues in Corporate Finance", *European Economic Review*, Juillet 1988; et C. Mayer, "The Assesment: Financial Systems and Corporate Investment", *Oxford Review of Economic Policy*, vol. 3, n° 4, hiver 1987.

12. Cf. R. Litan, *What Should Banks do?*, Brookings Institution, 1987.

13. On trouvera un bref exposé de ce problème ainsi que son application à l'analyse de la déréglementation dans l'article de D. Encaoua, "Règlementation et concurrence: quelques éléments de théorie économique", *Economie et Prévision*, 1986, n° 76.

14. Cette solution semble être celle privilégiée par G. Corrigan, président de la Fed. de New York, Cf. "Financial Market Structure: A Longer View", FRB de New York, Rapport annuel 1986.

15. Ces questions ont été débattues dans un numéro spécial de la revue *Challenge* de novembre-décembre 1987. On y trouve en particulier des articles de J. Tobin, G. Corrigan, R. Litan et W. Seidman.

16. Cette proposition est faite dans l'ouvrage déjà cité de R. Litan. On la retrouve dans l'ouvrage de L. Bryan, *La banque éclatée*, Inter Éditions, 1989.

17. F. Hayek a beaucoup contribué à la promotion de cette idée. Il l'évoqua une première fois dans son ouvrage, *Monetary Nationalism and International Stability*, Longmans Green, 1937. On trouvera une petite histoire de ce débat dans l'ouvrage de Ch. Goodhart, *The Evolution of Central Banks*, MIT Press, 1988. Cf. aussi l'article de G. Gorton et D. Mullineaux, "The Joint Production of Confidence: Endogenous Regulation and Nineteenth Century Commercial-Bank Clearinghouses", *Journal of Money Credit and Banking*, novembre 1987.

18. "Bank Runs, Deposit Insurance and Liquidity", *Journal of Political Economy*, 1983, p. 416.

19. Conceptuellement l'assurance-dépôts peut être considérée comme une option de vente. Dans le cas de faillite l'organisme d'assurance récupère les actifs de la banque pour un prix (d'exercice) égal au moment de la valeur assurée des dépôts. En partant de ce principe on peut calculer le prix optimal de la prime d'assurance. C'est R. Merton qui le premier a suggéré le traitement du problème en ces termes. Cf. "An Analytic Derivation of the Cost of Deposit Insurance and Loan Guarantees", *Journal of Banking and Finance*, juin 1977. Plusieurs applications en ont été faites, qui ne sont pas toujours très convaincantes du fait des hypothèses qu'elles supposent. Cf. A. Marcus et I. Shaked, "The Valuation of FDIC Deposit Insurance using Option-Pricing Estimates", *Journal of Money, Credit and Banking*, novembre 1984; et E. Ronn et A. Verma, "Pricing Risk adjusted Deposit Insurance:

An Option based Model", *Journal of Finance*, septembre 1986.

20. Cf. par exemple la démonstration de M. Koehn et A. Santomero, "Regulation of Bank Capital and Portfolio Risk", *Journal of Finance*, décembre 1980.

21. Cf. D. Kim et A. Santomero, "Risk in Banking and Capital Regulation", *Journal of Finance*, décembre 1988.

22. Cette idée avait été défendu par M. Friedman à l'origine dans un seul objectif de régulation monétaire. Elle est aujourd'hui soutenue par des auteurs sans rapport avec le monétarisme aux seules fins de contrôle prudentiel.

23. Cette idée est rigoureusement analysée dans l'ouvrage de Ch. Goodhart, *The Evolution of Central Banks*, MIT Press, 1988. Elle est également défendue par J. Kareken dans son article survey "Federal Bank Regulatory Policy: A Description and some Observations", Journal of Business, janvier 1986.

24. Cet argument est développé par: D. Diamond et P. Dybvig, "Banking Theory, Deposit Insurance and Bank Relation". *Journal of Business*, janvier 1986; et par Ch. Goodhart, *The Evolution of Central Banks*, op. cit. (chapitre 7).

25. On trouvera une présentation de cet argument dans: E. Baltensperger et J. Dermine, "Banking Deregulation", *Economic Policy*, n° 4, avril 1987.

26. Cette idée a été développée par B. Smith dans: "Private Information, Deposit Interest Rates, and the Stability of the Banking System", *Journal of Monetary Economics*, novembre 1984.

XIX. Issues in Banking Supervision and Regulation from the Perspective of a Banking Supervisor

PETER A. A. M. CORNET

INTRODUCTION

In recent years, financial institutions have been confronted with significant changes and developments. Generally speaking, the banks would appear to have reacted adequately, even if in some cases considerable effort was required. In the years ahead, too, the management of financial institutions should expect to be faced with new, often strategic challenges, not least on account of the move towards the completion of the internal EC market after 1992. This paper takes a look at the Second Council Directive on the coordination of banking legislation, which will have a major impact on European banking, as well as at the international accord which has meanwhile been reached on a minimum capital standard. It also discusses some of the principal developments now facing supervisory authorities, special attention being paid to the supervision of holding companies with a banking subsidiary.

PAST

Growing concern about the solvency position of international banks

From a financial and economic viewpoint, the past two decades contrasted sharply with the preceding ones. The abolition of the system of fixed exchange rates in 1972 seems to have marked the onset of a period in which relative stability gave way to increasing uncertainty about the course of macro-economic developments. Exchange rates and interests rates were marked by sharp fluctuations, as were the prices of commodities and securities. The financial markets reacted by introducing new financial instruments such as swaps, options, futures and FRAs. These instruments were designed to eliminate or, in any case, reduce uncertainties with regard to such factors as movements in interest rate levels and exchange rates. The global recession of the early 1980s certainly had a weakening effect on the financial position of the banking system. In contrast to earlier recessions, the banks' problems

D. E. Fair and C. de Boissieu (eds), Financial Institutions in Europe Under New Competitive Conditions, 275–291.
© 1990 *Kluwer Academic Publishers, Dordrecht. Printed in the Netherlands.*

were not confined to losses in respect of local, private customers. Major problems were also encountered in the area of sovereign lending. In the second half of 1982 Mexico, Brazil and Argentina successively found themselves in payment problems: the debt crisis was a stark reality. The central bank governors of the G-10 countries, holding that the solvency positions of their (international) banks should not be allowed to weaken further, responded by charging the Basle Committee on Banking Regulations and Supervisory Practices in 1984 with the task of designing internationally comparable solvency ratios and with devising ways for achieving greater convergence of banks' solvency ratios in the G-10 countries. Within the EC, work was also done in this field. Since 1981, within the framework of its discussions on observation ratios for solvency, the Banking Advisory Committtee had already been working on a definition of banks' own funds. In this context it closely monitored developments in the banks' solvency positions. The discussions within these two forums were coordinated, where possible.

This period (from 1981 to 1985) saw a clear change internationally in supervisory approaches to the solvency position of banks. After years of steadily declining national solvency requirements (denoted by some as a competition in laxity), the supervisory authorities decided to join forces not just to put an end to this situation, but to redress it. Conditions in the financial markets evidenced that banks' solvency positions were approaching the boundaries of acceptability. In the United States in particular, certain enterprises were succesful in obtaining lower-cost funding than banks. As such a situation cannot but undermine the function of banks, it is hardly surprising that, on the whole, the banks did not oppose the tendency towards new solvency requirements. They probably agreed that the supervisory efforts to ensure a stronger capital base, if applicable to all competitors as well, would benefit the entire banking sector.

The European dimension

In the summer of 1985 the European Commission published its White Paper on the completion of the internal market. The Paper indicated the specific impediments which stood in the way of economic unification of Europe and outlined ways to eliminate them. The liberalization of the financial sector was given separate attention. The Commission proposed not only liberalization of capital movements within Europe, but also complete freedom of financial services. From the banks' point of view, the second banking coordination Directive, the Directive on own funds and the Directive on an EC solvency ratio are among the most important elements of the development towards the internal market. Other important subjects are recommendations on a large-exposure rule and on a deposit guarantee scheme. Eventually, the new

EC legislation will lead to a free banking market in the European Communities, with banks operating under equal competitive conditions.

The plans prompted feverish activity not only within the financial sector but also in other segments of the production and services industries. Europhoria appeared to have set in. Suddenly the future looked different and brighter. Many enterprises set up strategic planning departments or upgraded existing ones. Banks increased their focus on mergers and acquisitions. The high hopes centred on the completion of the internal EC market were macroeconomically underpinned by the well-known Cecchini report, which presented figures showing that, ultimately, the financial sector, too, stood to gain materially from the single market. The report also indicated, however, that the increased competition could initially lead to an erosion of interest margins and to a reduction in other income for banks. But better prospects for cross-border operations as well as additional economic growth consequent on the completion of the internal market would ultimately tip the balance for the financial institutions.

PRESENT

The Basle accord on a solvency ratio

The mandate given to the Basle Committee by the central bank governors of the G-10 countries to achieve a level playing field for international banks and the European Communities' drive towards a free banking market after 1992 prompted great activity in the area of banking supervision. In line with established practice, under which supervisors first discuss new regulations with the banking system, the banks and/or their representative organizations were invited to comment in detail on the various proposals worked out in this connection. Most of their comments are reflected in the ultimate texts.

In July 1988 the Basle Committee reached agreement on a capital standard, to be introduced on a multilateral basis. The accord provides for a risk ratio, which relates capital to the sum of risk-weighted assets and off-balance-sheet items. This ratio thus differed from the gearing ratio which was still used at that time in a number of countries, including the United States; the gearing ratio relates only the balance sheet total to capital. The risk ratio approach entails advantages in that it does better justice to differences in balance sheet structure (and, hence, in risk profile) and assigns a lower weighting to assets involving a lower average degree of risk. Conversely, however, banks engaging to a relatively large extent in high-risk operations must hold a proportionally higher amount of capital. The risk ratio approach also takes account of the fast-growing off-balance-sheet activities of banks.

In the Basle accord, capital is defined as *core capital* (equity capital and disclosed reserves) plus *supplementary capital* (undisclosed reserves, revaluation reserves, general provisions, hybrid debt capital instruments and subordinated debt). In the calculation of the risk ratio, supplementary capital may be included up to 100 per cent of core capital, subordinated debt being counted up to 50 per cent of core capital. The assets side of the balance sheet is divided into five risk categories, which are assigned weights of 100 per cent, 50 per cent, 20 per cent, 10 per cent and 0 per cent. The central focus of this framework is credit risk (risk of counterparty failure) and, as a further aspect of this risk, country transfer risk. Other risks relating to lending, such as exchange rate risk, interest rate risk and position risk, are not at present allowed for as such in the calculation of the risk ratio. Supervisory authorities are currently working on simple methods to measure such exposures, a process which could be viewed as a first step towards international coordination of supervisory approaches to market risks. Off-balance-sheet items are incorporated into the calculation using a credit conversion factor. The accord culminates in a standard for the risk ratio. This standard has been set at 8 per cent, to be observed by the end of 1992 (a numerical illustration of the Basle accord is given in Annex I).

Both the definition of capital and the weighting percentages have been the subject of intensive negotiations among the members of the Basle Committee. It proved immensely difficult (and in some cases even impossible) to make allowance for the often historically conditioned, typical characteristics of banks in the different G-10 countries in a manner satisfactory to all parties. For example, the supervisory perception of the risks attaching to claims secured by mortgages or to claims on national local authorities differs widely among the various countries. In the end, a delicate compromise was reached, based on mutual concessions among all the parties. The accord on a minimum capital standard may be instrumental in effecting the necessary improvement in the banking system's financial position (or, phrased differently, its rating). In addition, it represents a most important step forward towards comparable competitive conditions for the banks in the major industrialized countries. However, the complete removal of all competitive distortions will take more than a uniform capital standard. The authorities responsible for fiscal legislation, too, will have to work towards convergence of tax régimes. In addition, ways should be sought to ensure that non-banks offering the same products to the financial markets as banks will be liable to comparable (capital adequacy) rules, since there is little point in achieving a level playing field for banks if this should put the banking sector as a whole at a competitive disadvantage.

Progress in Brussels

The European Commission closely monitored developments in Basle. It was able to do so not only because the Basle Committee allowed Commission representatives to participate in its meetings in the interests of continuing harmonization, but also because a number of countries represented on the Basle Committee are EC Member States. As a result, the proposed own funds Directive and solvency ratio Directive are very closely in line with the Basle accord. The minimum solvency ratio of 8 per cent, adopted both at Basle and at Brussels, definitely does not represent an easy target for all the parties involved. Trial calculations have shown that a considerable number of banks will have to strenghten their capital base in the near future. On the other hand, it may be assumed that supervisors will not easily allow the presently more highly capitalized banks to bring their solvency ratios down to the minimum level (or, in other words, allow them to weaken their relative positions).

For the banks in countries which are members of both the EC and the G-10, the coordination reached between Basle and Brussels has a considerable advantage in that they will not be confronted with different reporting systems. Furthermore, it is to be expected that the individual EC Member States will bring their national reporting systems closely into line with the Brussels and Basle framework. For international banks in particular, this may lead to a considerable reduction in reporting effort and cost. To complete the picture, it should be noted that, contrary to the Basle accord, the EC Directives must ultimately be incorporated into the Member States' national legislation. Compared with a Directive, the Basle accord represents a gentlemen's agreement involving a moral obligation. Another difference is that the EC Directives will apply to all banks, whereas the Basle accord, in principle, covers only banks which operate internationally. In the United States, however, the supervisory authorities have declared the Basle risk ratio applicable to all banks (including savings banks) and bank holding companies of any substance.

In its drive towards the completion of the internal market after 1992, the European Commission has also presented a draft second Directive on the coordination of banking legislation. The decision-making process in respect of this Directive is now in an advanced stage. The second coordination Directive was preceded by earlier Directives concerning access to and the conduct of banking in the European Communities. Instances are the first coordination Directive and a Directive concerning supervision on a conso-lidated basis. On the one hand, the second coordination Directive provides for the opening-up of markets and the reinforcement of market forces leading to keener competition; on the other hand, it sets minimum conditions for the prudential supervision of banks. The latter aspect seeks to maintain and, where possible, improve the financial stability of the existing banking systems. In order to obtain a banking licence a credit institution should, in principle, have initial capital of at least ECU 5 million. Furthermore, the second Directive will enable the competent authorities to obtain the necessary information regarding the identity of major shareholders of enterprises applying for a banking license or envisaging the acquisition of an existing bank. Moreover, the Directive provides for a limitation of banks' participations in any non-financial institution to 15 per cent of own funds. The total of such participations should not exceed 60 per cent of own funds. These requirements are more stringent than current practice in a number of EC countries.

Among the consequences which the liberalization aspect of the second Directive may be expected to have, the first is what can be termed the *geographical effect*. The introduction of the system of the single banking licence (one licence will suffice to engage in banking throughout the EC) means that the authorities of a host country may no longer demand that a licence should be obtained for the establishment of a branch, nor will they be permitted to demand a certain minimum amount of own funds. Another important effect is *product deregulation*. The list of permitted banking operations is based on the universal banking model, so that it includes all forms of securities business (a survey of permitted operations is given in Annex II). This will have consequences for those Member States in particular which still maintain a separation between commercial banks and investment banks. The second Directive may be expected to speed up the process of despecialization in the financial sector, since national authorities will be loath to put their domestic banks at a disadvantage by prohibiting them from engaging in types of business open to their competitors from other Member States.

The second Directive provides that, in the liberalized EC market, prudential supervision will be underlain by the principle of *mutual recognition* of national supervisory systems. This removes the need for full harmonization of banking legislation at the European level. It stands to reason that this principle is acceptable only if the Member States are agreed on a certain *minimum level of harmonization of essential supervisory requirements*. In this context, it is important to note another principle embedded in the Directive: that of *home state control*. Home state control means that the supervision will be exercised by the competent authorities of the Member State where a legally independent institution has its head office. Hence, home state control will encompass all of that institution's operations conducted within the Communities, whether through the provision of direct cross-border services or through operations of branches in other Member States. Whereas at present a bank operating branches in various EC countries has to deal with different national supervisory authorities, in the situation after 1992 it will only be confronted with the supervisor of the country where its European head office is located. For these banks the new situation will no doubt be marked by considerable supervisory deregulation.

It may be wondered – and some do – whether harmonized banking supervision in the EC on the basis of a number of minimum requirements might lead to minimal (and, hence, weakened) supervision. However, for as long as the minimum requirements are not minimal but ambitious, the ultimate supervisory system will be anything but minimal. Consequently, supervisors do not expect that banks will transfer their head offices to those Member States where they hope to find the lightest supervisory régime. If, in some isolated cases, banks were to contemplate such a move, they might be restrained by the predictable reactions of (potential) creditors and rating agencies.

It was noted above that mutual recognition of the national supervisory systems removes the need for full harmonization of banking legislation at the European level. Yet, it would appear that there are still some areas where further convergence could be meaningfully pursued. A case in point is deposit insurance. At present there is an EC Recommendation under which each Member State should operate a deposit guarantee scheme as from 1 January 1990. Most of the EC countries already have such a scheme (see Annex III). In Ireland, Luxembourg and Portugal legislation on this score is in the final stages, while the Greek system is still in the preparatory stage. The Annex shows that the existing systems differ considerably in terms of amount and scope of coverage. Although thus far deposit guarantee schemes do not seem to have had any discernible effect on depositors' selection of banks, this situation might change with the financial integration of Europe. Consequently, further harmonization of the various systems seems desirable. It is noteworthy that the proposals for two of the systems in preparation, like the operational systems of the United Kingdom and Italy, provide for a limited deductable amount. Experiences in the United States might have indicated that full coverage for high amounts is not invariably conducive to stability in the financial sector as it may tempt depositors to entrust their moneys lightly to institutions which are less than sound.

FUTURE

New possibilities for financial institutions

For financial institutions, the period ahead will blur both sectoral and geographical frontiers. This will, of course, be most pronounced in the process of the completion of the single European market. However, the internationalization of the financial system will not be confined to the European Communities alone. European banks will no doubt continue to expand their worldwide networks of branches, if only to be able to continue to serve their customers. On the other hand, banks from major countries such as the United States, Japan and Switzerland will increasingly seek to penetrate the large EC market. It is, incidentally, interesting to note that the EC establishments of banks from these countries generally do not operate in the retail market but tend to offer specialized services (such as export finance and securities transactions). Sectoral boundaries will also fade internationally. At present the segregation (statutory or otherwise) between banks, insurance companies, securities firms and investment institutions is clearly becoming less strict. In the United States and Japan, which traditionally maintained a strict separation between banking and security business, distinct tendencies are apparent to pull down the walls between the two types of financial business. Furthermore, forms of cooperation between banks and insurance companies are increasingly evident.

In this environment of globalization of financial markets, a process made possible not least by rapid technological innovation, individual institutions are faced with a number of choices. The basic choice concerns the scale of operation; larger-scale operation could increase the potential to benefit from the new market opportunities. To achieve this, a number of options are available:

a the establishment of branches at home and/or abroad;
b the acquisition of, or a merger with, a domestic institution (in the same sector);
c the acquisition of, or a merger with, a foreign institution (in the same sector);
d the acquisition of, or a merger with, a domestic or foreign institution active in a different sector.

Combinations are, of course, also possible. It is interesting to note that the reasons why institutions opt for one of these variants may differ widely. In all cases, however, the key consideration is ultimately profitability. Other considerations may include the retention or expansion of market shares. However, it might be noted in this context that a deliberate choice for a market niche need by no means imply that the institution concerned will suffer in terms of competitive power, as there will continue to be a need for specialist financial services in the future as well.

New tasks for supervisors

How should or could supervisors react to these developments? The use of the plural 'supervisors' is deliberate since most of the variants set out above involve more than one supervisor. Generally, supervisors will have to cooperate more intensively than they did in the past. This means that they will have to step up their consultations and exchange more information if they are to be able to exercise adequate supervision over the new and diverse (combinations of) financial institutions. These consultations should not be confined to banking supervisors but should include insurance supervisors and securities regulators as well, and should be both national and international. As yet, there is no adequate institutional framework for such national and international consultation among these supervisors of the various financial sectors. For the years ahead, achieving such a framework constitutes a major task. Its achievement could proceed along the same lines as the evolution of the consultation among banking supervisors, which, after more than twenty years, has now more or less reached maturity. Roughly, the following successive stages will have to be completed: the acquaintance phase, where supervisors learn to know and trust each other, the codification phase, where stock is taken of best practices, and finally the normative phase and the multilateral cooperation phase, where harmonized regulations, including standards, are formulated.

In some EC countries consultations among supervisors of various financial sectors are already being held on a regular basis. At Basle, discussions are in progress between banking supervisors and securities regulators from the G-10 countries. For the required further evolution of the European infrastructure and regulation in this area, the European Commission would appear to have a major coordinating role to play for as long as there are still at least twelve supervisors for each financial sector. Ultimately, European banking supervision should be among the tasks of the future European central bank.

For the time being, the individual supervisor should concentrate on his primary task (the protection of creditors' interests), while ensuring that the banks under his supervision can compete on an equal footing with other banks and financial institutions (level playing field).

First, this requires consolidation and further improvement of the supervisory framework as it is taking shape at Basle and Brussels. The establishment of a harmonized minimum capital standard constitutes a major step towards a stronger banking sector. However, much remains to be done. One example of further work in this area is the establishment of a large-exposure rule to counter undue concentrations of risk. On this subject, the EC has already issued a Recommendation, which does not, however, have binding force for the Member States. A Directive, which does have binding force, would be preferable. The subject of deposit guarantee schemes has already been discussed above. Both at Basle and at Brussels, work is now in progress to come to regulations concerning the so-termed market or position risk in respect of banks' securities positions. Developments on the stock exchanges in October

1987 have clearly shown that, by holding portfolios of securities (both trading and investment portfolios), the banks were running considerable risks. It is the supervisor's task to ensure that such risks are kept within acceptable limits, for instance by relating the maximum size of the positions to the bank's capital or by subjecting them to solvency requirements. Work should also focus on systems for measuring open foreign exchange positions and interest rate risk. In respect of the latter, many banks already employ (sophisticated) methods to compute the effect of changes in interest rates on their financial results. for purposes of prudential supervision a simpler but uniform system will probably suffice.

Another area where major efforts are still required concerns the adequate supervision of financial conglomerates. Within the EC, this challenge has been taken up and work has started on a revision of the Directive for consolidated supervision of credit institutions. Ultimately, this Directive should also provide for the supervision of holding companies which own at least one bank. If the holding company itself is not a bank it will generally not be subject to direct supervision even if its subsidiaries include a bank. Although it is true that a banking supervisor is primarily concerned with this bank, he cannot adequately perform his task if he has no insight into the other companies of the group and into the holding company. The fact is that developments within the other group companies of the holding company may substantially affect the banking subsidiary. Consequently, ways must be sought to get a measure of supervisory grip on the holding company. Important elements in this respect are:

- The *capital structure* of the holding company. Supervisors must be able to ascertain that the capital provided by the holding company to the subsidiary is actually available as such within the holding company.
- The *spread of risks*. The supervisor must have a clear insight into the financial relationships between the bank and the other group companies.
- The *trustworthiness of the management of the holding company.*
- The holding company's *participation policy.*

The supervision of financial conglomerates should seek to make the complex of intra-group financial links as transparent as possible. To this end close cooperation will have to be established with the other agencies in charge of the supervision of certain segments of the group. If developments within the group should be such as to pose a threat to the interests of the bank's creditors, the supervisor should have the power to isolate the bank from the rest of the group or even to revoke its banking licence. The need to isolate a bank from the rest of a group is probably most distinct if the group as a whole is acquired by investors planning to split it up and sell it as separate entities. In such a situation, the bank must clearly be able to continue business on its own.

Finally, in respect of the supervision of banking groups, it is important that these groups should not be faced with an excess of regulations. In practice, this will probably mean that supervisory tasks and responsibilities will have to be divided. Whether this will lead to joint supervision, delegated supervision or lead supervision is as yet unclear, as are the precise definitions which will be given to these terms. One thing, though, is clear: intensive consultation will be required. Individual supervisory authorities have already taken initial steps in this area, in response to concrete forms of cooperation between existing banks.

SUMMARY

Recently, following a period of gradual deterioration of banks' capital positions, agreements were made to improve the banks' financial credibility. To this end banks will have to strenghten their capital ratios. One way to achieve this is by improving profitability; the completion of the European internal market holds out prospects in this regard. The enlargement of the market will speed up the process whereby national and sectoral boundaries are increasingly fading. For the supervisory authorities this development calls for closer cooperation. A major new supervisory area will be that of financial conglomerates.

ANNEX I

Stylized example of the modalities of the BIS framework of capital adequacy measurement.[1]

Assets	(Amount)	(Risk weights)	Bank X (Risk-weighted assets)	Liabilities		
– cash	10	(0%)	0	– domestic banks	230	
– central; governments and central banks (preferential zone)[2]	140	(0%)	0	– foreign banks	250	
– banks (preferential zone)[2]	150	(20%)	30	– deposits	1,275	
– banks (other)				– bonds	150	
• residual maturity ≤ 1 year	175	(20%)	35	– paid-up share capital	50	
• residual maturity > 1 year	175	(100%)	175	– disclosed reserves[3]	100	
– residual mortgages	400	(50%)	200	*Capital elements tier 1*		150
– claims on private sector	750	(100%)	750	– undisclosed reserves	20	
– securities (private sector)	300	(100%)	300	– asset revaluation reserves	25	
– investment participations				– subordinated term debt	150	
• in non-financial companies	50	(100%)	50	(to a max. of 50% of tier 1)	75	
• in financial companies (unconsolidated)	50	(deducted from capital base)	–	*Capital elements tier 2*		
– premises	50	(100%)	50	(to a max. of 100% of tier 1)		120
Total	2,250		(1,590)		2,250	
				Total capital base		270

Off-balance-sheet activities

	Amount	Credit conversion factor	Risk weights	Risk-weighted off-balance-sheet activities
– Guarantees which are to be considered as direct credit substitutes (private sector)	750	100%	100%	750
– Revolving underwriting facilities (RUFs) (private sector)	100	50%	100%	50
– Documentary credits (private sector)	100	20%	100%	20
– Stand-by facilities (original maturity > 1 year) to banks in preferential zone[2]	300	50%	20%	30
– Other commitments (original maturity ≤ 1 year)	75	0%	–	–
			Total	850

$$\text{'Risk ratio'} = \frac{\text{Capital base} -/- \text{Deductions}}{\text{Total risk-weighted activities}} \times 100\%$$

$$= \frac{270 -/- 50}{1{,}590 + 850} \times 100\% = 9\%$$

Capital standard = 'risk ratio' $\geq 8\%$

[1] Committee on Banking Regulations and Supervisory Practices, *International convergence of capital measurement and capital standards*, July 1988.
[2] The preferential zone comprises countries which are full members of the OECD or which have concluded special lending arrangements with the IMF associated with the Fund's General Arrangements to Borrow.
[3] Excluding asset revaluation reserves.

Note: This highly stylized example does not include the effects on the fictitious Bank X's solvency position of, for instance, national regulations to ensure the spreading of risk (large item rule), to limit interest and exchange rate exposure or to enforce provisions for lending or country risks.

ANNEX II

Types of business that are classed as integral to banking and included within the scope of mutual recognition in the Second Banking Directive.

1. Deposit-taking and other forms of borrowing.
2. Lending including:
    – consumer credit;
    – mortgage lending;
    – factoring and invoice discounting;
    – trade finance (including forfaiting).
3. Financial leasing.
4. Money transmission services.
5. Issuing and administering means of payment (credit cards, travellers cheques and bankers drafts).
6. Guarantees and commitments.
7. Trading for own account or for account of the customers in:
    – Money market instruments (cheques, bills, CDs, etc.);
    – Foreign exchange;
    – Financial futures and options;
    – Exchange and interest rate instruments;
    – Securities.
8. Participation in share issues and the provision of services related to such issues and advising in the field of mergers and acquisitions and corporate finance.
9. Money broking.
10. Portfolio management and advice.
11. Safekeeping of securities.
12. Credit reference services.
13. Safe custody services.

ANNEX III

Bank deposit guarantee schemes in Member States

	Belgium	Denmark	France	Germany	Italy	Netherlands	Spain	UK
A. Nature of the schemes								
1. (i) Is membership voluntary or compulsory?	Voluntary	Compulsory	Compulsory	Voluntary	Voluntary	Compulsory	Voluntary	Compulsory
(ii) Are the arrangements statutory?	No	Yes	No	No	No	No	Yes	Yes
(iii) What proportion of banks are covered by the scheme?	All	All	All	All (minor exceptions)	90% of banks. No overseas bank branches belong.	All	All	All
2. Is the scheme administered officially or privately?	Officially	Officially	Privately	Privately	Privately	Officially	Officially	Officially
B. Funding arrangement								
3. (i) How is the scheme funded?	Calls on participating institutions in event of loss	Contributions from participating institutions. Funds's resources to reach a max of Dkr 3bn	Calls on participating institutions. In event of loss	Contributions from participating institutions	Calls on participating institutions in event of loss. Ceiling of funding fixed at L 4 trillion	Calls on participating institutions in event of loss	Contributions from participating institutions	Contributions from participating institutions. Ceiling of funding fixed at £6mn
(ii) Is the scheme a standing fund?	No	Yes	No	Yes	No	No	Yes	Yes

ANNEX III (continued)

Bank deposit guarantee schemes in Member States

	Belgium	Denmark	France	Germany	Italy	Netherlands	Spain	UK
C. Scheme coverage								
4. (i) Does coverage extend to deposits denominated in any currency?	B.Fcs only	All	F.Fcs only	All	All	All	All	£ only
5. Does coverage extend to deposits held with:								
(i) Domestic branches of foreign banks?	Yes	Yes	Yes	Yes	Yes	Yes	Yes	Yes
(ii) Foreign branches of domestic banks?	No (but yes if not covered by foreign scheme or only partly covered)	No (but yes if no compulsory scheme in host country)	No	Yes	No (but yes if not covered by foreign scheme)	No	No	No
6. Level of protection available to depositors?	B-Fcs 0.5mn per depositor (but overall limited to assets available in Fund)	Dkr 0.25mn per depositor	FF 0.4mn per depositor	Max=30% of bank's liable capital per depositor as per audited accounts (Commercial banks only)	i) 100% on claims to L200mn ii) 90% between L200mn and L1.0bn iii) 80% between L1.0bn and L3.0bn (li-	DFl 40,000 per depositor (variable 3 yearly)	Ptas 1.5mn per depositor	75% of deposit up to £20,000 (ie £15,000 maximum payment)

ANNEX III (continued)

Bank deposit guarantee schemes in Member States

	Belgium	Denmark	France	Germany	Italy	Netherlands	Spain	UK
					mits doubled for C/Ds and svgs certs)			
ECU rates as at 10 July 1989	= ECU 11,500	= ECU 31,100	= ECU 57,300		Max cover = ECU 1.7mn	= ECU 17,200	= ECU 11,500	Max cover = ECU 22,000

291

XX. Home Country Control and Mutual Recognition

JEAN DERMINE*

The European Commission has worked for nearly thirty years on the integration of banking and financial markets. Freedom of establishment and entry was achieved in 1973, but further efforts to harmonize banking regulations and promote cross-border services proved to be very slow. This process led to a genial idea, incorporated in the 1985 White Paper on the Completion of the Internal Market, the opening of markets prior to harmonization. Regulation and supervision are guided by the principles of home country control and mutual recognition according to which each country will accept the regulation and supervision enforced by other countries on their domestic firms operating abroad. These principles are very broad: they apply to all products, banking and financial services included. The issue raised in this paper concerns the application of these two principles to banking services. Is there anything special in banking that would justify a different approach?

In reference to the economic theory of regulation, we analyse the characteristics of banking products which call for public intervention. This leads to a discussion of deposit insurance, lender of last resort and the links between banking, insurance, industry and commerce.

The main conclusions of the paper are as follows. The major reason for intervention in banking is the need to ensure the stability of banking markets. This does not imply the systematic protection of depositors. The current design of deposit insurance systems and lender of last resort imply that the principles of home country control and mutual recognition must be complemented with *host country supervision*. As long as national monetary authorities do not delegate their power to a supranational authority, they should keep full supervisory responsibility for their domestic markets. Moreover, fair competition is likely to entail further harmonization of the coverage of the various deposit insurance systems and of the links between banking, commerce, insurance and industry.

The paper is organized as follows. Section I summarizes the main char-

* The author acknowledges extensive discussions with Professor Baltensperger.

D. E. Fair and C. de Boissieu (eds), Financial Institutions in Europe Under New Competitive Conditions, 293–303.
© 1990 *Kluwer Academic Publishers, Dordrecht. Printed in the Netherlands.*

acteristics of the single market proposal. Section II reviews the specific characteristics of banking services calling for public intervention. Finally, Section III evaluates the European proposals from the perspective of their ability to ensure the stability of banking markets.

I. EUROPEAN BANKING, FROM 1957 TO 1992

To understand fully the prudential issues at stake and the process of European banking integration, it is useful to review the major actions undertaken by the Brussels Commission and the Council of Ministers. Three time periods can be distinguished: deregulation of entry to domestic markets from 1957 to 1973, various attempts towards harmonization of banking regulations from 1973 to 1983 and the recent proposal of freedom of cross-border services, single banking licence, home country control and mutual recognition.

Deregulating entry 1957–1973

In July 1965, the Commission made a proposal for a Directive on the Abolition of Restrictions on Freedom of Establishment and Freedom to Provide Services in Respect of Self-employed Activities of Banks and other Financial Institutions. Adopted by the Council in June 1973, this Directive ensures the equal treatment of national and other firms of Member States on entry in domestic markets and on conditions to which banks are submitted during their activity. As Clarotti (1984) notes, very little discrimination remains as to entry in Member States. However, the objectives of the initial Treaty were still far from being met. Although the original Treaty and the 1973 Directive called for it, international competition through the supply of cross-border services was severely limited by restrictions on capital flows. Furthermore, there was no coordination of banking supervision, so that banks operating in different countries could be subject to different rules. This led to the second phase of attempts to harmonise regulations.

1973–1983 harmonization of banking regulations

Progress in harmonization came in 1977 with the adoption of the First Directive on the Coordination of Laws, Regulation and Administrative Provisions Relating to the Taking up and Pursuit of Credit Institutions. This Directive establishes a definition of credit institutions (article 1): "Undertakings, whose business is to receive deposits and other repayable funds from the public and to grant credit for its own account". The principle of Home Country Control was established. The supervision of credit institutions operating in several Member Countries will gradually be shifted from the host country to the *home country* of the parent bank. The 1977 Directive is a first step towards the harmonization of regulation. It is a general programme which, without providing any specific regulation, calls for further Directives.

After the 1977 First Banking Directive and the above-mentioned Directives, the European banking markets were still far from full integration for four major reasons:
- a bank wishing to operate in another country still had to be authorized by the supervisors of the other country,
- it remained subject to supervision by the host country and its range of activities could be constrained by host country laws
- in most countries, branches had to be provided with earmarked endowment capital as if they were a new bank,
- finally, as already mentioned, the supply of cross border services was severely impaired by the restrictions on capital flows.

The tasks of full harmonisation of national regulations seems to be a tentacular task which prompted a new approach towards European integration.

The completion of the internal market by 1992: 1983-1992

Following various European Councils, the Commission proposed at the Milano meeting in 1985 its White Paper on the completion of the internal market by 1992. In short, the Paper calls for the removal by January 1st 1993 of the physical, technical and fiscal barriers in all industries.

In the context of banking, the White paper calls for a single banking license, home country control and mutual recognition. These principles are incorporated in the 1989 Second Banking Directive. All credit institutions authorized in one European country will be able to establish or supply financial services without further authorization. They will be able to undertake all the activities listed in the annex of the Second Directive provided that these activities are not forbidden by the home country supervisor.

The list includes most activities of universal banks, the delivery of insurance services excepted. The Directive calls for home country control on solvency and large exposure but recognizes explicitly that host country regulation would apply for monetary policy reasons and for market position risk. Recognizing that full competition requires a fair level playing field and minimal harmonization of regulation, the Second Banking Directive calls for minimal equity (5 millions ECU), supervisory control of major shareholders and of banks' permanent participation in the non-financial sector. The Second Directive is accompanied by two Recommendations on large risks exposure and on deposit insurance and by proposals for Directives on reorganisation and winding up, own funds, solvency ratios and the accounts of foreign branches.

From this review of the Directives, Recommendations and proposals for Directives, it appears that the objective pursued by the European Commission is threefold: free entry and provision of financial services throughout the Community, the establishment of a fair level playing field with single banking licence, home country control, mutual recognition and minimal harmonization on equity, accounting, ownership and participation in the non-financial sector and, finally, consumer protection. In this respect, references (e.g. the 1985 White Paper or Clarotti, 1987) are often made to the European Court of Justice case 'Cassis de Dijon' according to which control on the quality of a product is warranted but can be met fully by the *home country supervisor*. However, references are also made to the 1986 non-life insurance court case according to which controls by host authorities can be accepted as long as they are justified on the ground of the 'public interest'. A second major illustration of the perceived need for consumer protection is the Directive and Recommendation on deposit insurance:

> Member States shall ensure that the deposit-guarantee schemes that exist in their territory cover the deposits of branches of institutions having their head office in another Member State. As a transitional measure, pending entry into force of a deposit-guarantee scheme in all Member States, the latter shall ensure that the deposit guarantee scheme, in which the institutions that have their head office in their territory take part, extend cover to deposits received by branches set up in host countries within the Community which have no deposit-guarantee scheme, under the same conditions as those laid down to guarantee deposits received in the home country (article 16).

From the reading of the proposals for Directives, it appears that one of the major reasons for public intervention in banking is the premise that *consumers of financial services need to be protected.* In order to assess the European framework, it is useful to review the banking literature and analyse the sources of potential market failure and the economic need for banking supervision. This is the object of the second Section.

II. THE ECONOMICS OF BANKING REGULATION

Following the approach in Baltensperger-Dermine (1987, 1989), the major services provided by banks and the analysis of the potential sources of market failure are reviewed. Although the services provided by banks are interrelated, it is convenient to distinguish four categories: portfolio management, payment (transmission) mechanism, risk sharing and monitoring or information-related services.

Portfolio management: at low cost, investors can acquire a diversified portfolio of liabilities issued by deficit spending units. The pure case is the SICAV, mutual fund or unit trust which allows the holder of a share to have access to a diversified portfolio of liabilities.

Payment mechanism: a second role for banks in the economy is the management of the payment system, that is to facilitate and keep track of transfers of wealth among individuals. This is the bookkeeping activity of banks realized by debiting and crediting accounts.

Risk-sharing services: an essential function of banks is to transform the risks faced by the parties, that is to supply risk-sharing contracts. First, banks not only provide a diversified asset, they also organize efficiently the distribution of the risky income earned on the asset pool. The deposit holders (the depositors) receive a fixed payment while the shareholders receive the residual income. Another insurance service includes liquidity insurance (option for the deposit holder to withdraw quickly at face value).

Monitoring or information-related services: banks perform a useful function in reducing the cost of screening and monitoring borrowers. As Diamond (1984) has shown, private information held by borrowers results in contracting problems and the delegation of screening and monitoring to banks is an efficient allocation mechanism. In addition to the classical lending function of banks, one can include in the information-related services most of the 'investment banking' activities such as underwriting and distribution of securtities, trust or fiduciary services, merger and acquisition and risk/treasure management.

As has been argued in the literature (e.g. Fama, 1980), if banks were to provide only the first two services – portfolio and transmission –, there would be no special need for banking regulation. However the recent literature on insurance and montoring services shows that the contract that emerges – *illiquid loans financed by short term deposits* – creates a potential market failure and a need for public intervention. Three independent explanations can be advanced: the public good character of information gathering and monitoring, the macroeconomic externality resulting from a bank default and the potential for bank runs and systemic crisis.

Information and consumer protection

The first argument is that the evaluation of bank risks is a costly activity which has the nature of a public good. Once it is produced, it is available to consumers at very low transfer cost. As such the monitoring and evaluation of banks should not be undertaken by each depositor but could be delegated to a public agency or a private rating firm. Furthermore, since small-account holders may find the cost of interpreting the rating high and/or since they care about risk-free deposits only, two alternatives could be developed. The first is to have deposit insurance. The second is to create risk-free banks, that is intermediaries investing all deposits in risk-free securities. Depositors would have the choice between banks offering a higher but risky return and those providing quasi-risk-free deposits.

Our view on public information is that, in this respect, the banking industry does not differ much from any other industry. The major difference is that a large set of depositors may prefer a risk-free deposit. As such, this does not require public intervention besides what is required for the securities industry in terms of disclosure of information.

Macro-domino externality

The second possible source of market failure is that the insolvency of one bank or group of banks (domino effect) is costly because information on borrowers is being lost. Borrowers would need to turn to other banks at more expensive credit terms. The externality does not arise from the loss of information per se – this is a private cost and borrowers should deal with safe banks – it comes rather from a macroeconomic effect which is not internalised by the borrower. More expensive credit terms imply lower investment and unemployment. Although it is likely that large failures in the banking industry would produce this effect (Bernanke, 1983), we find one reason to disregard this argument. Insolvent banks are taken over by other banks in most cases, precisely to avoid the costs arising out of losses of information. Therefore, one has to rely on other sources of market failures to justify permanent banking regulation.

Bank runs

This argument, recently formalised by Diamond-Dybvig (1983) and further expanded in Postlewaite-Vives (1987), Jacklin-Bahattacharya (1988) and Freeman (1988), is that an important activity of banks is to finance illiquid assets with short term deposits. This creates the potential risk that savers run tot withdraw their funds. A run can be triggered by bad news about the value of bank assets or by any unexplained phobia. In both cases, there is a cost since illiquid assets may have to be sold at a loss. Moreover, a bank failure could eventually trigger a signal on the solvency of other banks, leading to a systemic crisis. A market failure occurs because a cooperative solution among depositors cannot be enforced. Collectively, there is no incentive to run but, individually, there is the incentive to be the first on the line to collect the deposit at full face value. In our view, it is the financing of illiquid assets with short term deposits and the potential for bank runs which explains the need for public intervention and the establishment of a safety net to guarantee the stability of the financial system.

III. SHOULD HOME COUNTRY CONTROL AND MUTUAL RECOGNITION APPLY TO BANKING?

There is a striking difference between the approach taken by the European regulators and the rationale for banking regulation discussed in the literature. Leaving aside the freeing of entry and the development of fair competition, banking regulation seems to be perceived as a necessity to protect consumers against losses. In contrast, the banking literature is not concerned with risk per se. In an efficient market, as long as information flows properly, the risk will be priced into higher deposit rates and investors will have a menu ranging from risk-free to 'junk' banks. What is of concern is *the stability of the banking industry* and the fear that there can be circumstances leading to bank runs. Therefore a case is made for some form of insurance – deposit insurance or lender of last resort intervention – to prevent runs. Although a lender of last resort policy is not mentioned in the European Commission proposals, there are references to the deposit insurance systems created in European countries recently:

Table 1. Deposit insurance systems in Europe

Country	Coverage (domestic currency)	Coverage (ECU)
Belgium (1985)	BEF 500,000	11,574
France (1979)	FF 400,000	57,970
Germany (1977)	30% of equity	–
Netherlands (1972)	D.G. 35,000	14,957
Spain (1977)	pes 1,500,000	10,585
United Kingdom (1979)	75% of deposits up to £ 20,000	20,833

Sources: Baltensperger-Dermine, 1989 and Pecchioli, 1987.

Three features of the European insurance systems make them unique. The first is that, contrary to the FDIC in America, they are totally ignored by the public. Publicity is even forbidden in Germany. The argument seems to be that the announcement of their creation could destabilize confidence in the banking system. Since deposit insurance systems are unknown and since the coverage is small (incomplete in the UK), they are unlikely to contribute much to stability and one would have to rely on lender of last resort interventions of central banks to ensure stability. Secondly, since the coverage is different across countries, it could be destabilising if depositors start to chase the best coverage. There is casual evidence that corporate treasurers diversify their deposits among several banks in accordance with the coverage of the deposit insurance systems. A third feature of European deposit insurance mechanisms is that they cover the deposits of domestic and foreign banks operating locally. This could create potential difficulties. Indeed, any insurance activity requires the monitoring of the risks taken by the insuree, but the principle of home country supervision would not allow the control of foreign entities by the domestic deposit insurance agency. A similar argument applies to lenders of last resort who, being primarily responsible for the stability of their domestic markets, might want to bail out both national banks and affiliates of foreign banks. In this case too, the monitoring of risks should be undertaken by the relevant lender of last resort.

Since European deposit insurance systems are not widely known by the public, it seems certain that they do not meet the objective of preventing runs on banks. One is left wondering about the motivation for their recent creation. European deposit insurance systems can be interpreted as a tool to create small risk-free deposits while putting part of the cost of bailing out on the insurance fund funded by the banking industry. Being responsible in the end, the banking industry would act as a 'Banking Club' which would regulate its members (Goodhart, 1985). These motivations are understandable but it would seem that alternative institutional mechanisms can meet the same objectives: the creation of risk-free banks would provide risk-free deposits to those who wish to hold them and the financing by the banking sector of the cost of bailing out an institution can be enforced without resource to a deposit insurance system. Recently in France for instance, the banking community was forced to finance the losses incurred by Al Saudi Banque.

It is our view that the current European proposals with domestic deposit insurance, home country control and mutual recognition, provide adequate consumer protection but that they do not meet the main issue of the stability of banking markets. Three ways can be used to achieve stability. The first is to adapt the current framework with its deposit insurance and lender of last resort facilities. A second approach is to rely exclusively on discretionary lender of last resort interventions, while the third is to abandon completely the safety net while adapting the contractual terms of the liquid deposits.

The current approach could be improved if the various deposit insurance systems would offer the same coverage and if domestic supervision would apply to all institutions, domestic or foreign, covered by the insurance or the lender of last resort safety nets. This implies the abandonment of home country control as both deposit insurance and, especially, lenders of last resort are essentially concerned with domestic losses, be they incurred by national banks or by the affiliates of foreign banks. Moreover, these insurance systems should be advertised. The major weakness with this system is that it reduces private incentives to monitor risks. The adoption of flexible insurance premiums would solve the problem, but so far, no one has succeeded in putting this proposal into practical use.

The second approach would be to abandon deposit insurance and to rely exclusively on the lender of last resort. As has been argued by Tobin (1987) and Goodfriend-King (1987), this is a function of the central bank that should be used extremely rarely. Indeed, there are strong presumptions that, in case of problems, deposits tend to flow to well managed banks so that one has not to fear massive runs. The major advantage of a discretionary safety net as opposed to a more systematic insurance is that it increases private incentives for monitoring and evaluating bank riskiness. As in the first proposal, the safety net is still in place and would be made available only to institutions financing illiquid assets with short-term deposits. The cost of bailing out would be borne by the banking industry which would find it necessary to monitor its members. In this case too, as monetary authorities are likely to feel primarily responsible for the stability of their own domestic markets, they should be able to supervise all banks operating domestically.

The third approach already discussed in Baltensperger-Dermine (1987) is to attack the problem of bank runs at its root. Since it is the absence of cooperation among depositors and the hope to be the first to withdraw which causes the run, why not impose the cost of bankruptcy 'ex post' on all current and former depositors. The incentives to run would be reduced since there would be no place to hide to avoid the losses. The two difficulties with this proposal are the definition of the time of failure and the enforcement of the 'ex post' penalty. The time of failure needs to be defined so that the penalty falls only on those who have withdrawn their funds after the failure. Enforcement of the penalty would require the means to identify depositors and the ability to tax them. A major difference between the 'ex post' penalty and a public safety net is that in the first case losses are borne by depositors while in the second case they are shifted to the public agency. The complete privatization of costs is a clear advantage.

Recognising that, under current legal systems, the enforcement of the 'ex post' penalty would be difficult, we would favour the second proposal, a discretionary intervention system with a lender of last resort. The objective of financial stability is being met with this proposal while the private incentives for monitoring risk still remain since public intervention is uncertain. This proposal implies that as long as national monetary authorities are primarily responsible for the stability of their domestic market, they should keep full control on all banks operating domestically. It is in the 'public interest' to keep such controls.

As it is well known that implicit guarantees on deposits reduce the private market incentives to monitor the risk taken by banks and price it correctly into higher deposit rates (the so-called moral hazard problem), there is the necessity for central banks to limit the size of their 'umbrella' and to introduce various types of regulation. This includes traditionally ratios on capital and liquidity plus large-risk exposure. It involves also the specialization of credit institutions and the separation between banking and commerce. If there is a Directive harmonizing the control of own funds and a Recommendation on large risks, this is not the case for the separation of banking, insurance and commerce. Each regulator can control the ownership of banks (the 'fit and proper' criteria) and the participations of banks in the non-financial sector. One must confess empirical ignorance as to the competitive edge that could be gained by conglomerate firms, but if it was to exist, it should be clear that least-regulated banks would be in a better position (Dermine, 1989). It would seem useful to harmonize at least the links between banking and insurance.

IV. CONCLUSIONS

We have argued that the 'home country control' and 'mutual recognition' principles are sound as far as the protection of depositors is concerned. However, when one turns to the major economic reason for public intervention, the stability of banking markets, the efficiency of these two principles is very much weaker. As long as national monetary authorities bear the responsibility for national and foreign banks operating domestically, they should keep full supervisory controls on all institutions. There is a strong case for *joint supervision by home and host country authorities*. Deposit insurance systems in Europe do not appear necessary. The objective of protecting the 'small and uninformed' depositor can be achieved with the creation of risk-free banks. If deposit insurance systems are being kept, their coverage must be fully harmonized. Finally, the need to limit the size of the 'umbrella', with constraints on the links between banking, insurance, commerce and industry, raises the need for further harmonization. As is being said on the other side of the Channel, the 'jury is still out'.

REFERENCES

Baltensperger E. and J. Dermine (1987) "Banking Deregulation in Europe", *Economic Policy*, April.

Baltensperger E. and J. Dermine (1987) "The role of Public Policy in Insuring Financial Stability: A Cross-Country Comparison Perspective", in *Threats to International Financial Stability*, R. Portes and A. Swoboda (eds), Cambridge University Press, London.

Baltensperger E. and J. Dermine (1987) "European Banking, Prudential and Regulatory Issues", in *European Banking in the 1990's*, J. Dermine ed., Basil Blackwell, Oxford, forthcoming.

Bernanke B. (1983) "Non-monetary Effects of the Financial Crisis in the Propagation of the Great Depression", *American Economic Review*.

Clarotti P. (1984) "Progress and Future Developments of Establishment and Services in the EC in Relation to Banking", *Journal of Common Market Studies*.

Clarotti P. (1987) "Comment batir l'Europe des Banques", *Revue Banque*.

Dermine J. (1989) "The Specialization of Financial Institutions, the EEC Model", mimeo, INSEAD, Fontainebleau.

Diamond D. and P. Dybvig (1983) "Bank Runs, Deposit Insurance and Liquidity", *Journal of Political Economy* 91.

Diamond D. (1984) "Financial Intermediation and Delegated Monitoring", *Review of Economic Studies*.

Fama E. (11980) "Banking in the Theory of Finance", *Journal of Monetary Economics* 6.

Freeman, S. (1988) "Banking as the Provision of Liquidity", *Journal of Business* 61.

Goodfriend-King (1987) *Financial Deregulation, Monetary Policy and Central Banking*, Rochester.

Goodhart C. A. (1985) *The Evolution of Central Banks*, The London School of Economics and Political Science, London.

Pecchioli R. (1987) *Prudential Supervision in Banking*, OECD, Paris.

Postlewaite A. and X. Vives (1987) "Bank Runs as an Equilibrium Phenomenon", *Journal of Political Economy* 95.

Tobin J. (1987) "The Case for Preserving Regulatory Distinctions" in *Restructuring the Financial System*, a Symposium sponsored by the Federal Reserve Bank, Kansas City.

XXI. Banking Structure and Banking Stability after 1992

FORREST H. CAPIE and GEOFFREY E. WOOD

INTRODUCTION

The EC's Second Banking Directive (of 1988) when first reported in the press was said to advocate a "home country rule" for banking regulation. This would permit an EC bank to do anywhere in the EC whatever it is allowed to do in its home country. Subsequently it transpired that to this simple rule had been added "host country rules of conduct". The combined effect would be that whatever freedoms a bank might have at home, it was elsewhere constrained by its host's rules. This is of course a more restrictive form of the directive. In this paper we analyse the likely implications of the basic home country rule for the structure of the banking industry in Europe, and then consider whether the changes that we think such a rule would produce would enhance or diminish the stability of that industry, and what the regulatory implications of the changes might be. Our purpose in following this procedure is to clarify what the results of the simple rule would be, and thus to isolate which additional benefits come from the additional instructions.

Our analysis is supported by a comparison of the experience of countries with different regulatory and banking structures. The main countries involved in this comparison are the United States and the United Kingdom; reasons for this choice will emerge below. But we also draw on aspects of experience in Continental Europe.

The main body of the paper has two parts; the first considers how banking is likely to evolve under the Second Directive, and the second examines what can be said about the stability of that system and draws out the regulatory implications.

An essential preliminary, however, is to specify our assumptions about what kind of monetary system Europe will have. These assumptions are as follows. Each country will continue to issue its own currency. But despite that, certain steps towards monetary integration will be taken. Exchange controls will be abolished, both within and around Europe. (The former is already a firm commitment.) Legal tender laws will be abolished; courts will enforce contracts made in any European currency; and citizens of every

D. E. Fair and C. de Boissieu (eds), Financial Institutions in Europe Under New Competitive Conditions, 305–318.
© 1990 *Kluwer Academic Publishers, Dordrecht. Printed in the Netherlands.*

European country will be allowed, if they so wish, to have in their own country bank accounts denominated in any European currency. These assumptions ensure that there are no government-imposed restrictions on trans-national competition in banking.

That completes our preliminary observations. We can now turn to the main work of this paper.

I. WHERE WILL WE GO?

(i) Theory

There is some basic economic theory on regulation that is worth alluding to. Regulation can be regarded as a tax and can be analysed in the same fashion. A tax on sales raises prices to the consumer and lowers prices received by producers. The imposer of the tax collects revenue which he may distribute in whichever way he chooses. But the imposition of the tax has still meant a net welfare loss to the community.

The size of the net welfare loss depends both on the size of the tax and on the respective elasticities of demand and supply. Regulation is similar but just as in the case of the recently developed "voluntary" export restraints in international trade, regulation does not produce any revenue for the government which imposed it.

Deregulation therefore provides welfare gains. It removes some of the "tax" and so lowers the price to the consumer, and raises the price received by the producer. To estimate the gains in banking we would need to know the scale of the deregulation, estimate its tax equivalence, and employ the respective elasticities. The empirical difficulties would be considerable in any estimation of precise welfare gains. But the direction of change can be hinted at and an indication of gains given.

If the essence of the EC Directive remains the home country rule then the expectation must be that banks will aim to locate themselves in the most favourable regulatory environment. There is an alternative hypothesis that suggests that banks might seek out the most severe regulatory environment in order to gain some prestige, but there is no evidence that banks have ever done this in the past. National authorities might be expected to promote their banking industry by lowering the regulatory barriers. This could obviously lead to competitive deregulation, resulting in considerable welfare gains. Prices to the consumer would be bid down to their market value and prices to the producer bid up to their market value.

The extent to which the volume of trade in banking services would increase depends on the relative strength of the trade creating and trade diverting aspects of the move to a customs union. These depend on the extent of regulation in the various countries – in this case those of the Community and those of outsiders, the latter being principally the US, Japanese and EFTA countries.

Sometimes it has been argued, and illustrated from history, that moving from regulated to less regulated financial conditions contains some risks. The main argument is that if the move is made too suddenly it can produce the instability that it is the intention to escape. However all the signs are that Europe will not be making sudden moves but rather moving at a steady pace towards the new regime.

(ii) The experience

There are interesting historical examples of different banking structures operating under various regulatory frameworks. These contain some lessons for Europe in the 1990s. There is for example a contrast in North America between US and Canada. Banks in the US have for a long time been under the control of the individual states. State branching laws have restricted deposit banking.

A consequence of these state laws has been that American banks have had to hold undiversified portfolios of assets and liabilities, leaving them exposed to credit and interest rate risk. And a further consequence has been a long history of bank failure. (E. White 1984) Some recognition of this has meant that in the past decade or so several states have allowed out-of-State banks to open in their states, and evidence has emerged that these banks have proved stronger than those restricted to one state. Diversification has increased and stability improved.

What is striking though is that just across the border, in a not dissimilar economic structure, environment, and culture, the Canadian banking system has proved more robust. Canada has a nationwide system, with large banks and nationwide branching and they have experienced great stability; even in the depth of the Great Depression of 1929–32 when thousands of American banks failed. A similar contrast could be made with the UK.

(iii) Structure

Recent experience with deregulation of financial services in both the US and the UK together with the entry of Japan provides pointers to the kinds of changes that can be expected. The likely outcome is a development of large 'banks' with branching networks.

When restrictions on individual activities are removed an obvious consequence will be the emergence of institutions that cover the whole range of financial services. These institutions are sometimes called Universal banks.

This still leaves the possibility of small and highly specialised institutions.

Some European countries are familiar with these large banks; Germany is the most obvious example. Germany has for long allowed and even encouraged banks to offer a wide variety of services and to operate across the country. A likely outcome of the Second Directive is that banks in other European countries will move to this kind of institution once the obstacles are removed. The likely benefits are improved financial stability and economic development. The possible costs are those of concentration of power and conflicts of interest. But the recent evidence on Germany is that firms with bank ownership and presence on their boards have been more profitable than firms without. (Benston, 1989)

The inference behind this forecast is that there are some economies of scale to be reaped. In financial services there are large fixed costs, and these are best spread across a large number of customers. Also, participation in capital markets is generally cheaper the larger the transaction. There is the further possibility that a large diversified bank can subsidise one area of its operations that may come under extreme pressure by using the profits from another area of its operations. There are related aspects, sometimes referred to as "economies of scope", such as the ability of a large international bank to provide a larger range of services to its customers. There is evidence that moves are already taking place along these lines. In Spain the big seven have become the big six. In West Germany there have been mergers between regional banks in attempts to compete with the large national banks. There has also been some cross border activity such as the share swaps between Scottish and Spanish banks.

(iv) Branches

Another feature that seems to follow from this analysis is that trans-European banks would be likely to develop substantial branching networks. If for example France were an attractive country from the point of view of regulation and banks made their headquarters there, they would do that with a view to establishing themselves in other countries also.

They would therefore establish a considerable branch network. This in our view would have clear benefits for the stability of the banking system and so of the economy.

This widespread branching was the feature of the English banking structure that developed in the late nineteenth century and has lasted until now: a few large banks with headquarters in London and substantial branch networks throughout the country. It is of note that this structure never once experienced a financial crisis. Many individual banks failed of course, as is the way in business enterprise, but this never led to a crisis. We would hypothesize that such a structure allowed banks a wide source of deposit funds and gave them a portfolio thoroughly diversified across the whole economy. In England at this time the Bank of England stood ready to act as lender of last resort and should also be given some credit. But it is striking that British banking was so stable for so long in contrast to North America and European failures, even though both the latter had central banks ready to act as lender of last resort.

II. STABILITY, STRUCTURE, AND REGULATION

Having suggested how the banking systems of Europe are likely to evolve, we turn now to the regulation of that system. We first consider why banks are regulated. That leads to an examination of what restrictions bank regulators impose, and then to problems regulators are likely to face in the changed banking structure produced by the Second Banking Directive. That prepares the way for examination of how regulation may evolve.

(i) Why regulate

What is regulation? George Stigler provides a useful definition. Regulation is "..... any policy which alters market outcomes by the exercise of some coercive government power".

Two features of that definition are worthy of note. It distinguishes clearly between influences on outcomes by coercion and by incentive – tax and subsidy policy may well be intended to "influence market outcomes", but it is not regulation. Second, and very important, it contains no hint of the *direction* of influence, or of who its beneficiaries might be. Both features are important. The first narrows the area of discussion most usefully. The second reminds us that there are two sharply contrasting theories of why industries are regulated.

What is best thought of as the economist's traditional view of regulation has recently been set out very clearly by John Kay and John Vickers (1988). They sum up the traditional view by a simple maxim: "Competition when possible, regulation where necessary". (p. 287) Regulation, in that view, seeks to identify market failures that prevent an industry functioning competitively, and to correct these failures.

Regulation can thus be either of structure or of conduct. There can be regulation by some public authority, self regulation, or regulation within a statutory framework. But whoever does it, and whether it be of structure or of conduct, regulation should on this view be targeted on market failure. That is of course a normative theory of regulation – it tells us what regulation "ought" to do.

The second approach is identified particularly with George Stigler. He asked, in a pioneering series of studies (e.g. 1962, 1964, 1971), what regulation actually achieves. Who does it benefit and who does it harm? Over a wide range of industries (not, it is worth emphasising, including banking) he has found that regulation was either totally ineffective or worked to the benefit of existing firms in the industry. It did not eliminate harmful market failures.

Both views of regulation, the normative and positive, are worth taking seriously; for both yield predictions on the scope of regulatory constraints on financial sector.

We therefore next turn to the sources of market failure that regulation in this area seeks to remedy, and, ask, what shape would regulation thus targeted take? Then we consider what a Stiglerian view of regulation would predict for banking and financial services.

(ii) Regulation and market failure

Traditional analysis distinguishes between externalities and market power as sources of divergence from the competitive ideal. (See Bator, 1958) More recently, asymmetric information has been added as a third source of market failure. These information problems are the principal rationale for the regulation of financial services. But there are also important externalities in this area. There is one between bank's customers, and another, closely related to the first, between banks.

If a large number of depositors all simultaneously seek to withdraw their funds from a bank, there is a possibility that the bank will have insufficient funds to meet their claims. There is a clear negative externality between depositors – one gains at the expense of another. Indeed, two sources of market failure are endemic to financial markets.

There is inevitably asymmetric information between buyers and seller – a bank management inevitably knows more about its balance sheet than even the best-informed depositors. Second, there is considerable benefit to the economy as a whole in sustaining confidence in the financial system.

There is no doubt that the maintenance of confidence in the banking system and the avoidance of bank runs is a major benefit to the nation at large. Any doubts on this are readily dispelled by reading Milton Friedman and Anna Schwartz's account of the consequences of a wave of bank failures in the United States. (Friedman and Schwartz, 1963, ch. 7)

The maintenance of adequate capital, and adequate readily realisable capital, is central to this. This has clear implications for the present discussion.

In terms of encouraging confidence in the system, and promoting its stability, the above argument would seem to point to the following conclusions. Structure should be regulated so as to enhance the stability of the key elements of the banking system – these being banks which take deposits from the public and are responsible for maintaining the money supply. Measures of capital adequacy should therefore be developed, and attention devoted to developing measures of the riskiness of *portfolios*, i.e. both assets *and* liabilities. Deposits insurance could be important. There should be rules for capital adequacy because of the existence of externalities. We may wish to encourage competing regulatory domains – for consumers can then choose where to buy these services. There could be self-regulation – reputation is an investment, but it may need regulation to produce adequate investment in it because of the externality aspects.

All this has specific implications which will be drawn out. But before doing so, it is useful next to develop the implications of the Stiglerian view of regulation.

(iii) Regulation as self interest

The former view sees regulation as a way of eliminating or reducing market failure. The view now being set out sees regulation as a way of producing market failure – of producing monopoly profits. How is that done? The essence of monopoly is that new entry is difficult – in the (rare) case of natural monopoly, impossible.

How could a regulatory regime discourage new entry to banking? There are three obvious routes. Again, they involve regulation of structure and regulation of conduct. Essentially, all would operate to make entry except on a large scale very difficult. Structure regulation would allow nationwide branching. With nationwide branch networks to compete against, a small entrant to commercial banking would find it difficult to threaten well established firms. Substantial capital adequacy requirements would exercise a similar deterrent effect. There should be a good measure of self-regulation; for the existing members could make entrance to the club difficult.

What is striking about this is how self interest would lead to regulatory proposals similar at any rate in outline to those which would be produced by public interest.

(This may be part of the explanation of why the Stiglerian view of regulation has not as yet been widely applied to banking – the two theories make similar predictions, so tests to distinguish the two models are difficult to design.) From the point of view of the theorist of regulation that is inconvenient, but from the present view point it is useful. That the central predictions of the two theories are the same means that whatever view of regulation gives a better general description of its practice, we can anticipate similar regulatory constraints.

(iv)   Prospective regulatory structure

It has been argued so far that, regardless of motive, the regulatory framework will have certain key characteristics. There will be nationwide branching permitted – Europe-wide, in the present context. There will be capital requirements. There will be deposit insurance. There will be both self-regulation and competing regulatory domains. Traditionally, in addition to the above, there has been separation of commercial banking from what is seen as the more risky activity of investment banking.

It should be pointed out immediately that the last of these ways of regulating the system is already breaking down. Separation between commercial and investment banking is no longer widely enforced and, as argued above, banks will increasingly move to regulatory regimes where a wide range of activities is permitted. Competitive pressures are eliminating the possibility of that particular control by structure, and unless there is a Europe-wide agreement to reverse this trend (and unless the decision is reinforced by a "ring-fence" around Europe), then such regulation is no longer possible.

We must, therefore, pay heed to the very important implications of the combination of investment and commercial banking. There are three separate questions involved.

They are as follows:
1. What kind of risks do banks face?
2. How can regulation help stabilise the system? Are there other means that might be used? (And notice the emphasis on the *system* as opposed to the firm.)
3. What complications are caused by co-mingling of commercial and investment banking?

(v)   The risks facing banks

Bank failures increased in the 1970s and 1980s. UK supervision was a reaction to this (See Gardener 1986). There have been waves of banking failures in the USA – 1966, 1969–70, 1974–75, and now of course the insolvency, but for unfunded government guarantees, of the savings and loan industry in the US. The failure of Bankhaus Herstatt in 1974 is notable in recent German banking. What risks led to these failures?

Banks have been lending to governments. Despite having done that for centuries they appear to have discovered only recently the concept of sovereign risk. Government *can* go bankrupt, and, much more often, do refuse to pay. Banks are exposed to credit risk: private sector borrowers can go bankrupt. (Bankhaus Herstatt was unfortunate. It was brought down by a risk bankers had then not had to face to a significant extent for many years

– foreign currency risk.) Banks also face interest rate mismatch and maturity mismatch risk. And finally, as a result of the increasingly common practice of lending money first and then borrowing it afterwards, they face funding risk; as a result of liability management they have tended to become "asset driven".

All these risks, if they turn out badly, bear on two aspects of a bank's balance sheet – its capital and its liquidity. To stabilise themselves, banks must increase their capital/risk assets ratios, and restore their liquidity. (Notice, by the way, we are so far concerned with the individual bank; there are features which can also protect the system.)

The co-mingling of different types of bank will make regulation to protect against these problems much more difficult. The reason was highlighted by Haberman (1987). To quote,

"Since the most basic need for capital is to protect an institution from the risk of insolvency, capital should be sufficient to absorb losses while an institution adapts to adverse developments". (p. 88) As Haberman goes on to point out, firms whose primary business is as an investment house can and do adjust their portfolios quickly, and, of course, can have their positions go wrong quickly and have to pay up quickly. They thus require to be able to draw on large amounts of capital on short notice.

Commercial banks are different. Although specific transactions may have short maturity, customer exposures usually span many years. The risks facing these banks *in their traditional business*, should they turn out badly, tend to drain capital fairly slowly.

Because of that difference investment houses are traditionally evaluated on a liquidation basis, and their accounting is mark to market. In contrast, commercial banks are evaluated as going concerns; their accounting is based on original cost. And not only is their capital evaluated differently; a greater proportion of that of investment houses is expected to be "liquid" – that is to say, readily marketable.

The structure of banking is rapidly moving to one where banks engage in both types of activity. How will regulation evolve in the face of this increasingly complex task?

(vi) What do regulators need to know?

Supervisors need to know what kinds of business a bank engages in. They need to know how much capital a bank has, and, in interaction with the first requirement, how exposed that capital is to shocks. They need to know how liquid that capital is. And they need to know all this frequently, the frequency of course varying with the risk of the business. The frequent gathering of this information both compensates for the asymmetry of information between banks and their customers, and ensures that banks are not, as a result of the perverse incentives provided by deposit insurance and lender of last resort, undertaking risks at the expense of the taxpayer.

There must be measures of solvency and liquidity. In tabular form, the most basic requirement is as follows:

1. regular information on ratio of capital to liabilities;
2. regular information on liquid assets as proportion of portfolios.

As an example of these, the Bank of England has for some years required regular information on solvency (capital adequacy) and on the ratio of "free reserves" (shareholders' funds less fixed and capital assets) to public liabilities (current and contingent liabilities.)

This is of course both basic and historic. It is basic in that the information does not reveal the nature of the exposure. Is the bank exposed to foreign exchange risk. Is it exposed to one larger customer, and thus not benefiting from portfolio diversification? And it is historic in the sense that if the bank fails tomorrow, what it was worth yesterday is of little interest to depositors or those who pay compensation to them.

There must be measures of large exposure risk, and adjustments for the risk of business (noting in particular the co-mingling of commercial and investment banking). Further, information on the past variably of the bank's position is useful, so that *projections* can be made of how the bank is likely to fare in conceivable future states of the world. This could enable regulators better to calculate "risk adjusted" capital and liquidity requirements.

One basic problem of course remains. How much capital and liquidity is enough? In a most useful survey of Bank of England attitudes, Gardener (1986) wrote "Controls tend to be based on a mixture of historical precedent, subjective assessment, industry norms, intuition and supervisory preferences." (p. 40) Provide what information we may, supervisors will still be relying on judgement.

(vii) The basic information summarised

Supervisors will be concerned to evaluate the solvency of banks under various situations. They can do this either by continually carrying out projections of future solvency; or, as a substitute, risk – adjusting historic (book) data. Either way, they will require information which lets them evaluate capital and liquid assets behaviour in the past in response to the kind of risks to which the bank is exposed. They will therefore require information on foreign exchange exposure, large exposure to one party, interest rate exposure, exposure as a result of maturity transformation; and even then judgment will be required.

It appears, then, that the structure of banking which will evolve as a result of the Second Banking Directive is one where the task of regulators in maintaining stability will be much more complex than it is now. More regulatory authorities will want information, and the information, once obtained, will be harder to interpret. Banks will move to the least regulated regime; but that could still be one of strict regulation.

Will we therefore inevitably have a banking system which is simultaneously both more regulated and less stable because of the difficulty of regulating it than it is now? In our view, such a result is possible. But it not inevitable. Indeed, increased instability is more likely to be produced the *more* regulators interfere in the decisions of individual banks. Regulation can evolve in two directions as a result of the market pressures we have identified. One is towards increased complexity as outlined above. The other is towards much greater simplicity. We shall argue in the next section of this paper that evolution towards greater simplicity can produce a regulatory regime which can do all that we require, and which is more likely to be effective than the complex one discussed above.

III. THE SYSTEM, NOT THE BANKS

(i) It is useful at this point to recollect why there is concern with banks to a much greater degree than with most other firms. The basic reason is that the failure of one bank can lead to the failure of others, perhaps the collapse of the whole system, and, via the working of the money multiplier, a collapse in the stock of money. This chain of events comes about because depositors are led to fear that their bank is not safe if they see one bank failing. They therefore fly to cash, and, as banks operate on a fractional reserve system, banks which are solvent and liquid enough for normal times are brought down by a surge in the demand for liquid money.

This danger was diagnosed, and the remedy set out, in the 19th century. Henry Thornton provided a clear but completely uninfluential statement of what to do. Subsequently Walter Bagehot, by a series of articles in the *Economist*, and subsequently in *Lombard Street*, persuaded the Bank of England to act "a lender of last resort". This involves lending cash *on security to the banking system* in the event of a run for cash on the part of the public.[1]

A vivid description of what to do is provided by Jeremiah Harman, a director of the Bank of England at the time of the panic of 1825.

"We lent it (i.e. gold) by every possible means and in modes we had never adopted before; we took in advances on security, we purchased exchequer bills, we made advances on exchequer bills, we not only discounted outright but we made advances on the deposit of bills of exchange to an immense amount, in short, by every possible means consistent with the safety of the

Bank and on some occasions we were not over nice! Seeing the dreadful state in which the public were, we rendered every assistance in our power."

This policy worked. There is no need for central banks to go further, and involve themselves in supervision and regulation. Such detailed inspection of banks is necessary to prevent moral hazard only if individual institutions are implicitly underwritten by the central bank, and it is a crucial part of the "Bagehot Rule" that they are not.[2]

If central banks operate as classic lenders of last resort, then they need not supervise banks. They need maintain only a check on the quality of paper offered to them for discounting – or even rely on private rating agencies for the task. The problems of supervision outlined above can therefore be safely ignored.

This policy is sometimes criticised on social grounds. Small depositors, it is said, may suffer losses, and 'caveat emptor" should not apply because such depositors simply do not have the knowledge or the time to assess a bank's solvency. The way to deal with this problem is a system of deposit insurance, restricted to small depositors *only*. Such a restriction would mean that it would be very difficult for banks to engage in risky investments at the potential expense of the taxpayer – for large depositors would monitor their behaviour, and expect high returns for high risk. Information asymmetries are much less important for large depositors; and if more information were required, professional rating agencies could become involved.

Stability

(ii) How frequently would the LLR need to act? As argued above (Section I ii) this question is best answered by a comparison of two sharply contrasted banking systems, the UK and US. The former has not had a serious banking crisis since 1866. The latter is still plagued by bank failures and resulting fears in the financial markets. The crucial difference is that since the late 19th century Britain has had a banking system very widely diversified regionally, and essentially nationwide since early this century.

Banks in the US are prohibited from such diversification. Because this portfolio restriction is imposed on US banks, they are much more vulnerable to shocks in their local area.

A collapse in the oil price shakes the Texas banking system, because of how it is compelled to obtain its funds. But a collapse in the oil price has no effect whatever on the British banking system, although a few branches in Aberdeen may become somewhat less profitable. A similar lesson is given by the Credit Anstalt failure. (See Schubert, 1990). Although that bank had many problems imposed on it, the crucial one seems to have been the sudden loss of a large part of its widely diversified branch network with the break up of the Austro-Hungarian Empire.

This analysis and evidence (of which much more detail can be found in Schwartz (1986)) has an important implication for banking stability in Europe. By allowing – indeed, encouraging – Europe-wide banking, the Second Banking Directive promotes banking stability. It will produce a more widely diversified, and therefore more stable, banking system in Europe. For that reason the Directive will make a major contribution to European prosperity.

SUMMARY AND CONCLUSIONS

In this paper we have argued that the "basic form" of the Second Banking Directive could after 1992 lead to major changes in the structure of banking in Europe. These changes would affect the location of headquarters, and, economically much more important, lead to a banking system more diversified both geographically and by activity. This diversification by activity could make supervision and regulation much more difficult. In time this might lead to a retreat from detailed banking supervision to a role for central banks much closer to that of the classic lender of last resort. In any event, it is clear that the changes in structure would produce a banking system which is highly stable. As a result, although regulation might become more complex it could become much simpler, for it will be (apart from the prevention of fraud) much less necessary. In contrast, the "amended form" of the Directive would prevent the beneficent diversification process we have described. This in turn would inhibit the development of a more stable and efficient banking system, and make lightening of the regulatory burden less likely.

Furthermore, regulation would be much more complex than it is at present.

It is therefore very much to be hoped that the Directive takes the pro-competitive form; for in banking as in every other economic activity free trade brings benefits.

NOTES

1. Observe that it must be a run to cash. Flight from one bank to another is important for the bank which is losing deposits, but totally unimportant for the system. Note too that the Bank had adopted this policy before Bagehot wrote. His contribution was to argue that this should be a general principle of behaviour.
2. Charles Goodhart has recently argued for bail-outs on two grounds – to preserve the money transmission system, and to preserve customer relationships. (Goodhart, 1990). But aside from the enormous moral hazard problem created by that policy, there are other arguments against it. The money transmission system is an industry into which entry is easy when an existing firm fails – while money creation is a legally protected monopoly. And the customer

relationship, while important, is often not destroyed by a bank failure. The bank often continues operating under most of the same management, with new owners having bought the institution at a price which imposes losses on the previous owners. See Benston and Kaufman (1989) for a discussion of this latter point, and Wood (1990) for the former.

REFERENCES

Bator, F. (1958) "The Anatomy of Market Failure" *Quarterly Journal of Economics.*

Benston, G. J. (1989) in *"Global Asset Manager"*, Credit-Suisse, Zurich.

Benston, G. J. and Kauffman, G. (1989) *"Risk and Solvency Regulation of Financial Institutions: Past Policies and Current Options"*, Salomon Brothers Center for the Study of Financial Institutions, Graduate School of Business New York University.

Friedman and Schwartz (1963), *Monetary History of the United States*, Princeton University Press for NBER.

Gardener, E. M. (1986) *"U.K. Banking Supervision"*, Allen and Unwin.

Goodhart, C. A. E. G. (1990) "Are Central Banks Necessary?" in *"Competitive Banking"*, ed. F. H. Capie and G. E. Wood, Macmillan.

Haberman, G. (1987) "Capital Requirements of Commercial and Investment Banks", Federal Reserve Bank of New York Quarterly Review, Autumn.

Kay, J. and Vickers, J. (1988) "Regulatory Reform in Britain", *Economic Policy*, Cambridge University Press.

Schwartz, Anna J. (1986) "Real and Pseudo Banking Crisis" in *Financial Crises and the World Banking System*, ed. F. H. Capie and G. E. Wood, Macmillan.

Schubert, A (1900) *"The Credit Anstalt Crisis of 1931"*, Cambridge University Press.

Stigler, G. J. (1962) "What can Regulators Regulate? The Case of Electricity", *Journal of Law and Economics.*

Stigler, G. J. (1964) "Public Regulation of the Securities Market", Journal of Business of the University of Chicago.

Stigler, G. J. (1971) "The Theory of Economic Regulation", Bell Journal of Economics and Management Science, Spring.

White, E. N. (1984) *The Regulation and Reform of the American Banking System 1900–1929*, Princeton University Press.

Wood, G. E. (1990) "A Comment on Charles Goodhart's Paper" in Capie and Wood, *op. cit.*

XXII. Issues in Financial Regulation: Efficiency, Stability, Information

RAINER S. MASERA*

1. INTRODUCTION

Economic analysis suggests that regulation is justified and wanted when market mechanisms reveal shortcomings. Design and control of the financial industry and markets can be both explained and warranted along these lines.

The credit and monetary system is characterised by fundamental externalities, notably insofar as it affects overall economic welfare. The workings of monetary policy on the one hand, and, on the other, price stability, the efficient inter-temporal allocation of resources, sectoral resource transfers, and economic growth, all depend upon the correct functioning of the financial system.

Asymmetric information is an important feature of the financial sector, with opposite types of problems encountered, in principle, in the banking and in the insurance industries. On this count too, "failures" in the working of the market manifest themselves: both sources of market failure can be seen as instances of missing markets.

A third source of welfare-loss is related to market power. In this respect, among the many possible causes of market failure, non-competitive behaviour of existing firms with significant oligopoly power appears to be the most relevant one in financial markets. Lack of competitive pressures implies allocative as well as productive and dynamic inefficiencies.

The very functioning of financial markets requires therefore regulation, which should however be designed in the light of market deficiencies, and with a view to preventing them, or, at least, to warding off their negative effects, insofar as possible. In this framework, the process of regulatory design should be also steadily updated to reflect changes in relevant economic forces. Technological advance, modifications in savings patterns and modes, adaptations in instruments and techniques of monetary policy, market size..., are all factors which impinge upon failures in financial markets, and hence on the optimal design of regulation.

* The author is grateful to Drs. E. Barone, A. Bucci, S. Crawford, S. Del Punta, and G. Falchi for helpful comments on an earlier draft. He is naturally responsible for any remaining shortcomings.

D. E. Fair and C. de Boissieu (eds), Financial Institutions in Europe Under New Competitive Conditions, 319–343.
© 1990 *Kluwer Academic Publishers, Dordrecht. Printed in the Netherlands.*

In practice, instead, traditional divisions within the financial markets, often inherited from the 1920s and the 1930s, had ossified regulatory frameworks over a nearly fifty-year span. The Great Depression – which was at the time interpreted as a major endogenous market failure, related to and compounded by the close links between industry and finance – set off a flood tide of regulation, retreat, and disintegration of the national financial markets. This led notably in many countries to strict separation of functions and activities in the financial markets which implied a decline in contestability. In turn, this went hand in hand with an *increase* in oligopoly forces in financial markets. In some countries dominated by strong statist pressures, regulation of the financial sector took the extreme form of nationalization.

The regulatory process came thus to be flawed by a fundamental confusion of cause and effect. As is now abundantly clear, the Great Depression was the result of basic failures of monetary and fiscal policies of the major countries in a beggar-thy-neighbour context, not to specific failures of the financial system.

In the 1970s and in the 1980s fundamental economic forces set in motion a long overdue process of financial deregulation, first in the international markets, then domestically in all major countries, albeit to different extents and in different degrees, in part as a consequence of the profound diversity in inherited control systems.

However, it soon became clear that deregulation had to be accompanied by re-regulation. Because of the very nature of the financial system, the two processes should be seen as complementary. Rapid growth and diversification of financial transactions, technological change, new market dimensions, securitization and financial innovation proper, all required new approaches to "market design". Innovative regulation was – and is – required to create efficient market structures. Operative rules on intermediaries; methods, techniques and transparency of brokerage, dealing and settlement in securities and money markets; rules of conduct and definition of standard products and qualities in markets for financial futures, options and swaps: all these are instances which require specific, innovative and mutually consistent regulatory frameworks.

This paper is an attempt to put such processes of de- and re-regulation into an economic perspective, within the context of globalization of financial markets, with a view to improving both their efficiency and their stability. Section 2 offers an analytical assesment of regulation in financial markets, while Section 3 contains a brief overview of recent developments in Europe, Japan and the United States. Section 4 draws some general conclusions.

The emphasis will be on an internationally co-ordinated approach towards financial regulation leading to contestable markets, reducing information asymmetries, and improving information on product quality; this, in turn, stresses the relevance of reputation-building and capital adequacy. This approach to financial regulation departs form the received wisdom, which should be critically reassessed and often may not withstand analytical scrutiny.

2. FINANCIAL REGULATION AND SUPERVISION: WHY AND HOW?

2.1 Reasons for control of financial markets

Market failures can be related to three well-defined causes:
- the existence of externalities, i.e. of disparities between private and social costs or benefits, in conformity with the analytical framework of welfare economics;
- problems regarding the power to control the market, complicated by the sometimes conflicting requirements of static allocative efficiency on the one hand, and innovation and dynamic efficiency on the other; information problems, with special reference to situations of unequal access to information about the quality of products and services by potential buyers and sellers.

All these factors are encountered in financial markets. Traditionally, attention has been focused on the first two; recent literature instead places special stress on the importance of asymmetrical information. Investors' lack of information on the range of opportunities available in all sectors of financial markets (banking, securities, insurance, foreign exchange, futures, options and swaps) is the key reason for the proliferation of services for the indirect professional management of savings. The problem concerns both the quality and the price of the products available. The main response of the market itself to information short-comings is to establish "reputation".

The market power of providers of financial services represents a second motive for regulation. The traditional approach, which emphasized the factors affecting the static allocative efficiency of markets of a given size, should be re-examined in order to take into account the economies of scale and scope and the resulting dynamic efficiency and positive externalities created by the globalization of financial markets. In principle, monopolistic firms operating in a given market tend to fix prices well above the marginal costs of supplying goods and services, and have little interest in seeking dynamic productivity gains. It is questionable however, whether this hypothesis is relevant when the market has a world, or even a European dimension, taking into account the number of existing players. On the world scale, even the largest financial institutions hold very small market shares. In any event, if financial markets are contestable, i.e. entry and exit are free and without costs on both sides, allocative and operative efficiency can be achieved even with a small number of intermediaries.

When considering the real or potential existence of gaps between private and social costs or benefits, two points must be taken into account. The first is that banks play an indirect, but fundamental, role in the determination of overall monetary equilibrium, and second that the stability of the financial system is a necessary condition for the correct allocation of resources and the creation of efficient links between financial savings and productive investments. In both cases it is clear that the actions of individual banks and economic agents influence the collective welfare. Conduct-of-business rules (notably reserve requirements and capital adequacy ratios) meet the need for financial controls at the macro level and, themselves, exploit the existence of externalities.

Before reviewing the factors that may affect controls, let me outline briefly traditional regulation typology.

2.2 Traditional types of controls and levels of implementation.

The economic analysis of regulation is conducted within the framework of the principal/agent approach. The former has his own objectives, which are imposed in various ways on the latter, who is usually a direct actor and possesses greater operational scope and knowledge at a more disaggregated level. The approach can be applied at each of the three principal stages of the decision-making process: (1) at the parliamentary or governmental level, (2) at the level of the sectoral or monetary authorities responsible for controls over firms, and (3) at the level of firms operating in the financial sector.

Controls are of differing *degrees of severity* or comprehensiveness and can be grouped in four categories: (1) nationalization, (2) regulation by one or more public entities, (3) self-regulation by an industry group or operators within that sector, (4) internal controls established and maintained by individual firms.

There has been a great deal of discussion as to how the transformation of the principles of banking and the stress on the entrepreneurial nature of the banking market has affected methods and instruments of control. In all the major countries there has been a shift towards implementing controls at lower, less centralized levels. These have also been strengthened and extended, in line with the developments of agents' autonomy in the trans-national market as one of the underlying principles of the organization of the financial systems. This issue will be developed later when dealing with the on-going process of both de- and re-regulation in financial markets.

The *manner* in which regulation is performed can be classified into three main categories, as described below.

Structural regulation primarily involves creating a separation between functions and activities, such as those erected between banks and non-bank financial intermediaries; between dealers and brokers; between dealer-brokers and investment managers, and so on. Functional separation is often reinforced by specific regulations governing ownership linkages within the financial sector and between the financial and non-financial sector. Of especial importance is the issue of separation between "banking and commerce".

The second main form of regulation comprises conduct-of-business rules. These prescribe how mandataries must behave and impose restrictions on their freedom of action. At the simplest level, this type of rule can consist in the definition of standard market products, methods and techniques. More generally, they impose constraints on behaviour, for instance by establishing minimum equity/liability (or asset), ratios, or by setting credit ceilings. A fundamental distinction in this area should be drawn between administrative and market-related rules. The administrative approach is based on the same concept of direct control that – in conjunction with the Great Depression – also led, in some countries, to nationalization. Both aspects of regulation, its form and level, thus need to be re-examined. While administrative directives are the easiest way to control behaviour, actually achieving the desired result is generally an inefficient process. Administrative controls tend to be evaded, and are therefore multiplied, ultimately generating inefficiency and welfare losses.

The third main form of financial regulation basically concerns information; it involves two fields of intervention on:
– minimum standards for the quality of the financial products;
– transparency requirements, regarding both the quantity and the quality of information.

The whole approach to regulation in any of its above-mentioned forms can be based on a cost-benefit analysis of information with reference to savers, professional operators, and intermediaries. Information is of crucial importance because it allows and stimulates the independent assessment of opportunities among which economic agents can choose in a transparent market.

Information improvement and transparency are two related concepts and if transparency is necessary to stability then it follows that the improvement of information within the financial system will be one of the most important contributions one can make to enhance stability. In the extreme case of perfect information, risk would be voided, thereby cementing financial stability.

The traditional typology of regulation, as well as its partition amongst different levels of implementation have been deeply modified by recent trends in financial markets, thus calling for a re-appraisal of its underpinnings. Basic concepts and canons have been altered by the changes in financial frontiers and instruments.

2.3 Factors affecting control features and objectives

The traditional approach of regulation theory is based on the distinction between banking, the securities industry and risk insurance. On the basis of these "objective" separations, regulation has followed well-defined paths that often led to separate regulatory authorities for each of the corresponding markets and to a definite correspondence between the typology of contracts and the issuing institutions. But financial innovation, together with techonlogical progress and the consequent attempt by financial operators to modify the supply of financial instruments to face new challenges and differentiated demands by investors, have gradually eroded the differences between traditional categories.

This trend revealed many complex forms such as the globalization of financial markets, the development of new contractual arrangements, the reduction of transaction costs, and the extension of negotiable areas. New technology has been boosting gross financial transactions at a very fast pace. The massive fall in costs of data processing and instantaneous information transmission are facilitating in ways previously not feasible the development of a broad spectrum of complex financial instruments which can be tailored to the hedging, funding and investment needs of a growing array of market participants. Some of this has involved an unbundling of financial risk to meet the increasingly specialized risk avoidance requirements of market participants. Currency and interest rate swaps together with financial futures and options have become important means by which currency and interest rate risks can be hedged and shifted between firms. The proliferation of financial instruments in turn implies an increasing number of arbitrage opportunities, which tend to further boost gross financial transaction volume in relation to output.

More generally, the synergic interaction of: (i) the uncertain economic environment of the past two decades, characterized by very high volatility of inflation, interest rates, exchange rates and unprecedented imbalances in current accounts; (ii) rapid technical progress in data processing and tele-communications; and (iii) greater reliance on the allocative efficiency of a properly functioning price system, created an irresistible drive towards overall financial deregulation, which should be stretched to include the move towards liberalization of capital movements.

This ebb tide is still continuing, but the question is more and more correctly posed in terms of adapting the existing regulatory structures, with a view to integrating national financial systems in a coherent framework: an analysis of this on-going complex process will be conducted in the following section, with specific reference in Section 3 to the experience in the United States, Japan and Europe.

Matching regulatory structure to the continuously changing financial markets requires the re-organization of the instruments and responsibilities of controls, bearing in mind the main objectives of an "optimal" monetary and financial system. In broad terms these are: (1) the functioning of the monetary payments mechanism, (2) the transfer of funds from surplus to deficit economic agents (sectors), (3) the selection of investment projects, and (4) the re-distribution of risks resulting from the production process.

The fulfilment of these objectives calls for regulation aimed at improving market effeciency and transparency without sacrificing overall financial stability, i.e. the implementation of measures to improve information and prudential controls. In other words, both efficiency and stability issues should be dealt with in the deregulation/re-regulation process that emerges from the necessity to review previous regulatory frameworks. The main question remaining to be asked is whether and how efficiency and stability can be positively correlated by means of the implementation of regulatory controls.

2.4 Different patterns of relationship between stability and efficiency

The complexity of the links between efficiency and stability deserves a foreword.

The concept of stability has to be clearly defined. This calls for the evaluation of the links between firm stability and systemic stability. A Schumpeterian phase of "creative destruction" appears to be an inherent part of the quantum jump in the size of the market against a background of technological and financial innovation. The nature of competitive markets implies that company crises should also be seen from the stand-point of market renewal. The fact that the market is open to new initiatives logically requires that others should be expected to drop out, especially in a context that already shows signs of overcapacity in certain areas. The question has acquired new connotations in a context of: (i) enlarging market frontiers, both geographically and from an operational viewpoint, and (ii) greater effective competition in each area. In this case, the fall of a single unit should not entail noteworthy negative externalities and may, on the contrary, lead to higher efficiency and overall stability because it can bring firms within the market to adjust their own concepts of efficiency, and reputation to dynamic market conditions, thanks to a positive "contagion effect". This is clearly the opposite with respect to the traditional "contagion theory", whereby failure of one firm would send amplified destabilizing waves to the whole system.

The inside-money character of depository intermediaries produces negative externalities in the case of a bank default. Social cost exceeds the private cost borne by depositors and shareholders of the defaulting bank mainly on three counts: (i) the destruction of deposits may affect negatively overall savings behaviour, because of the perception of risk on assets usually regarded as safe; (ii) the corresponding reduction in the real money stock leads to excess demand for monetary balances, which works towards depressing economic activity, (iii) the evaporation of a fraction of the transactions network affects the overall cost of monetary transactions, since the cost of making connections in any transactions network is exponentially related to the proportion of the network destroyed.

All these factors indicate that social costs of bank default will appreciably exceed private costs if, and only if, a significant share of bank deposits is affected. This, in turn, can happen either in the case of a default by a very large bank, compared to market size, or when the fall of one bank extends to others, through a domino effect. In this latter situation panics may develop in the absence of an adequate lender-of-last resort function towards illiquid, but solvent institutions. Both failures have considerably less relevance now compared to half a century ago, also as a consequence of the imposition of reserve requirements and deposit-equity ratios, with a view to compelling the banking industry to internalize external diseconomies. The trend is – correctly I believe – evolving by placing greater reliance on capital requirements. These can be shown to be generally cheaper than a non-interest bearing reserve requirement to the intermediary, to achieve a given reduction of default risk.

We have here the vexed question of safety nets for depositors in the event of bank failure. These schemes are meant to operate both as an instrument to protect consumers unable to evaluate the strength of the institutions to which they entrust their savings, and to preserve the stability of the monetary system, which, as we have indicated, has the characteristics of a public good.

It is however clear that, in many instances, practical implementations of this approach have revealed major shortcomings. These experiences are not inconsistent with economic analysis. The very existence of a safety net has important negative side-effects which should not be neglected. Both depositors and banks tend in fact to become indifferent to risk exposure. Depositors concentrate their attention on the direct yield of their savings, without concern for the "credibility" of the institutions. In turn, the costly attempt by banks to build up credibility – notably by enhancing their capital base, by improving risk monitoring (through both asset and liability management and credit evaluation techniques) and by ameliorating internal control procedures – is thwarted. Banks are indeed tempted to excessive risk exposure in order to maintain a competitive edge with institutions which are ready to offer high interest rates on their liabilities.

Risk-taking displays two forms. There is, first, the more direct way of venturing into higher credit, interest rate, and exchange rate risk loan activity. Even more important, however, is the weakening of the internal control system.

As indicated, the first line of defence in assuring the safety and stability of financial institutions rests with their own mechanisms of internal control. High prudential standards require therefore maximising incentives to encourage the building up of reputation. To the extent that deposit guarantee schemes impair these incentives, they may well ultimately affect in a negative way the very systemic stability which they are meant to promote. An appropriate balance may be achieved if these schemes are geared to a risk-based determination of premium charges. The full disclosure of the banks' situation – in line with the emphasis attached to information and transparency considerations in this paper – would help the constant assessment by economic operators, directly or indirectly, through the monitoring of specialized agencies. This is a trend which, in fact, is clearly detectable under present circumstances.

Another issue arising from the problem of ascertaining the proper dosage of stability and efficiency concerns the nature of the relationship between banks and firms. This is a key problem in the process of European financial integration, bearing in mind that the development of financial markets as separate entities is more advanced in economies in which the role of banks is less pervasive, especially as regards the links with other sectors of the financial system and industry itself.

The crucial problems become those concerning the minimal harmonization process, and in particular, the differences that exist in the ways "mixed" banks are viewed. In certain countries separation between financial and other enterprises is regarded as a prerequisite for both stability and allocative efficiency. The contrary view is taken by other countries. Academic views are equally divided. It is by no means manifest who should bear the burden of proof; on the one hand, there is the traditional argument of conflict of interest set forth by those who favour strict separation; on the other hand, it must be acknowledged that the rapid growth and the relative stability of the German and the Japanese economies, in contrast to the British and the US performance, corresponds to much closer ties between banks and industry in the case of the first two countries.

Today's theoretical apparatus enables us to enrich our analysis. For example, information appropriation theory suggests that the link between investment and finance may be closer and more effective when banks' relations with firms are more direct and more concerned with the substance of the latter's activities. In technically "efficient" financial markets (i.e. markets where prices reflect immediately all available information) analysts may instead rely excessively – or exclusively – on the performance of company stock to infer otherwise costly information about its position, projects and prospects. These considerations may offset the traditional arguments in favour of two-way separation of banks and "commerce". In terms of this analysis, the question should instead be posed in the framework of antitrust legislation, account being taken of the new market dimensions.

The relationship between efficiency and stability depends on what assumptions are made about: (1) the relationships between efficiency and controls on the one hand and stability and controls on the other; and (2) the different time horizons taken into consideration.

In the short run, it is realistic to assume a positive correlation between financial stability and the stringency of controls. This is likely also as a result of the fact that transition periods – such as the current one – characterized by financial innovation are potentially more prone to speculative waves, insofar as agents have not yet assimilated past experiences, thereby contributing to the dispersion of risk. In this case institutional controls foster stability. However economic theory suggest to the contrary that efficiency and controls are negatively correlated where allocative as well as X-efficiency are contemplated. Both of these considerations cloud, in the short run, the nature of the relationship between efficiency and stability.

In the medium to long run the question appears to be somewhat different. A specification of controls is necessary at this point. As was argued, there is no question about the fact that markets need rules, but these have to be determined according to economic principles. In other words there is a choice to be made between "good and bad" controls. If, for instance, regulation is aimed at reducing entry barriers to licensing and certification, and at improving information diffusion, i.e. increasing market contestability and transparency, and, in general, to force intermediaries to internalise externalities, then it is welcomed and will improve both efficiency and stability. The shift to cross-market and cross-country operations in an innovative environment, may suggest the risk of contagious development of speculative bubbles. To prevent and contain this negative externality, circuit breakers may be appropriate, as suggested in the Brady Report, to give professional dealers time to look further forward and act so as to provide "solidity" to the markets.

This type of regulation is by no means a substitute for competition; on the contrary, it represents a prerequisite for the competitive forces to prevail. On the other hand, structural controls which hinder the system's ability to adapt to market stimuli and the challenges brought by innovation clearly have the opposite result. Even if the immediate consequence of the abolition of controls of this latter type can lead to instances of instability, this by no means implies a positive long run relationship between controls and stability. In this case, it is the previous reliance on the inappropriate controls that led to inefficiencies; with the opening up of the markets these inherited distortions come into the open.

Overall therefore, if controls are selected according to the economic principles outlined above, there can be little doubt that, over a sufficiently long period of time, both efficiency and systemic stability go hand in hand.

3. FINANCIAL REGULATION IN EUROPE, THE US AND JAPAN: THE CHALLENGES POSED BY GLOBAL MARKETS

Regulatory environments have changed considerably in recent years, and the process of deregulation is now superseded by a more complex approach. Deregulation and re-regulation coexist in the face of financial innovation.

The pace of adjustment has accelerated with Europe's move towards the Single Market and the ever-increasing integration of the world's financial markets. It is important to stress in this regard that in the US and Japan, as well as in Europe, structural changes are hastened by the globalization process.

3.1 Europe and the single market

Mainly owing to their respective historical legacies and despite recent reforms, the structures of EC financial markets remain substantially different. Speaking broadly, two basic models can be detected in Europe: the "market-oriented" model – typical of the United Kingdom – and the "institution-oriented" model – exemplified by Germany.

The main difference between the two approaches can be found in the relative centrality of the banking sector, which implies in turn a role of less importance for the capital markets.

The British market is characterized by a high level of equity and bond financing on the part of firms and specialization of financial intermediaries. The German system, instead, is based on the prevalence of the universal bank and features tight links between banks and industrial firms, although the Monopoly Commission indicates that bank participations in non-financial enterprises should be limited to 5 per cent of the capital of any individual company in which participations are held.

In France and Italy the banking sector traditionally has tended towards the "institution-oriented" model and has also been prone to regulatory control at the most comprehensive level, that of nationalization. While in France a substantial portion of the banking system has since been privatized, in Italy it remains uncertain whether privatization will be chosen as a strategy. Both countries featured specialization of intermediaries as well as strict limitations to the links between banks and industry.

Existing differences in Europe in the very structure of the financial system and in the regulatory frameworks make the system-competition inherent in the Single Market a major challenge. Freedom of capital movements which will come fully into effect as of 1 July 1990, eliminates the restrictions on financial flows between countries. The freedom to provide financial services, which will become effective on 1 January 1993, implies the right for any entity authorized to undertake banking business in a member country to carry out a broad spectrum of financial operations throughout the European market in accordance with the regulations and under the supervision of its home country.

The problem lies in the dosage of minimal harmonization and mutual recognition which is likely to lead, via the second of these principles, to competition between supervisory frameworks with a gradual convergence on the arrangements that best meet the needs of the market. The harmonization carried out pursuant to Community provisions, and hence in accordance with the supranational prudential framework, will be supplemented by that carried out in response to competition and the need of each national credit system to compete on equal terms with the others. One, far from easy, objective of the preliminary formulation of a homogeneous core of supervisory rules is thus to prevent excessive deregulation and limit the risks of distorted competition.

The bed-rock of minimal harmonization will consist of the measures already approved in earlier years – mainly of the conduct-of-business and information types – and others that are being prepared.

As for those already approved, the harmonization of the legislation on credit business includes:
- Directives, which are binding for the member states, on the minimal conditions for authorization to engage in credit business (the First Coordination Directive, 1977), on the supervision on a consolidated basis of credit institutions that own interests in other credit institutions (1983), on the specific features of banks' accounts (annual accounts and consolidated accounts of credit and financial institutions), compared with those laid down for other companies (1986), and on the definition of the concept of 'own funds' (1986);
- two 1987 Recommendations, which only have the force of proposals or suggestions, on the supervision and control of credit institutions' large exposures and the introduction of bank deposit guarantee schemes.

The measures that are planned for adoption before 1992 comprise two other Directives on:
- the minimum requirements for credit institutions to be able to operate in countries other than their home country in accordance with the principel of mutual recognition (the Second Coordination Directive);
- the introduction of a standard for credit institutions' capital in relation to their risk-weighted assets.

The last of these proposed Directives is based on an approach analogous to that followed at the BIS by the Group of Ten countries and Luxembourg in setting its recently adopted capital adequacy requirements.

The mutual recognition of home country prudential regulations and controls means that banks with their head offices in different countries will operate in the same markets, but come under different regulatory systems as regards prudential supervision and monetary policy. Responsibility for the former is entrusted to the home country, while that for the latter lies with the host country, which, until further coordination is achieved, is also responsible for monitoring liquidity and the regulation and control of the "market risk' arising in connection with securities business.

The purpose of minimal harmonization of the criteria underlying prudential supervision is to prevent the less strictly regulated countries from enjoying a competitive advantage that would provoke across-the-board deregulation towards the lower standards. Ex ante, it is not easy to determine the point at which the balance should be struck between the conflicting requirements involved. In particular, it is clear that the application of Community legislation on capital ratios and consolidated accounts for banking groups will provide the basis for uniform supervision of credit institutions in all the member states, but cannot in itself guarantee the stability of their banking systems or remove the disparities that exist today between credit institutions subject to very different regulatory systems.

3.2 United States

Caution against concentrating in the hands of a few the power to allocate credit to the public has been a constant motivation in American banking law going back to the 1800s. Historically, this has created a bias favouring specialized kinds of banks which, in turn, has encouraged the development of specialized kinds of markets, as well as a specialized (some would say fragmented) regulatory framework. In this context the McFadden Act (1927) and Glass Steagall Act (1933) are landmark laws. The first permitted interstate branching by federally-chartered banks, thus coaxing back under federal rule scores of institutions which had been re-organized under more permissive state charters. The second generally enforced a separation of companies 'principally involved' in the securities business and the member banks of the Federal Reserve system.

Even more strictly than in the McFadden Act, free interstate banking was prohibited by the Bank Holding Company Act of 1956. This included the so-called Douglas Amendement which barred bank holding companies from acquiring out-of-state banks unless specifically permitted by the statutes of the recipient state. This effectively froze the pattern of interstate banking until 1975, when the state of Maine, hoping to draw new investment, did pass such legislation. Since then, the pendulum has swung back towards interstate banking, with nearly every state in the Union having passed some form of reciprocal recognition legislation by the end of 1987.

The passage in 1988 of a California law that will broaden the scope of that state's reciprocity arrangements to the rest of the nation (notably including New York) by January 1, 1991 promises to soon facilitate the knitting together of East and West Coast institutions.

This should not be taken to mean that the deep distrust of concentration in finance has disappeared from American public life. Instead that concern has been balanced by two more pressing and contemporary realities. Most of the early interstate combinations involved the acquisition of a troubled or failing credit institution by a stronger out of state institution. The public interest was clearly benefited by facilitating rather than blocking such purchases. Thus interstate banking, in part, represented successful improvisation on the part of supervisors and law-makers. No less, important, however, has been the growing awareness that concentration among banks and the concentration of credit no longer corresponded in any strict sense.

By contrast, the Glass Steagall Act has been progressively eroded through clever lawyering, mostly at the initiative of the larger New York-based banks and assisted by a largely receptive Board of Governors. The US Supreme Court established a key initial ruling in 1984 upholding the Board and permitting the purchase by Bank of America of discount broker Charles Schwab & Co. The Board went further in December, 1986, permitting Bankers Trust to place commercial paper through an affiliate. Six months later, the Board ruled favourably again on requests initiated by Citicorp, JP Morgan and Bankers Trust to set up the same holding company-to-affiliate structure to cover the sale of municipal revenue bonds, mortgage-backed securities and securities backed by consumer receivables. At the end of the Reagan Administration, it appeared possible to repeal the Act altogether, but Congress ultimately decided not to take up the issue.

The recent FIERA legislation (Federal Institutions Emergency Recovery Act), which establishes the Resolution Trust Company (potentially the largest bank in the country), could dramatically alter the US financial system. Underlying the debate on what to do about the thrifts are broader questions of system structure within the context of an increasingly global market and, as always, in the face of immediate needs to restore a large portion of the system to health. In the US too, one debated topic is whether to permit closer ties between industry and credit institutions. The Federal Reserve is strongly against relaxing what has been a rigorous separation, a position other American monetary authorities and bankers find unrealistic. Notable among them is William Seidman, head of the Federal Deposit Insurance

Corp., who has recently observed that "the Federal Reserve system [. . .] believes that separating commerce and finance is the 11th commandment [. . .]. But I'm convinced that in the future not even the Fed or the bankers will be able to offset the push towards a system of universal banking, such exists in Germany or Switzerland."

3.3 Japan

The banking sector is the centre-piece of the Japanese financial market which, following our typology, should be considered an 'institution-oriented' market. A peculiarity of this market is the strict system of regulatory control applied according to a framework of functional segmentation among financial intermediaries, the most important being Article 65 of the Securities Law which prohibits banks from engaging in the securities business. Within banking further segmentations exist between commercial and trust banks, and short- and long-term finance. A hard line also separates banking from insurance, while the insurance industry is further sub-divided (life insurance and casualty insurance).

Under Japanese law (anti-monopoly law) no entity engaged in financial business can own more than 5 per cent (10 per cent in the case of an insurance company) of the total outstanding stock of any Japanese company not engaged in same business. It is widely recognized that the links are nonetheless very tight between banks and industrial firms.

The process of financial innovation in recent years has strengthened competition between banks and securities companies, in the process reducing the divisions which had kept them out of each other's businesses. For example, banks may now supply financial products linked to government bond transactions, and they have been permitted to engage in limited securities placement connected with the underwriting of public bonds. On the other hand securities companies may now lend funds collateralized by public bond holdings, without there being restrictions on the use of those funds.

The rules that foster such deep segmentations in the domestic market are not applied so strictly overseas. Securities houses have been permitted to set up wholly-owned banking subsidiaries abroad, while IBJ – the most important long term credit bank – was allowed to operate a brokerage activity in the London market.

A debate is underway also in Japan about the desirability of changing the financial market's structure where it concerns the banking and insurance sectors. It seems probable that a full review of the core principle of the system, the division of activities by type of institution, will be necessary and will, in all likelihood, increase the liberalization of the system.

A subcommittee of the Financial System Research Council, a study group established by the Ministry of Finance, recently completed a report reviewing alternative policies aimed at removing the existing barriers dividing banking from the securities business. Significantly, the subcommittee's next major project will focus on how to deal with the insurance industry, which is eagerly seeking mechanisms for branching out into both the banking and securities areas.

In the present work, the subcommittee proposes five reform options:
– to create a European-type universal banking system;
– to establish a holding company formula;
– to allow the creation of investment banks by both banks and securities houses;
– to authorize wholly-owned subsidiaries in each of the specified financial service areas;
– to institute an overlapping system that allows various financial entities to enter one another's territories gradually.

The subcommittee suggested that 'in the distant future' a European-style universal banking system should be introduced by the government. For the time being, however, the group adopted the third and fourth options as immediate recommendations to assist the Japanese financial industry to better cope with the effects of globalization.

In this case, not only will commercial banks be allowed to set up securities houses as subsidiaries and vice-versa, but both securities houses and banks will be allowed to establish investment banking subsidiaries to provide corporate finance services.

4. CONCLUSIONS

Trade in financial services is acquiring global dimensions. Market entry requirements and rigid conduct rules are gradually being relaxed. Barriers between banking and credit, investment services and securities operations, collective investment, insurance, and foreign exchange operations are being removed, within national markets and across borders. Securitization and financial innovation link the various markets in forms hitherto unknown. Alongside the traditional spot markets, index futures, options and swaps markets have acquired paramount importance, and permit a much more sophisticated use of financial and credit investments. Individual and "unaware" saving is being replaced by collective, professional management of loanable funds. Freedom of capital movements puts into competition national currencies and financial systems.

The developments of global financial products, under the thrust of strong technological and economic forces is both made possible by and acts as a spur on a general trend towards deregulation and more contestable financial markets.

The creation of the European single market must be assessed in this perspective, and should be seen as a fundamental part of the process itself. Not only will it create the largest unified market, but it will spur, through the stimuli of reciprocity, closer financial ties across the world. This will happen both directly and indirectly; i.e., by fostering the interpenetration of market segments within the domestic boundaries of the US and Japan.

Intensified competition in contestable markets will promote efficiency, while the implementation of regulation will respond more to economic principles. X-inefficiency is a typical characteristic of financial enterprises regulated on the basis of historically dictated norms, which are not – or no longer –related to economic arguments, i.e., directed to correct "failures" in the workings of the market. Financial markets overly protected by regulation are characterized by inefficient use of inputs. Human and non-human capital alike are artificially inflated, without attention to productivity and cost efficiency. Both theoretical and empirical studies suggest that the risk of X-inefficiency is particularly high in the case where the most stringent degree of control – nationalization – is combined with functional separation and administrative conduct-of-business rules. In this situation, capital market monitoring is absent, internal monitoring by public shareholders can be conducted on the basis of political considerations, and managers may not be motivated by cost-efficiency and revenue maximization.

The supply and resource allocation response to increased competition and deregulation of the type described above will materialize only over a relatively long time horizon, while the squeeze on financial margins may be more rapid. The positive effects on both productive and allocative efficiency require and imply rationalization, concentration of investment, exploitation of the economies of scale and scope potentially created by technological advance and by combination of complementary financial products and services.

The short-term consequence of unleashing competitive forces and deregulation in financial markets previously shielded by prudential and border barriers may well be an increase in the level of risk. To some extent, this is, however, the inevitable cost to be paid before the benefits of increased competition are fully felt.

The complex search for dimension, fields of specialization, and combinations of services will imply a potentially painful transition phase. This shall be accompanied by pressures, possibly arising also from the financial enterprises already in the market, to re-introduce traditional regulatory instruments. This paper calls instead for an approach which involves re-regulation being enacted together with deregulation, as indeed we are, to some extent, currently witnessing. Along with the move towards contestable markets, specific attention must be given to reducing information distortions, while capital adequacy ratios should help maintain stability and confidence in the system. With the disappearance of the fences between financial sectors, institutional de-specialization rules will also have to be introduced, to prevent conflicts of interest and insider trading.

Transparency and full information on product quality will lead to an active search for reputation building, which should include effective self-regulation of the various sectors (the Club approach), and individual firms (internal company controls).

The pursuit of stability will increasingly require the active search at the microeconomic level – which is, however, more and more represented by informed professional operators, rather than by uninformed individuals – for institutions, instruments and operations involving known and limited risks.

This approach, which is predicated upon the existence of a transparent trade-off between risk and return, implies and requires that the law of the market should not be impeded at the micro level, with regard to the destiny of unsuccessful institutions and projects. In is only in this way that operators will incorporate risk-of-default considerations into their financial decision-making process.

Banks naturally occupy a central position in the financial system and their failure would entail externality losses. However, if the insolvent bank is small in relation to market size, negative externalities may not be noteworthy. Deposit insurance schemes can reduce further social costs. The moral hazard problem of undifferentiated deposit-guarantee schemes has, however, been stressed in this paper, together with the need to adopt a risk-based determination of premium charges.

Microeconomic default need not represent a risk of systemic instability, it can indeed help prevent this from materializing, especially when reference is made to the new dimensions of financial markets. Following these lines, the principal actions to prevent systemic instability consist, on the one hand, in re-regulation aimed at improving information, setting standards, and checking conflict of interest; and on the other hand, let it be stressed here, in the pursuit of co-ordinated economic policies, consistent with non-inflationary growth. The imbalances in both current and government accounts in some large countries represent the most serious causes of systemic financial risk.

The complex process of deregulation and re-regulation which is advocated in this paper implies a thorough re-examination of the relevant regulatory and supervisory arrangements. Far reaching changes and adjustments will be necessary if today's national systems, based on widely differing principles, are to coexist in a stable integrated environment. The solution of these fundamental problems should not be left to competition between regulatory systems; competitive deregulation cannot be the answer to the problems posed by those "market-failure" instances which require regulation in the first place. Within the contestable market approach advocated here, the thrust of intervention is, however, well defined along information and reputation lines. Consistent capital adequacy, disclosure, transparency, and product quality requirements on both on- and off-balance sheet operations are also a fundamental regulatory response to negative externalities: they can, in particular, prevent and damp down the spreading of bank runs, which would imply systemic failures.

The general trend towards integrated markets at the global level represents a quantum jump, with playing fields which are much larger than previous ones, and which intersect in previously unforeseen ways. What is important now is that a basic set of transparent rules should be gradually defined, together with the referees responsible for their interpretation and application.

In terms of today's trans-national operations, which cut across previous functional separations, the existing domestic and functional regulatory approach must itself evolve towards a much more integrated model, at European as well as at world levels. In the reshaping of the regulatory system for financial markets, the recent advances of economic theory in this area should be taken into account, together with the experience of market operators. This conference, I believe, should be seen in this perspective.

BIBLIOGRAPHY

AA.VV. (1986) *La metropoli finanziaria*, Proceedings of the 3rd International Conference of Project Milan, IRER – Istituto Regionale di Ricerca della Lombardia, Milan, 15-16 November 1985.

AA.VV. (1986) *Donato Menichella. Testimonianze e studi raccolti dalla Banca d'Italia*, Editori Laterza.

AA.VV. (1988) *Banca e mercato. Riflessioni su evoluzione e prospettive dell'industria bancaria in Italia*, Società Editrice Il Mulino.

AA.VV. (1988) *Le regole della moneta*, Biblioteca della Libertà, Le Monnier.

Akerlof, G. (1970) "The Market for Lemons: Qualitative Uncertainty and the Market Mechanism", *Quarterly Journal of Economics*.

Allen, F. (1984) "Reputation and Product Quality", *Rand Journal of Economics*.

Arcelli, M. "Considerazioni Generali", in Parrillo F. (ed.) (1987), *Efficienza e stabilità dei sistemi finanziari: un raffronto internazionale*, Conference Proceedings, Associazione Bancaria Italiana, Rome, May.

Arcuti, L. (1982) *Finanziamento degli investimenti negli anni '80: il ruolo delle istituzioni finanziarie*, Opening address to the international conference celebrating the 50th anniversary of the foundation of IMI, 29–30 October.

Armento, A., Belli, F., Bertelli, R. and Brozzetti, A. (1987) "Un ventennio di crisi bancaria in Italia 1963–1985", in Belli et al. (eds) *Banche in crisi 1960–85*, Editori Laterza.

Arthur Andersen (1989) *European Capital Markets*, Strategic Forecast Economist Publications.

338

Assireme and A.N.I.C.A. (1984) Proceedings of the conference on: *Economia reale e credito: la specializzazione degli intermediari creditizi ed il finanziamento degli investimenti.* Fondazioni Cini – Isola di S. Giorgio.

Averch, H. and Johnson, L. (1962) "Behaviour of the Firm under Regulatory Constraint", *American Economic Review.*

Banca d'Italia (1984) *Italian Credit Structures. Efficiency, Competition and Controls,* Euromoney Publications.

Banca d'Italia (1988) *Ordinamento degli enti pubblici creditizi. L'adozione del modello della società per azioni.*

Banca d'Italia (1989) *Intermediazione finanziaria non bancaria e gruppi bancari polifunzionali: le esigenze di regolamentazione,* Temi di Discussione del Servizio Studi, n. 113.

Banca d'Italia (1989) *La tassazione delle rendite finanziarie nella CEE alla luce della liberalizzazione valutaria,* Temi discussione del Servizio Studi, n. 114.

Bank for International Settlements (1986) *Recent Innovations in International Banking.*

Bank of England (1987) "Change in the Stock Exchange and Regulation of the City", *Bank of England Quarterly Bulletin.*

Baron, D. P. and Myerson, R. B. (1982) "Regulating a Monopolist with Unknown Costs" *Econometrica.*

Bator, F. (1985) "The Anatomy of Market Failure", *Quarterly Journal of Economics.*

Baumol, W. J. (1982) "Contestable Markets: An Uprising in the Theory of Industrial Structure", *American Economic Review.*

Baumol, W. J., Panzar, J. C. and Willig R. D. (1986) "On the Theory of Perfectly Contestable Markets" in Stiglitz J. E. and Mathewson G. F., *New Developments in the Analysis of Markets Structure* MacMillan, London.

Belli, F., Minervini, G., Patroni Griffi, A. and Porzio, M. (eds.) (1987) *Banche in crisi 1960–1985,* Editori Laterza.

Bingham, G. (1988) "New Financial Instruments: Economic and Financial Policy Implications", OECD Symposium on *New Financial Instruments,* Paris.

Bleeke, J. A. and Bryan, L. L. (1988) "The Globalization of Financial Markets", *The McKinsey Quarterly.*

"Brady Commission Report" (1988) *Report of the Presidential Task Force on Market Mechanisms,* January.

Bryan, L. L. and Allen, P. (1988) "Geographic Strategies for the 1990s", *The McKinsey Quarterly.*

Camera dei Deputati (1988) *Sistemi creditizi a confronto,* Servizio Studi.

Capriglione, F. (1983) *L'impresa bancaria tra controllo e autonomia,* Giuffrè Editore.

Caranza, C. and Cottarelli, C. (1987) *L'innovazione finanziaria in Italia: un processo disuguale.*

Carbonetti, F. (1983) "La gestione delle crisi bancarie in Italia: prospettive e problemi di una riforma", in *Banche in crisi,* op. cit.

Carli, G. "Tipicità dei dissesti bancari", in *Banche in crisi,* op.cit.

Carli, G. (ed.), (1978) *La struttura del sistema creditizio italiano.* Società Editrice Il Mulino.

Cassese, S. (1983) "The 'Division of Labour in Banking'. The Functional and Geographical Distribution of Credit from 1936 to Today", *Review of Economic Condition in Italy.*

Cassese, S. (1984) "The Long Life of the Financial Institutions set up in the Thirties", *The Journal of European Economic History.*

Cassese, S. (1985) "Problemi delle banche pubbliche", in *Banche in crisi,* op. cit.

Cassese, S. (1987) "Le società bancarie pubbliche", *Bancaria.*

Castaldi, G. and Clemente, C. (1981) "Il controlli di vigilanza sugli enti creditizi", *Bancaria.*

Castelnuovo, R. A. (1989) *Teoria dell'innovazione finanziaria: una rassegna critica e ipotesi di metodologia di analisi,* Research on the Changes of the Italian Financial System: Innovation and Regulation, LUISS Ceradi.

Cesarini, F. (1985) "Osservazioni in merito allo svolgimento delle crisi bancarie in Italia", in *Banche in crisi*, op. cit.

Cesarini, F. (ed.), (1985) *Il rafforzamento patrimoniale delle banche. Ricorso al mercato e quotazione in borsa*, Società Editrice il Mulino.

Cesarini, F. (1988) "La strategia delle aziende di credito nella prospettiva delle direttive Cee". Paper presented to the national conference on: *Banks, Financial Intermediation and Related Tax Problems in the Perspective of the 1990s*, Faculty of Economics, Rome University, "La Sapienza", Rome, 25–26 October.

Ciampi, C. A. (1988) *Liberalizzazione valutaria e integrazione finanziaria europea*, speech delivered at the Accademia della Guardia di Finanza, Bergamo, 14 October.

Ciampi, C. A. (1988) *Attività conoscitiva preliminare all'esame dei documenti di bilancio dell'anno 1988*, Statement by the Governor of the Bank of Italy before 5th Committee of the Senate and the Chamber of Deputies in joint session, 7 October.

Ciampi, C. A. (1988) *Indagine conoscitiva sullo stato di realizzazione dello spazio unico europeo*, Statement by the Governor of the Bank of Italy before the Senate Commission for EC Affairs, 28 July.

Ciocca, P. (1987) *L'instabilità dell'economia*, Giulio Einaudi Editore.

Coase, R. H. (1960) "The Problem of Social Cost", *Journal of Law and Economics*.

Cornini, C. and Schianchi, A. (1987). *La nuova finanza. Instabilità e innovazione nei mercati internazionali*, Edizioni del Sol 24 Ore.

Corrigan, E. G. (1987) Statement before the United States Committee on Banking, Housing and Urban Affairs, Washington D.C. June 18.

Costi, R. (1986) *L'ordinamento bancario*, Società Editrice Il Mulino.

Demsetz, H. (1968) "Why Regulate Utilities?", *Journal of Law and Economics*.

Desario, V. (1983) "L'attività di vigilanza: le crisi bancarie", in *Banche in crisi*, op. cit.

Dini, L. (1988) "The Italian Financial System in the Perspective of 1992", Conference on *Target 1992*, The Italian Chamber of Commerce for Great Britain, London.

Dini, L. (1988) "Deregulation in 1992: Strategies and Opportunities", International Financial Institutions Conference, Salomon Brothers International Limited, Venice, 9 September.

Dini, L. (1988) "Financial Markets Revolution: International Diagnosis and Implications for the Banking Sector", 20th Congress of the Confédération International du Crédit Populaire, Marrakech, 20 October.

Domberger, S. Meadowcroft, J. and Thompson, D. (1986). "Competitive Tendering and Efficiency", *Fiscal Studies*.

Dornbusch, R. (1988) *Money and Finance in European Integration*.

Einaudi, L. (1911) "Appunti", in *Origini e identità del credito speciale*, op. cit.

Einaudi, L. (1935) "Di altri scatoloni pseudo-commerciali e pseudo-bancari", in *Origini e identità del credito speciale*, op. cit.

Eisenbeis, R. A. (1987) "Eroding Market Imperfections for Financial Intermediaries, the Payments System, and Regulatory Reform". Paper presented to the Symposium on *Restructuring the Financial System*, Federal Reserve Bank of Kansas City, Jackson Hole, Wyoming, 20–22 August.

Farrel, J. and Saloner, G. (1985) "Standardization, Compatibility and Innovation", *Rand Journal of Economics*.

Fazio, A. (1988) Introductory speech to the national conference on: *Banks, Financial Intermediation and Related Tax Problems in the Perspective of the 1990s*, Faculty of Economics, Rome University.

Feller, G. and Vigorelli, M. (eds.) (1986) *Banca Anni '90*, Arthur Andersen & Co. – ABI report on the Italian banking system, Edizioni del Sole 24 Ore.

Fisinger, J., Hammond, E. M. and Tapp, J. (1985) "Insurance: Competition or Regulation?

A Comparative Study of the Insurance Market in the United Kingdom and the Federal Republic of Germany" *IFS Report* Series 19. Institute for Fiscal Studies, London.

Folkerts-Landau D. F. I. (1982) *On the Regulation of Banking Intermediaries in the International Financial System* IMF, Research Department, 17 March.

Franklin R. E. (1987) "Can regulatory reform prevent the impending disaster in financial markets?". Paper presented to the Symposium on *Restructuring the Financial System*, op. cit.

Freedman, C. (1987) "Financial Restructuring: the Canadian Experience". Paper presented to the Symposium on *Restructuring the Financial System*, op. cit.

Gennotte, G. and Pyle, D. (1987), *Capital Controls and Bank Regulation*, Temi di discussione, Servizio Studi Banc d'Italia.

Golberg, V.P. (1976) "Regulation and Administered Contracts", *Bell Journal of Economics.*

Goodhart, C. (1985) *The Evolution of Central Banks: A Natural Development?*, Suntory Joyota International Centre for Economics and Related Disciplines, London School of Economics.

Goodhart, C. (1987) "The Economics of 'Big Bang' ", *Midland Bank Review.*

Gower Report (1984) *Review of Investor Protection*, Cmnd. 9125, HMSO, London.

Greenspan, A. (1988) *Testimony before the Committee on Banking, Housing & Urban Affairs*, by the Chairman, Board of Governors of the Federal Reserve System, February 2.

Grossman, S. and Stiglitz, J. E. (1980) "On the Impossibility of Informationally Efficient Markets", *American Economic Review.*

Grossman, S. (1981) "The Informational Role of Warranties and Private Disclosure About Product Quality", *Journal of Law and Economics.*

Group of Thirty (1988) *International Macroeconomic Policy Coordination.*

Heal, G. (1976) "Do Bad Products Drive out Good?", *Quarterly Journal of Economics.*

Hellwig, M. (1989) "Asymmetric Information, Financial Markets and Financial Institutions: Where are we currently going?" *European Economic Review*, 33.

Hicks, J. (1989) *A Market Theory of Money*, Oxford University Press.

Huertas T. F. (1988) "Redesigning Regulation – The Future of Finance in the United States". Paper presented to the Symposium on *Restructuring the Financial System*, op. cit.

International Currency Review (1988) "US Banking Sector: Federal Safety Net Bankrupted by Deregulation".

Japan Times (17 May 1989) *Financial Body Issues Draft Options on Ways to Unify Banking Securities.*

Johnson, C. (1988) "Banking and 1992", presented at the conference on *The Changing of European Banking*, Business Research International.

Kane, E. G. (1987) "Discussion of 'Eroding Market Imperfections' by R. Eisenbeis". Paper presented to the Symposium on *Restructuring the Financial System*, op. cit.

Kareken, J. and Wallace, M. (1978) "Deposit Insurance and Bank Regulation: A Partial Equilibrium Exposition", *Journal of Business*, July.

Katz, M. and Shapiro, C. (1985) "Network Externalities, Competition and Compatibility", *American Economic Review.*

Kay, J. A., Mayer, C. and Thompson, D. (eds.) (1986) *Privatisation and Regulation: The UK Experience*, Oxford University Press.

Kay, J. A., (1988) *The State and the Market. The UK Experience of Privatisation*, Published by the Group of Thirty.

Kay, J. A. and Vickers, J. (1988) "Regulatory Reform in Britain", *Economic Policy.*

Klein, B. and Leffler, K. (1981) "The Role of Market Forces in Assuring Contractual Performance", *Journal of Political Economy.*

Laffont, J. J. and Tirole, J. (1986) "Using Cost Observation to Regulate Firms", *Journal of Political Economy.*

Lamfalussy, A. (1988) "International Co-ordination of Macro-economic Policies". Sixth Annual Lecture – Irish Banks' Chair in *Banking and Finance*, Dublin.

Lamfalussy, A. (1988) "Globalization of Financial Markets: International Supervisory and Regulatory Issues". Symposium: *Financial Market Volatility*, Jackson Hole, Wyoming (USA).

Lanciotti, G. "La vigilanza sulle banche a dimensioni multinazionale e il fenomeno dei centri offshore", in *Banche in crisi*, op. cit.

Leland, H. (1979) "Quacks Lemons and Licensing: A Theory of Minimum Quality Standard", *Journal of Political Economy*.

Loehnis, A. (1987) "Financial Restructuring: the UK Experience". Paper presented to the Symposium on *Restructuring the Financial System*, op. cit.

Mankiw, N. G. and Whinston, M. D. (1986) "Free Entry and Social Inefficiency", *Rand Journal of Economics*.

Marzano, A. (1988) "Partecipazioni di imprese non finanziarie al capitale bancario", *Banche e Banchieri*.

Masera, R. S. (1989) "Monetary and Financial Markets in Europe: Regulation and Market Forces", *Review of Economic Conditions in Italy*, Banco di Roma, n. 1

Mayer, C. (1987) "Financial Systems and Corporate Investment", *Oxford Review of Economic Policy*.

Micossi, S. (1987) "The Single European Market", paper presented at the Conference *Towards the Single European Market*, London.

Milgrom, P. and Roberts, J. (1986) "Price and Advertising Signals of Product Quality", *Journal of Political Economy*.

Minervini, G. "Banca d'Italia e Consob nel caso Ambrosiano. Il problema del coordinamento delle organizzazioni di controllo", in *Banche in crisi*, op. cit.

Minervini, G. (1984) "Note sull'assicurazione dei depositi bancari", in *Banche in crisi*, op. cit.

Monti, M., Cesarini, F. and Scognamiglio, C. (1983) "The Italian Credit and Financial System", Report of the Committee appointed by the Minister of the Treasury, *BNL Quarterly Review*, special issue.

Monti, M. (1988) "L'integrazione monetaria e finanziaria in Europa: convenienze, pressioni, prospettive", ISPI, Quaderni-Papers.

Morelli, G. and Pace, C. (eds) (1984) *Origini e identità del credito speciale*. Franco Angeli Editore.

Mottura, P. (1988) *Efficienza del sistema finanziario fra proprietà pubblica e proprietà privata*, SDA Bocconi, Business School.

NEDO (1976) *A study of UK Nationalised Industries – Their Role in the Economy and Control in the Future*, HMSO, London.

Nelson, P. (1974) "Advertising as Information", *Journal of Political Economy*.

Nuzzo, A. (1989) *Articolazioni sul sistema finanziario tedesco*, Research on the Transformation of the Italian Financial System: Innovation and Deregulation, LUISS Ceradi.

Occhiuto, A. (1979) Introductory speech to the round table on: *La tutela del risparmio bancario*, Ente per gli Studi Monetari, Bancari e Finanziari "Luigi Einaudi", 7–8 April.

Oda, H. and Grice, R. G. (1988) *Japanese Banking Securities and Anti-Monopoly Law*, Butterworths.

OECD (1985) *Competition Policy and the Professions*, Paris.

Onado, M. "Le banche centrali di fronte alle crisi degli anni ottanta", in *Banche in crisi*, op. cit.

Padoa-Schioppa, T. (1987) "Verso un ordinamento bancario europeo", paper presented to the conference on: *New equilibria between financial intermediaries, savings and firms*, Milan, 23 October.

Padoa-Schioppa, T. (1988) "The Blurring of Financial Frontiers: in Search of an Order", speech to the conference on *Financial Conglomerates*, Commission of the European Communities,

Banca d'Italia, *Economic Bulletin*, October.

Padoa-Schioppa, T. (Study Group) (1987) *Efficiency, Stability and Equity*, report of the group appointed by the Commission of the European Communities and chaired by T. Padoa-Schioppa.

Parrillo, F. (ed.) (1987) *Efficienza e stabilità dei sistemi finanziari: un raffronto internazionale*, Conference Proceedings, Associazione Bancaria Italiana, Rome, Italy.

Peacock Report (1986) *Report of the Committee on Financing the BBC*, Cmnd. 9824, HMSO, London.

Pera, A. (1989) "Deregulation in an Economy-wide Context", *OECD Economic Studies*, Spring.

Pescatrice, D. R. and Trapani, J. M. (1980) "The Performance and Objective of Public and Private Utilities Operating in the United States", *Journal of Public Economics*.

Prometeia, (1988) in cooperation with ABI. *Analisi dei bilanci bancari*, May.

Ricci, R. (1989) *Esame delle diverse opinioni emerse nel confronto con le conclusioni della ricerca*, Research on the Changes of the Italian Financial System: Innovation and Deregulation, LUISS Ceradi.

Roll, R. (1988) "The International Crash of October 1987", *Financial Analysts Journal*.

Ronchi, C. "L'evoluzione della normativa riguardante gli istituti di creditio speciale", in *Gli istituti di credito speciale*, op. cit.

Rothschild, M. and Stiglitz, J. (1976) "Equilibrium in Competitive Insurance Markets: The Economics of Markets with Incomplete Information", *Quarterly Journal of Economics*.

Ryan, R. (1988) "Strategie di mercato in tempi di deregolamentazione", *Bancaria*.

Salop, S. and Stiglitz, J. (1977) "Bargains and Ripoffs: A Model of Monopolistically Competitive Price Dispersion", *Review of Economic Studies*.

Sarcinelli, M. (Committee) (1987) *Ricchezza finanziaria, debito pubblico e poltica monetaria nella prospettiva dell'integrazzione internazionale*, report of the Committee appointed by the Minister of the Treasury and chaired by M. Sarcinelli, Istituto Poligrafico e Zecca dello Stato (abridged English version in *BNL Quarterly Review*, September 1987).

Sarcinelli, M. (1988) "Prospettive di internazionalizzazione dell'economia e della finanza", *Economic Review*.

Schlesinger, P. "La struttura degli organi della banca pubblica", in *Banche in crisi*, op. cit.

Segrè, C. (Group of Experts) (1967) "La formazione di un mercato europeo dei capitali", report of the group of experts appointed by the Commission of the EEC and chaired by C. Segrè, *Bancaria, serie Documenti*.

Shaked, A. and Sutton, J. (1981) "The Self-regulating Profession", *Review of Economic Studies*.

Shapiro, C. (1982) "Consumer Information, Product Quality and Seller Reputation", *Bell Journal of Economics*.

Shapiro, C. (1986) "Investment, Moral Hazard and Occupational Licensing", *Review of Economic Studies*.

Shliefer, A. (1985) "A Theory of Yardstick Competition", *Rand Journal of Economics*.

Soda, A. P. (1987) "La 'Prudential Regulation' con riferimento alle operazioni 'fuori bilancio' ", *Banche e Banchieri*.

Spence, M. (1983) "Contestable Markets and the Theory of Industry Structure: A Review Article", *Journal of Economic Literature*, Vol. XXI.

Spence, M. (1984) "Cost Reduction, Competition and Industry Performance", *Econometrica*.

Steiner, T. D. and Teixeira, D. (1988) "The Changing World of Banking: Technology is more than just a Strategy", *The McKinsey Quarterly*.

Suzuki, Y. (1987) "Financial Reform in Japan: Developments and Prospects". Paper presented to the Symposium on *Restructuring the Financial System*, op. cit.

Suzuki, Y. (1987) *The Japanese Financial System*, Clarendon Press Oxford.

Suzumura, K. and Kiyono, K. (1987) "Entry Barriers and Economic Welfare", *Review of Economic*

Studies.

Szego, G. (1986) *L'assicurazione nell'attività bancaria*, Temi di discussione, Servizio Studi Banca d'Italia.

Seidman, W. (1989) "This is Dirty Business", *Fortune*, May.

Tobin, J. (1987) "The Case for Preserving Regulatory Distinctions". Symposium: *Restructuring the Financial System*, Jackson Hole, Wyoming (USA).

Vaciago, G. (1988) "L'integrazzione finanziaria in Europa: costi e benefici per l'Italia", paper presented to the conference *Europe conviene?*, Milan, 18 January 1988.

Vaciago, G. (1988) "Il nuovo mercato die titoli di Stato: efficienza e liquidità", paper presented to the conference on: *Prospettive e operatività dei mercati monetari e finanziari dopo le recenti trasformazioni*, Banco di Roma, 1 December.

Vickers, J. S. (1985) "The Economics of Predatory Practices", *Fiscal Studies*.

Vickers, J. S. and Yarrow, G. (1988) *Privatization - An Economic Analysis*, MIT Press.

Visentini G. (1988) *Le recenti evoluzioni nella disciplina dell attività finanziarie. Appunti*, LUISS (mimeo).

Wallich, H.C. (1984) *A Broad View of Deregulation*, Conference on Pacific Basin Financial Reform, San Francisco, Ca, 12 December.

Williamson, J. (1986) *The Economic Function of Futures Markets*, Cambridge University Press.

Williamson, O. E. (1976) "Franchising Bidding for Natural Monopolies - In General and with Respect to CATV", *Bell Journal of Economics*.

Whittaker, A. M. (1988) *Regolamentazione dei servizi finanziari nel Regno Unito*, Research on the Transformation of the Italian Financial System: Innovation and Deregulation, LUISS Ceradi.

Yanelle, M. O. (1989) "The Strategic Analysis of Intermediation", *European Economic Review*, 33.

Part F
Concluding Address

XXIII. General Report on the Colloquium

CHRISTOPHER JOHNSON

I am delighted to see such a big audience here. I am going to give you a health warning in English to start with. This is directed to my English and English-speaking friends. When you hear me give the first part of my talk in French, don't go out. You might even understand some of it. As we all know in England, foreign languages are very easy to understand when they're spoken very slowly and haltingly by a member of your own race. It's only when foreigners speak them that they're really difficult to understand. So stay with me, and I shall in fact be moving into English when I come to the more detailed discussion of the Commissions.

(The following section has been translated by the author from the original French)
For the British, in the context of 1992 it is important to tackle foreign languages, but not to massacre them, which we do from time to time. I regret this, but we are making a big effort. You mustn't all learn English, because then our efforts would be wasted and we would be able to speak to you in our own language, which isn't very good from a "marketing" point of view. I am already using a term in "Franglais" and I must point out that during this conference I have collected several choice examples of Franglais which have been used by French speakers. They told us that the "Big Bang" didn't create a "level playing field" because the "price earnings" ratios vary so much between one "stock exchange" and another. It must also be said that governments don't play their part. They have a bad "policy mix", and the markets have to do some "arm-twisting".

A great deal has been said about asymmetry during this conference, particularly asymmetry of information. But I draw your attention to several other types of asymmetry. We have just spoken of language asymmetry, which works in favour of English, and there is monetary asymmetry, which works in favour of the D-mark. I have tried to find an asymmetry which works in favour of France. This must surely be cooking and hotels such as we have found in the Nice area. Long may it last, to our great satisfaction. You are giving a public service to the whole of Europe, and we hope that we shall be able to harmonize the quality of our cooking, but in an upwards

D. E. Fair and C. de Boissieu (eds), Financial Institutions in Europe Under New Competitive Conditions, 347–361.
© 1990 *Kluwer Academic Publishers, Dordrecht. Printed in the Netherlands.*

and not a downwards direction.

I must also tell you that there are very few of us British here. The man on the newspaper stand told me that he never saw any Englishmen here, and I drew his attention to the street name "Promenade des Anglais". He told me: "That's history. Now they haven't got enough money to make use of their own promenade." The pound is going through a difficult period, but we hope it will soon recover so that we can come to the Riviera more often.

I would like to thank the other rapporteurs. Without the Commission rapporteurs, the rapporteur-general would not be able to do anything. He can't be in four places at once, and I was very happy to find such a team of brilliant young men from the Bank of France. I am very grateful to them. Nevertheless I managed to visit all the Commissions in person and because of this I dressed in very relaxed style, in shirt-sleeves without a tie. Like that no one could be in any doubt about the presence of the rapporteur-general in their Commission at least for part of the time. If you didn't all see me, it was because you were asleep.

I shall start with some remarks about the three keynote speeches which we heard on the first morning of the conference. I draw your attention to the theme of the conference, which was "New conditions of competition for financial institutions in Europe", which wasn't an exact translation of the English title "Financial institutions in Europe in new competitive conditions". However, I won't linger over the nuances of the translation.

What are the competitive conditions which the speakers discussed? National deregulation, European harmonization of rules, on which Mr Fitchew addressed us, and global liberalization of financial services in GATT; no one spoke about this, because we are in Europe; but Europe is part of the world, one must not forget. Then there is innovation – innovation of technology, products, and banking structures. We spoke about universalization and specialization in banking structures. Finally, perhaps the most important topic, on which M. Lagayette addressed us, was monetary integration. "What are the monetary implications of financial integration?" was his title. One could reformulate the question: "What are the financial implications of monetary integration?"

We shall have the final abolition of exchange controls, notably in France and Italy in July 1990, and later in Spain and Ireland. This will have a big influence on the ability of bank customers to deposit their money anywhere they want to. As M. Lagayette said, it isn't enough to free demand; one must also free supply. That is being done by the Second Banking Directive, which will give banks freedom to go and look for deposits which individuals will be free to deposit in foreign banks in foreign currencies.

There is also the question of monetary policy, which concerns the use of interest rates as an economic policy weapon. One must ask whether this doesn't throw out the calculations on which competition is based. In Spain interest rates are too high for balanced international competition. They are attracting more capital than they need. In the UK, we tried the same experiment, attracting capital by raising interest rates, but the capital doesn't want to know; apparently interest rates are still not high enough even now.

Against this danger of having divergent interest rates for monetary reasons, there is what M. Lagayette called the "viscosity of savings". I like that word, which I came across in the works of Jean-Paul Sartre. In *L'Etre et le Néant* you can read a chapter on "The viscous". In Sartre's work, it is something rather unpleasant, but clearly when M. Lagayette used it, it simply meant that savers are conservative, and market instruments are not perfect substitutes, whether between banks, currencies or products. Saving doesn't always go where the yield is highest, at least not without a time-lag. That is perhaps a defence against the worst kind of instability which competition could bring.

There are other monetary questions, for example measures taken by central banks. Host country central banks will still be responsible for monetary policy in their territory. Here we find an extraordinary divergence in the level of obligatory bank reserves which banks have to keep at the central bank, and restrictions on interest rates which still exist in France and other countries. One may wonder whether it isn't also necessary to harmonize methods of monetary control. We are a long way off this. In Britain, we have practically abolished any instruments of monetary control. No one should have been surprised to find that the broad monetary aggregates were not being controlled. In other countries, such as Spain, a high level of bank reserves is obligatory.

I draw your attention to the main problem of monetary integration, that is whether we are going towards fixed exchange rates and a common currency, because, as M. Lagayette said, a single market can function efficiently only with a system of single prices. Without fixed exchange rates, I would even say without a common currency, there is no law of one price in the market. Competition risks being distorted by considerations of the value of such and such a currency rather than such and such a banking product. Consumers are in danger of going into the stronger currencies, even at lower interest rates, rather than into the less reliable currencies.

Perhaps one way out of this dilemma would be the wider use of the ecu, about which M. Lagayette spoke. He mentioned the possibility of a big stock market denominated in ecu. This goes to the heart of the London Stock Exchange's desires, where they are discussing a product of this kind. In one field at least, the UK isn't altogether backward. I hope that we shall join the EMS exchange rate mechanism, but we are already very active in the ecu market.

We must discuss in good faith the different routes to the summit, as M.

Lagayette put it. If we want alternatives to the Delors project, there must be other routes to the summit, but they must be routes which really do lead to the summit. What M. Lagayette meant, in a very diplomatic manner, is that Mr Lawson's project of competition between currencies doesn't really lead to the summit of a common currency, because the main area of competition between currencies is in the fluctuation of their values. If currencies are fixed against each other then the competition is merely illusory.

To turn now to Mr Fitchew's speech, he gave us the regulatory framework of this new financial market in Europe. Although he described very well what had been done in the Second Banking Directive and all the other directives, what I noted was the lack of progress in a number of areas which are of great importance to the financial world. There is little or no harmonization in areas such as company law, taxation, consumer protection, investment regulations for insurance and pension funds, and also the question of capital adequacy for securities operations. There is a whole series of new Directives which we hope to see coming out of Brussels in the years ahead. That is to say the 1992 programme is open-ended. It will not end in 1992. We shall need other Directives to complement those which will already have been decided. Otherwise we risk finding that it is host country and not home country regulation which plays the biggest part. This will cause the survival of twelve national markets.

I also found interesting what Mr Fitchew told us about insurance. This is a very important field, not only for the insurance companies themselves, but also for banks, which are trying to diversify into insurance in their domestic markets and in the wider European market. Progress has been agonizingly slow. There has been resistance from Germany and other countries in the name of consumer protection. They are very reluctant to relax their strict regulations. One can hope that the new Directives yet to be issued will cover mass risks, first for non-life and, even more important for the banks, life insurance. Home country regulation must prevail, if not totally, at least enough to allow insurance companies to supply products from their own national territory, without having to set up costly networks in host countries.

Then M. Lévy-Lang, a banker, shared with us some of his fairly revolutionary secrets. He showed us at least one strategy for the future which other banks might follow. He emphasized the differences between national banking markets; differences of technical environment, such as telecommunications, computer software, and electronics standards; differences of taxation and regulation, and so on. He also hinted at a future in which the substantial margins which now exist in retail banking would be squeezed by competition. It was the vision of the Cecchini Report, which practically no one here mentioned – perhaps they are suspicious of the Price Waterhouse data. One must expect to see competition bringing down excessive margins, especially for mass consumer products.

In this field, M. Lévy-Lang introduced a concept familiar to investment banks which lend to big companies, that is to say, transaction banking rather than relationship banking. Are we going in the direction of transaction banking for individuals, where they can go shopping on their screens for products from a whole range of banks, or do they prefer to give all their business to one bank, instead of going on errands here and there to find bargains? Truly one can envisage both solutions at once. There is consumer inertia, which ensures that for most banking products he stays with his own bank, unless he is extremely dissatisfied, which can happen, unfortunately. In that case he will go and find another bank for a specific transaction. For banks, and consumers, both solutions are valid. There can either be a universal bank which offers every product to the same customer list; here one sees economies of scope come into their own. Or there can be banks which go looking for customers everywhere, particularly from their rivals' lists. One sees both strategies being pursued at once. It is not a bad idea to try to keep one's existing customer base faithful while hunting the customers of other banks.

All this raises the question of the future of branch networks. Clearly a network is partly a function of the loyalty of the customer base. What is the future of home banking, where the consumer is much freer to make his choice? Even relationship banking is helped by home terminals, in cases where the branch network is already handling as many personal visits as it can within its own physical limitations.

(The translation from French ends here. The remaining part was given in English)

COMMISSION I

Commission I was in a way the heartland of the conference. It was about the central topic of competition in banking. It had a rather Latin flavour to it, because three out of the five papers were in French. It had a French chairman, but of course, as is customary nowadays, we had a German co-chairman in order to impose a certain monetary discipline on the French way of doing things.

The three case studies were also all somewhat of a Latin hue because they covered France, Italy and Spain, the countries where more remains to be done by way of deregulation in order to at least start off by having domestic competition as a pre-condition of proper international competition. I was sorry we didn't have a contribution from Ireland because Ireland is one of the more interesting newcomers to this competition. Ireland has such a small home market that nobody else is going to be interested in invading it, but it has such a favourable regime for foreign banks that they may use Ireland as a launching pad from which to invade other countries in Europe. Winston Churchill once called it an aircraft carrier stationed off the British coast. So watch out for low flying aircraft flying the Irish flag.

We had a very European introduction from Steinherr of the European Investment Bank. In the course of his title and his talk, he managed to bring in all the big abstract nouns – innovation, internationalization, deregulation, integration. I was sorry he didn't introduce the concept of despecialization, because that was on the order paper. Anyway the links between these abstract concepts were an important part of the subject matter. As a devil's advocate, I thought I would try to write down the opposites of all these abstract nouns, and what I got was tradition, regionalization, reregulation, disintegration, respecialization, and bankerization, as the opposite to securitization. Now that is a bit of reverse Franglais. The French have this wonderful word *bancarisation* which doesn't exist in England, but should. It refers to the spread of the banking habit. I wondered whether my second set of abstract nouns were not at least as close to the trend that we are going to see as the first set. They are not mutually incompatible.

Steinherr asks the question "Why is it all happening now?" There are several possible answers. One is, of course, "Why not?". It is as good a time as any other. The next answer is: "Well, perhaps it isn't happening". Perhaps the opposite is happening. We may not have noticed yet. Or at least it may not be happening yet, and it may not be happening everywhere.

There is also an interesting concept in the paper by Metais and Lubochinsky, which had this wonderful idea of variable geometry. I reflected on what this might mean. As I sat up late last night trying to write, I decided that it meant that one could always adopt the horizontal position instead of the vertical position. I therefore went sound asleep. When I woke up the next morning I had had some further thoughts about variable geometry. There is of course the variable geometry aircraft, which as you know was a complete technical flop. Most of them crashed. But it was a nice idea. It was an aircraft that could either be a fighter, or if it spread its wings out, it could become a bomber. (The original; F-111 American variable geometry aircraft had considerable technical problems, which were overcome in subsequent aircraft, such as the French Mirages.) This is a bit like the commercial bankers thinking that they can also become investment bankers if they just make a few adjustments to their wing span. I am afraid some of them crashed. One may wonder whether it is in fact possible to be quite as adaptable as that. Clearly adaptability is highly desirable. One has got to be realistic about whether one can achieve it.

There is another meaning that the authors may have had for variable geometry, and that is in the context of the EEC when it means that certain countries can choose to integrate for all purposes – the twelve member community – or for certain purposes you can have fewer, you can have eight countries agreeing to do something, and the others don't agree to do it. So it's rather closer to the *à la carte* idea, that you can decide how many different businesses you want to be in. You can move in and out of them, and the example they gave was that banks could decide for example to have just a broking function in insurance or securities, or they could decide to act as principals – one can move from one to the other.

Now we look at the case studies in Commission I. De Juvigny told me a lot I didn't know about the degree of regulation which still exists in France. There are six categories of bank. Here we have to have another bit of Franglais. What we need is *banalization*, which again I wouldn't like to translate into English. It means something like just being a normal bank rather than a special kind of bank. So they need to banalize these different categories of bank. Controlled interest rates still exist, notably zero interest on sight deposits. There are all kinds of tax breaks still on bonds, and different kinds of savings deposits. They even have controlled hours in banking. In Britain we have never had control on banking hours. The wishes of the staff are quite enough to ensure that most banks do not open for very long hours. So that is a case where the free market produces its own form of regulation. But one can say that there is no level playing field in France at the moment, except perhaps for the airports through which all the rich Frenchmen take their money when they have some serious business to do. So France has got some way to go.

Italy also has some way to go. Here we have different considerations, where regulation tends to favour small regional banks, as shown in the paper by Onado. One might ask whether this has got certain social externalities – that people in a region or town rather like the idea of their own bank. One finds this very much in the United States, where a lot of small towns like to have their bank, and indeed they will give it deposits at very low interest, because, who knows, they might need to borrow money from it some time. So there is a localization of credit factor in Italy which one ought to think carefully about before sweeping it away in the interests of uniformity.

In Spain the emphasis in Maldonado's paper was more on bank mergers. One might query whether the best response to European competition is to start forming national champions, to start merging all the big domestic banks which are probably already quite big enough to be enjoying economies of scale. Do they really need to be bigger to compete in the European market, because for a long time there is not going to be a perfect European market? One might be in danger of creating monopoly situations in the domestic market in the name of the Single European Market. I did feel that we ought to have heard a little bit about the Spanish mergers that didn't happen as well as the ones that did happen, but for any of you that read Spanish there is an amazing book about Banesto and its recent gyrations called *Asalto al Poder*, by Jesus Cacho. It is the first time in history that a book about banking has been the top of the best seller lists, but I can tell you that there are some very colourful characters there. I met a few of them on the Costa del Sol a few weeks ago.

The issues raised by Commission I were some of the fundamental ones about the theme of the whole conference. Does innovation cause deregulation? Is the fact that banks want to innovate and bring pressure to bear one reason why regulations are swept away? Or is it more, as we were told, that innovations happen because of regulations? There are ways of getting round regulations, so you might say that deregulation might make some innovations unnecessary, even though it would permit others to take place, which were already in the wind.

The next issue about competition is as somebody put it, Hamlet-like, "to be or not to be". This refers to "to be or not to be" a universal bank. The consensus seemed to be that in countries which have universal banks, and are satisfied with the way they operate, it would seem sensible to keep them. One thinks of the advantages to German industrial development of having close bank-industry relations. On the other hand, where a country does not have a universal banking structure, it would seem to go against the whole idea of home country regulation – doing it the way it is in your home country – to start creating universal banks just to be like everybody else.

The Second Banking Directive clearly makes universal banks possible. It allows banks to carry out all the functions of a universal bank – investment banking as well as conventional banking – but just because it makes it possible that does not mean that it makes it necessary. If you try to eat everything on the menu, you may well get indigestion. One compromise that was indicated in discussion was that banks, if they were universal at home – enjoying economies of scope in that way – might still want to operate on a more selective basis abroad. They might want to find a niche. Incidentally "niche" is not a French word. It's an English word. The French for niche is *créneau*. But anyway the niche or *créneau* strategy has clearly been very popular among banks.

Here we have to draw a distinction between on the one hand global banking, and on the other hand universal banking. Global banking can cover just one product. If you have a good product, like treasury operations, you can attempt to sell it through your branches all over the world. On the other hand you can be a universal bank without going overseas at all. You can simply cover the whole range of banking products in your home market. So the key to strategy is the extent to which one wants to be global, the extent to which one wants to be universal, and the interaction between the two strategies.

This raises the whole question of networks. Are banking networks a good thing to have? Is it like a railway where the branch lines act as feeders for the main lines, or is it again like a railway in that in spite of that the branch lines always lose money, and if you want to be efficient you have to shut them down. Advances in banking technology are going to raise a number of questions over networks. At present the debate is a bit like that about "Is the glass half empty, or is it half full?" If half your customers never come to the branch does that show that the branch is useless and you should be finding other delivery systems, but if half of them do still come, are they just going to switch to another bank if you close the branch?

The one topic that was not perhaps fully covered in the discussion in Commission I was that of contestability; the idea that ease of entry rather than actual entry is important for competition. The fact that somebody could enter the market will keep prices down; will keep banks efficient, whether they do in fact enter or not. My own view is that contestability applies more to products than to institutions, and it goes with economies of scope. A bank which already has a branch network, and a customer list, can quite easily develop a new product on the back of it, as the British clearing banks did with mortgage finance, for example. It is a lot more difficult for a new institution to enter a market because here you have the problems of reputation. It takes time and money to build up a reputation before you can compete. Good banks are like some good French wines – they don't always travel. Many foreign banks have found this in the UK retail market.

For the contestability theory to work you have to have not only ease of entry, but ease of exit. This can be a problem. A bank may spend a lot of money trying to get into a market. It may then not be able to get its money back. If you had a pleasant evening in the casino here at Nice, you spent a lot of money, but you enjoyed the experience, you got a lot of thrills out of it. You really can't go up to the croupier and say: "I'd like my money back". That is not the way things are done. But never mind. Salvation is at hand. We now have an exit route. Whenever one of our ventures in a foreign market doesn't succeed, we can simply sell it to a Japanese bank. So the Japanese are doing a great deal to ensure contestability in European competition.

COMMISSION II

Commission II was in some ways related to Commission I. It extended the concept of competition both to financial centres, and to non-bank business such as insurance and securities. Here we had a rather more Nordic line-up than in Commission I. We had an Anglo-Danish chairmanship, and there were also British and Danish papers, and papers from a German and a Belgian, which was in French, I am glad to say, so it wasn't entirely monolingual. We had the insurance, mortgage credit and securities industries all represented. However, among the financial centres we had a paper only about Frankfurt, and the merits of the other centres had to be advanced, as they were, in the discussion.

Llewellyn's paper covered the questions of competition, diversification, and structural change in the UK, and obviously the implication was that these three things go together. Johnson gave more of a warning note, with particular reference to competition in retail banking. His title was "Threat or Promise". Indeed I would say that he was so worried about the problem of bad debts and consumer banking that he would never make a good banker. Any banker who never has a bad debt is immediately demoted as not being nearly enterprising enough. If you operate at the margin you have to go over it sometimes. We had the specialist talk by Lumsden about housing finance and the building societies. Aerthøj gave us an unusual example of an insurance company moving into banking, and successfully setting up a bank within its group. The only thing we missed here was something on the whole question of competition in offering money transmission services, which could be one of the important results of 1992.

What are the main issues here? First of all, diversification. Clearly it is one form of competition, and it is a way of driving down monopoly rents in protected sectors, which have been the preserve of one type of institution. Indeed it may also be a way towards offering the consumer a better deal, and the benefits of one-stop shopping, if he wants to get more than one basic product from his bank. On the other hand one could also see diversification as being some kind of step towards a universal banking structure with all the merits and demerits which that entails.

There is a paradox in this type of competition, because if the new competitors are entering markets by under-selling – saying like John Lewis "We are never knowingly undersold" – then how is it that profits appear to have increased so much in these areas where competition is taking place? One reason is that new entrants to a market always try to share the monopoly rents which exist in it instead of driving them down, and thus making it uneconomic to enter that market. If you're the marginal producer, there is no point in trying to get such a big market share that you can operate at lower cost. Your first strategy is to try and share in those juicy monopoly rents. There is also the point that supply creates its own demand in this case. Banks and other institutions have discovered a great shut-in borrowing capacity on the part of people who didn't know they had it, indeed will perhaps turn out not to have it. Nevertheless many sound new loans have been made to people who always regarded being able to borrow money as a privilege which went with having a bank and not a building society account, and they didn't know they could open a bank account.

Let us think how diversification may have risks. This was an aspect drawn attention to by Johnson, and his answer was that other types of business are not fully understood by banks. There are culture differences. We have seen the mistakes which banks have made when entering investment banking. One way of limiting these risks is for banks to act in an agency role, as brokers rather than as principals, in insurance for example. This is the way most banks got into insurance. Then you inevitably have a further development. After some years banks feel that they understand insurance. They don't see why they should share their profit on it with somebody else, and they end up going into the insurance business, as my own bank did buying a majority share in Abbey Life. So risks have to be understood, but if understood they can be taken.

Much of the more successful diversification that has taken place has been in the insurance market. Here there is some element of a joint product. There are definite economies, because product design may be going more towards having products which have a partly insurance and a partly banking character. There are many other forms of diversification, which are closely related to banking business, as for example estate agencies related to mortgage finance. The insurance of buildings and contents is clearly also related to mortgage finance. Such activities have the merit of bringing in fee income, and thus improving the return on assets because they do not require any additional assets; but they may cause the cost-income ratio to worsen.

Finally, diversification into securities is quite obviously something where the banks are following the demands of their personal customers, and indeed where we now find in the UK that the main discount broking services are no longer offered by stockbrokers, but by High Street banks. This is where the economies of scale operate in a big way. The paper by Martin and van Turenhoudt showed how the Belgian stock exchange, somewhat after London, has been opening itself up to ownership by the banks.

Financial centres were the other topic of Commission II. It is quite clear that the reason why Frankfurt has been backward as a financial centre is the degree of product regulation, and indeed regulation of who can do what, which still exists in the German market. This regulation is gradually being abolished, under pressure from people like Norbert Walter himself, but one does have to ask to what extent the very close control over monetary aggregates which is exercised in Frankfurt is partly due to the degree of regulation of banking products. One could indeed put the proposition the other way round, and ask whether the degree of banking deregulation in London is not partly responsible for the complete inability of the authorities, even if they wished, to control the monetary aggregates.

A number of claims were put forward for rival centres. London will always have a future as a world, and not just as a European financial centre. The Americans and the Japanese would rather deal with one centre, or at least some kind of integrated European market. Luxembourg is already doing well with UCITS unit trust type vehicles, but will have to learn to stand on its own feet without special tax privileges. Here the competition is coming from places like the Channel Islands and Monaco. Maybe we should have had a speaker from Monaco not at the reception, but here in this conference to explain the merits of Monaco, as a rival to Frankfurt. It was also perhaps slightly surprising that we had nothing about Paris as a financial centre, but then the French believe in doing good by stealth. While we have been having "Big Bangs" in London, the French have had a series of small controlled underground explosions, which nevertheless seem to be working towards an extremely efficient and impressive financial centre.

There is a danger that we shall have competition in laxity among financial centres in order to get business. We shall end up with a polycentric structure where there is no one centre, where the markets are on screen. We shall have a disembodied market with a federal-type organization. The alternative would be, to use an airport metaphor, the hub-and-spokes approach, with one main market, and others as its satellites.

COMMISSION III

Commission III was slightly at a tangent to the main discussions. It was a session for the investment bankers on the role of financial institutions in the restructuring of industry. Indeed one might include the banking industry as one which needs other banks to restructure it. We had case studies from Switzerland and Belgium, as well as a Swiss-Belgian chairmanship. Schwietert gave us a study about the Swiss watch industry. It is a wonderful example of our saying: "The exception proves the rule". Because here the Swiss bankers broke all the rules of prudent banking. They took huge equity stakes in their customers. They told the customer how to run his business, and they got the central bank to relax the capital adequacy rules. But nothing succeeds like success. They saved that great national treasure, the Swiss watch industry. I wish that when the British banks were persuaded to give similar treatment to the car industry, they'd had a few people on their boards who knew how a car was put together, who might have perhaps had an equally good result in that case.

We also had a stimulating case study by Ugeux describing the turn-round operation in Société Générale. That was fascinating in itself. I cannot dwell on it, but the moral of it was that when the customer is choosing banks, it's a question of horses for courses. No bank should expect to be chosen for every single banking function by any customer, however loyal. There are quite different functions attached to commercial banks which lend you money, preferably for long periods, banks which do your treasury business for you, banks which arrange for the issue of equity, banks which advise you on mergers and acquisitions, and banks which give you other corporate financial advice. Here we are beginning to get some interesting new competition from the lawyers, the accountants, and the management consultants, who are usurping many of the traditional advice functions of investment banks.

Those were the case studies in Commission III, and the general issues involved were the obvious ones of whether commercial banks were either able to, or indeed should be in the mergers and acquisitions business. Can you deal with conflicts of interest simply by having Chinese walls, and if you have an arm's length relationship between a commercial bank and its investment banking subsidiary, what is the point of it? You are not going to get any synergy out of it, and you're probably not going to know enough about it to control the risks. So the merits of that particular diversification may be rather questionable. Banks may end up specializing in M&A work for their middle market customers, who are perhaps not as well served by the big names in investment banking.

There is also a big field opening up for M&A type work as a result of 1992, and the desire of industrial companies to get together with friendly, or take over rival companies, in order to form different European groupings. Here one has to ask whether we don't need several different routes towards industrial restructuring. The contested takeover is not the only route, not necessarily the best route, and it is a route which is not even open in many European countries. In Britain and America we are accustomed to the contested takeover. It has become more popular in France. It is still quite difficult in Germany and Italy. Therefore one has to look at other ways of bringing about industrial restructuring, which may in some cases be considerably less costly in terms of transactions costs. One can legitimately have a few doubts about some of the evidence which was presented by the speakers here.

Ravenscraft, as he admitted, was basing his experience of the poor results of mergers on American experience, and there are undoubted benefits even there to the shareholders of the target companies, who get an immediate benefit from being taken over. There is also the paper by Caytas and Mahari, which raised many of the problems I have discussed when it comes to what banks should be doing in the M&A business.

Commission IV was on the key question "Is there an efficiency/stability trade off?" As far as I know nobody even attempted to give a satisfactory definition of either efficiency or stability. Your answer to the question may depend on how you define these two things.

Here we had a very good French-American chairmanship, but I should say that probably the American would be regarded by most of us as an honorary European. We had a number of academics who have gone into banking. We had Artus and Pollin on the effects of regulation on bank behaviour, and we had Masera on the central question of efficiency versus stability. We had a very provocative essay from the academics, from Wood and Capie, querying whether regulation was required at all. We also had a paper from Dermine on home country control, and on mutual recognition from Cornet, giving a very important perspective of somebody who is actually a supervisor.

The different types of regulation have very different effects on banks. Deposit insurance is one of the favourites of the academic community. It is easy to prove that deposit insurance can be counter-productive because it can lead banks to behave in a much more risky manner than if it didn't exist. I am a bit dubious about this. Most depositors don't even know that they have deposit insurance, so one can hardly say that it influences their behaviour a great deal. Banks were shockingly badly managed long before we had deposit insurance in most countries, and good banks continue to be well managed even with deposit insurance, because the people who manage them don't much fancy losing their jobs in the event of the bank taking unacceptable risks, and being found out. So while I would welcome the moves to harmonize deposit insurance in the EEC, which is one of the later things on the agenda, one can exaggerate its effects.

Similar remarks can be made about capital adequacy ratios. You could say that once a bank is living up to its Cooke ratios, it can then take any risk it likes, and indeed it will have an incentive to move into higher yielding assets in order to earn enough capital in order to keep its Cooke ratios up to scratch. Again, a well managed bank is not going to manage its balance sheets solely by looking at the Cooke ratios. They are much too crude – they deal only with generic risks, and not with risks specific to a particular borrower. In other words they don't deal properly with specific counter-party risk. So again, this type of regulation does not necessarily lead to greater banking instability.

We also have monetary controls – liquidity ratios which are designed to protect the system against shortages of liquidity and monetary panics. This would be regarded by most people as a way of at least improving the efficiency of the system, although it can't cater for the individual bank, which is short of liquidity because it is badly managed, and should be allowed to go under. There is one type of regulation which I think we must all agree is necessary whatever you think of the others, and that is the regulation of banking concentration. One can argue about whether banks need to be more concentrated than they are at present in Europe to achieve efficiency, but most people have doubts about whether the economies of scale really go all that far up the scale. One might on the other hand reason that it is better for the banking industry to remain relatively disaggregated in order to provide sufficient competition – certainly within each individual country – even though these banks may be small by the European scale.

I conclude with a few general issues about regulation and deregulation. There does seem to be some kind of trade-off. We assume that deregulation leads to more competition, which leads to more efficiency, and thus there is a trade-off. Less regulation, more efficiency. On the other hand, one might also reason that from the point of view of social efficiency a certain minimum amount of regulation is necessary. This is an argument about the externalities – values external to banking itself, like the importance of having a good payments system, the safeguarding of people's wealth, the protection of the investor, and indeed the allocation of funds between savers and investors. So we are looking for the banking system to be not just efficient in itself by its own measurements, but also to play a role which is efficient for the economy as a whole. These two do not necessarily coincide.

I would like to end with something inspired by M. Cornet's paper, perhaps reversing something I said about academics in banking. I would say that this shows that very often supervisors make good commercial bankers. Banks have a strategic choice in three dimensions; organic growth or take-over, own product or new product, domestic or foreign. Between the extremes of organic growth in own products at home, or take-over in new products abroad, many options are possible, and different choices may apply to each type of business.

To sum up the conference, competition means being free to make mistakes, and supervision means being free to try to prevent them. Since prevention is better than cure, we should all be grateful to the supervisors.

FINANCIAL AND MONETARY POLICY STUDIES

* 1. J.S.G. Wilson and C.F. Scheffer (eds.): *Multinational Enterprises*. Financial and Monitary Aspects. 1974   ISBN 90-286-0124-4

* 2. H. Fournier and J.E. Wadsworth (eds.): *Floating Exchange Rates*. The Lessons of Recent Experience. 1976   ISBN 90-286-0565-7

* 3. J.E. Wadsworth, J.S.G. Wilson and H. Fournier (eds.): *The Development of Financial Institutions in Europe, 1956–1976*. 1977   ISBN 90-286-0337-9

* 4. J.E. Wadsworth and F.L. de Juvigny (eds.): *New Approaches in Monetary Policy*. 1979   ISBN 90-286-0848-6

* 5. J.R. Sargent (ed.), R. Bertrand, J.S.G. Wilson and T.M. Rybczynski (ass. eds.): *Europe and the Dollar in the World-Wide Disequilibrium*. 1981   ISBN 90-286-0700-5

* 6. D.E. Fair and F.L. de Juvigny (eds.): *Bank Management in a Changing Domestic and International Environment*. The Challenges of the Eighties. 1982

    ISBN 90-247-2606-9

* 7. D.E. Fair (ed.) in cooperation with R. Bertrand: *International Lending in a Fragile World Economy*. 1983   ISBN 90-247-2809-6

  8. P. Salin (ed.): *Currency Competition and Monetary Union*. 1984

    ISBN 90-247-2817-7

* 9. D.E. Flair (ed.) in cooperation with F.L. de Juvigny: *Government Policies and the Working of Financial Systems in Industrialized Countries*. 1984   ISBN 90-247-3076-7

  10. C. Goedhart, G.A. Kessler, J. Kymmell and F. de Roos (eds.): *Jelle Zijlstra, A Central Banker's View*. Selected Speeches and Articles. 1985   ISBN 90-247-3184-4

  11. C. van Ewijk and J.J. Klant (eds.): *Monetary Conditions for Economic Recovery*. 1985   ISBN 90-247-3219-0

* 12. D.E. Fair (ed.): *Shifting Frontiers in Financial Markets*. 1986   ISBN 90-247-3225-5

  13. E.F. Toma and M. Toma (eds.): *Central Bankers, Bureaucratic Incentives, and Monetary Policy*. 1986   ISBN 90-247-3366-9

* 14. D.E. Fair and C. de Boissieu (eds.): *International Monetary and Financial Integration*. The European Dimension. 1988   ISBN 90-247-3563-7

  15. J. Cohen: *The Flow of Funds in Theory and Practice*. A Flow-Constrained Approach to Monetary Theory and Policy. 1987   ISBN 90-247-3601-3

  16. W. Eizenga, E.F. Limburg and J.J. Polak (eds.): *The Quest for National and Global Economic Stability*. In Honor of Hendrikus Johannes Witteveen. 1988

    ISBN 90-247-3653-6

* 17. D.E. Fair and C. de Boissieu (eds.): *The International Adjustment Process*. New Perspectives, Recent Experience and Future Challenges for the Financial System. 1989   ISBN 0-7923-0013-0

  18. J.J. Sijben (ed.): *Financing the World Economy in the Nineties*. 1989

    ISBN 0-7923-0090-4

FINANCIAL AND MONETARY POLICY STUDIES

19. I. Rizzo: *The 'Hidden' Debt*. With a Foreword by A.T. Peacock. 1990
ISBN 0-7923-0610-4

*20. D.E. Fair and C. de Boissieu (eds.): *Financial Institutions in Europe under New Competitive Conditions*. 1990   ISBN 0-7923-0673-2

*Published on behalf of the *Société Universitaire Européenne de Recherches Financières* (SUERF), consisting the lectures given at Colloquia, organized and directed by SUERF.

Further information about *Economy* publications are available on request.

Kluwer Academic Publishers – Dordrecht / Boston / London